LEARNING IN ORGANIZATIONS

Learning in Organizations: An Evidence-Based Approach examines the variety of systematic approaches and strategies for learning and development used in the workplace through the implementation of formal training, guided instruction, developmental job experiences, and self-directed learning.

The hallmark of *Learning in Organizations* is an emphasis on research evidence of what is and is not known about learning and learning strategies and the translation of that evidence to guide best practices in workplace learning and development. The book features evidence on learning principles, new learning technologies, and strategies for developing individual, team, and leadership capabilities. The content of the chapters is enhanced by the inclusion of key learning goals for each chapter, case studies, chapter summaries, best practice recommendations, and a hands-on project for use in the classroom.

Learning in Organizations provides researchers with a detailed investigation of learning practices to help drive future research. For learning practitioners, research evidence is translated into best practices that can be applied to enhance workplace learning and development. For undergraduate and graduate students, the book provides an up-to-date review of the key concepts and ways of thinking about and studying learning in the workplace.

J. Kevin Ford is Professor of Psychology at Michigan State University. He has published over 100 articles, chapters and books and is a consultant on individual, team, and organizational development. Dr. Ford is a Fellow of the Society for Industrial and Organizational Psychology.

LEARNING IN ORGANIZATIONS
AN EVIDENCE-BASED APPROACH

J. Kevin Ford

Routledge
Taylor & Francis Group

NEW YORK AND LONDON

First published 2021
by Routledge
52 Vanderbilt Avenue, New York, NY 10017

and by Routledge
2 Park Square, Milton Park, Abingdon, Oxon, OX14 4RN

Routledge is an imprint of the Taylor & Francis Group, an informa business

Library of Congress Cataloging-in-Publication Data
A catalog record for this title has been requested

ISBN: 978-0-367-20187-6 (hbk)
ISBN: 978-0-367-20189-0 (pbk)
ISBN: 978-0-429-26001-8 (ebk)

Typeset in Palatino
by SPi Global, India

To:

Dr. Irwin L. Goldstein who started me on my journey
in Industrial and Organizational Psychology

and

my wonderfully supportive family –
Melanie, Kate, Ty, Megyn, and Reilly

CONTENTS

PREFACE

In 1974 Irwin Goldstein produced *Training in Organizations*, which was one of the first books to provide a systematic review of training research and practice organized around the instructional systems design model. As an undergraduate psychology major at the University of Maryland, I took a class from Irv in my junior year, which introduced me to the book and grabbed hold of the attention around the importance of learning-related issues at work. This class and Irv's wonderful support helped lead me to my career in Industrial and Organizational Psychology. Irv went on to produce two more editions – in 1986 and in 1993. For the fourth edition, I had the distinct honor of being asked by Irv to partner with him on revising the book, which was published in 2002. As we noted in the preface for that fourth edition, organizations were moving from an industrial to a knowledge society and the dynamic, fast-moving and complex work environment made for an especially exciting time to revise the book.

Learning in Organizations is a logical extension and expansion to the fourth edition of *Training in Organizations*. Organizations see even more clearly the importance of learning and development for competitive advantage, organizational effectiveness, and adaptability. The book title shift from "training" to "learning" recognizes that training is only one part of a variety of systematic approaches and strategies for enhancing learning and development in the workplace of today. We know much more today about the effective implementation of formal training, guided instruction through coaching and mentoring, developmental job experiences, and autonomous or self-directed learning. The hallmark of the book is an emphasis on research evidence and the translation of that evidence to guide best practices in workplace learning and development.

Needs assessment, objectives, design, and thoughtful evaluation continue to form critical foundations for effective learning and development approaches within the context of the dynamic changes facing organizations today. *Learning in Organizations* highlights these issues as well as the delivery of learning content through traditional face-to-face instruction and through learning technologies such as virtual reality, serious games, and mobile learning. The research evidence and best practices are identified for developing individuals from newcomer status to high levels of proficiency, imparting the knowledge and skills to create effective teams and building needed leadership capabilities throughout the organization. In addition, larger societal issues around learning and development are described. These issues include the need to increase workforce readiness to facilitate youth employment, address issues of employee skill obsolescence, and build skills in areas to aid reemployment.

The goal of this book is to the capture the excitement of the many research and learning system issues that abound around workforce learning and development. In particular, *Learning in Organizations* provides researchers with a detailed investigation of what we know and what we do not know to help drive future research. There is an extensive set of references for each chapter for those interested in examining the original work. For learning practitioners, research evidence is translated into best practices that can be applied to enhance workplace learning and development. The top ten best practice guidelines are given at the end of Chapters 3 through 10 resulting in 80 guidelines for practice. For undergraduate and graduate students, the book provides an up-to-date review of the key concepts and ways of thinking about and studying learning into the workplace. Questions at the start of each chapter directs attention to key issues. Whether researcher, practitioner, or student, my hope is that reading this book stimulates your thinking and generates insights that you did not have previously about the incredibly interesting area of human learning within the context of the workplace.

Message to Instructors: An appendix to this book presents a hands-on project that I have used for my undergraduate and graduate level classes to bring the issues around building an effective training and onboarding programs to light. The project asks students to develop a systematic approach to train a newcomer to a job that they have picked and can interview people in that job (or their supervisor) to gain the information needed to complete the project. The project requires students to conduct a training needs assessment, prioritize training needs, create training objectives, develop a plan of instruction that includes strategies for enhancing learning and training transfer, and plan out an evaluation process. The full complexity of the project for graduate students is provided in the Appendix – the projects can be modified to be a better fit for undergraduate courses. I have found that combining the science of learning based on research evidence with hands-on practice through this project helps maximize student learning (and hopefully retention and transfer after the class). In this way, students can experience the myriad of decisions that have to be made when developing a training intervention. Please contact me directly at fordjk@msu.edu if you would like an electronic version of the project so you can modify it to fit your needs or to discuss how I have incorporated this project into my classes.

ACKNOWLEDGMENTS

In closing, I would like to acknowledge the current and former faculty members in the Industrial and Organizational Psychology program at Michigan State University (you know who you are) who have created such a supportive learning and productive work environment for me. I am also indebted to our former and current graduate students in our PhD program in Industrial and Organizational Psychology who have taken my workplace learning and development course and helped stimulate my thinking about the key issues in the field. Thanks to Brent Donnellan my psychology department chair who provided me with the precious resource of time to work on this book.

I want to especially thank Christina Chronister at Routledge who encouraged me to go ahead and write this book and provided invaluable advice along the way. Danielle Dyal, her editorial and administrative assistant, was incredibly patient with all my questions about formatting, permissions, writing style and the like. Thanks also to the production staff at Routledge especially Ting Baker and Natalie Hamil for working with me every step in the way to take my final draft submission to this much more polished finished product. Finally, I want to acknowledge my debt of gratitude to Kate and Megyn Ford who helped their dad by working diligently to produce the high-quality camera-ready figures that grace this book. Clearly, this level of skill was beyond me!

ABOUT THE AUTHOR

 **J. Kevin Ford** (PhD, The Ohio State University, 1983) is a Professor of Psychology at Michigan State University. His major research interests involve improving learning and retention in the workplace through training and other learning activities. He is known for his work on understanding key criterion work constructs such as learning and performance and in particular the study of factors impacting the transfer of learning to the job. Kevin also concentrates on strategies for facilitating organizational change and approaches for building continuous learning and improvement orientations within organizations. He has published over 100 articles, chapters, and books. He has been part of a number of funded research projects from the National Institute of Health, The National Institute for Justice, The State of Michigan, the National Science Foundation, and the Air Force Resources Directorate. Kevin is an active consultant on training, development, and organizational change in both private industry and the public sector. These efforts include learning needs assessment, design, and evaluation as well as organizational visioning and strategy development. Kevin's contribution to the field of psychology has been recognized as he is a Fellow of the Society of Industrial and Organizational Psychology.

PART I

Foundations

CHAPTER 1

The Learning Enterprise

Questions

✓ What are the key learning challenges faced by organizations?
✓ How can learning professionals take a systematic approach to creating and sustaining the learning enterprise?
✓ What do we mean by evidence and how can it be used to drive best practices for learning and development?

This is a critical time for work organizations. Competition is intense and organizations operate in a highly technical and global environment. The work force is becoming more diverse and more interconnected. Advances in technology have created jobs that are more cognitively complex and demanding. Organizations have become leaner resulting in broader responsibilities for workers. Across industries there is increased emphasis on softer skills such as interpersonal and communication skills as well as an emphasis on collaboration and teamwork. Expectations have risen for leaders to take on roles of coaching, mentoring, and facilitation as well as traditional leader roles. Work is becoming more knowledge driven requiring a deeper combination of information sharing and expertise helping lead to more effective problem-solving skills that can be applied to decisions or situations (Kraiger & Ford, 2007).

The Global Human Capital Trends report and survey by Deloitte of over 10,000 human resource and business leaders across 140 countries (Walsh, 2017; Abattiello et al., 2018) examined the challenges ahead for how organizations organize, manage, develop, and align people. One of the top ten trends is the need to enhance knowledge and skills of employees in "real time, all the time." These learning efforts likely need to be intensified given projected global skill shortages estimated to be 85 million jobs by 2030 (Mishra & Bisui, 2019). The rapid advance of technology in areas such as automation, artificial intelligence, machine learning, and neural networks could impact as many as 375 million workers globally or about 14% of the workforce in terms of job transitions and needed skill upgrades by 2030 (Manyika et al., 2017).

Given these expected trends, it is not surprising that businesses are allocating resources to the learning and development of their workforce to increase competitiveness, improve services, and enhance adaptability. One industry report noted that companies are spending over $90 billion dollars on training and development activities in the U.S. alone (Ho et al., 2016). Based on a benchmarking survey of over 300 companies, they report that the direct expenditure per full time employee for learning related initiatives was $1284.00, which represented about 4% of payroll expenses. Companies on average are providing over 34 direct learning hours per employee with a cost of about $1900.00 per learning hour. This provides some idea of the level of investment in learning activities. Companies noted as particularly strong in supporting and leveraging a continuous learning orientation were found to provide 42.7 learning hours per employee every year.

This chapter begins with learning realities and the importance of the learning enterprise in addressing key learning challenges. The chapter then describes frameworks around types of learning approaches and a learning systems model for creating effective learning processes. The third section of the chapter discusses the importance of evidence-based research and using findings to drive best practices to facilitate workplace learning. This includes cautionary stories of myth making around the learning enterprise. The chapter ends with a description of the organization of the book.

LEARNING WITHIN CONTEXT

The clear need for a robust learning enterprise in organizations is often not met by the reality. This book hopefully provides insights to where gaps may exist in the learning enterprise and strategies for reducing the gaps. What makes closing gaps difficult is the fact that the learning enterprise is embedded in and affected by other parts in the organization as well as affected by changes in the external environment. The challenges (and opportunities!) in meeting organizational, leadership, team, and individual needs are large.

A Levels of Analysis Perspective

Learning is typically thought of as rooted in individual learners. Certainly, learning as indicated by changes in knowledge and skills, occurs within an individual. Nevertheless, individuals are part of groups of workers, groups of workers form departments and functions, departments and functions are embedded within an organization, and organizations are embedded within types of industries and societies. Because organizations consist of multiple levels, any event or action should be viewed within their larger context. This means that learning and development activities cannot be considered in isolation from influences from other levels.

One implication for workplace learning is recognizing that goals and actions can have a cascading effect down and across the various levels of analysis. For example, governmental policies such as protecting individuals with disabilities can impact organizational practices regarding employee training and development. The extent to which organizations value immediate performance goals over longer-term learning goals can impact the amount of resources developed to learning initiatives. Departmental norms and expectations around learning can affect team goals and team performance. Teams can impact how much opportunity individuals have to obtain new knowledge and skills. Effects can also be upward in their influence across levels of analysis. Individuals can become active learners who help teammates, which in turn drives team effectiveness. Teams can experiment and move forward on improvement strategies that can lead to the diffusion of the innovation across functions and departments. Organizations can lobby government agencies for help in increasing the pool of qualified applicants by funding such projects as school-to-work transition or the retraining of displaced workers.

A second implication is that learning is social and relational rather than simply a solitary, individual level phenomenon. The success of new learning initiatives such as cross-training team members relies not only on the development of individuals within the team but also the coordinated efforts of team members and team leaders to be committed to supporting cross-training. The motivation and ultimate success of an individual applying new knowledge and skills to the job is affected in part by the support level of the group surrounding the individual. Organizations also have history, customs, worldviews, and stated values that can facilitate or hinder learning processes within the organization such as capabilities to transmit best practices and diffuse learning innovations across departments, functions, and levels in the organization. These cross-level effects must be considered to build an effective learning enterprise.

A third implication is that understanding learning requires seeing the interrelationships or patterns throughout the organization rather than only seeing learning as individual events (Senge, 2006). Existing policies and practices can lead to where the "whole" (in terms of learning) is more (or less) than the sum of its parts. For example, improvements in the selection system, resulting in people with higher job relevant skills and capabilities, can have a dramatic effect on reducing the level of learning required to get newcomers up to speed. Effective leadership development efforts can result in a greater pool of qualified persons for promotions. A levels perspective also points to the need to understand the extent to which root causes of learning problems reside within the broader context rather than for simply assuming employees are not interested in upgrading their skills. Thinking levels of analysis emphasizes the need to understand the effectiveness of feedback loops in the organization about what is working and not working relevant to organizational efforts to foster learning (Ford & Foster-Fishman, 2012).

Learning Challenges

Throughout our lives, learning experiences can be an important source of stimulation for enhancing one's knowledge and skills. While educational systems provide a potent source of those learning experiences, organizations need employees to build on that foundation to effectively perform their jobs. How to build and implement effective learning experiences given competing goal and resource demands poses four challenges.

INITIAL AND SUSTAINED DEVELOPMENT One challenge is how to develop talent as quickly, efficiently and as effectively as possible – from front-line workers to leadership positions (Ready, Hill, & Conger, 2008). It can take many weeks or months for a newcomer to become an independent worker. Weak starts can be quite costly to organizations by lengthening the time for a new-comer to become fully job proficient. Speed to proficiency is a key competi-tive advantage (Byham, 2008). Organizations need to examine what they are currently doing for onboarding, training, and socializing newcomers to more adequately address the speed to proficiency issue.

In addition to effective start-ups for newcomers, there is also a need to accelerate and enhance the development of employees' deep and special-ized knowledge that goes beyond this initial level of proficiency. This rapid advancement requires individuals to not only become technically proficient in their present job duties but also develop more generalizable skills and compe-tencies such as communication and decision-making skills. The development of these more generalizable skills across job incumbents helps organizations to build the talent base that is more fluid and adaptive to changing realities (Schmitt et al., 2003). There is a challenge of how and when to facilitate the acquisition of required technical as well as critical interpersonal, problem solv-ing, and other more generalizable skills.

SKILL UPGRADING AND TRANSITIONS   A second challenge concerns developing talent to meet the emerging strategic goals of an organization. Organizations are faced with changing environments that often require shifting priorities and adopting new strategic goals and plans. A learning challenge this leads to is how to minimize skill obsolescence by upgrading worker capabilities to take on new roles and responsibilities. There can be immediate issues of obsoles-cence due to the introduction of new technologies such as automation and robotics that threaten workers in many job categories. Companies must decide whether to retrain those individuals to new types of positions or invest heavily in learning.

Governments are seeing the need to partner with organizations to mini-mize skill shortages and to help workers maintain employment. For example, the Singaporean government started the SkillsFuture initiative in 2016. They identified 23 key industries tied to future growth and opportunities and cre-ated strategies to help individuals gain the skills needed to transition into those industries or to upgrade existing skills to maintain employment in those sec-tors. The initiative now has identified 33 industries and by 2019 about 500,000 individuals and 1,400 enterprises had benefited from SkillsFuture programs in sectors such as information and communication technology, productivity and innovation, and food and beverage and emerging skill areas in data ana-lytics and advanced manufacturing. More specifically, over 124,000 midcareer individuals were given subsidies and training supports (www.skillsfuture.sg/NewsAndUpdates/).

Individuals with advanced education and training can also face skill obsolescence without additional attention to skill enhancement. For example, estimates are that an engineer's education has a half-life of five years, mean-ing that half of what is learned in school is obsolete five years after gradua-tion (Kruchten, 2008). An illustration of this need for updating is the story of AT&T in Table 1.1. They faced a quickly changing technology to cloud-based computing, interconnectivity, and machine learning with a workforce whose existing base of knowledge and skills were becoming obsolete. This massive effort at retraining and reskilling is a critical piece in AT&T's efforts to meet new business priorities. Within the first three years of this strategic initiative,

TABLE 1.1   Spotlight: Retraining Efforts at AT&T

AT&T had dominated the phone business for a long time. Yet, the telecommunications giant has had to reinvent itself given the reality of the move from hardware to the cloud. This means that many of the existing jobs would soon become obsolete. With an average tenure of over 20 years for technical and managerial jobs outside of call centers, AT&T has chosen to invest in its future by placing large resources into retraining programs for its employees in its effort to compete with organizations such as Google. Given the move to wireless networks, there are major technical training needs in areas such as cloud-based computing, connectivity, and machine learning. Much of the initial effort was around a comprehensive learning needs assessment in order to determine skill gaps given what roles were needed in the organization to compete effectively in the future. Then a planning process was conducted to identify and develop programs internally and to identify appropriate credentialing through partnering with outside vendors and schools. The number of job titles in the organizations were dramatically reduced with an emphasis on broadening the types of tasks required for each of the newly created roles. For example, 17 job titles were reduced to one title of software engineer – with the expectation that the role encompasses a number of the tasks that had been divided into those roles.

After the learning needs and planning process was completed, employees were provided with a number of tools for self-management around career opportunities and individual skill development planning. The tools allowed employees to identify their own skill gaps given the new and changing job requirements, point to job opportunities, and identified how the required skills could be developed. With this type of information, employee meetings with their managers could focus on what made the most sense in terms of career options moving forward and how to best gain the skills. In other cases, managers and team members were assigned new roles and responsibilities given organizationally identified needs. Either way, the managers and employees were expected to get the skills through internal or externally identified sources on their own time. Given this requirement, a large amount of the courses taken are on-line with many leading to formal certifications and, in some cases, with high-in-demand jobs, employees could earn a master's degree in computer science through its partnership with a university. Successful completion is required to receive tuition reimbursement. This strategic effort clearly puts the onus on the individual to manage their own career. Within the first three years, about 50% of the workforce were engaged in upgrading existing skills or acquiring skills for newly created job opportunities through traditional training and education programs, professional development opportunities, and tuition assistance. In many cases, employees were expected to complete skill development programs on their own time. In addition, the reward and compensation system was updated to focus more on the market value of various in demand job categories and deemphasizing job tenure. With the enhancement of skills also came the raising of performance expectations to fill the identified needs. As with any major organizational change effort, some employees have concerns about their ability to transform their skills in order to meet these increasing demands leading some to question their future job prospects at AT&T for the existing workforce. Layoffs and relocations continue to be an option the company can use to remain profitable. In addition, AT&T is also investing in youth through programs such as Year Up and Girls Who Code for those aged 18–24 to gain technical as well as softer skills such as networking and public speaking. Individuals from those programs can then obtain internship positions to put their skills to work.

Sources: Donovan, J., & Benko, C. (2016, October). AT&T's talent overhaul: Can the firm really retrain hundreds of thousands of employees? *Harvard Business Review*, 69–73; Fast Company (2019, September 04). AT&T: Preparing the workforce for tomorrow.

about 50% of the workforce has been engaged in upgrading existing skills or acquiring skills for newly created job opportunities through traditional training and education programs, professional development opportunities, and tuition assistance. Whether this impressive effort is enough to sustain the company is yet to be determined.

ENHANCING TEAMWORK AND COLLABORATION   A third challenge is the need to enhance collaboration and cooperation and the sharing of knowledge across individuals, team members, and functions in organizations. Given the more permeable organizational boundaries and concomitant needs for communication across business functions and geographically dispersed facilities, organizations are employing more team-based and collaborative strategies to drive performance effectiveness and to enhance innovation. The coordination needs are expanded when organizational have global reach and global market.

To be effective, these virtual and face-to-face permanent or ad hoc teams must be seamless in their integration of activities, drive best practices, and actively support the diffusion of innovations. This points to the challenge of not only individual level competencies but also teamwork competencies. These teamwork competencies include areas such as anticipating needs of team members, coordinating activities, exchanging information, and focusing on team rather than individual goals. In addition, specific skills in areas such as setting goals, conducting effective team meetings, problem solving and dealing with interpersonal conflict must be developed while meeting day-to-day realities facing organizations.

LEADERSHIP DEVELOPMENT   A fourth challenge is around leadership and leader development. The changing dynamics for organizations puts additional attention on how leaders are being developed to deal with ongoing issues in effective ways. CEOs are being asked to be more active in regards to corporate social responsibility. Global reach requires leaders well trained to work effectively with different cultures. Leaders are being asked to work more collaboratively across departments and functions as well as with different stakeholder groups inside and outside organizational boundaries (Volini et al., 2019).

Organizations desire that first line and middle management commit more time and attention to coaching and mentoring while at the same time handling the continued pressure for maintaining and enhancing efficiency and organizational effectiveness. While there are many approaches to developing leadership skills, how to create meaningful experiences to build leader competencies while maintaining or meeting short term performance goals is a major challenge for organizations.

LEARNING FRAMEWORKS

The challenges facing organization require systematic frameworks around intentional learning and development. One organizing framework is around the types of learning approaches that organizations can engage in or encourage. A second framework is around a planned approach to the identification of learning needs, the design of an effective learning process, competent delivery and evaluation.

Types of Learning Approaches

Learning experiences need to be carefully specified and crafted to be aligned with the strategic goals of the organization and the continuing evolving needs of the organization. Learning at work has traditionally been synonymous with training. Clearly there has been a shift to thinking more broadly about learning and ways of thinking about various approaches to enhancing learning processes at work (Poell, Van Dam, & Van den Berg, 2004). Figure 1.1 depicts the four key types of learning approaches identified that can facilitate building employee capabilities. Each of these types are described next.

FORMAL TRAINING One type of learning approach most frequently associated with learning at work and the development of people is through the creation and delivery of formal training programs. The programs are created to meet an organizational need, are designed to meet learning objectives, and are delivered through face-to-face instruction or presented virtually through web-based and mobile platforms. Learning technologies such as training simulators and augmented reality can be used to place trainees in realistic scenarios to practice and improve upon key skills.

Recent research evidence lends support to this belief of training effectiveness as the overall level of investment in training has been found to have important benefits for organizations. For example, Kim and Ployhart (2014) examined 359 firms over 12 years and found that the amount of internal training investment over time influenced firm profit growth through their impact on firm labor productivity. Sung and Choi (2014) examined 260 companies using a time-lagged analysis that showed expenditures on internal training affected learning practices within the companies and these practices were then linked to higher levels of innovative performance. Another study found that across a

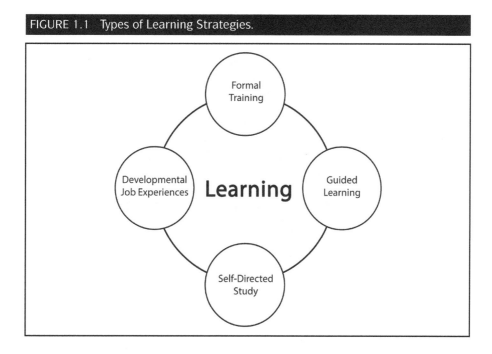

FIGURE 1.1   Types of Learning Strategies.

variety of leadership training studies that the estimated return on leadership development investment averaged positive financial return (Avolio, Avey, & Quisenberry, 2010). Therefore, there is strong empirical evidence to support the attention paid by organizations to enhancing employee knowledge and skills through formal training experiences.

GUIDED LEARNING   A second type of learning approach consists of individualized and guided learning processes such as on-the-job training where a newcomer is paired with an experienced worker to observe and learn the job. Formal training can rarely provide all the knowledge and skills required on the job leading to the need for more one-on-one instruction and coaching. The hallmark of guided instruction is that it is carried out at the workplace and delivered while the learner is engaged in the performance of job tasks. Guided instruction can also come in the form of one-on-one coaching (often for leaders) as well as supervisory and peer mentoring programs for less experienced employees. Both types of guided instruction vary in terms of how well structured or unstructured the learning experience is and in terms of how valuable it is to the development of the learner. Interestingly, 51.4% of companies surveyed reported using on the job coaching by supervisors and/or peers (Ho et al., 2016). Dahling et al. (2016) present research evidence that managerial coaching frequency and skill level are related to annual sales goal attainment by the sales representatives that they directly supervised – demonstrating the importance of effective coaching strategies.

DEVELOPMENTAL JOB EXPERIENCES   A third type of learning approach is the creation and implementation of developmental job assignments. Developmental job assignments are intended to stretch an individual's skills through placing the individual in new job situations. These situations are chosen to provide a more expansive job experiences that require the development of new or enhanced knowledge and skills. For example, an employee with high potential could be assigned to lead an important project that requires managing work that is broader in scope and requires additional job responsibilities than the person had been faced with in the past. Through this job experience in project management, the individual has to coordinate teams activities, delegate tasks, and create systems to monitor and track work being accomplished. These types of developmental activities have been found to help accelerate learning (McCauley et al., 2006). A recent study showed that 66.8% of the companies surveyed emphasized job learning through developmental experiences as an important part of the learning enterprise (Ho et al., 2016).

SELF-DIRECTED LEARNING   A fourth type of learning approach has been called self-directed or autonomous learning. Self-directed learning is voluntary actions taken by employees to understand their own development needs and proactively initiate developmental opportunities to improve their knowledge and update skills (Ellingson & Noe, 2017). Organizations encourage this voluntary autonomous learning through building a continuous learning and improvement culture. Creating a learning culture requires a heavy investment in the learning enterprise that is closely tied to the strategic goals of the organization. It requires a commitment by leaders to create learning opportunities for growth, modeling learning, valuing collaboration and team learning, encouraging experimentation and creating systems to capture and share learning across the organization (Marsick & Watkins, 2003).

There are intentional strategies that help individuals in more informal learning situations to see the need to learn, improve and develop such as being transparent as to skills needed to support future organizational changes. Organizations can also provide mechanisms for feedback from supervisors, peers and subordinates on knowledge and skill gaps. Setting performance expectations, structuring performance reward systems, and establishing accountability systems aligned with a continuous learning orientation can nudge individuals towards continued personal growth. Leaders can also provide constructive feedback after a learning event or experience such as a developmental job assignment to guide future actions. After a coaching experience, the coach can provide time for an individual to reflect on what was gained and what learning needs remain (Tannenbaum, Beard, McNall, & Salas, 2010). Specific initiatives to support self-directed learning include creating suites of resources that are easily accessible for individuals who want to enhance their skills. In addition, organizations can play a role in encouraging self-directed learning by having generous tuition reimbursement plans to gain a college degree as well as strong incentive systems around obtaining various professional certifications to upgrade knowledge and skills.

Learning Systems Model

The strategic goals that organizations hope to achieve vary widely such as producing quality goods in a shorter time period, reducing accidents, developing more effective teams, implementing a management system that is more service-oriented, and increasing health-oriented approaches to life styles as a way of reducing absenteeism due to illness and stress. The potential number of goals is unlimited. Learning interventions are not a panacea for all work-related issues. Individuals may have the requisite knowledge and skills but not be given the opportunity to apply those knowledge and skills on the job. If learning gaps are identified, well-conceived and organized approaches to learning must be enacted to achieve beneficial results for individual growth and development, team effectiveness, and organizational success.

An overarching framework that provides a backbone structure of this book is the Learning Systems Model (LSM). The LSM is rooted in the work over the last 50 years on instructional systems design (ISD) training models applied to the systematic development and implementation of learning programs (Goldstein & Ford, 2002). The foundations for such a systematic approach to creating learning opportunities was well articulated years ago by Viteles (1932) as he noted that

> *a well-organized training program, based on a sound analysis of the job and applying well established learning principles, enables the worker to employ the most effective methods in the performance of his task. Systematic instruction speeds the rate of acquisition of skills and thereby reduces the time required for training. (p. 393)*

FIGURE 1.2 Learning Systems Model.

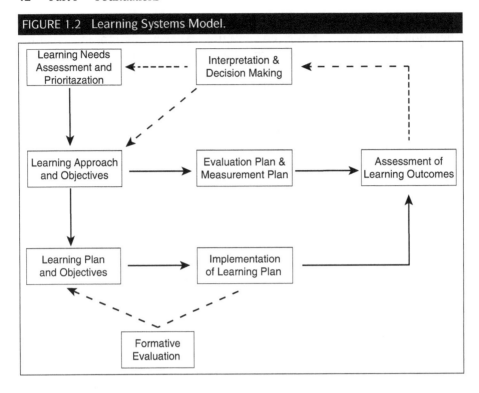

The LSM as presented in Figure 1.2 identifies the important components in building an effective learning system and the interrelationships among the components. The components include assessing learning needs, determining the learning approach and objectives to be attained, the development of a learning plan and the methods to be used, the implementation of the learning plan, and the evaluation or assessment of learning outcomes. The evaluation components provide evidence as to the extent to which learning needs have been met leading to the feedback loops (the dotted lines in the LSM) needed to reassess needs as well as to continuously improve the learning system. The model shows that a learning event or experience is never totally a finished product as feedback provides the information to continually modify the learning process to better meet learning goals. While the chapters to follow in Part II of this book provide more detail on these components, this chapter provides an overview that describes the basics of the model.

The model begins with the assessment of learning needs. Learning needs require looking at the organization as it currently stands as well as where the organization wants to go in the future and how these issues affect the type and level of learning and development needed. Based on needs assessment information, learning priorities can be developed for individual employees, teams, functions or the organization as a whole.

Once learning needs have been assessed and prioritized for each learning opportunity, the first decision is which type of learning approach would be best to meet the learning need identified. For example, looking at learning needs of newcomers in an engineering function may lead to considering the importance of technical training early in the process along with a strong guided learning approach with a coach. Once the type of approach is decided, a blueprint can be created that describes the objectives to be achieved by the learner upon completion of the learning opportunity. A learning objective is a tangible statement of what one wants to see that the learner has acquired as a function of the learning approach to be taken. They specify what the learner should show they have accomplished as a function of the learning approach.

Once the type of learning approach and learning objectives have been set, the next step is to plan out and design the learning intervention. This is a delicate process of determining the appropriate content to cover, the best way to sequence the content to build on each other, and the learning principles to incorporate that have been found to facilitate learning. The plan also identifies the appropriate methods to use to best convey the learning content. This includes making choices about the use of lectures, discussions, demonstrations, practice, and feedback. In addition, what learning technologies might be gainfully employed as delivery mechanisms such as serious games or simulations must be contemplated in developing the plan. Programs that do not achieve their full potential benefit are often a result of a limited understanding of the specific learning needs (necessary knowledge, skills, and competencies) of the individual employees or teams. For example, learning specialists can be sold on an approach such as the use of a team-building program without a clear understanding of the underlying needs and whether the techniques being considered for implementation would be useful in meeting those learning needs.

As shown in Figure 1.2, a parallel activity to developing the learning plan is the development of an evaluation plan to assess learning outcomes. Learning outcomes measures must be developed such as whether the learners obtained the knowledge and skills detailed in the learning objectives. An evaluation plan can also be developed to examine learning transfer or the extent to which the learner is actively applying the newly acquired knowledge, skills, and attitudes on the job to enhance effectiveness. For example, if we expect new technology specialists to be able to troubleshoot a malfunction after initial training, then one could set up the practice scenario at the end of training and measure how quickly and accurately the learner was able to identify and successfully address the malfunction. Then, on the job, the evaluation plan could specify the measurement of how well the learner is now handling the less routine and more complex machine malfunctions on the job.

Once the instructional and evaluation plans are determined, the next step is the delivery of the instructional plan. During delivery, a formative evaluation can be performed to determine if the learning content delivered is consistent with the learning plan of instruction. Such information can be helpful in making quick corrections to the implementation or making an adjustment to the learning plan (or methods) to better meet the learning objectives. From such an evaluation, it might become obvious to the observer that learners are not given enough skill development leading to changes in the learning plan to add in more time for practice and feedback.

After all the work to identify learning needs and designing the plan, the evaluation plan is implemented to gather the type of data needed to determine if the learning approach met the learning goals to address the learning gaps in the organization. Evaluation is often easier said than done (Salas &

TABLE 1.2 Challenges in Evaluation
A community agency was offering a program for previously unemployed individuals to help them obtain jobs. Training consultants were invited to visit and offer suggestions about improvements to the program. Questions about the success of the program were answered by reference to the excellent curricula and the high attendance rate of the participants. A frank discussion ensued related to the objectives of the program, with particular emphasis on the criteria being utilized to measure the adequacy of the program – that is, how successful the participants were in obtaining and holding jobs. This discussion led to the revelation that the success level simply was not known because such data had never been collected. Of course, it was possible that the program was working successfully, but the information to make such a judgment was unavailable. Thus, there was no way to judge the effectiveness of the program or to provide information that could lead to improvements. Basically, unless there is information about the effectiveness of the programs in helping trainees to find jobs, it is not possible to know whether it made sense to revise or where to place the efforts when revisions were necessary.
Source: Goldstein, I. L. & Ford, J. K. (2002). *Training in organizations: Needs assessment, development, and evaluation*, 4th ed., Wadsworth, Belmont, CA.

Cannon-Bowers, 2001). Table 1.2 presents a case example of some of the difficulties faced when asked to evaluate a learning opportunity, in this case a training program to help unemployed individuals obtain a job.

The final phase is the feedback loop where the data from the assessment of learning outcome is interpreted and then used in making decisions about future learning steps. The development and implementation of a learning approach is an evolving process. In some cases, the evaluation may indicate that the learning need has been met for the individual or teams that were the focus of the learning intervention. In this case, the information from the evaluation could identify the reasons why the learning program was effective. This information would be quite helpful in improving the effectiveness of other learning approaches. On the other hand, the evaluation may point to limited success leading to questions of how to better meet the learning needs. The information could be used to improve the relevancy of the learning content, revise learning objectives, refine learning design, or point to more effective delivery options. The assessment information can also help in reassessing and reprioritizing learning needs.

While the two-dimensional representation of the LSM in Figure 1.2 presents a somewhat linear step-like perspective, the cyclical nature of the model is clear from the dotted lines of the feedback loops. In addition, rather than lines only going in one direction, it is helpful to think that there are reciprocal or bidirectional links among the components. Once a plan of instruction is created, it might become obvious that the learning objectives are not be realistic given time constraints imposed on the learning opportunity leading to revising the objectives or adding more hours to instruction. The delivery of learning may point to problematic areas that require revising the plan of instruction. So, the reciprocal processes and feedback loops are not only relevant at the end of the model after formal evaluation but take place throughout the processes in enacting the LSM.

As a final note on this organizing model, much of what we know about building and sustaining effective learning systems comes from training research. Nevertheless, it is important to point out that best practices found from training research have direct implications for enhancing the success of other types of learning approaches – as this is all about learning! There are well-developed strategies for conducting a thorough training needs assessment to identify what knowledge and skills are needed to be enhanced in employees. Such strategies can also be used to identify what types of developmental job experiences are needed to enhance those knowledge and skills beyond formal training. We also have strong empirical evidence of learning principles that facilitate learning during training. One such principle (to be discussed more fully in Chapter 5) is incorporating generative learning into a training session. Generative learning refers to having trainees work with an issue or problem prior to a more formal lecture and discussion of the issues in order to enhance readiness to learn. This principle is certainly relevant to incorporate when mentoring or coaching individuals by asking good questions and posing problems that the individual addresses prior to obtaining an on-the-job learning experience.

AN EVIDENCE-BASED APPROACH

Organizations often look to what other organizations are doing. This can lead to fads such as today we focus on transformational leadership while tomorrow we abandon that and target strategic leadership training. Without adequate evaluation of techniques, the cycle of fads continues. This is particularly true about learning technologies. As noted by Clark (2010),

> with each new technology wave, enthusiasts ride the crest with claims that finally we have the tools to really revolutionize training. Yet, in just a few years, today's latest media hype will fade, yielding to the inexorable evolution of technology and a fresh spate of technological hyperbole. (p. 12)

The increasing emphasis on accountability makes it more likely that organizations will correctly insist on understanding the impact of the learning programs where much time and resources have been invested. In addition, the organization's need to control costs in order to compete in today's economy puts an emphasis on the added value of the learning enterprise. This section describes ways to find and interpret evidence that can inform best practices for enhancing learning. The use of meta-analysis to combine findings across studies is then described. A cautionary tale of statements made that may or may not be evidence base is then presented. The section ends with a discussion of evidence-based approach taken in this book.

Finding Evidence

Moving from the cycle of fads requires a focus on what has been termed "evidence-based practice." This approach means that choices made about the organizational learning enterprise is informed by the best evidence available at that time. The medical field has embraced this notion making evidence-based practice a critical component in the care of patients. As one example, constant reminders for care givers to wash hands to reduce the chances of infection has been found to have positive impacts on patient care (Heath & Heath, 2008). While becoming more common, companies have typically underutilized the evidence that is available to help enhance learning and developmental activities.

Evidence-based practice is a disciplined approach to understanding the choices that are possible and making decisions based on the explicit use of the best available evidence so as to lead to desired outcomes (Rousseau & Gunia, 2015). Evidence-based practice requires taking a number of steps before quality decisions can be made. As an initial step, one must turn a practical issue into a question to be answered such as whether an organization should invest more in team building. With this question being asked, one can search for and retrieve evidence that is available around the value of team building, when teambuilding is most useful, and how to enhance its effectiveness. Based on this evidence, individuals in decision-making positions can critically judge the trustworthiness and relevance of the evidence acquired. This may require aggregating across sources that may present somewhat contradictory evidence. Then the evidence can be adequately assessed to determine if a team-building activity would be appropriate to incorporate into the development of team members in one's organization (Barends, Rousseau, & Briner, 2014). A nice discussion of evidence based practice as well as articles, tools, and presentations can be gleaned from the Center for Evidence-Based Management at www.cebma.org.

In regard to the learning enterprise, organizations can look to three main sources for helping understand "what works." The sources differ in how closely tied they are to research evidence acquired through rigorous evaluation. A first level of evidence is to understand what other companies identified as having best practices are doing and potentially copying some of the components to improve one's own learning enterprise. There can be a fine line between a fad and companies identified as exemplars of best practices. Many companies seen as great at one point in time may not be seen that way at a later point in time. Nevertheless, learning specialists may obtain useful ideas on ways of enhancing the learning enterprise from examining what companies labelled as exemplars are doing relevant to what they are investing in relevant to learning and development in their workplace.

The Association for Talent Development identifies and provides a yearly BEST award to companies seen as innovative around learning and development. Table 1.3 presents three examples of the recent winners and a short description of what they did to be awarded. One explicit goal of the Association in writing about the excellence exemplified by the award winners is to help organizations with ideas on how to improve their learning enterprise. Of course, one would need much more detailed understanding of the approaches in these exemplar companies and give much thought about what could be applied successfully in one's organization that may vary from the winners on a number of dimensions. While awards are given, it is also important to recognize that there may be only preliminary or limited objective evidence metrics that validate the impact of the best practice approach.

A second level for best practice revolves around judgments made by experienced learning specialists who have been in the trenches and reflect on what has and has not worked to facilitate learning and the application of learning to the job. These expert judgments are based on direct observations and personal experiences as well as reflections and attempts to continuously improve learning outcomes. The conclusions reached can be quite valuable

TABLE 1.3   Association for Talent Development "BEST" Award Winners
Each year, the Association for Talent Development presents awards to companies that have been selected for exemplary efforts at learning and development. The awards are meant to recognize organizations that use talent development as a key strategic tool to become more effective. This means that the organizations go beyond just providing a set of individual learning opportunities. The award winners must show that they have a well-defined talent development strategy, a structured approach to sequencing learning and creating innovative pathways for life-long learning and development as well as evidence of success and an indication of how developing talent is valued in the organization.
Wipro Limited, Bangalore, India: Serves global clients with cutting edge technology solutions Wipro Limited focuses on enhancing skill agility and establishing a culture of continual upskilling and reskilling. The company mandates reskilling in areas that are rapidly advancing so employees can be "future ready." For example, employees choose to be certified in digital and other skills based on career aspirations and future needs of the company. Career advancement is based on completing learning programs, successfully completing certifications, and performance improvement.
Verizon, New York, USA: Global telecommunications Verizon updated it business model and priorities. One priority is more closely linking business strategies to leadership skills to help lead a culture change. The Leadership Edge program was developed in partnership with the CEO and executive group to facilitate the application of the new business model and priorities to daily work throughout the organization. There is also a leadership academy, which is a one-week intensive learning experience for sales and service people to build coaching and collaboration skills using learning technologies such as virtual reality and augmented reality as well as serious gaming to help learners gain the most from the experiences. There is also a Women of the World grassroots program to building a leadership talent pipeline for women who are currently working front-line jobs.
Danone, Turkey: Global food and Beverages Danone has created a self-driven learning system that flows from the employees' career aspirations. Employees know that they are the sole drivers of their own learning and development with support from managers and human resource personnel. Managers are trained to be coaches and facilitators of career discussions with employees helping to design the learning opportunities that best fit the career paths desired. The learning opportunities include short, on-the-job learning including cross-functional, cross-division, and cross-company intensive programs. There is also a six-month program for high potentials matching them with mentors in the business areas the employee would like to explore and develop skills to match that career direction. The goal is for everyone to be a learner and a coach in order to develop the unique talents in the organization.
Source: Castellano, S. (2019). Leading through change. *Talent Development* (October: Association for Talent Development BEST Award Winners Revealed). ATD, Alexandria, VA.

in identifying strategies and approaches for optimizing learning. To illustrate, experienced learning specialists designed, delivered, and modified a set of learning workshops for teaching medical "fellows" for how to teach and coach others. This emphasis on continuously improving the workshops over the course of over 25 years led to a strong understanding of what works for enhancing both learning and the transfer of the knowledge and skills from the workshop to the job. Table 1.4 presents the 12 "tips" shared with the broader learning community about specific steps to take to facilitate transfer. These

TABLE 1.4 Reflections on Strategies for Facilitating Learning Transfer

Strategy	Description
Assess developmental needs	Systematically identify needed competencies and use the information to develop overall program goals and to specific knowledge and skills to acquire
Communicate the expectation of application	Provide continual messages to participants prior to and during the workshops that the design of the workshops was intentionally focused on direct application to the job by focusing on highly job relevant knowledge and skills based on the needs assessment
Secure support for application	Before attending the workshops, ensure there is a formal agreement with the participant's supervisor for release time not only for the learning events but also for the project development time in between learning sessions
Prepare instructors and coaches to teach for transfer	Have the instructors gain knowledge prior to the learning workshops regarding an assortment of practical and effective methods that can be readily applied and broadly adapted by participants given their job context and needs
Teach principles and methods	Ensure that the learning sessions include specific steps within a method so learners could be directed to ways of doing something as well as conveying the underlying principles of why the methods are effective
Motivate to apply	Present evidence-based best practices and logical reasons for use of the methods and principles and present examples showing the practicality or ease of application
Provide tools to aid recall and application	Convert instructional material into easily digestible and accessible job aids to provide application guidance such as diagrams, checklists, decision aids, charts, models, principles, skill steps and mnemonics
Demonstrate an application	Demonstrate the desired methods, steps, and behaviors prior to having the learner practice by telling the learner what to look at and to look for before the demonstration and then ask the learners to commit the steps to memory

(continued)

TABLE 1.4 (Continued)   Reflections on Strategies for Facilitating Learning Transfer

Strategy	Description
Provide authentic practice	Arrange ample time for skill practice with increasing challenge with contexts similar to job situations
Require an application project	Have learners design with input from their supervisor a job relevant and feasible project that is begun immediately once back on the job so as to provide the opportunity to apply the principles and skills gained
Establish a feedback cycle	Teach participants how to give useful, respective, and honest feedback to learning peers and provide time for self-assessment and reflection as well as group and instructor guidance on how to improve
Evaluate transfer	Use qualitative and quantitative evaluation methods and design to determine what has been applied to the job and why so as to continuously improve instruction

Source: Yelon, S. L., Ford, J. K., & Anderson, W. A. (2014). Twelve tips for increasing transfer of training from faculty development programs. *Medical Teacher*, 36, 945–950.

suggestions provide decision makers with choices for adopting some or all of the tips to improve their own learning enterprise.

The third level for deriving best practices comes from empirically based research. Empirically based research is where data is gathered to test a set of propositions or hypotheses. Data can be collected leading to qualitative (e.g., categorizing data from interviews) or quantitative (e.g., survey responses) analysis. While both types of analyses provide information that can be turned into evidence, the emphasis here is on quantitative approaches to testing hypotheses.

Figure 1.3 presents visually four different types of research models that could be tested though systematic data collection and quantitative analysis. For example, one might be interested in the extent to which individuals' motivation to learn prior to attending a training program affects the extent to which they apply the knowledge gained from the program to the job – an issue of training transfer (talked about in Chapter 5). This type or research would require measuring an individual's level of motivation through say a survey asking questions such as on a scale (from 1 = to no extent to 5 = to a great extent) how motivated are you to learn from the upcoming training program. Such a study would also need to measure the extent to which the leaners applied or transferred new knowledge to the job. Learners could be asked the extent to which they are now using the knowledge or skills taught in the training program. Conducting such a study would lead to analyzing the data to test whether there is a direct relationship between the scores on the motivation to learn and the transfer measures such that people high on motivation to learn

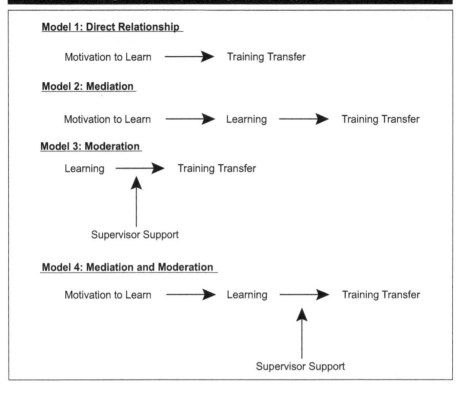

FIGURE 1.3   Testing Relationships through Various types of Research Models.

are found to have higher levels of training transfer. A more complicated model could include testing for what is called a "mediation" effect. This second research model might specify that the level of motivation to learn impacts how much is learned from the training program and this level of knowledge gained is what affects the extent to which the learner applies the knowledge gained as measured by say positive changes in job behavior. With this model, motivation to learn impacts transfer through its influence on how much an individual learns from the program. In a third model, one could contend that the extent to which learning from training leads to transfer or changes in job behavior is affected by the level of supervisory support in the workplace. In this case, we would hypothesize that the level of supervisory support "moderates" the relationship between knowledge gain and transfer. One way this moderation effect would be shown is if individuals who gained much knowledge in training showed high levels of application when the supervisor was supportive but lower levels of application when supervisor support was low. For those who did not gain much from the learning program, the amount of transfer would likely be low regardless of the level of support. A further increase in complexity is shown in the last model that hypothesizes both a mediation and moderation effect such that motivation to learn affects knowledge gain (as above), which impacts the extent of transfer, but that the relationship of the level of knowledge gain leading to the application to the job depends on the level of supervisory support for the training. Clearly, models that are to be tested can be much more complicated that these presented but they give a basic idea of what empirically based testing is all about.

Analyzing and Combining Evidence

Empirical findings must be interpreted as to their importance for driving best practices. Taking the example above, we typically would calculate a correlation (r) between motivation to learn and transfer to find how strong the relationship is. The higher the r the stronger the relationship with a correlation of zero showing no relationship between the two such that the level of motivation has nothing to do with the amount of knowledge gained. So, let us assume the study finds that highly motivated learners gain more knowledge and are more likely to apply this knowledge when performing the job than those with lower levels of motivation to learn. In addition, the study also finds from interview data that highly motived individuals perceive the training as more job relevant than those with low motivation to learn. This finding provides some evidence for understanding why there are differences in the levels of motivation to learn across individuals. An implication for best practices, then, would be to either ensure that learners are selected if the training is a good fit for their job duties or that the relevance of the learning opportunity is made clearer to all learners prior to attending the program. On the other hand, if findings show that leader support is critical for individuals to transfer their knowledge to the job, then the focus of attention would need to be on enhancing that level of support by the leaders such as having them attend the program prior to their employees.

The research findings from individual studies provide evidence as to what factors are relevant to understanding and predicting learning outcomes. Once a number of studies have been done testing similar relationships such as motivation to learn and transfer, a next step is to integrate or synthesize the findings across those studies. In this way, across studies that differ in many ways (types of jobs, measurement of study variables, etc.), one can uncover what has been found in the research literature to help drive best practices.

One way to do this is by conducting a systematic and critical review of the research findings across studies. For a systematic review, the researcher assembles the full weight of evidence available pertaining to a given research question, which is then evaluated in terms of its scientific rigor and excellence and considered as part of the formal review of research findings (Hodgkinson & Ford, 2014). The researchers examine the evidence and provide a summary of what has been found in the research. Systematic reviews are one of the cornerstones of evidence-based approach for building best practices (Briner, Denyer, & Rousseau, 2009). A limitation is the potential for subjectivity on the part of the researcher in choosing what studies to review, how the findings are summarized, and interpreting the implications of the findings for best practices.

A quantitative approach to examining findings across multiple studies is through the use of meta-analytic reviews. Meta-analysis is the application of statistical procedures to aggregate findings across studies in order to synthesize and discover the patterns in the findings to clarify the state of the science at any given point in time (Hunter & Schmidt, 2004). As an illustration, a meta-analytic study on training transfer found 89 studies that have investigated factors that could affect the application of trained knowledge and skills to the job (Blume et al., 2010). The studies were coded for what factors were measured in the studies and how transfer was measured. For example, the researchers found 29 studies with 3,844 learners in those study and looked at the relationship of motivation and transfer as use. They found 29 studies with

3,844 learners that looked at the relationship of between .18 and .30. Given that this interval does not include zero we can be confident that transfer rates are higher for those with greater motivation to learn – although modest in strength. They also found that the relationship of the supportiveness of the work environment and transfer across 35 studies with 5,017 learners was .30.

The study was also able to study moderators of the relationships being studied. The researchers were able to show that the level of work environment support was much more important when training general principles and guidelines (e.g., how to give feedback to coworkers) than when training on technical skills. Other researchers have also used meta-analytic evidence to study more complex sets of mediation effects. For example, one study examined how the effects of individual characteristics such as conscientiousness as well as work environment support affected training transfer through their impact on learning (knowledge and skill) and motivation to transfer (Huang et al., 2015). The bottom line is that we now have many meta-analytic studies that have been completed to understand the factors that impact learning and transfer. In this book, many of these types of studies are described to provide the best evidence that we have at this point in time around the science of learning.

Cautionary Tales

While the focus of this book is on best evidence, it is also important to point out areas where the "hype" or some commonly accepted statements do not meet an evidence-based test. As noted by Weick (2006) in his article on better guesses in an unknowable world, "a fundamental property of everyday life is that people believe ahead of the evidence" (p. 1724). Two areas that provide a cautionary tale regarding beliefs and evidence around learning and transfer are provided next.

LESS THAN 10% OF WHAT IS TRAINED IS APPLIED TO THE JOB   This statement (and many other similar statements) make the claim that little of what is trained is applied to the job implying that training has only a small impact on job performance. Practitioners and researchers have invoked this notion that only a small percent of what is learned is transferred to justify the need for more studies on the factors that can affect transfer and to spur trainers and training designers to be more effective in promoting transfer.

While this claim may have good intentions and "feel" right, there is no empirical evidence for this claim (Ford, Yelon, & Billington, 2011). The origin of this statement is based on a hypothetical statement asked within the context of a discussion about the cost of training. For sake of an argument, Georgensen (1982) noted "how many times have you heard training directors say … I would estimate that only 10% of content which is presented in the classroom is reflected in behavioral change on the job." As noted by Fitzpatrick (2001), Georgenson (1982) was using a rhetorical device to catch the audience's attention. Yet, the claim has qualities of a "sticky idea" (Heath & Heath, 2008). People tend to accept and keep ideas that are consistent with six principles of being simple, unexpected, concrete, credible, emotional, and tell a good story. Ford, Yelon, and Billington (2011) show how these six principles seem to fit quite nicely with the 10% transfer idea. They point out the inherent problem that the 10% estimate has no clear referent – 10% of something could mean many things such as only one of ten principles taught are applied on average across all learners or only one in ten trainees applied all ten principles. The conclusions one would draw about the training would be quite different depending on which interpretation was more representative of reality. The statement also is not clear on what sort of learning was or was not transferred and implies that transferring general knowledge principles, simple or complex skills, or attitudes is relatively easy to measure objectively in order to calculate a percentage – when in reality measurement of transfer (e.g., behavioral change) is quite difficult to accomplish. The bottom line is a cautionary tale that researchers and practitioners may assume that the extent of transfer is low because of its repeated assertion rather than because of its empirical support. The lesson is that to be wary of and question "all-encompassing statements that supposedly represent conventional wisdom and to search for convincing evidence and to critically analyze assumptions behind generalization" (Ford, Yelon, & Billington, 2011, p. 20).

THE 70-20-10 RULE   This rule contends that 70% of what is learned by employees is from on-the-job experiences such as working on tasks and problems, 20% is from coaching and feedback and only 10% of what is learned comes from formal training courses. This claim implies that most learning occurs informally and that formal training accounts for a minimal amount of the accumulated knowledge and skills of employees and leaders in organizations. There is limited empirical evidence to support the 70-20-10 claim or the implied assumption that this rule is generalized to any type of job in any type of organization.

This does not mean that informal learning experiences from job experiences are not important but that one must be careful in the conclusions one draws. The 70-20-10 rule of thumb seems to indicate that formal training "is at best only marginally contribute to employee learning and development, perhaps approaching the point of being a waste of time and resources" (Clardy, 2018, p. 12). As noted earlier in the chapter, research provides strong evidence that investments in training can have a strong impact on organizational success.

Clardy (2018) provides four methodological problems with the studies cited as supporting the 70-20-10 rule. First, a number of studies gathered data from high-level executives through interviews and surveys. These efforts resulted in a highly restrictive sample of participants making it hard to generalize to all types of jobs and functions. Second, many of the studies cited as supporting this rule of thumb had "loaded" open-ended interviews that emphasized questions on informal learning opportunities – in fact, some studies did not have any prompts for respondents to talk about the impact of formal education and training experiences. Third, the problem with coming up with percentages has been discussed above with the 10% rule of thumb for transfer and has relevance to the 70-20-10 rule. In terms of calculating fractions, how does one know what the numerator (above the line) and denominator (below the line) is? Fourth, given the overreliance on self-reports, the rule of thumb has no objective data to back up this rule. As noted by Marsick (2003), the nature of informal learning makes it "prone to self-distortion because it is by its nature, tacit, opportunistic and not typically highly conscious (p. 391). In addition, the interconnectedness of learning is not recognized by this rule.

Formal training has been the impetus for more self-guided learning or a greater focus on enhancing skills through seeking out mentors and coaches. The lesson moving forward is to how to improve all learning experiences, especially those that are more informal and unstructured.

There are other issues about learning that are covered in this book that separate facts based on evidence from fiction. These issues include effective ways of learning, whether learning styles matter, and how long it takes to become an expert in one's field. In addition to these issues, Chapter 10 on leadership development comes back to the issue of the 70-20-10 rule. A detailed examination of other learning myths is described in a recent book by Quinn (2018) on *Millennials, Goldfish, & other Training Misconceptions*.

BOOK ORGANIZATION

This book is divided into three parts. Part I is on foundational issues around learning.

Chapter 1 has highlighted the need for effective learning and development in the workplace as well as pointed to its challenges. It has also provided a framework on types of learning approaches as well as a Learning Systems Model to guide our understanding of how to create effective learning opportunities. The need to take an evidence-based approach has also been highlighted. Chapter 2 points to the important fundamental reality that the learning enterprise resolves around learning! The chapter defines what learning is (and is not) and presents a multi-dimensional framework around knowledge, skill, and affective indicators that learning has occurred.

Part II examines in detail the components and interrelationships in the Learning Systems Model. Chapter 3 describes the learning needs assessment process that includes organizational, work, and person analyses. It highlights the critical role of identifying current and future learning needs in an organization. Based on this effort, priorities can be set for learning and the learning strategy can be chosen. Once learning needs have been prioritized, Chapter 4 describes the steps to develop learning objectives to provide clear directions to meeting each learning need. Based on learning objectives, the learning plan can be created to best meet the learning objectives. The chapter also focuses on the learner and the critical issues of enhancing learner readiness and motivation to learn. While learning is clearly foundational, the ultimate key for organizations is what learners do on the job after acquiring new knowledge and skills. This issue of learning transfer is described in Chapter 5 with a focus on understanding the person, work environment, and learning design factors that have the strongest impact on the retention and application of new knowledge and skills on the job. Chapter 6 examines the role of evaluation by describing the importance of developing reliable and valid measures of learning and transfer. The chapter also emphasizes the use of rigorous research designs to allow for more confidence in the results obtained from assessing changes in learning and on the job behavior. The next chapter describes the methods used to deliver the learning plan including more traditional approaches such as lecture, discussion, demonstration, and practice. Chapter 7 also addresses emerging learning technologies that have been advanced as helping to facilitate learning.

Part III investigates the best practice evidence for a variety of learning strategies for building individual, team and organizational effectiveness. Chapter 8 examines the evidence around learning approaches to build individuals from a relative novice stage to becoming an expert in their job. This includes reviewing strategies such as initial onboarding efforts as well as subsequent skill updating and career management for individuals in an organization. The move to designing jobs around permanent teams and ad hoc team-based project work in organizations is highlighted in Chapter 9. Learning strategies for enhancing teamwork and team development are described. Chapter 10 examines the role of leaders in organizations and the variety of strategies to develop effective leadership from front-line supervisors to the executive C-Suite. The final chapter examines ways that organizations can facilitate a learning culture by becoming what has been called a learning organization. Chapter 11 also goes beyond individual companies by focusing on learning needs at the societal level that have implications for work organizations. In every chapter, what we know from research evidence is highlighted as well as what we still need to know to help drive best practices.

References

Abattiello, A., Agarwal, D., Bersin, J., Lahiri, G., Schwartz, J., & Volini, E. (2018). *Global Human Capital Trends 2018: The rise of the social enterprise*. New York: Deloitte Insights.

Avolio, B. J., Avey, J. B., & Quisenberry, D. (2010). Estimating return on leadership development investment. *The Leadership Quarterly*, 21(4), 633–644. doi. org/10.1016/j.leaqua.2010.06.006

Barends, E., Rousseau, D. M., & Briner, R. B. (2014). *Evidence based management: The basic principles*. Amsterdam: Center for Evidence-Based Management.

Blume, B. D., Ford, J. K., Baldwin, T. T., & Huang, J. L. (2010). Transfer of training: A meta-analytic review. *Journal of Management*, 36(4), 1065–1105. doi. org/10.1177/0149206309352880

Briner, R. B., Denyer, D., & Rousseau, D. M. (2009). Evidence-based management: Concept cleanup time? *Academy of Management Perspectives*, 23(4), 19–32. doi.org/10.5465/amp.23.4.19

Byham, W. C. (2008). *Strong start to job success: What leaders can do to shorten time to proficiency, increase job engagement, and reduce early turnover*. Pittsburg, PA: Development Dimensions International, pp. 1–22.

Castellano, S. (2019). Leading through change. *Talent development* (October: Association for Talent Development BEST Award Winners Revealed). ATD, Alexandria, VA.

Clardy, A. (2018). 70-20-10 and the dominance of informal learning: A fact in search of evidence. *Human Resource Development Review*, 17(2), 153–178. doi. org/10.1177/1534484318759399

Clark, R. C. (2010). *Evidence-based training methods: A guide for training professionals*. Washington, DC: American Society for Training and Development Press.

Dahling, J. J., Taylor, S. R., Chau, S. L., & Dwight, S. A. (2016). Does coaching matter? A multilevel model linking managerial coaching skill and frequency to sales goal attainment. *Personnel Psychology*, 69(4), 863–894. doi.org/10.1111/peps.12123

Donovan, J., & Benko, C. (2016, October). AT&T's talent overhaul: Can the firm really retrain hundreds of thousands of employees? *Harvard Business Review*, 69–73.

Ellingson, J. E., & Noe, R. A. (Eds.). (2017). *Autonomous learning in the workplace*. New York: Taylor & Francis Group.

Fast Company (2019, September 4). *AT&T: Preparing the workforce for tomorrow*. New York: Fast Company, Mansueto Ventures.

Fitzpatrick, R. (2001). The strange case of the transfer of training estimate. *The industrial-organizational Psychologist*, 39(2), 18–19.

Ford, J. K., & Foster-Fishman, P. (2012). Organizational development and change: Linking research from the profit, nonprofit, and public sectors. *The Oxford handbook of organizational psychology*, 2, 956–992.

Ford, J. K., Yelon, S. L., & Billington, A. Q. (2011). How much is transferred from training to the job? The 10% delusion as a catalyst for thinking about transfer. *Performance Improvement Quarterly*, 24(2), 7–24. doi.org/10.1002/piq.20108

Georgenson, D. L. (1982). The problem of transfer calls for partnership. *Training and Development Journal*, 36, 75–78.

Goldstein, I., & Ford, J. K. (2002). *Training in organizations: Needs assessment, development, and evaluation* (4th edition). Belmont, CA: Wadsworth.

Heath, C., & Heath, D. (2008). *Make to stick: Why some ideas take hold and others come unstuck*. New York: Arrow Books, Limited.

Ho, M., Jones, M., Julien, T., & Body, J. (2016). *2015 state of the industry*. Alexandria, VA: Association for Talent Development.

Hodgkinson, G. P., & Ford, J. K. (2014). Narrative, meta-analytic, and systematic reviews: What are the differences and why do they matter? *Journal of Organizational Behavior*, 35, 1–5. doi.org/10.1002/job.1918

Huang, J. L., Blume, B. D., Ford, J. K., & Baldwin, T. T. (2015). A tale of two transfers: Disentangling maximum and typical transfer and their respective predictors. *Journal of Business and Psychology*, 30(4), 709–732. doi.org/10.1007/s10869-014-9394-1

Hunter, J. E., & Schmidt, F. L. (2004). *Methods of meta-analysis: Correcting error and bias in research findings*. Thousand Oaks, CA: Sage.

Kim, Y., & Ployhart, R. E. (2014). The effects of staffing and training on firm productivity and profit growth before, during, and after the Great Recession. *Journal of Applied Psychology*, 99(3), 361. doi.org/10.1037/a0035408

Kraiger, K., & Ford, J. K. (2007). The expanding role of workplace training: Themes and trends influencing training research and practice. In L. L. Koppes (Eds.), *Historical perspectives in industrial and organizational psychology* (pp. 281–309). Mahwah, NJ: Lawrence Erlbaum Associates.

Kruchten, P. (2008). The biological half-life of software engineering ideas. *IEEE Software*, 25(5), 10–11. doi.org/10.1109/MS.2008.127

Manyika, J., Lund, S., Chui, M., Bughin, J., Woetzel, J., Batra, P., & Sanghvi, S. (2017). *Jobs lost, jobs gained: Workforce transitions in a time of automation*. New York: McKinsey Global Institute, 150.

Marsick, V. J. (2003). Invited reaction: Informal learning and the transfer of learning: How managers develop proficiency. *Human Resource Development Quarterly*, 14, 389–395. doi.org/10.1002/hrdq.1075

Marsick, V. J., & Watkins, K. E. (2003). Demonstrating the value of an organization's learning culture: The dimensions of the learning organization questionnaire. *Advances in Developing Human Resources*, 5(2), 132–151. doi.org/10.1177/1523422303005002002

McCauley, C. D., Drath, W. H., Palus, C. J., O'Connor, P. M., & Baker, B. A. (2006). The use of constructive-developmental theory to advance the understanding of leadership. *The Leadership Quarterly*, 17(6), 634–653. doi.org/10.1016/j.leaqua.2006.10.006

Mishra, R. R., & Bisui, R. (2019). *The global talent crunch: Talent development as a means to bridge the gap*. Los Angeles, CA: Korn Ferry.

Poell, R. F., Van Dam, K., & Van Den Berg, P. T. (2004). Organising learning in work contexts. *Applied Psychology*, 53(4), 529–540. doi.org/10.1111/j.1464-0597.2004.00186.x

Quinn, C. N. (2018). *Millennials, goldfish & other training misconceptions: Debunking learning myths and superstitions*. American Society for Training and Development.

Ready, D. A., Hill, L. A., & Conger, J. A. (2008). Winning the race for talent in emerging markets. *Harvard Business Review*, 86(11), 62–70.

Rousseau, D. M., & Gunia, B. C. (2015). Evidence-based practice: The psychology of EBP implementation. *Annual Review of Psychology*, 67, 667–692. doi.org/10.1146/annurev-psych-122414-033336

Salas, E., & Cannon-Bowers, J. A. (2001). The science of training: A decade of progress. *Annual Review of Psychology*, 52(1), 471–499. doi.org/10.1146/annurev.psych.52.1.471

Schmitt, N., Cortina, J. M., Ingerick, M. J., & Wiechmann, D. (2003). Personnel selection and employee performance. W. C. Borman, D. R. Ilgen, & R. J. Klimoski (Eds.), *Handbook of psychology: Industrial and organizational psychology*, Vol. 12 (pp. 77–105). Hoboken, NJ: John Wiley & Sons Inc.

Senge, P. M. (2006). *The fifth discipline: The art and practice of the learning organization*. New York: Broadway Business.

Sung, S. Y., & Choi, J. N. (2014). Do organizations spend wisely on employees? Effects of training and development investments on learning and innovation in organizations. *Journal of Organizational Behavior*, 35(3), 393–412. doi.org/10.1002/job.1897

Tannenbaum, S. I., Beard, R. L., & McNall, L. A., & Salas, E. (2010). Informal learning and development in organizations. In S. W. J. Kozlowski & E. Salas (Eds.), *Learning and development in organizations*, 330–331. New York: Routledge.

Viteles, M. S. (1932). *Industrial psychology*. New York: Norton.

Volini, E., Schwartz, J., Roy, I., Hauptmann, M., Van Durme, Y., Denny, B., & Bersin, J. (2019). *Leading the social enterprise: Reinvent with a human focus*. New York: Deloitte University Press.

Walsh, B. (2017). *Rewriting the rules for the digital age 2017: Deloitte global human capital trends*. New York: Deloitte University Press.

Weick, K. E. (2006). Faith, evidence, and action: Better guesses in an unknowable world. *Organization studies*, 27(11), 1723–1736. doi.org/10.1177/0170840606068351

Yelon, S. L., Ford, J. K., & Anderson, W. A. (2014). Twelve tips for increasing transfer of training from faculty development programs. *Medical Teacher*, 36, 945–950. doi.org/10.3109/0142159X.2014.929098

CHAPTER 2

Learning about Learning

Questions

- ✓ What do we mean by learning and what is the opposite of learning?
- ✓ What happens internally within learners as they acquire new knowledge, skills, and attitudes on the road to job expertise?
- ✓ What are the observable indicators that can be measured to determine that learning has occurred?

The foundation of any learning enterprise in organizations – not surprisingly – is learning! The goal of training, guided instruction, developmental job assignments and self-directed instruction is for the learner to gain something from those experiences. How do we understand what could be gained and what can we look towards to indicate that some amount of learning has taken place? The purpose of this chapter is to define what is meant by learning, categorize what can change as a function of a learning experience, and to detail the stages of learning over time and across one's career.

LEARNING DEFINED

What do we mean by learning? How about starting with saying something about what learning is not. The opposite of learning is to miss, overlook, or to pass over. Other opposites include to neglect, ignore, or to disregard. A final characteristic is to forget – which is to fail to remember or to be unable to recall (Dictionary.com). Forgetting implies that some knowledge or skill was gained but that after some time (e.g., without any opportunity to practice) what was gained is now not accessible to the learner. Shulman (1999) has noted that one of the most frequent pathologies of learning is "amnesia" or forgetting what was learned. He also states that learners can also fall prey to "fantasia" or the illusion that one is confident they understand something that they do not; or be a victim to "inertia" – something that is not forgotten but is not organized in memory in such a way that leads to any useful purpose. An example of this is someone being able to spout a fact but having no idea why the fact is important or how it could be used for some purpose.

Learning, then, must be where something that could be learned is not missed (or fail to comprehend, sense, or experience), overlooked (to look past), ignored (refuse to take notice of; to reject as ungrounded), or forgotten (failed to be remembered). Table 2.1 provides examples of what *is* defined as learning. An examination of the definitions of what is learning and what is the opposite of learning points to three key characteristics.

One characteristic in defining learning is that there is some type of change from prior to and then after an experience or set of experiences. Some definitions focus on changes in knowledge and skills while others describe learning more generally as changes in one's capabilities. Others note that learning leads to changes in behaviors or at least changes in the potentiality of a greater range of behaviors that may or may not be seen until there are opportunities to "show" that learning has taken place. Still others note that learning can be observed in terms of changes in affect (e.g., attitudes, values, motivational orientation, anxiety) that are seen through changes in behavioral tendencies or decisions made to be consistent with the changes in affect. To take one example, if one attends a safety training program and comes away with seeing the value in being safer on the job, the individual may decide not to take the shortcuts to safety that the person had been making prior to the training intervention. The definitions also highlight that the changes in the learner are a direct result of how the learner attends to, interprets, and responds to the learning experience.

TABLE 2.1 Definitions of Learning

A change in human disposition or capability that persists over a period of time and is not simply ascribable to processes of growth.
* *Gagne*, 1970

The relatively permanent change in knowledge, skill, and affect produced by experience
* Weiss, 1990

The acquiring, distributing or interpreting of information that changes the range of potential behaviors
* Huber, 1991

The process whereby knowledge is created through the transformation of experience.
* Kolb, Boyatzis, & Mainemelis, 2001

A process that leads to change, which occurs as a result of experience and increases the potential for improved performance and future learning
* Ambrose, Bridges, DiPietro, Lovett, & Norman, 2010

The process of acquiring new knowledge and behaviors as a result of practice, study, or experience
* Salas, Tannenbaum, Kraiger, & Smith-Jentsch, 2012

Acquiring knowledge and skills and having them readily available from memory so you can make sense of future problems and opportunities.
* Brown, Roediger, & McDaniel, 2014

A second characteristic is that the changes in knowledge, skill, and/ or affect must be relatively permanent to be called learning. While change unfolds over time, an issue is how long can one expect to "see" the changes in knowledge, skills or attitudes after the learning experience to conclude that any changes are not fleeting but are long lasting. The challenge of learning is "getting knowledge that is inside to move out, and getting knowledge that is outside to move in" (Shulman, 1999; p. 11). To "move in" is to acquire knowledge (or skill or attitudes) from sources outside the self that remains within the individual learner. To "move out" is about the permanence of the change and the ability to apply something gained to the job.

A third characteristic derived from the definitions in Table 2.1 is that learning is an inferred process – that is, we infer that learning is taking place when we observe or measure changes in the learner according to some expectation. Learning is, therefore, a process to understand not just a product of an experience. Yet, one can only know if something has changed in a learner by what one observes in terms of some knowledge or skill measures such as a multiple choice test, behavior in a work simulator, or in terms of job performance (Ambrose et al., 2010). We therefore need well-developed conceptual frameworks of what those changes could be in order to appropriately target what to observe so that measures can be developed to examine the extent to which learning has occurred.

The definitions of learning do not, however, assume that all changes in knowledge, skills and/or affect lead to improvement in job behaviors and performance. As noted by Huber (1991), we can "incorrectly learn, and they can correctly learn that which is incorrect" (p. 89). For example, to continue with the safety training example, a newcomer can learn from an experienced coworker short cuts that can increase the probability of the newcomer having an accident. Clearly, the hope or goal of the learning approach is oriented towards seeing observable changes in knowledge, skills, and/or affect that lead to behavioral changes linked to enhanced efficiency or effectiveness in job performance – but the extent to which this occurs is an empirical or testable proposition!

LEARNING TAXONOMIES

So, what changes might one expect as a function of a learning experience or intervention? Based on strong research evidence, taxonomies have been created to identify the variety of learning changes that could arise. The word "taxonomy" comes from the Greek word "taxis," meaning arrangement or division, and "nomos," meaning law. Thus, a taxonomy is the science of classification according to some predetermined system. Similarities and differences are used to develop a classification framework. A classification scheme presented in Figure 2.1 identifies key learning constructs that have been used to create taxonomies. The model divides learning construct into cognitive outcomes that reflect concepts like knowledge and cognitive strategies, skill-based outcomes, and attitudinal or motivational outcomes such as self-efficacy and goal setting (Kraiger, Ford, & Salas, 1993a). Knowledge, skill, and affective taxonomies provide frameworks for understanding the underlying components of learning. The taxonomies point to what can be observed and measured to be able to "see" whether learning has occurred.

FIGURE 2.1 A Classification Scheme of Learning Constructs.

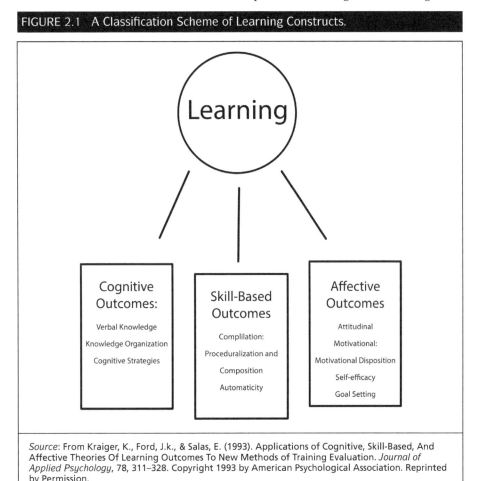

Source: From Kraiger, K., Ford, J.k., & Salas, E. (1993). Applications of Cognitive, Skill-Based, And Affective Theories Of Learning Outcomes To New Methods of Training Evaluation. *Journal of Applied Psychology*, 78, 311–328. Copyright 1993 by American Psychological Association. Reprinted by Permission.

Knowledge

An important taxonomy of knowledge that has stood the test of time is one developed by Bloom et al. (1956). The taxonomy as revised identifies two dimensions to help us understand what it means when we say someone has more knowledge now than before a learning opportunity (Krathwohl & Anderson, 2009). The "knowledge" dimension targets the various types of knowledge that can be gained while the "cognitive" dimension focuses on the complexity of the knowledge that can be gained from learning experiences.

Four types of knowledge are presented in Table 2.2. One type of knowledge is factual or what is called verbal or declarative knowledge. Factual knowledge includes the knowledge of specific terminology and definitions, and knowing specific details or characteristics pertaining to a concept or idea. For example, you can now state the definitions of learning presented in Table 2.1! One could also have factual knowledge of a principle or the components of a model. One example would be that the learner is able to describe the principle of spaced practice (e.g., spaced practice as described in Chapter 5 as spreading out practice over time). These form the basic informational level a newly hired worker needs to know if they are to understand their job and the

TABLE 2.2 Structure of Knowledge
A. Factual knowledge – The basic elements such as terminology and special details that the learner must know to be acquainted with a discipline or solve problems in it B. Conceptual knowledge – The relationships or categories among the basic elements within a larger structure that lead to the development of general principles and models of how the elements function separately and together C. Procedural knowledge – How to enact the elements using specific skills, techniques, and methods D. Metacognitive knowledge – Strategic knowledge of context and situations of when to apply (or not apply) procedural knowledge and an awareness and understanding of self-knowledge
Source: Krathwohl, D. R. (2002). A revision of Bloom's taxonomy: An overview. *Theory into Practice*, 41(4), 212–218.

tasks to be performed. A new machinist would need to know the names and function of the various tools used to set up a machine prior to learning how to operate the machine.

A second type of knowledge is conceptual knowledge. With factual knowledge, a learner has bits and pieces of information that are, to some degree, isolated from one another and seen as relatively discrete. With conceptual knowledge, the learner begins to have a greater understanding of how the bits of information fit the whole. Facts are now tied together in a more organized way in memory and similar parts are connected and dissimilar pieces of knowledge are more distant. The learner has more of an organized mental model around concepts and ideas that helps the learner combine the various bits of information around a task in an "interconnected, non-arbitrary, and systematic manner" (Anderson et al., 2001; p. 42). For example, an airline pilot after initial training may now possess distinct mental models that provide an organizing structure for what to do during preflight, take-offs, and landings.

The third type is called procedural knowledge, whereby a learner knows the steps that need to be taken to accomplish a task based on the factual and conceptual knowledge accumulated. At this stage, the learner has a good sense of what works and what does not work in various job situations. A manager may now know that there are different approaches for performance coaching depending on the employee's level of performance and years of experience. Therefore, procedural knowledge includes knowing when and where it is appropriate to use a procedure, method, or technique given a specific job situation. The sequence of steps to complete a task may be fairly routine where steps are completed in the same order every time or the steps might change depending on the result of actions on previous steps such as reacting to an employee who disagrees with issues identified by the manager around a performance problem.

The fourth type is strategic knowledge that includes the development of generalizable principles and strategies for job performance. While procedural knowledge is useful for one type of task or procedure, with strategic knowledge, the accumulation of learning through experience leads to the development of guiding principles that can be used across tasks and various procedures. Thus, strategic knowledge involves a deeper understanding of the complexities of various tasks and problems that occur on the job and recognizing when and where those principles could be appropriately applied to various job situations. For example, an individual might learn how to use a means-ends analysis (i.e., a strategy in which a person identifies and then eliminates any differences between their current position in a problem and the goal state) to solve a problem with one particular task. Then later, when faced with a different job context or situation, the individual is able to determine whether the application of a means-ends analysis is the best approach. Strategic knowledge is also related to self-reflection and questioning whether the principles and steps of applying a strategy like a means-ends analysis need to be modified or adapted to better fit the new situation.

The cognitive dimension of the knowledge taxonomy consists of elements that provide indicators or ways of observing whether knowledge has been gained as a function of a learning experience. The elements are ordered in a hierarchical fashion in terms of level of complexity of the cognitive processing required. The simplest cognitive process element is being able to remember or retrieve relevant knowledge from one's long-term memory when asked. The next level is not just remembering something but showing that one has an understanding of that something. For example, a new human resource person might know what questions to ask in a selection interview and what questions not to ask relevant to employment discrimination issues. The next level of complexity is being able to describe or apply the steps in a procedure (e.g., how to set up a machine) given a situation or context (routine or non-routine setup) the learner finds he/she is in.

A more complex level of cognitive processing is to be able to analyze or break down learning content into parts and to detect how the parts relate to one another – to have an organized mental map that aids in taking a systematic approach to solve troubleshooting problems. Figure 2.2 presents the mental model or knowledge map of a person well trained in a computer software program versus a minimally trained relative novice. In this study, the researchers applied a technique called Pathfinder to present a visual representation of how people view the relationship among various knowledge concepts. An examination of Figure 2.2 reveals that novices could not distinguish among the various concepts and therefore every concept seems related or similar to each other. For the trained individuals, the concepts were more tightly categorized into three main groupings of similar or related concepts within each grouping tightly connected with one (Kraiger, Salas, & Cannon-Bowers, 1995).

The highest level of complexity includes evaluating or being able to make judgements about the appropriate actions based on a specific set of criteria and standards. Job experts can evaluate options and create or put things together to form novel solutions to a problem based on their extensive experience base. As will be discussed later in the chapter, experts are relied on for being able to address non-routine situations by coupling their wide experience base with their ability for creativity addressing those types of situations.

Skills

A skill is a learned, goal-directed activity entailing a wide range of human behaviors that involve an organized sequence of activities (Fitts & Posner, 1967). This section examines what types of skills are learned followed by a description of a skill development taxonomy.

FIGURE 2.2 Comparison of (a) Novice and (b) Expert Mental Model Solutions for Knowledge of A Statistical Programming Package.

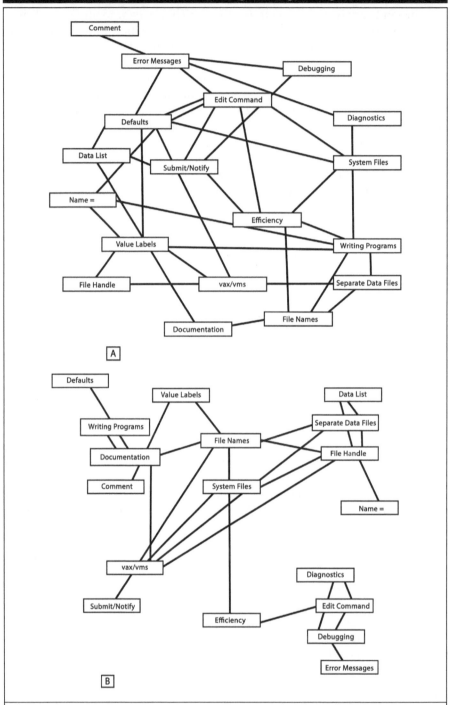

Source: Ford, J. K., & Kraiger, K. (1995). The Application of Cognitive Constructs and Principles to The Instructional Systems Model of Training: Implications for Needs Assessment, Design, and Transfer. In C. L. Cooper & T. Robertson (Eds.), *International Review of Industrial and Organizational Psychology*. Copyright 1995 by John Wiley & Sons. Reprinted by Permission.

TYPES OF SKILLS A skill can be grouped into three categories based on the capabilities most important for accomplishing the goal-directed activity of a job – cognitive, perceptual, and motor. A cognitive skill involves knowing what to do and when to do it or under what circumstances the skill is most appropriate to employ. In this way, a cognitive skill is represented in the knowledge domain as procedural and strategic knowledge requiring high levels of analysis and evaluation. Success relevant to applying computer-programming skills at work would be an example of a task that requires strong cognitive skills.

Perceptual skills include the capability to see or recognize important aspects in the work environment that affect the learner's ability to identify when and how to act given the work context. Perceptual skills are about detecting information and discriminating what is or is not relevant to attend to when deciding to act (Edwards, 2010). A computer programmer cannot appropriately troubleshoot a problem that has arisen with running a program unless first identifying the cues embedded in why the program is not functioning. Perceptual skills are also involved in determining spatial patterns and relationships such as speed and distance and sounds. For example, in terms of perceptual skills, high-level tennis players are superior to less advanced players in anticipating the trajectory of the ball – highlighting the importance of visual search and decision-making behaviors (Williams et al., 2002). In terms of a work example, I was conducting a job analysis with a first line supervisor in his office when he suddenly stopped talking, listened for second and then noted calmly to me that a machine operation close to where we were talking was experiencing a problem that needed troubleshooting. Amidst the ongoing hum of many machines and forklifts in the facility, he was able to hear something amiss that I had not heard or understood.

Cognitive skills emphasize knowing what to do, while perceptual skills emphasize being attuned to and obtaining information relevant to completing a task or solving a problem with a task. Motor skills focus directly on action and doing the steps relevant to accomplish a task in the appropriate manner. Therefore, motor skills concern the coordination of movement. Examples can vary from mundane and routine tasks such as typing a document using a word processing package to highly specialized motor skills such as being able to efficiently complete complex set-up procedures for highly sophisticated machinery.

SKILL TAXONOMY Clearly all three categories of skills contribute in some manner to the completion of job activities. With skill development, the learner progresses in their cognitive, perceptual, and motor skills over time relevant to the sets of job tasks. Learners begin to link the various acts required in a sequential and organized manner. The progression is also hierarchical in nature across three definable phases of initial acquisition, skill integration or compilation, and skill automaticity. Table 2.3 provides a summary of these three phases of development in relation to the goal of each phase, the typical learning activity associated with that phase and the performance level at each phase.

Initial acquisition is rudimentary with a heavy emphasis on cognitive skills and the transition from factual or declarative knowledge to an understanding of the procedures (i.e., knowledge of each step in a task and the sequence of actions relevant across the steps). Identifying and understanding the basic perceptual and motor skill components of doing a task are also part

TABLE 2.3	Stages of Skill Acquisition		
Stage	**Goal**	**Activity**	**Performance**
Initial Phase	Understand task steps and task components	Explanation and demonstration of steps with attempt to mirror exactly what has been trained	Erratic, focus on individual steps and closely following directions without deviation
Integration Phase	Comprehend and perform tasks	Deliberate practice and feedback and repetition	Somewhat fluid, less effortful thinking needed to complete steps in task, need for some support or help from time to time
Automation Phase	Perform tasks with speed, efficiency, and effectiveness	Effortless performance requiring little cognitive input, focus is on refining skills	Continuous, fluid, seamless task performance as well as being able to adapt effort depending on situation faced

Sources: Adapted from Fitts, P. M., & Posner, M. I. (1967). *Human performance*. Oxford, UK: Brooks/Cole; and Reznick, R. K., & MacRae, H. (2006). Teaching surgical skills – changes in the wind. *New England Journal of Medicine*, 355(25), 2664–2669, p. 2665.

of this phase. At this initial phase, performance is erratic with the learner continuing to focus on each step as a separate, discrete process to be mastered rather than viewing the task as a whole. The learner is attempting to absorb a lot of information and to memorize the steps leading to high levels of mental effort. Accordingly, task performance is slow and the learner's capacity to attend to distracting elements (hearing what others are saying while concentrating on the steps of a task) or other relevant steps in a task is low. They also need assistance with completing the task such as asking questions about what steps to take next in the task sequence.

Compilation or integration occurs with continued practice of the steps of the task. The goal of additional experience and learning is to comprehend and complete the actions required for the whole task. Performance is characterized by faster less error-prone actions. The integration of discrete steps is more seamless as it can be observed as a single more free-flowing and fluid act requiring less supervision or help. In this phase, learners begin to generalize what they are learning about performing specific tasks to different context and problems. For example, a computer programmer can now not only debug one particular type of problem but can apply elements of the debugging strategy used for solving a different type of problem. The learner is also in a better position to understand what skills are useful or not useful for the circumstance and to modify or adapt steps in a task depending on the situation.

The third automaticity phase occurs with continued practice, experience, and feedback with the outcome of enhanced precision, speed, and efficiency such as completing the task with the fewest steps or movements. Performance is fluid and accomplished. The learners not only perform tasks quickly and accurately but can do so with little conscious thought or mental effort. We know the learner has reached this phase when they can perform well on a task regardless of distractions and situational pressures. In addition, the learner can shift attention back and forth to another task with its own set of required cognitive, perceptual, and motor skills without affecting the original task performance. It is important to note that learning is still occurring during the automaticity phase as the skill capabilities continue to be fine-tuned leading to further, albeit smaller improvements in accuracy and speed. We often call such people continuous learners who are striving to become not just competent but to become the expert in their job domain (more about expertise later!).

A nice example of the differences among these three phases is the skill progression of medical students learning a surgical skill from the initial acquisition (cognitive stage), compilation (integrative), and autonomous phases:

> *In the cognitive stage, the learner intellectualizes the task; performance is erratic, and the procedure is carried out in distinct steps. For example, with a surgical skill as simple as tying a knot, in the cognitive stage the learner must understand the mechanics of the skill—how to hold the tie, how to place the throws, and how to move the hands. With practice and feedback, the learner reaches the integrative stage, in which knowledge is translated into appropriate motor behavior. The learner is still thinking about how to move the hands and hold the tie but is able to execute the task more fluidly, with fewer interruptions. In the autonomous stage, practice gradually results in smooth performance. The learner no longer needs to think about how to execute this particular task and can concentrate on other aspects of the procedure. (Reznick & MacRae, 2006; p. 2664)*

As another example, in baseball there is revolution in the use of technology to improve performance. Batting simulators can now track the use of visual, auditory, and tactical information relevant to the outcome of a baseball swing (Gray, 2009). Research shows that batters combine information across these factors but place most weight on visual cues to improve their swing. Differences in skill acquisition also indicate that highly skilled batters perform better when attention is focused on external cues such as the sound of the ball leaving the bat. Less skilled players learn better when they focus attention on skill execution such as the movement of the hands and the movement of the bat during a swing (Castaneda & Gray, 2007).

Affect

Affect is defined as an individual's attitudes, values, feelings, emotions, and motivational tendencies. Synonyms of affect include words such as influence, move, inspire, engage, interest, and to captivate or fascinate. These words convey the point that a learning event can inspire an individual to want to learn more about an issue after say attending a training program on diversity. A learning experience can also lead to disquiet, distress, concern, and discomfort. For example, after a supervisor is trained on how to more effectively coach others, the learner may feel that they did not gain enough of the knowledge and skills leading to lower levels of self-efficacy – the belief in a capability of performing behaviors that lead towards a goal. The examples show that affect involves the internal response of the learner to those ideas and principles underlying the learning activity (Anderson et al., 2001).

An attitude is defined as a *learned* predisposition to respond in a consistently favorable or unfavorable manner with response to a given issue or situation (Fishbein & Ajzen, 2015). Attitudes are formed and become stronger or weaker as people attach feelings and change their beliefs towards the target of learning experiences. Human resource professionals undergoing training to become organizational change agents within their own organizations may form an attitude that the change in job duties is misguided or unneeded. One could predict from these attitudes that they would not be inclined to learn change relevant strategies during training or apply principles to lead change efforts in their organization. Instead, they would more likely to act in ways to support the status quo.

A taxonomy of the affective domain is organized around increasing levels of internalization of the attitude or particular belief – from simple attention to an idea, strategy, method, or technique that may not have much impact on behavior to a high level of internalization where an idea or strategy comes to consistently guide how one makes decisions or acts given certain contexts and situations. With internalization, the value underlying the beliefs become part of who the person is. Therefore, as one moves up the affective hierarchy, one becomes more involved, committed and internally motivated (Krathwohl, Bloom, & Masia, 1964).

Figure 2.3 presents the five levels of increasing internalization of attitudes in an affective based taxonomy. *Receiving* or attending is the lowest level in the

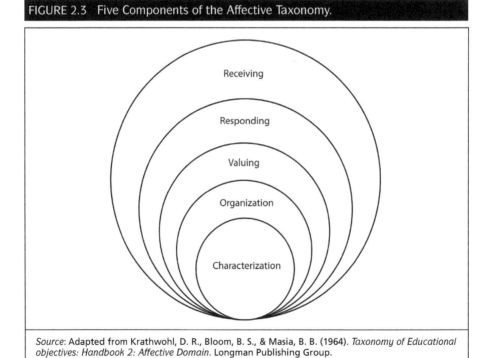

FIGURE 2.3   Five Components of the Affective Taxonomy.

Receiving

Responding

Valuing

Organization

Characterization

Source: Adapted from Krathwohl, D. R., Bloom, B. S., & Masia, B. B. (1964). *Taxonomy of Educational objectives: Handbook 2: Affective Domain*. Longman Publishing Group.

hierarchy as it concerns paying attention to a new idea or principle during a learning experience (remember that ignoring is the opposite of learning!) and having some self-awareness of how one feels about the idea or principle. The second level of *responding* is being more proactive in freely talking about an idea or principle with others. At this level there is feelings of satisfaction or dissatisfaction with the dialogue or discussion. The third level is *valuing* where a learner can see the worth of an idea, principle, or skill and thus accepts or evaluates it as good. At this level, the learner is poised to commit to learning more about something as it is viewed as worthwhile. The fourth level is *organizing* or placing the new value within the set of values one already holds. When faced with a situation, one then decides which value takes precedent or priority in guiding job behaviors. One can state that fairness is an important value but also hold that mercy is also a value. In a situation faced by a leader to either hold everyone accountable to the same standard or to allow one individual to not uphold the standard due to some mitigating circumstance, one value must be prioritized over the other. So, the more likely that a value "wins" out over other values across various situations and people provides a window into how one has internalized the value and prioritized it. The highest level in the hierarchy is called the *characterization* of a value in which there is consistency in one's decisions and actions related to a set of values that have been organized and prioritized. This is where the internalization is ingrained into one's "philosophy of life."

An Integrated Perspective

While the three types of taxonomies and frameworks have been presented separately, clearly there are interrelationships and reinforcing loops among them. Procedural knowledge is a precursor to being able to demonstrate one has the skills to carry out the steps required to perform a task. A key assumption underlying one training method called behavioral modeling (discussed in Chapter 10) is that skills must first be developed through observation, demonstration, practice, and reinforcement. Once the new skills have been developed and subsequent behavioral patterns are found to be effective by the learner in addressing problems in their job, the learner will come to recognize the value of these new and effective behaviors. Once that value is demonstrated, the learner is much more likely to internalize attitudes and values congruent with the new behavioral patterns (Taylor, Russ-Eft, & Chan, 2005).

From a career development perspective, there is a need to progress in all three domains of knowledge, skill, and affect. Learners must not only think in certain ways but also perform skills and act in ways consistent with the norms, values, and conventions of the professions (Shulman, 2005). The implication for learning in organizations is that while knowledge and skill must be developed, there is also progress in "acting" which includes the internalized dispositions and commitment to particular courses of action.

Shulman (2002) developed a table of learning that classifies these interrelated aspects of learning. The circular nature of this typology presented in Figure 2.4 highlights the interrelatedness and continuous nature of learning. Learning begins with engagement by the learner with what is to be learned. With engagement, the learner is not just passively going through the motions of paying attention but is trying to attend to the information relevant to the learning experience. Engagement and motivation lead to enhancing knowledge and

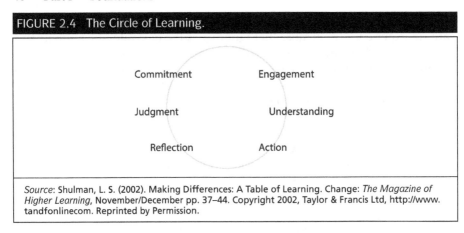

FIGURE 2.4   The Circle of Learning.

Commitment   Engagement

Judgment   Understanding

Reflection   Action

Source: Shulman, L. S. (2002). Making Differences: A Table of Learning. Change: *The Magazine of Higher Learning*, November/December pp. 37–44. Copyright 2002, Taylor & Francis Ltd, http://www. tandfonlinecom. Reprinted by Permission.

understanding the material being presented. Understanding is a prerequisite to becoming capable of acting or displaying a new skill. Once a skill is displayed over time and situations, the learner can reflect on the behavior exhibited relevant to the skill and think more clearly (and at a higher order thinking) of what works and does not work. This reflection can result in ideas on how to improve upon the behaviors exhibited based on continual enhancement of knowledge, skills, and affect. The learner is now prepared to address new situations with different contexts, people, and events by making a judgement on which knowledge and skills are required to be performed in those new situations or decisions on how to adapt behaviors to best fit the new situation. Over time, these judgements and decisions tied to effective performance lead to higher levels of commitment and personal identity – consistent with the affect taxonomy and moving up the internalization hierarchy. The repeatable cycle implies that as one attains a high level of internalization and commitment, the learner is then better prepared to and willing to attend to and seek out further learning experiences in this area. The learning cycle illustrates the continual development that can occur over time relevant to learning at work across one's career.

LONG-TERM DEVELOPMENT

Various models have been proposed to describe the changes that occur within learners over time. The most influential model identifies five stages: novice, advanced beginner or apprentice, competent, proficient, and expert (Dreyfus & Dreyfus, 2005). There is a stepwise but not necessarily linear progression of knowledge, skill, and affect in the development of expertise. The move from novice to expert requires substantial changes in what the learner can do as well as the strategies used to approach a task and make decisions (Kinchin & Cabot, 2010).

Stages of Development

The novice stage is where a newcomer in an organization is acquiring knowledge about the specific facts and learning the "ropes" of the job. The learner is beginning to recognize the steps required for a job and procedures to follow in a rote manner through continual practice. Rules are relatively simple and straightforward. The learner at this stage may lack of sense of the whole or overall tasks as the focus is on specific steps of key tasks and getting them right. For a new machinist, this would entail learning the names of all the parts and accessories needed for setting up a machine while also learning what specific buttons to push and in what order to run routine or easy jobs.

In the advanced beginner stage, the learner is now developing an understanding of the interrelatedness of the step-by-step procedures and how different situations may affect what the learner is to do. Therefore, the learner is beginning to see more of the whole task – due to the frequent opportunities to practice routine situations during the novice stage. The learner is also gaining knowledge of what not to do (e.g., what happens if the buttons are pushed in the wrong order) based on feedback from oneself or from others about the impact of mistakes on task performance. The advanced beginner is starting to develop an internal set of rules that link situations to effective actions. For example, a newly promoted first line supervisor now knows what should be recorded on the documentation for the job and understands how that information is helpful in tracking what is happening on the shop floor.

A competent performer now has a large repository of job experiences to develop a more organized understanding of the tasks and the priorities that are needed to be set across tasks. The learner is developing a growing capability to manage different situations and adapt to new situations and understands the job well enough to learn some efficiencies that help propel stronger performance. The learner is now moving up the affect domain by becoming more invested in the job and the outcomes of the actions taken to complete tasks and engaging in more self-reflection and self-evaluation. To illustrate, a computer programming engineer at this stage is now able to deal with a variety of programming needs by considering various approaches that can be taken while seeing the value of working in a certain way for different types of problems.

A person who is at the proficiency stage level can now recognize situations quickly (the sensing part of skill development) and analyze the situation in terms of similarities and dissimilarities with past experiences. Based on this analysis, action can be taken that is effective for the new problems based on what has worked or not worked in the past and adapting an approach if viewed as necessary. The learner is in a better position to experiment with new ways of doing things when there are opportunities and reflecting on why the new approach did or did not lead to the expected results. This requires a level of confidence gained to feel comfortable with experimentation as a function of one's experience, feedback, and reflection.

What distinguishes experts from others who are highly competent and proficient in their job? The expert has now reached the highest levels in the hierarchies across the knowledge, skill, and affective taxonomies. This high level is characterized by the capability to create and invest new ideas and solutions to problems, accurately evaluate if ideas and solutions are good ones, and to persuade others of the value of an idea and implement them effectively (Sternberg, 2003). From a cognitive perspective, the expert can perform tasks autonomously without conscious thought and with fluid and efficient performance. An example from dentistry showed that while all performers did the basic steps the same way, the more expert performers eliminated superfluous activity while also combining steps in a seamless way to be more efficient in their actions leading to less time to complete the tasks (Chambers, 2012). From the affect side, the person has now reached a high level of internalization in which one's identity is connected to the job and the tasks being performed.

Expertise can be thought of as having two components of routine and adaptive expertise (Carbonell et al., 2014). Routine expertise consists of the knowledge and skills that individuals apply to well learned and familiar contexts and situations in an efficient and effective manner. Individuals compile declarative knowledge into procedural, condition-action knowledge and continued practice leads to automatic and highly efficient performance. Adaptive expertise involves the capability to integrate simultaneously multiple sources of knowledge for use in effectively addressing changing conditions and unfamiliar situations. The concepts of routine and adaptive expertise are consistent with instructional design concepts of recurrent and nonrecurrent skills. As noted by Young et al. (2014), individuals become highly proficient in a job through the development of recurrent skills i.e., practicing tasks that are consistent from typical problem situations and problem solutions. This development of recurrent skills continues throughout a career as an individual comes to automatize certain tasks and develops more efficient and effective strategies relevant to these recurrent skills. When moving beyond this high level of competency, an expert also develops non-recurrent skills in which the effectiveness of job behaviors and possible solutions differs across more challenging problem situations. The development of non-recurrent skills builds upon the foundations laid by developing competencies in the recurrent skills.

Characteristics of tasks impact the need for routine or adaptive expertise. In dynamic conditions relevant for many of today's work tasks, goals are often shifting and may even be competing with other goals. Problems are often ill-structured and the information available to the individual is incomplete and ambiguous. Action feedback loops are lengthy in dynamic situations, making the connection between behavioral cause and effect more difficult to establish to know what works and what does not work. Dynamic conditions also require an individual to recall multiple perspectives and schemas to determine the meaning of the situation or problem before moving to solutions (Hoffman et al., 2014).

Adaptive expertise is observed when individuals are able to invent new procedures based on their knowledge and skills. They can also make accurate predictions regarding possible outcomes that may occur depending on the strategy taken. Adaptation requires an understanding of deeper principles underlying the task, capabilities to recognize and identify changed situations and knowledge of whether or not the existing repertoire of strategies can or should be applied (Smith, Ford, & Kozlowski, 1997). If the situation requires individuals to reconfigure procedures, extensive knowledge about a variety of procedures as well as how to select and combine them is necessary. The progression from competent to adaptive expert is indicated when how an individual comes to decisions and acts is described by that person as intuitive. Many people at work are competent and highly proficient but only a few can be labelled as truly an expert in their domain. This high level of routine and adaptive expertise may "take longer to reach than any of the intermediate stages, if it's ever reached at all" (Kinchin & Cabot, 2010; p. 155). That is why it is so important to retain experts. It is also important to develop new talent ahead of time to replace the experts when they retire.

Qualitative Shifts

The stage model highlights that the knowledge, skill and affect of an advanced beginner, for example, is not just an incomplete version of that of an expert. One qualitative difference concerns the depth of knowledge, skill and affect which has been called deep specialization (Ford, Webb, & Showler, 2017). With specialized knowledge, the learner has changed so that not only can individuals recall facts and figures like an advanced beginner but the person can distinguish between situations when that knowledge (or skills) is applicable and when it is not applicable. This leads those with deep specialization to use their depth of knowledge in the appropriate context and at the appropriate time to achieve superior performance. Over time, the individual with more depth of knowledge can do a better job of relating information to changing demands and predicting what might happen next given the current situation. The confidence gained from being able to perform tasks effortlessly can lead to higher levels of internalization regarding work tasks.

A second qualitative difference involves the development of self-regulatory skills that involves the capability to know what the appropriate strategies are to facilitate further knowledge acquisition (Lord & Hall, 2005). Individuals who have achieved deep specialization are able to more accurately monitor or assess their own mental states and are more likely to know when they have understood task relevant information. Experts are also more likely to discontinue a problem-solving strategy that would ultimately prove to be unsuccessful than those at the competence level. They are also better able to estimate the number of trials they will need to accomplish as task. For example, a highly valued information technologist has superior understanding of ideal working strategies and has a better awareness of performance strategy options (Sonnentag, 1998).

A new and exciting area of research on qualitative shifts or differences is the examination of brain functioning through the analysis of functional magnetic resonance imaging (fMRI). This research is exploring neurological differences as tasks are being performed as well as examining differences between experts and those who are at an earlier stage (Kok & de Bruin, 2018). The research shows that more experience and practice results in more connections and associations in memory. In terms of task performance, Bahrami et al. (2014) found that medical students performing laparoscopic surgery tasks in a simulated environment had higher brain activation in different parts of the brain as the complexity of the surgery tasks increased. Another study examined clinical decision-making and investigated how knowledge and various work experiences are related to differences in neural activity. Second year medical students and experienced gastroenterologists diagnosed 16 clinical cases that varied in terms of analytical complexity. As expected, the expert clinicians were better than the relative advanced beginners in terms of accuracy of diagnosis and speed of diagnosis. Results also indicated that for the complex cases there were noticeable differences between the two groups in terms of activations in various regions in the brain. Interestingly for simple cases, novices had "activations in the neural regions associated with factual rule-based knowledge whereas in experts we observed right hemisphere activation in neural regions associated with experiential knowledge" (Hruska et al., 2016; p. 992). Callan et al. (2013) studied pilots and non-pilots watching a simulation of a glider landing. They discovered that the seasoned pilots had increased activities in different parts of the brain (e.g., premotor cortex) compared to the novices. Others have found higher levels of neural efficiency for experts reflecting an increase in automaticity in elite over competent athletes (Callan & Naito, 2014). In support, other research findings show that for experts there is less brain activity in the control regions of the brain supporting the concept of automaticity (Diedrichsen & Kornysheva, 2015). We should expect continued advancements in our understanding of changes in brain activity and efficiency for work-related tasks that can shed light on how to accelerate the rate of learning and retention.

In sum, throughout the progression from novice to competent to expert, there are cognitive mechanisms at work. As individuals increase in skill level, they become increasingly reliant on the situation to inform them of the problem, take a more holistic approach to recognizing patterns in the problem, base decision-making on intuition, and become absorbed in their performance. Hoffman et al. (2014) provide behaviorally based indicators to distinguish between those who are competent and good in their jobs from those who are experts. The indicators include: (1) is highly regarded by peers because of their highly organized body of knowledge; (2) shows consummate skill, qualitatively different strategies, and has economy of effort; (3) deals effectively with rare cases that others cannot address; (4) recognizes aspects of a problem that make it novel and adapts strategies to solve tough cases; and (5) contributes new knowledge and procedures.

How Long to Become an Expert?

Clearly not everyone who has a large amount of work experience becomes an expert – they may be proficient but not be considered by others as an expert. Experts are highly valued by companies as they are the go-to people when there is a need for creative ideas and solutions especially around non-routine situations. Experts are widely recognized for their talents and wisdom. They have also been called the star performers who are valued as they are extraordinary in their level of production or output compared to those who merely proficient in their job (Aguinis & O'Boyle, 2014).

As noted in Chapter 1, a key foundation is the evidence or findings used to form best practices for learning. An illustration of a controversy over research evidence and what it can mean for best practice revolves around the questions of how long it takes to become an expert. A large research stream has examined the role of deliberate practice in the development of expertise. Researchers have emphasized the importance of the focused and effortful practice activities of the learner with the explicit goal of continual improvement of skills and performance (Keith & Ericsson, 2007). Ericsson and his colleagues have studied deliberate practice effects in a variety of skill domains such as chess, hockey, and music. They have made the claim that the differences in task performance of experts over others who are merely competent can be explained by the amount of deliberate practice employed by the learner. Examining these domains led to the conclusion that at least a decade of experience with at least 10,000 hours of deliberate practice is needed to become an expert (Ericsson et al., 2018). This stream of research and deliberate practice estimate has been picked up by the popular press including books such as *Outlier* (Gladwell,

2008) and *The Talent Code* (Coyle, 2010). These authors emphasized the importance of practice over natural talent as the key to excellence. Soon, everyone seemed to be talking about this estimate as a strong indicator of the time to become an expert.

This notion that 10,000 hours of deliberate practice is all that is needed to become an expert was put to the extreme test by Dan McLaughlin who attempted to become an expert golfer by building up the hours of practice. Table 2.4 presents this colorful story and how it ended.

While the McLaughlin story is fun to read about, one point of controversy is about the generalizability of the 10,000-hour rule and the role of individual differences in talent. The number of hours it takes to become an expert in hockey or chess may or may not generalize to jobs in organizations that vary greatly in terms of complexity to learn. For example, one estimate is that it takes over 26,000 hours to become an expert astrophysicist in terms of obtaining a PhD, writing some major impactful studies, and authoring some well-received books. An expert in the culinary arts is said to need over 13,000 hours of training in culinary school at home and abroad and then have additional work across varied experiences in order to move their way up through various experiences across restaurants to be viewed as a top chef by *Food &*

TABLE 2.4 The Curious Golfing Story of Dan McLaughlin

This is a story of Dan McLaughlin who took this idea of 10,000 hours to the extreme. He quit his day job as a professional photographer after reading about deliberate practice and focused his efforts to become a golf professional and making the PGA tour, which is the highest level of competitive golf. Dan become the poster boy of the 10,000 hour "rule." Dan worked on his game and created a blog called the Dan Plan (thedanplan. com) to document this quest to become a golf professional. He had a coach for guidance on his golf swing and golf strategy. He had a strength trainer and someone called a "goal guru." He followed the advice of learning experts including Ericsson around the grit and determination needed to concentrate on learning and improving. He plotted his improvement over time and only counting his concentrated practice time as hours towards the 10,000. Dan had a blog that documented his journey.

His golf scores did improve over time. At 2,500 hours of deliberate practice his golf handicap was a 9. A handicap is calculated by taking into account the player's score for 18 holes as well as taking into account the difficulty of the course played. The lower the number the better the player with a scratch golfer being someone who has a handicap of 0. With 3,500 hours of deliberate practice, his handicap went down to 6 and at 4,500 hours his handicap was 5. By 6,000 hours of practice, the handicap had dropped to close to 3. Clearly this level of handicap is good and is achieved by a small number of amateur golfers. Yet, these efforts came nowhere near what it would take to be considered a scratch golfer let alone be in the ballpark of trying to become a tour professional – his goal of being recognized as an expert golfer.

Interestingly, after 6,000 hours Dan ran out of gas as his back gave out with all the effort. There were weeks where he could rarely practice. As reported in a story on the "Dan Plan," Dan had to undergo months of physical therapy before being able to play again somewhat free of pain. Given his injuries, his handicap started to go up from the low of 3.1 to 3.9 and then when he stopped it was 5.5. When asked about his experience he did note that perhaps he could recommit to deliberate practice when he became older to make a run for the senior golf tour!

Sources: Crawford, A. (2017, March 16). What happened to the Dan Plan? www.golfwrx. com/437894/what-happened-to-the-dan-plan/; Phillips, S. (2017, August 11). The average guy who spent 6003 hours trying to be a professional golfer. www.theatlantic.com/health/archive/2017/08/ the-dan-plan/536592/; www.thedanplan.com

Wine magazine. The Electric Power Research Institute contends that it takes up to 25 years to become an expert in some key mission critical activities rather than simply being good (proficient) at what they do (Moon, Hoffman, & Ziebell, 2009). Another way of thinking about expertise is to calculate the time to achieve a PhD and then after work experience and additional learning being seen as having obtained a high level of achievement or becoming the go-to person: https://9qo7v4bolm-flywheel.netdna-ssl.com/wp-content/uploads/2012/08/11.11.22_Experts-1.png

A second issue around this controversy is the underlying premise of the research on deliberate practice that other factors such as natural talent is not important for explaining the trajectory of skill development. The claim that individual differences in performance are largely accounted for by the level of deliberate practice has been effectively challenged. A meta-analytic study of performance in sports found that deliberate practice had a small impact on differences among elite athletes and that elite athletes tended to start their sport later in childhood in comparison to lower skill performers (MacNamara, Moreau, & Hambrick, 2016). Another study found that only 34% of the variance in performance among chess players and about 30% of the variance in music performance could be attributed to the amount of deliberate practice (Hambrick et al., 2016). Ullén, Hambrick and Mosing (2016) contend that expertise is determined by a variety of genetic, ability, motor skills, and personality factors. They also note the role of working memory capacity or the ability to maintain information in an active and accessible state over a short period of time as a critical individual difference factor. Interestingly, a study of twins (identical and fraternal) found that heritability accounted for a large amount of variance in musical aptitude such as melody discrimination (Ullén et al., 2014).

Clearly, deliberate practice with help and feedback from coaches and mentors is useful and needs to be considered as one strategy for developing talent in organizations. Organizations can likely do a better job of leveraging everyday job situations as learning opportunities with a focus on building expertise over time. Strategies for developing talent are presented in Part III of this book. On the other hand, from a best evidence perspective, the research findings point to being cautious about broad claims about the impact of deliberate practice on learning and performance as well as the specific claim of 10,000 hours to become an expert. There are a variety of other factors that impact the development of expertise. That is why organizations also need effective selection and promotion systems to find the best talent!

CONCLUDING REMARKS: THE FOUNDATION OF LEARNING

This chapter started out with the simple notion that the foundation of the learning enterprise is understanding the concept of learning. The organizational challenge is how to develop individuals in a way that accelerates the move from novice to competence to high proficiency and for some – expertise.

The knowledge gained from this chapter on learning about learning is integral to the content in the following chapters. Assessing learning needs require some identification of what level relative to the taxonomies of knowledge, skill, and affect is required by the organization for various jobs and what level individuals need to obtain within what timeframe. Designing a learning experience such as a formal training program requires identification of what changes in knowledge, skill or affect are expected as a function of that training – something we will cover when talking about the objectives of the learning experience. Instructional design requires an appreciation for learning principles and how they can impact gains in knowledge, skills, and affect. How to facilitate the transfer of the gains from a learning experience such as guided one-on-one instruction requires attention to what has already been learned and how to further enhance that learning as the learner continuous to work on the job. The chapters in Part II target these issues of learning needs, designing for learning, learning transfer, evaluation and methods for delivering learning content.

References

Aguinis, H., & O'Boyle Jr, E. (2014). Star performers in twenty-first century organizations. *Personnel Psychology*, 67(2), 313–350. doi.org/10.1111/peps.12054

Ambrose, S. A., Bridges, M. W., DiPietro, M., Lovett, M. C., & Norman, M. K. (2010). *How learning works*. San Francisco, CA: Jossey-Bass.

Anderson, L. W. and Krathwohl, D. R., et al (Eds.) (2001) *A taxonomy for learning, teaching, and assessing: A revision of bloom's taxonomy of educational objectives*. Boston, MA: Allyn & Bacon.

Bahrami, P., Graham, S. J., Grantcharov, T. P., Cusimano, M. D., Rotstein, O. D., Mansur, A., & Schweizer, T. A. (2014). Neuroanatomical correlates of laparoscopic surgery training. *Surgical Endoscopy*, 28(7), 2189–2198. doi.org/10.1007/s00464-014-3452-7

Bloom, B. S., Engelhart, M. D., Furst, E. J., Hill, W. H., & Krathwohl, D. R. (1956). *Taxonomy of educational objectives: The classification of educational goals. Handbook 1: Cognitive domain*. New York: David McKay.

Brown, P. C., Roediger III, H. L., & McDaniel, M. A. (2014). *Make it stick*. Cambridge, MA: Harvard University Press.

Callan, D. E., & Naito, E. (2014). Neural processes distinguishing elite from expert and novice athletes. *Cognitive and Behavioral Neurology*, 27(4), 183–188. doi.org/10.1097/WNN.0000000000000043

Callan, D. E., Terzibas, C., Cassel, D. B., Callan, A., Kawato, M., & Sato, M. A. (2013). Differential activation of brain regions involved with error-feedback and imitation based motor simulation when observing self and an expert's actions in pilots and non-pilots on a complex glider landing task. *Neuroimage*, 72, 55–68. doi.org/10.1016/j.neuroimage.2013.01.028

Carbonell, K. B., Stalmeijer, R. E., Könings, K. D., Segers, M., & van Merriënboer, J. J. (2014). How experts deal with novel situations: A review of adaptive expertise. *Educational Research Review*, 12, 14–29. http://dx.doi.org/10.1016/j.edurev.2014.03.001

Castaneda, B., & Gray, R. (2007). Effects of focus of attention on baseball batting performance in players of differing skill levels. *Journal of Sport and Exercise Psychology*, 29(1), 60–77. doi.org/10.1123/jsep.29.1.60

Chambers, D. W. (2012). Dental education's involvement with dentists' learning in practice: Data and theory. *Journal of Dental Education*, 76(1), 107–117.

Coyle, D. (2010). *The talent code: Greatness isn't born, it's grown*. New York: Random House.

Crawford, A. (2017, March 16). What happened to the Dan Plan? http://www.golfwrx.com/437894/what-happened-to-the-dan-plan/

Diedrichsen, J., & Kornysheva, K. (2015). Motor skill learning between selection and execution. *Trends in Cognitive Sciences*, 19(4), 227–233. doi.org/10.1016/j.tics.2015.02.003

Dreyfus, H. L., & Dreyfus, S. E. (2005). Peripheral vision: Expertise in real world contexts. *Organization Studies*, 26(5), 779–792. doi.org/10.1177/0170840605053102

Edwards, W. H. (2010). *Motor learning and control: From theory to practice*. Cengage Learning.

Ericsson, K. A. (2006). The influence of experience and deliberate practice on the development of superior expert performance. In K. A. Ericsson, N. Charness, P. Feltovich, & R. R. Hoffman (Eds.), *Handbook of expertise and expert performance* (pp. 683–706). Cambridge, UK: Cambridge University Press.

Ericsson, K. A., Hoffman, R. R., Kozbelt, A., & Williams, A. M. (Eds.). (2018). *The Cambridge handbook of expertise and expert performance*. Cambridge, UK: Cambridge University Press.

Fitts, P. M., & Posner, M. I. (1967). *Human performance*. Oxford, UK: Brooks/Cole

Fishbein, M., & Ajzen, I. (2015). *Predicting and changing behavior: The reasoned action approach*. New York: Routledge.

Ford, J. K., & Kraiger, K. (1995). The application of cognitive constructs and principles to the instructional systems model of training: Implications for needs assessment, design, and transfer. In C. L. Cooper & T. Robertson (Eds.), *International review of industrial and organizational psychology*. London, UK: John Wiley & Sons.

Ford, J. K., Webb, J. M., & Showler, M. (2017). Building deep specialization through intentional learning activities. In K. G. Brown (Ed.), *The Cambridge handbook of workplace training and employee development* (p. 228). Cambridge: Cambridge University Press.

Gagne, R. M. (1970). *The conditions of learning* (4th edition). New York: Holt, Rinehart & Winston.

Gladwell, M. (2008). *Outliers: The story of success*. London, UK: Hachette UK.

Gray, R. (2009). How do batters use visual, auditory, and tactile information about the success of a baseball swing? *Research Quarterly for Exercise and Sport*, 80(3), 491–501. doi.org/10.1080/02701367.2009.10599587

Hambrick, D. Z., Macnamara, B. N., Campitelli, G., Ullén, F., & Mosing, M. A. (2016). Beyond born versus made: A new look at expertise. In B. H. Ross (Ed.), *The psychology of Learning and Motivation*, Vol. 64, (1–55). San Diego, CA: Elsevier Academic Press.

Hoffman, R. R., Ward, P., Feltovich, P. J., DiBello, L., Fiore, S. M., and Andrews, D. H. (2014). *Accelerated expertise*. New York: Psychology Press.

Hruska, P., Hecker, K. G., Coderre, S., McLaughlin, K., Cortese, F., Doig, C., … Krigolson, O. (2016). Hemispheric activation differences in novice and expert clinicians during clinical decision making. *Advances in Health Sciences Education*, 21(5), 921–933. doi.org/10.1007/s10459-015-9648-3

Huber, G. P. (1991). Organizational learning: The contributing processes and the literatures. *Organization Science*, 2(1), 88–115. doi.org/10.1287/orsc.2.1.88

Keith, N., & Ericsson, K. A. (2007). A deliberate practice account of typing proficiency in everyday typists. *Journal of Experimental Psychology: Applied*, 13(3), 135. doi.org/10.1037/1076-898X.13.3.135

Kraiger, K., Ford, J. K., & Salas, E. (1993a). Application of cognitive, skill-based, and affective theories of learning outcomes to new methods of training evaluation. *Journal of Applied Psychology*, 78(2), 311. doi.org/10.1037/0021-9010.78.2.311

Kinchin, I. M., and Cabot, L. B. (2010). Reconsidering the dimensions of expertise: From linear stages towards dual processing. *London Review of Education* 8, 153–166. doi.org/10.1080/14748460.2010.487334

Kok, E. M., & de Bruin, A. B. H. (2018). The neuroscience of motor expertise in real world tasks. In D. Hambrick, G. Campitelli, & B. Macnamara (Eds.), *The science of expertise*. New York: Routledge.

Kolb, D. A., Boyatzis, R. E., & Mainemelis, C. (2001). Experiential learning theory previous research and new directions. *Perspectives on Thinking, Learning, and Cognitive Styles*, 1(8), 227–247.

Kraiger, K., Ford, J. K., & Salas, E. (1993b). Application of cognitive, skill-based, and affective theories of learning outcomes to new methods of training evaluation. *Journal of Applied Psychology*, 78(2), 311–328. https://doi.org/10.1037/0021-9010.78.2.311

Kraiger, K., Salas, E., & Cannon-Bowers, J. A. (1995). Measuring knowledge organization as a method for assessing learning during training. *Human Factors*, 37(4), 804–816. doi.org/10.1518/001872095778995535

Krathwohl, D. R. (2002). A revision of Bloom's taxonomy: An overview. *Theory into Practice*, 41(4), 212–218. doi.org/10.1207/s15430421tip4104_2

Krathwohl, D. R., & Anderson, L. W. (2009). *A taxonomy for learning, teaching, and assessing: A revision of Bloom's taxonomy of educational objectives*. New York: Longman.

Krathwohl, D. R., Bloom, B. S., & Masia, B. B. (1964). *Taxonomy of educational objectives: Handbook 2: Affective domain*. New York: Longman Publishing Group.

Lord, R. G., & Hall, R. J. (2005). Identity, deep structure and the development of leadership skill. *The Leadership Quarterly*, 16(4), 591–615. doi.org/10.1016/j.leaqua.2005.06.003

MacNamara, B. N., Moreau, D., & Hambrick, D. Z. (2016). The relationship between deliberate practice and performance in sports: A meta-analysis. *Perspectives on Psychological Science*, 11(3), 333–350. doi.org/10.1177/1745691616635591

Moon, B., Hoffman, R., & Ziebell, D. (2009). How did you do that? *Electric Perspectives*, 34(1), 20–29.

Phillips, S. (2017, August 11). The average guy who spent 6003 hours trying to be a professional golfer. www.theatlantic.com/health/archive/2017/08/the-dan-plan/536592/

Reznick, R. K., & MacRae, H. (2006). Teaching surgical skills – Changes in the wind. *New England Journal of Medicine*, 355(25), 2664–2669. doi.org/10.1056/NEJMra054785

Salas, E., Tannenbaum, S. I., Kraiger, K., & Smith-Jentsch, K. A. (2012). The science of training and development in organizations: What matters in practice. *Psychological Science in the Public Interest*, 13(2), 74–101. doi.org/10.1177/1529100612436661

Shulman, L. S. (1999). Taking learning seriously. *Change: The Magazine of Higher Learning*, 31(4), 10–17.

Shulman, L. S. (2002). Making differences: A table of learning. *Change: The Magazine of Higher Learning*, 34(6), 36–44.

Shulman, L. S. (2005). Signature pedagogies in the professions. *Daedalus*, 134, 52–59.

Smith, E., Ford, K., & Kozlowski, S. (1997). Building adaptive expertise: Implications for training design strategies. In M. A. Quinones & A. Ehrenstein (Eds.), *Training for a rapidly changing workplace: Applications of psychological research*. Washington, DC: American Psychological Association.

Sonnentag, S. (1998). Expertise at work: Research perspectives and practical interventions for ensuring excellent performance at the workplace. *European Journal of Work and Organizational Psychology*, 7(4), 449–454. doi.org/10.1080/135943298398493

Sternberg, R. J. (2003). WICS: A model of leadership in organizations. *Academy of Management Learning & Education*, 2(4), 386–401. doi.org/10.5465/amle.2003.11902088

Taylor, P. J., Russ-Eft, D. F., & Chan, D. W. (2005). A meta-analytic review of behavior modeling training. *Journal of Applied Psychology*, 90(4), 692. doi.org/10.1037/0021-9010.90.4.692

Ullén, F., Mosing, M. A., Holm, L., Eriksson, H., & Madison, G. (2014). Psychometric properties and heritability of a new online test for musicality, the Swedish Musical Discrimination Test. *Personality and Individual Differences*, 63, 87–93. doi.org/10.1016/j.paid.2014.01.057

Ullén, F., Hambrick, D. Z., & Mosing, M. A. (2016). Rethinking expertise: A multifactorial gene–environment interaction model of expert performance. *Psychological Bulletin*, 142(4), 427. doi.org/10.1037/bul0000033

Weiss, H. M. (1990). Learning theory and industrial and organizational psychology. In M. Dunnette (Ed.), *Handbook of industrial and organizational psychology* (Vol. 1, pp. 171–221). Palo Alto, CA: Consulting Psychologist Press.

Williams, A. M., Ward, P., Knowles, J. M., & Smeeton, N. J. (2002). Anticipation skill in a real-world task: Measurement, training, and transfer in tennis. *Journal of Experimental Psychology: Applied*, 8(4), 259. doi.org/10.1037/1076-898X.8.4.259

Young, J. Q., Van Merrienboer, J., Durning, S., & Ten Cate, O. (2014). Cognitive load theory: Implications for medical education: *AMEE Guide No. 86*. *Medical teacher*, 36(5), 371–384. doi.org/10.3109/0142159X.2014.889290

PART II

A Systematic Approach

Assessing Learning Needs

Questions

✓ How does one translate organizational strategies into learning needs?
✓ What are the differences between competencies and work tasks?
✓ How can information be collected from job experts to identify learning needs of relative newcomers in a job?

Learning experiences through training, guided instruction, job experiences, and informal self-directed activities should begin with what needs to be learned so that a plan can be developed. There is the temptation to begin a learning experience without a thorough analysis of needs; however, a reexamination of the learning systems model introduced in Chapter 1 emphasizes the danger of beginning any learning program or activity without an assessment of learning gaps and the learning environment. Learning objectives, criteria, and design of any learning activity should all stem from this type of analysis. Understanding the capabilities and needs of persons in the organization is part of the road map for enhancing learning at work. In addition, as conditions change, organizations must adapt to new realities that may require enhanced worker and leader capabilities. Physicians diagnose problems using X-rays, fMRIs and laboratory tests before they attempt to prescribe a course of action. Similarly, a comprehensive needs assessment is required to determine the best course of action to produce the desired result.

There are three components of an effective needs assessment system: organization-wide analysis, an analysis of the work performed, and an analysis of the persons performing the work. Figure 3.1 presents a model of the various elements within each type of assessment. Most of this chapter is devoted to a discussion of these elements but the quality of the needs assessment process as a whole is dependent on how well connected the linkages are. Organization-wide analysis involves a "learning audit" for the company including current

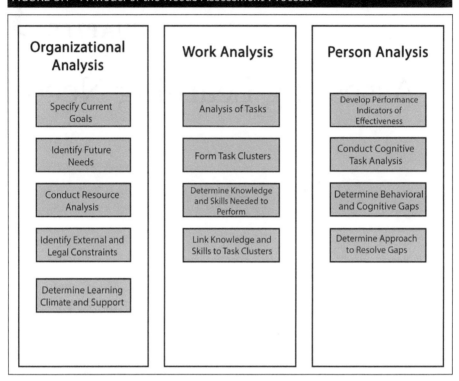

FIGURE 3.1   A Model of the Needs Assessment Process.

Organizational Analysis

Specify Current Goals

Identify Future Needs

Conduct Resource Analysis

Identify External and Legal Constraints

Determine Learning Climate and Support

Work Analysis

Analysis of Tasks

Form Task Clusters

Determine Knowledge and Skills Needed to Perform

Link Knowledge and Skills to Task Clusters

Person Analysis

Develop Performance Indicators of Effectiveness

Conduct Cognitive Task Analysis

Determine Behavioral and Cognitive Gaps

Determine Approach to Resolve Gaps

organizational learning needs as well as an analysis of future needs. A work analysis identifies what tasks, knowledge, skills, and capabilities are required, whether one is talking about jobs assigned to an individual or to a team such as flight crews. A person analysis targets the individual employee within a job or as a team member to identify specific gaps between what the current level of learning and development is for employees and what is the desired level. This gap analysis can then be examined to determine whether learning activities are the best solution for enhancing the contribution of the employee to individual, team, and organizational effectiveness, and if so what types of learning approach is best.

The needs assessment process is an intervention that requires input from organizational leaders, learning specialists and job incumbents. The success of the needs assessment process depends on the extent of the support for these efforts and the allocation of resources needed to conduct a systematic assessment. Realistic expectations need to be set as to the extensiveness of the process, the level of participation required, the time span for completion of the analyses, and the cost. To design an effective learning system, one must gain the cooperation of the key members of the organization. Successful interventions are characterized by highly motivated people who develop, early in the process, a two-way communication network with all pertinent stakeholders. A case example of a conflict around needs assessment is provided in Table 3.1. Rather than ignoring conflicts and hoping that they go away, the case shows that the consultant made an active attempt to refocus energy to meet the goals of the needs assessment process rather than allowing it to be undercut by on-going organizational conflicts.

TABLE 3.1 Top Management Support for Needs Assessment
I was invited by an organization's top management to design a needs assessment package that would be used to establish rating scales for performance appraisal. As part of that process, I requested that the first meeting be with a union-management committee, which I had heard about from top management. The committee had representatives from all parts of the organization. The hostility in the atmosphere at the meeting was made apparent by such questions as "What are you trying to sell us?"; "Did you ever do this type of work before?"; "Are you trying to stick us with a system you developed for someone else?" Finally, after several hours of "conversation," I learned that this committee had, at the request of top management, developed an earlier plan for the project. After countless hours of volunteer time, they submitted a report. On the same day their report was submitted, they were informed that an outside consultant had been asked to perform the same activity. Unfortunately for me, I was the chosen consultant. I decided not even to try to begin the project. Instead, we arranged for meetings between top management, the committee, and our research team to work out everyone's feelings and to establish appropriate roles for each group. Eventually, we proceeded with the project with everyone's cooperation. Months later, members of the committee noted that, if we had not met with them and if we had not resolved these difficulties, no one in the organization would have cooperated during the needs assessment; they had intended to subvert the entire needs assessment process. I have no doubt that they would have accomplished their purpose.
Source: Goldstein, I. L., & Ford, J. K. (2002). *Training in organizations: Needs assessment, development, and evaluation*, 4th ed., Wadsworth, Belmont, CA.

ORGANIZATIONAL ANALYSIS

Organizational analysis is a system-wide examination of the organization relevant to learning and development. Figure 3.2 provides an overview of the key elements. The first element is the organization's strategic goals. Goals can be formed around the current state of learning in the organization or focus on future learning needs. The second element is the four types of learning systems that we discussed in Chapter 1 – formal training programs, one-on-one guided instruction and coaching, developmental job experiences, and self-directed learning. The third element involves relevant organizational characteristics of resources, climate, and constraints on the learning enterprise

FIGURE 3.2 Components of Organizational Analysis.

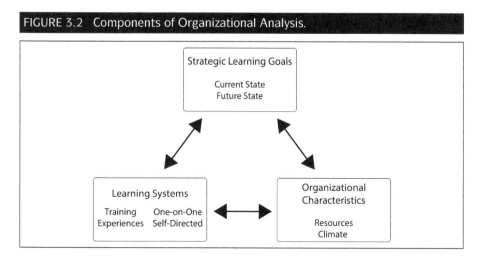

in the organization. An analysis of these three elements forms the basis for a "learning audit" of the organization. The two types of goals and three organizational characteristics are described below.

Strategic Learning Goals

Strategic learning goals examine the current state of learning in the organization as well as future learning needs given the direction of the organization. The examination of current state includes understanding how well the four types of learning strategies of formal training, guided learning, developmental job experiences, and self-directed learning are delivering what is expected and meeting organizational needs. This gap analysis of what is expected and what is the reality on the ground forms the basis for continuously improving those systems. For example, if an organization has prioritized over the last two years the need to actively pursue quality enhancement, one question for the organizational analysis is to ask if the learning needs relevant to this goal are being met and if not why not. This requires a discussion of the strengths of the learning enterprise in the organization as a whole as well as the identification of weaknesses. When the weaknesses are identified, the question becomes how to make those weaknesses into more of a strength by using evidenced based practices. Let us assume that one strength of the efforts around quality enhancement is that the training programs for incumbents are well designed and implemented and positively influences performance. The weakness in this system, though, is that many newcomers hired after the once-a-year formal training program are not being adequately trained through the one-on-one on-the-job training provided by the first line supervisors.

Organizations and their environments are not standing still so a look only at the current status of the learning enterprise and identifying gaps is not enough to provide for a comprehensive analysis. Organizations face changing realities and competitive pressures are also opportunities to expand and grow the business or redirect efforts. As the marketplace evolves, learning needs must be considered for jobs that may not even exist or existing ones that will need to be transformed. As one example of changing realities, state public state wildlife agencies are facing declining number of hunters – a main source of revenue – at the same time societal demands are pushing for the expansion of serviced provided by agencies to nontraditional stakeholders like recreational groups. One forward-looking state agency has conducted an extensive assessment of current state and futures states with input from multiple stakeholder groups in order to develop a five-year strategic plan. The plan has led to changes in the way the organization is structured as well as changing priorities. The changing roles and responsibilities with those new priorities along with a recognized need for a more adaptive management has had direct implications for learning needs within the agency. In this case, leaders saw the need to develop a more directed and intensive career-oriented approach, which led to the development of a career-learning academy.

Another example of future directions that I have been involved in is the move to community policing by a number of agencies. Police organizations spend considerable training on skill requirements such as operating a police vehicle or utilizing firearms or information requirements such as knowing the law regarding a felony as compared to a misdemeanor. However, when public safety organizations become involved in problem solving with community members as a function of this move to a community policing philosophy, they often discover the need to attend to other learning objectives – such as enhanced presentation skills and improved interpersonal relationships with the public. In these cases, it requires a reanalysis of learning goals across levels and functions relevant to the new vision and direction to identify the knowledge and skills that need to be embraced and enhanced. Table 3.2 presents the set of knowledge and skills identified by a team of officers, sergeants, and upper level managers regarding the changing roles of sergeants. As can be seen, many of the skills identified were softer type skills around building community and officer support. It is also important to note that some of the issues identified can be addressed through learning activities while other needs require structural changes and other organizational implementation strategies.

Core Competencies

A formalized approach to looking at capabilities needed across organizational levels and functions is the development of core competency models. A large percentage of Fortune 500 companies employ some form of competency modeling and assessment (Stone, Webster, & Schoonover, 2013). Competencies typically represent general capabilities that form the basis for talent management within an organization such as critical thinking and decision making. Core competencies are "patterns of behavior" considered important to the current and/or future success of the organization (Sanchez & Levine, 2009). The identified competencies send a signal to the employees about what behavioral patterns are valued by organizational leaders. In this way, these desired behavioral patterns can become the norm within the organization. The competencies also provide a common language prescribing what is expected regardless of level, function, or job.

A competency based approach is typically developed in a top-down way in order to identify a set of human resource capabilities that help meet the strategic goals of the organization and that are aligned with the vision for the organization (Campion et al., 2011). Leaders can better link the future direction of the organization with future job requirements. As an example, to meet mounting competitive pressures, organizations may see the need to enhance teamwork capabilities in the competency area of collaborative problem solving. Then work can be done to identify what type(s) of learning system strategies to best build those capabilities. In this way, one could see an increase in the behavioral patterns exhibited that are consistent with that competency (Neubert et al., 2015).

Many executive development and coaching programs are based on a leadership core competency model that include competencies such as taking risks and challenging the status quo or having mutual respect. Eight core competencies often desired of leaders including (1) leading and deciding, (2) supporting and cooperating, (3) interacting and presenting, (4) analyzing and interpreting, (5) creating and conceptualizing, (6) organizing and executing, (7) adapting and coping, and (8) enterprising and coping (Bartram, 2005). Adapting is defined as responding well to change, managing pressures, and coping with setbacks. The competency of creating and conceptualizing is defined as working well in situations requiring openness to new ideas and experiences as well as thinking broadly and strategically.

TABLE 3.2   The Move to Community Policing: Organizational Analysis

Skill Area	Short-Term Needs	Intermediate Needs	Long-Term Needs
Administration	-Time management -Knowledge of the law -Reinforce new vision and values	-Organizing / documenting skills (esp. tracking schedules) -Managing vs. Doing (personnel management) -Paying attention and tracking what officers are doing…becoming more involved with officers	-Focusing on performance outcomes other than numbers: identifying community policing behaviors -Rewarding CP behaviors -Changing performance evaluation measures
Community Orientation	-Facilitating/ teaching external community members -Gathering information from the community about their needs -Promoting officer ownership over areas	-Building community partnerships	
Personal Development/ Communication	-Team building -Listening skills -Accepting upward feedback -Opening lines of communication with officers -Providing expectations to officers (role clarity)	-Mentoring others -Communicating with fellow sergeants -Empowering officers -Delegating and following-through -Holding officers accountable for performing CP activities -Modeling CP behaviors	-Developing a customer service orientation towards officers (provide resources and support) -Giving officers the confidence to fail
Problem Solving	-Identifying problems -Enforcing a more proactive model of policing	-Setting good goals -Developing a long-term focus: continuous improvement -Managing geography vs. shift responsibilities	-Promoting officer creativity
Technology/Data	-Emailing (group messages) -Using computers (work processing, internet)	-Mining data -Printing data	-Crime mapping

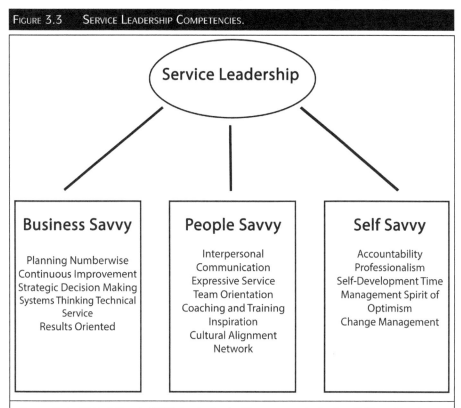

FIGURE 3.3   SERVICE LEADERSHIP COMPETENCIES.

Source: Testa, M. R., & Sipe, L. (2012). Service-leadership competencies for hospitality and tourism management. *International Journal of Hospitality Management*, 31, 648–658. Copyright 2012 by Elsevier Science and Technology. Reprinted by permission.

Leadership competencies have also been identified for specific industries. In the service industry, one model displayed in Figure 3.3 categorizes business (planning strategic decision-making, results oriented), people (interpersonal communication, coaching, cultural alignment) and self-focused (accountability, professionalism, time management, and self-development) competencies (Testa & Sipe, 2012). The inspiration competency is defined as engaging and inspiring others to do their best every day while numberwise is seen as incorporating data, reports, and trends to draw conclusions and inform decisions. The effectiveness of approaches to build these competencies can be examined during an organizational analysis.

Required Learning Needs

A comprehensive organizational analysis takes into account mandated learning requirements. Learning requirements such as federally mandated safety training programs require allocation of resources and personnel. Leaders may also identify internally mandated needs across levels of functions such as enhancing diversity and inclusion initiatives seen as critical for organizational effectiveness.

Two types of external conditions affecting learning needs include vertical and horizontal regulations (Frieden, 2002). The vertical regulatory system at the governmental level targets specific types of industries. For example, the trucking industry in the United States is regulated by the Interstate Commerce Commission (ICC) while the Food and Drug Administration (FDA) regulates the drug industry. Failure to provide the required training prescribed by these regulatory agencies can lead to fines and penalties. Horizontal regulation targets specific issues within organizations that are concerned with employee wellbeing and society related issues. In regards to wellbeing, a governmental entity like the Occupational Safety and Health Administration in the United States is concerned with job safety across all industries. From a societal perspective, in many other countries, equal employment opportunity committees have been created to address issues related to fair employment and discrimination regardless of industry type. Horizontal regulatory agencies have as their constituents the groups concerned with those specific issues or problems such as civil rights groups. They are less concerned with the mission of the organizations they regulate and more focused on employees across all organizations.

The regulations established by the vertical and horizontal regulatory agencies must be considered in an organizational analysis to determine if they are being adequately addressed. Fair employment practice guidelines have important implications for the needs assessment process, the selection of applicants, and even the type of records that must be maintained. In other cases, the requirement might be new governmental requirements that affect what learning goals must be enhanced, enlarged or even started within an organization. Rapid changes in technological advances have been a constant struggle for regulators in governmental agencies to adapt to new developments (Gasparini, 2014). Existing organizational learning programs may need to be evaluated to make sure they are consistent with new safety, health, and technology regulations.

Expenditures such as in-house educational assistance (to support self-directed learning) have to follow the rules to comply with governmental tax codes (Clardy, 2014). Assessments can also be conducted to examine if learning opportunities are providing reasonable accommodations for individuals with disabilities (Murphy, 2018). A recent study found evidence that older workers are less likely to receive opportunities for training and development, highlighting the importance of examining organizational fair employment practices (Czaja et al., 2015).

Although the emphasis here has been on regulations, other factors can affect the learning enterprise. As companies become more global, cultural issues must be considered. A company moving to become more global in reach and multinational should analyze and account for cultural differences and their implications for learning activities as incumbents are relocated to different countries.

Once organizational learning goals are established, the next step is to examine the organizational conditions surrounding the learning enterprise. This stage of the organizational analysis targets the (1) resources and support of the organization for the learning systems and (2) the climate for learning and developing self and others within the organization.

Resources

Resources relevant to the learning enterprise includes an analysis of people, time and money. In terms of people, one can examine the number of people in learning-related efforts throughout the organization and the capabilities that those people have relevant to enhancing the effectiveness of the learning enterprise. This could include an examination of the current state of training designers, trainers and evaluators of training (if separate functions) as well as an analysis of those providing on-the-job training, coaching, and mentoring to identify areas for continuous improvement. The need for enhancing the coaching abilities of key top leaders in the organization could be identified as a priority to provide the level of support and feedback needed for high potentials. These efforts would enhance the pool of potential managers seen as promotable into higher levels of leadership. Or, the identification of future directions may require projecting requirements like hiring of new personnel in the training department now in order to expand course offerings to meet future needs rather than responding only when a personnel crisis is occurring.

The issue of an analysis of time spent on learning programs and activities addresses the extent to which the organization is taking seriously the need for developing people. As noted in Chapter 1, the average number of hours trained per employee was reported to be about 34 hours of training per year. If an organization is expending far fewer hours per employee per year, a question could be raised about the amount of effort being placed on developing people. Also, if many trainers are part time, one could ask if that is sustainable given future learning needs in the organization.

The examination of monetary expenditures for the learning enterprise can also lead to an interesting discussion of the amount of support that might be needed to address current and future learning gaps. The use of new technology can have dramatic implications for the learning enterprise. In one manufacturing company I worked with, they had purchased expensive new machinery to meet identified future production needs. The purchased machinery was much more complex than the machines currently being used to make similar parts. While the potential for greater efficiency in production was clear to the top decision makers who made this investment decision, less attention was given to who would run the new equipment and the length of time to get people up to speed to meet this production pressure. It became clear after the new machinery was installed that the in-service training provided by the company who manufactured the new machinery was not good enough to build the capabilities of the people that were needed. In addition, it was recognized late in the game after installing the machines that the two expert machine operators and one first line supervisors would need time to train others in the organization slowing down the rate of production on the other machines. The new equipment laid idle or at low production rates longer than desired due to the lack of adequate foresight about learning needs. This story shows the importance of resource analysis around learning when planning to purchase and implement new technology.

Organizational Learning Climate

This element of an organizational analysis examines the extent to which a positive learning and development climate exists. It also includes ensuring that reward and reinforcement systems in the organization value investments in learning and development. Existing disincentives or obstacles to learning and development can also be identified. Persons who participate in formal training programs are required to learn something in one environment (training situation) and use the learning in another environment (on the job). Training programs can be judged to be a failure but the root cause for some program failures might be due to the lack of support in the workplace for using the knowledge or skills gained in training. In working with the military, we found that supervisors were a key gatekeeper as to what opportunities trainees were given to apply what they have been trained in as a new recruit (Ford et al., 1992). In other situations, a learner may have difficulty overcoming a situation where he or she arrives with a set of behaviors that are not consistent with the way the manager, supervisor, or peers prefer to have the job performed.

Table 3.3 provides some survey items that can be used to assess learning climate such as the extent to which existing managers make sure that new supervisors have the opportunity to use their new knowledge and skills immediately on the job. Research with fast-food restaurants found that learners assigned to units that had a more positive learning climate in terms of supporting trainees to use what they've learned and rewarding trainees for doing so demonstrated greater transfer of the trained behaviors to the job (Rouiller & Goldstein, 1993).

More generally, an assessment of the learning climate of the organization is particularly important when an organization is attempting transformational change. In one organization there was a realization of the need to espouse the importance of learning through a vision statement of we are committed to continuous learning at all levels of our organization with just in time delivery of learning activities and full support for knowledge and skill-based improvements in capabilities. The extent to which this espoused statement

---

TABLE 3.3   Examples of Learning Transfer Climate Items

Supervisors make sure trainees have the opportunity to use their training immediately.
Supervisors share their training experience and learning with others.
The equipment used in training is similar to the equipment found on the job.
An experienced co-worker helps trainees as needed back on the job.
Performance aids are available on the job to support what was trained
Supervisors acknowledge when they see trainees applying the knowledge and skills from a program.
More experienced workers ridicule the use of techniques taught in training (reverse scored).
Existing managers do not notice new managers who are using their training (reverse scored).
New managers who successfully use their training are likely to receive a salary increase.
Trainees who apply knowledge and skills effectively are given preference for new assignments.
Coworkers encourage trainees to try out new skills.
Supervisors help learners set realistic goals for performing the job after training.
Supervisors appreciate trainees who do their jobs as they were taught in training.
Failure to use what was trained on the job is discouraged.

Sources: Rouiller, J. Z., & Goldstein, I. L. (1993). The relationship between organizational transfer climate and positive transfer of training. *Human Resource Development Quarterly*, 4, pp. 377–390; Ford, J. K., Quinones, M. A., Sego, D. J., & Sorra, J. S. (1992). Factors affecting the opportunity to perform trained tasks on the job. *Personnel Psychology*, 45, 511–527; Thayer, P., & Teachout, M. (1995). *A climate for transfer model*. Human Resources Directorate, Technical Training Research Division, Brooks AFB, TX.

becomes reality is critical to showing employees that the vision has meaning in the organization (Cutcher-Gershenfeld & Ford, 2005). Statements given by leaders about the importance of development may be questioned by managers who are under high pressure to maintain production standards even when some of their employees are attending a three-day training program mandated by the organization! Another case study examined an organizational-wide assessment of learning needs in a large health care system that was undergoing significant changes around empowerment, partnerships, individual responsibility, and ownership for learning. They found that the emphasis on teamwork and collaboration helped drive the internal cultural changes required to move the effort forward (Reed & Vakola, 2006).

WORK ANALYSIS

A work analysis (traditionally called a task analysis in training literature) examines in detail the jobs within an organization. What does a human resource specialist or a civil engineer do? A comprehensive view of any job starts with the identification of the specific tasks completed by employees in the jobs of interest. A second type of information is the underlying knowledge and skills required to complete the tasks. It is important to note that the target of these types of analyses is not a description of any one person working on the job or an analysis of how well a person is doing in performing the job tasks – that is a part of the person analysis. A third type of information can be in the form or broader capabilities that are relevant to completing the job tasks such as deductive reasoning or the ability to apply general rules to specific problems. The work analysis can also go beyond individual jobs and focus jobs embedded within teams.

Task Analysis

To understand what it takes to do a job, one must identify the task activities or work operations performed (Brannick, Cadie, & Levine, 2012). The foundation of a task statement is to use a direct style that describes an individual task that is performed using the language of the people who perform the job. This requires one-on-one interviews or focus groups with job incumbents and supervisors. Job incumbents can be asked to describe what a "typical day" is like for them – what do they do at the beginning of their day, what do they do next, what they do at the end of the day, as well as what they do on an irregular basis, etc. From the information gathered, task statements are documented in this form: (1) begins with a functional verb that identifies the primary operation or action that is observable, (2) describes what work is accomplished, and (3) identifies why the worker does that task. A task statement for a first line supervisor ending a shift might be to inform (action) the next shift supervisor of the current status (what) to help provide a smooth transition of duties (why). Table 3.4 presents some example task statements. For practice, identify the three categories of action, how, and why for each of the statements.

It is important that the statements identify a complete task rather than specific steps that need to be taken to complete each task. In this way, the level of specificity of the task statements can be consistent with a focus on a whole task that makes sense to the worker. A task for a machine operator after producing a

TABLE 3.4   Examples of Tasks from a Variety of Jobs

1. Call job candidates to provide feedback and keep them informed during the pre-employment selection process.
2. Monitor the implementation of personnel procedures to ensure that provisions of the labor contract are maintained.
3. Interpret letters from the highway department concerning driver license revocation in order to verbally advise citizens on the appropriate course of action.
4. Observe and evaluate the performance of job incumbents for the purpose of salary review.
5. Evaluate workloads, priorities, and activity schedules to determine staffing requirements and assignments for areas of responsibility.
6. Inspect hospital facilitates to determine compliance with government rules and regulations pertaining to health practices.
7. Maintain written records and logs of contacts with customers to provide documentation concerning steps taken to resolve their service problem.
8. Provide verbal feedback to first line supervisors to assist them in critiquing their own performance after incidents to help them develop more effective ways of handling future situations.

Source: Goldstein, I. L., & Ford, J. K. (2002). *Training in organizations: Needs assessment, development, and evaluation*, 4th ed., Wadsworth, Belmont, CA.

part could be "detect ragged edges and deburr so as to have a finished product ready to ship." If necessary, one could then also identify the steps that one takes when completing that task (e.g., raise hand onto table, places fingertips on part, moves fingers to the right six inches, and so on). Usually, the breaking down of the tasks into a steps or a sequence of activities is useful only once it has already been determined that a task should be taught through some type of learning opportunity with the steps becoming part of the plan for instruction.

After a full task set is developed and verified for a job, another useful procedure is the development of *task clusters*. The purpose of clustering is to help organize the individual task statements into similar categories of job duties. A rational clustering approach involves the following steps:

1. Label and develop definitions of task clusters that describe broader functions than the individual tasks.
2. Have a group of subject matter experts (SMEs) such as incumbents, supervisors or human resource specialists independently sort each of the tasks into one of the identified clusters.
3. Establish a rule that defines the level of agreement needed to declare that a task is successfully clustered. For example, if ten people are performing the clustering, a rule might be that eight of ten people must agree on where the task should be clustered
4. Plan to rework the task cluster definitions. When disagreement occurs on the placement of a task, it usually provides very useful information concerning the development of either the task or the cluster.

Usually, disagreement occurs because the task has more than one work component in it, and different judges focus on different parts of the task or that the clusters themselves are too broad or poorly defined. This rational clustering process can lead to useful re-editing of the tasks and the cluster definitions to have a clearer understanding of the job. Table 3.5 illustrates an example of a task cluster and individual tasks for the job of a customer service representative.

TABLE 3.5 Example of a Task Cluster for the Job of a Customer Service Representative

Task cluster: Interaction with customer – communication between the customer service representative and the customer to determine what service difficulties have occurred

1. Determine what difficulties the customer is having in order to complete a service report.
2. Ask the customer for relevant information in order to provide all information needed by vendor to service the customer.
3. Call the customer to determine whether the problem has been resolved by the promised date and time.
4. Provide the customer with information so that the customer can follow up the call at a later time to obtain status information.
5. Provide instructions to the customer concerning basic self-checks that can be used to resolve the problem.
6. Provide information to the customer about services that are available to resolve the problem.
7. Inform the customer about possible service charges that may be billed to service the customer's equipment.

Source: Goldstein, I. L., & Ford, J. K. (2002). *Training in organizations: Needs assessment, development, and evaluation*, 4th ed., Wadsworth, Belmont, CA.

Knowledge and Skills

Whereas task analysis provides an understanding a job, from a learning perspective it is necessary to understand the knowledge and skills required to perform those tasks within each task cluster. *Knowledge* refers to an organized body of information, usually of a factual or procedural nature as we talked about in Chapter 2, which, if successfully applied, makes job performance possible. *Skill* refers to the capability to perform job operations with some degree of ease and precision. The specification of a skill implies a standard that is required for effective job operations.

A direct procedure to collect this type of information is to simply ask job experts to examine each task cluster (and tasks under that cluster) and identify what a person needs to know or needs to be able to do skill wise to complete the tasks in the task cluster. Information should be gathered on priorities, for example by asking what newcomers need to understand and execute immediately to become effective relevant to the tasks in the task cluster. Knowledge and skill statements from a job analysis of a police officer job are presented in Table 3.6. Each statement is direct and to the point – starting with the word knowledge or skill – and then describes exactly what is needed to perform the tasks in the task clusters.

Some of the guidelines for the development of such statements include:

1. Maintain a reasonable balance between generality and specificity relative to intended use.
2. Identify both knowledge and skills to perform the tasks in the task cluster. For example, a task might be "analyze hiring patterns to determine whether company practices are consistent with fair employment practice guidelines." One of the knowledge components for this task will involve knowledge concerning federal, state, and local guidelines on fair

TABLE 3.6   Example Knowledge and Skill Statements for the Job of Police Officer
1. Knowledge of what is or is not evidence and what constitutes its admissibility in court.
2. Knowledge of search and seizure laws and procedures.
3. Knowledge of proper procedures for stopping a vehicle with a known felon.
4. Knowledge of when an arrest can be made with or without a warrant.
5. Knowledge of methods and procedures for person searches.
6. Knowledge of community and social service agencies available for juveniles.
7. Knowledge of traffic laws.
8. Skill in securing the scene of an accident.
9. Skill in handling domestic violence or conflict situations (proper approach, calming techniques, problem solving strategies).
10. Skill in operating firearms.
11. Skill in operating and maintaining control of patrol car while involved in high speed pursuits.
12. Skill in communicating with, interviewing, and questioning citizens.

employment practices. Another component might involve skill in use of statistical procedures appropriate to perform analyses of hiring patterns.

3. Avoid including trivial information. For example, for a supervisor's job, "knowledge of how to order personal office supplies" is likely to be trivial.

Identifying Learning Needs

Once the tasks, knowledge and the skills are specified, obtaining further information is often required to determine learning needs. For example, it is usually necessary to know which task clusters are more important than others and within the clusters which tasks and knowledge and skills are more important. It may also be useful to obtain information on how frequently a task is performed or the tasks where there are high consequences for making mistakes. This type of information can be quite useful for prioritizing learning needs for newcomers such as what to focus on and what to avoid. Another piece of information could be how difficult it is to gain each knowledge or learn a particular skill. Designing a formalized training program around knowledge and skills that are not important or are easy to learn through experience would not make much sense.

Surveys permit the collection of great amounts of information in a relatively short period of time. The survey format makes it possible to collect ratings data from experienced job incumbents and/or supervisors (or other stakeholder groups) across large enough samples to ensure confidence in the results found. An example of an importance scale for a survey of task statements is given in Table 3.7. Similar scales for the importance of knowledge and skills can be similarly designed. One can also look to the future and ask the question as to whether task clusters, tasks, knowledge, or skills will become more or less important given future directions (Voskuijl, 2017). Raters can also be asked about where knowledge and skills are best acquired (before hire, initial training, later on-the-job) or the depth of knowledge required early in the job. The exact questions and ratings scales used on the survey can vary depending on the purpose.

TABLE 3.7   Sample Importance Scale for Tasks
Importance: How important is this task (or task cluster) to effective performance on this job? 1 = Not Important (improper task performance is not likely to have any consequences for people, things or places and requires no corrective action) 2 = Of Minor Importance (improper task performance leading to errors has only minor consequences for people, things or places and could be easily corrected) 3 = Moderately Important (improper task performance or errors on this task would create a problem for people, things or places) 4 = Important (improper task performance or errors on this task hampers the effectiveness of a unit or department) 5 = Critical Importance (improper task performance or errors on this task would likely result in *serious* consequences for people or *extensive* damages to things and places)
Source: Goldstein, I. L., & Ford, J. K. (2002). *Training in organizations: Needs assessment, development, and evaluation*, 4th ed., Wadsworth, Belmont, CA.

TABLE 3.8 Scale Linking Knowledge and Skills to Tasks	
2 = Essential	This knowledge or skill is essential to the performance of this task (or task cluster). Without this knowledge or skill one would not be able to perform this task effectively.
1 = Helpful	This knowledge or skill is useful in performing this task (or task cluster). This task could be performed without this knowledge or skill, although it would be more difficult or time consuming.
0 = Not Relevant	This knowledge or skill is not needed to perform this task (or task cluster). Having this knowledge or skill would make no difference in the performance of this task.
Source: Goldstein, I. L., & Ford, J. K. (2002). *Training in organizations: Needs assessment, development, and evaluation*, 4th ed., Wadsworth, Belmont, CA.	

To complete the analysis, as shown in Table 3.8, raters can be asked the extent to which specific knowledge and skills are essential, helpful or not relevant to performing the tasks within a task cluster. Looking at the required knowledge and skills and noting what types of tasks they are linked provides a roadmap for the design of learning interventions.

Whatever survey data is collected can then be analyzed to determine average responses (which tasks are seen as more important than other tasks), variability in responses across raters, and degree of agreement between the raters. Based on the average ratings of, say, importance, cutoffs can be set for the determination of which tasks and KSAs should be prioritized for learning. It might be decided that all tasks that earn an average value of 3.0 on a five-point rating scale (1 = not important; 2 = minor importance; 3 = moderately important; 4 = importance and 5 = critically important) and above are included in the next stage of the needs assessment process. The data can also be examined to determine if the work being examined is viewed the same way by job incumbents across a globally dispersed organization or by different units within the same location. To illustrate, the task cluster of interacting with customers can be analyzed to see if the ratings show a similar level of importance from different rating sources and across different countries where the same job is performed. Different groups of raters such as supervisors and job incumbents may not agree on the importance (or other scales) of tasks or knowledge and skills required to perform the job. In those instances, it is important to resolve the disagreement before any learning opportunity is planned and designed.

Methods for Conducting Work Analysis

The goal of a work analysis is to take an accurate picture of the job from multiple angles and perspectives. There are a number of different methods for collecting task, knowledge and skill, and capabilities information. Each method has unique characteristics that can affect both the kind and quality of the information obtained. The quality of information from an interview is dependent on the interviewer's skills. Surveys can be subject to sampling biases that can occur if a substantial number of relevant participants are not sent the survey or do not return the survey. Job observations may allow one to see only the routine parts of a job and therefore miss some non-routine tasks that are important. Focus groups may be dominated by some members of the group leading to incomplete analysis of the job. Given that each method has its own strengths and limitations, a good approach is to consider using more than one methodology. Steps can be taken to minimize possible disadvantages or limitation such as training interviewers in standardized protocols when conducting a work analysis. It is also important to avoid having only one person conduct interviews, job observations, or job panels.

Regardless of which methods are used, respondents need to represent a reasonable cross sample of those individuals with relevant information about the job. In this way, alternative viewpoints of the job and differences in how certain aspects are assessed on things like importance or consequence of error can be identified and clarified. In addition, if organizational members believe that learning systems are being designed with their help and input, they are more likely to lend support for the learning interventions that were subsequently developed.

One logical way to involve many participants is to have different individuals included in the various stages of the assessment procedure. For example, in working on the job of police officer, my research team started with job observations from riding with patrol officers to gain a perspective about the job. The team switched to individual interviews of officers to complete the identification of tasks. Then focus groups of sergeants were used to cluster the tasks into relevant categories and to identify the knowledge and skills necessary for the job. Based on this information, surveys of the entire police force of sergeants and officers were conducted to collect statistical information such as the importance of the tasks as well as the underlying knowledge and skills. Such information was used to determine if the current training program for new recruits was oriented appropriately on the important tasks, knowledge, and skills.

Capabilities and Work Team Analysis

The approaches described above provide detailed information about knowledge, skills and task relationships that can be used for the design of learning activities targeted for specific jobs. It is also possible to organize these link-ages into more general clusters around capabilities or abilities required for individuals to do their job well. In addition, many organizations have adopted team-based work systems as a way of meeting the increasing needs for greater integration and collaboration in the workplace. This requires an analysis of team tasks and the knowledge and skills needed by team members.

CAPABILITIES Broader human capabilities necessary to effectively perform the job tasks rather than the specific knowledge and skills involve the identifica-tion of what makes exemplary performers exemplary! Example capabilities for a technical job could include things such as strong analytical capabilities and mathematical reasoning ability. Worker capacities for jobs could also include what has been called softer "skills" such as time management, attention to detail, and ability to work under pressure.

Gathering information about capabilities for each individual job in an organization can seem overwhelming. An important source of information on jobs can be obtained from the Occupational Information Network or O*NET from the Department of Labor (www.onetonline.org/). It is a free online relational database of hundreds of jobs and career clusters of jobs that can be searched on a variety of characteristics including skill requirements. In regards to needs assessment, the data base includes information such as tasks and work activities by job title, high-level knowledge requirements, technol-ogy skills required, and abilities (e.g., inductive reasoning, written compre-hension). For example, for solar energy photovoltaic installers, tasks includes statements such as installing photovoltaic systems in accordance with codes and standards using drawings, schematics and instruction, and assembling solar modules, panels, and support structures as specified. Technological skills include the use of customer relationship management software and enterprise application integration software. Knowledge statements consist of principles involved in production of precision technical plans and blueprints as well as knowledge of quality standards for service. The job also requires capabilities such as problem sensitivity to be able to tell when something is wrong or likely to go wrong and visualization or the ability to see how something will look after it is moved around or reconfigured. Work activities include handling and moving objects to be able to install and position material and inspecting equip-ment, structures, and material to identify defects. The work context involves face-to-face discussions every day and being exposed to high places and expo-sure to weather. In addition, most of the time performing tasks is spent using hands to handle and control objectives. As such, this information is quite help-ful in getting started on a work analysis for learning. The material on capabili-ties is also well suited for thinking about hiring criteria or helping individuals think about career options.

TEAMS Needs assessments can also be conducted at the team level of analy-sis. For example, a manufacturing company might create work teams that take raw material, transform it into a part, conduct quality analyses and package the parts for shipping. Other teams may be temporary such as project teams working on an issue to be disbanded when the issue is adequately addressed and reformed into a different project team. Regardless, teams often need com-plementary skills as individuals work semi-autonomously on defined tasks.

Team members also have defined and differentiated roles and responsibilities but must rely on one another to accomplish team goals. To perform effectively, team members must develop an understanding of how their actions affect and are affected by others (Kozlowski & Ilgen, 2006).

The transformation of a group of individuals into an effective team requires that team members gain knowledge and skills beyond their individual job that helps the team succeed. Therefore, a work analysis needs to examine not only individual jobs within the team using the methods above but must also identify teamwork knowledge, skills, and competencies required for effective team performance. Teamwork skills target the interactions among team members independent of the task to be performed. Teamwork skills that distinguish effective and ineffective teams have been identified including behavioral indicators such as adaptability, shared situational awareness, team management, coordination, interpersonal relations, and decision-making (Salas, Cooke, & Rosen, 2008). Chapter 9 investigates the use of these foundational teamwork skills to build team effectiveness through a variety of learning approaches.

PERSON ANALYSIS

A work analysis helps to determine or cut down the list of "what" to consider incorporating into a learning approach. Once the "what" has been decided there is a need to understand the person issues relevant to the job. A person analysis examines "who" needs to be given learning opportunities to address knowledge or skill gaps that further the learning goals identified through the strategic planning process.

To identify the "who" requires a gap analysis. A gap analysis consists of two main parts – the current learning state of the person in question and the desired job behaviors and performance. Once these two parts are identified, the gap between the two can be described and then a decision can be made as to how best to reduce that gap. This section examines data that can be gathered to identify the gap. Once identified, one can then determine if a learning experience or experiences (or what type) is the best way to address that gap. The gap could be due to inadequate knowledge and skills but it is also possible that the gap is more about lack of incentives to perform at a high level, the lack of support in the workplace, inadequate job design, or lack of motivation. Therefore, a person analysis asks three questions in order to determine the next steps to be taken: (1) what do highly effective people do on the job to provide an indicator of desired performance levels; (2) what is the current level of effectiveness for the person(s) in question for targeted jobs; and (3) to what extent can identified gaps be reduced or eliminated through some type of learning intervention? In addition to current states, a person analysis can also detail gaps due to the need for individuals to upgrade skills to meet future or projected desired behaviors and performance levels. Figure 3.4 shows this dual purpose for person analysis on immediate and longer-term needs.

There are two main approaches for identifying standards for successful performance by people who have mastered tasks in the targeted job. One approach involves a cognitive analysis of experts in the job to identify how they go about addressing and solving the key challenges to performing the job tasks. A second approach is to identify the behaviors that separate what highly

FIGURE 3.4   Immediate and Longer Term Needs Analysis.

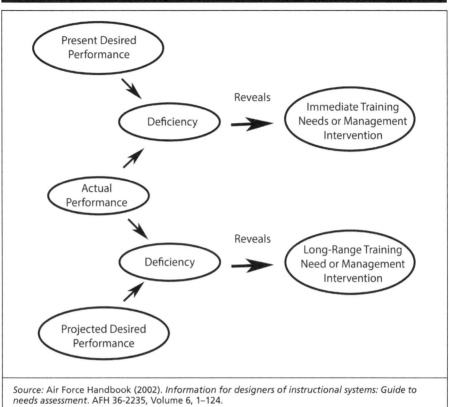

Source: Air Force Handbook (2002). *Information for designers of instructional systems: Guide to needs assessment.* AFH 36-2235, Volume 6, 1–124.

effective incumbents do over those who are not as effective. This cognitive and behavior-based information helps set what the performance expectations are for newcomers, incumbents, or those who transfer into that job.

Cognitive Analysis

A cognitive-based perspective addresses the underlying requirements to accomplish work tasks by revealing the thought processes that highly effective individuals in the job employ to achieve their superior performance (Crandall, Klein, & Hoffman, 2006). The analysis includes the mental aspects underlying performance – the goals, strategies, and decisions that have to be made to perform a task. An examination of differences between experts and relative novices or advanced beginners in terms of goals and actions helps identify areas for development as seen through the lens of an expert performer (Klein et al., 2018).

One example of a cognitive task analysis conducted by the United States Air Force is PARI or precursor, action, results, and interpretation. This methodology is used to understand the cognitive task requirements for complex situations requiring adaptability. The PARI procedure includes problem-solving situations where experts use their knowledge to respond to problems. The experts describe what they would consider in a job situation (precursor), solutions they would choose (action), and then are probed for the reasons behind their actions and what they see as the impact of their actions (results). The next step is to ask what the results mean to them and how they would respond to the feedback from results (interpretation). These procedures are especially useful in producing knowledge that is usually tacit or unspoken by job experts. Such an approach uncovers the expert's mental model or how they see connections among various elements in a problem as well as the linkage of the situation to possible actions (Dargue & Biddle, 2016).

The PARI methodology reveals the strategic knowledge used by experts in deciding what to do and when to act. For example, the expert in comparison to an advanced beginner may have a different approach to troubleshooting when a particular device failed when a test is being run such as:

1. Focus on the components that are active when the test failed, thus avoiding the examination of a large number of irrelevant parts.
2. Determine that the testing equipment is more likely to go bad than the piece of equipment being analyzed, thus picking the unit with the highest probability of failure.
3. Determine that one piece of equipment is much more difficult to troubleshoot, thus deciding to rule out the easier components first.

Each reason is directly tied to the knowledge of the equipment but involves considerably more knowledge than just how the equipment operates. Interestingly, when advanced beginners and experts are compared, they do not differ substantially in their knowledge of the basics in troubleshooting procedures (for example, taking measurements or checking connections). However, the advanced beginners cannot formulate the type of strategies described above. They tend not to generate hypotheses concerning the problem nor predict what result would occur from the use of their strategies. Often, advanced beginners focus on the use of outside sources for their strategies, such as deciding to perform a particular operation or test because a book or computer program instructs the learner to try this action. However, the learners often are uncertain about what they would learn from the test.

Researchers have explored the implications of a cognitive task analysis for developing more effective learning plans so as to accelerate learners to more quickly think and behave like a job expert. In an important study, a troubleshooting course for technicians designed from a traditional work analysis was compared to a new troubleshooting course developed from information gathered through a cognitive task analysis (Schaafstal, Schraagen, & van Berl, 2000). Both the new and traditional training course on troubleshooting were designed to improve the skills of relatively novice technicians on the identification of equipment malfunctions and the appropriate steps for taking corrective action and solving the malfunction. Based on information from experts, the new course design provided a more structured, explicitly discussed hierarchical approach to dealing with malfunctions. Findings highlighted a number of positive results in comparison to the program based on the traditional program. Technicians trained in the new troubleshooting course solved twice as many malfunctions, in less time, then those trained in the traditional way. The new training was also completed in less time (33% reduction of time) than the traditional training program. Individuals trained by the program designed based on cognitive task analysis were rated by experts as applying higher level reasoning skills when addressing troubleshooting problems.

Given that a number of similar studies have now been conducted employing cognitive task analysis, a meta-analysis across studies has been conducted. The analysis across 56 comparisons of training programs supports the conclusion from this original study that training content and design based on a cognitive analysis leads to more effective learning than designs based on traditional work analysis information (Tofel-Grehl & Feldon, 2013).

More recent studies using a scenario-based instructional approach called Shadowbox with programs designed from cognitive task analysis information have shown impressive results in accelerating learning. The scenarios provide novices or advanced beginners with opportunities to practice in realistic situations with embedded critical decision points and expert developed guided feedback to help the learner around those decision points. One study found a 28% improvement in performance for marines trained through Shadowbox as compared to a traditional training approach (Klein et al., 2016).

Behavioral Analysis

A cognitive analysis provides a framework for understanding how experts are using the knowledge, skills and capabilities to address tasks on the job. A second approach is to examine job behaviors – what successful people do on the job. These performance indicators can then become the standards of success that one is striving to develop in others.

A popular approach to identifying observable job behaviors is through the use of a critical incident technique developed during World War II to help with selecting aircrews in the air force (Flanagan, 1954). The critical incident technique is a qualitative methodology used to gather stories of effective and ineffective job performance. Interviews with knowledgeable people of the job in question provide rich stories that include three types of information: (1) a comprehensive description of the situation or event that occurred on the job; (2) the specific actions or response of the person on the job to that situation; and (3) the consequences or outcomes that were obtained based on the actions or response by the job incumbent. Obtaining a large number of stories for a particular job such as stories of what effective and ineffective coaches do in different types of situations leads to categorizing the behaviors that have been found to be particular effective (Butterfield et al., 2005). These effective behaviors can then be tangible indicators of what successful performance on the job looks like.

Stories from critical incidents have been used to investigate which elements in the interaction between a customer and a staff member are critical to the success of those interactions. This type of analysis identifies the key "trigger" factors embedded in ineffective customer interactions that result in customers thinking about switching companies for the service (Roos, 2002). In comparison, success stories can help identify how experts deal with situations such as customer special requests (Beatty et al., 2016). What separates an effective and ineffective response to a customer situation faced by pest control employees who are asked to put down a treatment around a structure that was not covered by the contract? Gathering stories around key events help to identify what are considered effective actions or responses and which responses are less effective. A learning plan can then incorporate the effective responses into the program.

What Is the Current State?

To perform a person analysis, it is necessary to develop measures of criteria that are accurate indicators of current work behavior and performance. Supervisory performance appraisal is typically seen as the system for understanding the current state of people in their jobs in terms of effectiveness. Another source of performance-based information is from personnel file data gathered as part of completing the work. An employee manufacturing parts can have data regularly gathered on parts produced per hour or shift, quality of work performed, and speed of performing machine set-ups. Examples from a sales marketing position might include sales volume, sales growth rate, sales from new accounts, product breadth, and market share.

Technology enhanced assessments are making it easier to capture data on individual performance. For example, onboard computer systems can track truck delivery times and the extent of safe driving behaviors. Similarly, text mining software can aid in analyzing performance in call centers and email communications. In addition to gathering this type of performance data, the current state of the person that is more directly related to possible learning issues can be determined through job knowledge tests, work sample performance, and developmental ratings (Campbell & Wiernik, 2015). These provide windows to understand or uncover knowledge or skill deficiencies impeding performance.

Job knowledge focuses on current state of knowledge (declarative, procedural, and strategic) with the assumption that individuals who have greater levels of technical and procedural knowledge have the capability to perform well on the job. This type of testing requires a close analysis of the job to ensure the test questions are job relevant. In addition, job incumbents can be interviewed and asked to describe in detail the steps they would perform to accomplish various job tasks as another option for measuring job knowledge (Knapp, 2014). The correlation between scores from well-designed job knowledge tests and performance measures has been found to be fairly high (Ployhart, Schneider, & Schmitt, 2006).

A work sample is an assessment in a realistic setting in which the participant works on a set of job tasks under observation and rated for their performance. For technical jobs, a work analysis is performed and critical tasks identified. The steps that must be taken and the sequence of these steps to successfully perform the task are identified. The military have developed various "walk-through performance" testing procedures where trained observers use a checklist of sequenced task steps to capture what the person should do relevant to completing the work sample (Hedge & Teachout, 1986). As one example of a walk-through test, a job incumbent who is asked to complete the task of installing a starter on the jet engine would be observed to see if the task steps such as lubricate the spline, index position of the starter, and install the locking device are performed correctly and in the correct sequence. Other criteria such as how long it takes to complete the task and the quality of the work completed can also be gathered.

For managerial jobs, an assessment center is often used to identify developmental needs. An assessment center is a structured off-the-job approach measuring job-relevant leadership capabilities or competencies such as planning and organizing, problem-solving, decision-making, interpersonal skills, and communication through a standardized set of simulated activities (Thornton &

Byham, 2013). Activities can include an in-basket exercise where the individual must deal with a number of work requests under time constraints as well as leadership discussion groups. Trained observers rate participants during these exercises and provide feedback relevant to the competencies. More information on assessment centers for leadership development is provided in Chapter 10.

Ratings can also be a source of information about developmental needs. Sources of ratings data can be obtained from supervisors, peers, subordinates, customers or other stakeholder group, and even from self-assessments. For example, 360° or multi-rater feedback systems gather ratings on core competencies from as many sources as possible. I was involved in such a project for a large transportation company with a focus on leader competencies such as strategist, motivator, change manager, coach, team builder, and relational partners. Feedback reports comparing results across rating sources (including self-ratings) were provided to identify strengths and areas for future development for each leader. Participants used the data to identify up to three areas to concentrate on improving based on the feedback with action plans to gain required knowledge and skills.

NEEDS ASSESSMENT STRATEGIES

There are a number of approaches organizations can use to conduct a systematic needs assessment. Four examples of approaches are described to give a picture of what can be done and provide food for thought when you have to conduct a needs assessment in your organization. The examples revolve around training needs assessment as that is the usual targeted focus.

Naquin and Holton (2006) describe a large-scale project to identify and prioritize training needs for over 7,200 governmental workers. As shown in Figure 3.5, the needs assessment strategy revolved around two tracks

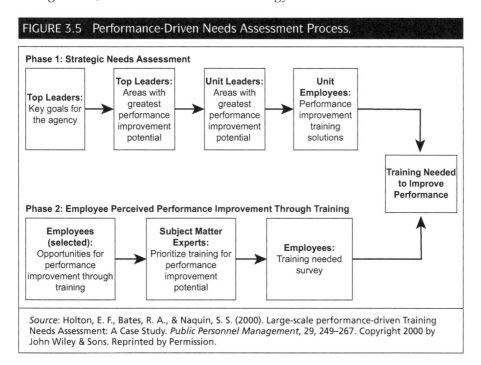

FIGURE 3.5   Performance-Driven Needs Assessment Process.

Phase 1: Strategic Needs Assessment

Top Leaders: Key goals for the agency → Top Leaders: Areas with greatest performance improvement potential → Unit Leaders: Areas with greatest performance improvement potential → Unit Employees: Performance improvement training solutions →

Training Needed to Improve Performance

Phase 2: Employee Perceived Performance Improvement Through Training

Employees (selected): Opportunities for performance improvement through training → Subject Matter Experts: Prioritize training for performance improvement potential → Employees: Training needed survey →

Source: Holton, E. F., Bates, R. A., & Naquin, S. S. (2000). Large-scale performance-driven Training Needs Assessment: A Case Study. *Public Personnel Management*, 29, 249–267. Copyright 2000 by John Wiley & Sons. Reprinted by Permission.

– a strategic training needs assessment process and an employee-felt need for training process. The strategic assessment process had top leaders identify the key goals for their agency and the areas that they saw having the greatest potential for performance improvement in the agency. The next level of management then took that list and refined it by identifying high, medium and low priority performance improvement goals. Interview data of other leaders and selected employees examined the high priority items to make a determination of what improvement strategies would make the most sense to address the performance needs identified. Focus groups were held to make training recommendations for the performance improvement priorities that were most likely addressed through enhancing knowledge and skills. For the second track, employees were divided into job groups and a random sample were sent a survey that asked them to describe the three to five issues that most affected the individual from being as productive on the job as they could be. They were then asked for each problem listed to identify any possible training solutions as well as other possible non-learning solutions. Subject matter experts from each job category who were identified as strong performers reviewed the data generated and categorize the results. A survey was created based on the proposed training solutions generated and employees were asked the extent to which their performance could be enhanced by completing training in that area (1 = to no extent up to 5 = a great deal). Results were analyzed and the highest rated training solutions were identified. The lists from the two tracks were then combined and a final list of training needs generated.

The second example illustrates a competency-based approach to identifying managerial competency gaps. A competency model for managers in the hospitality and tourism sector was systematically developed for career development (Horng et al., 2011). The process led to the identification of 18 competency domains divided into general leadership competencies such as problem-solving and communication and technical skill competencies such as financial management. In terms of expected mastery, 11 experts in the hotel industry were asked to complete a modified Delphi method leading to consensus ratings of the importance of each competency for the job. Then performance ratings of managers based on the 18 competencies were gathered from supervisors, peers, subordinates, and by self-assessment that were combined to produce a performance score for each manager. The importance of each competency was then mapped onto the performance ratings. The data were analyzed to determine competencies viewed as important but not performed well for a majority of managers. Based on this analysis, strategic management and field management (dealing with customer needs and problems) were identified as areas to concentrate training and developmental efforts for improvement (Horng & Lin, 2013).

A third approach is captured by a future-oriented training needs assessment around space exploration teams with the intent to eventually land people on Mars. The National Aeronautics and Space Administration in the United States recognizes that the success of what they call long-duration exploration mission teams is not only about the technical skills of the astronauts and mission control personnel but also about critical teamwork competencies. Therefore, there is a recognition of the need to have a well-developed training system that builds the types of knowledge, skills, and attitudes required for effective teamwork. A training needs assessment identified critical needs and gaps in the current training curriculum and provided recommendations for effectively addressing those curriculum gaps (Smith-Jentsch et al., 2015). The needs assessment included interviews with experts around training needs for teamwork skills as well as the strengths and weaknesses of the current teamwork relevant curriculum. In addition, there was an analysis of archival interview data collected from astronauts with long-duration space flight experiences and a review of astronaut job analyses to identify teamwork competency needs. During the interviews, the participants were asked to report on their experiences with team coordination, communication, cohesion, and stress during their missions. The job analysis information identified a number of behavioral competencies critical to mission success. Ratings data also helped identify which behavioral competences required the most development. The existing training materials were then studied to uncover the portions that addressed teamwork issues, the training methods employed, and any evaluations of improvement of teamwork skills as a function of these training experiences. The training content was examined to determine the extent to which the content was meeting the identified needs of teamwork development and to investigate the extent to which the training content was consistent with established best practices for team training and team building. This comprehensive needs analysis revealed 17 critical teamwork training gaps with 23 recommendations for addressing those gaps. Table 3.9 provides some example gaps and recommendations identified.

The final example of a needs assessment approach involves a manufacturing facility that I have worked with for a number of years. The company has reinvented itself to remain competitive including an extensive strategic planning effort to define their vision and values. The identification process led top leaders to generate objectives and strategies of how to meet the objectives including the move to a team-based work system where employees become owners of the manufacturing process leading to the finished product, investment in new technology, and upgrading skills. Employee groups developed specific tactics to meet the goals of the various strategies. A representative group was formed to identify the upgrades in knowledge and skills required for the strategic direction to teams to be successful. The knowledge and skills were turned into clusters of needed knowledge and skills such as print reading, geometric tolerance, gage usage, basic business and budgeting practices, teamwork skills, and problem-solving. Experts in each of the manufacturing functions (e.g., hobbing, drilling, deburring, machine set-up, CNC programming) were identified and with the help of consultants developed a detailed list of tasks and sequenced steps within each task for each function. The experts were then charged with assessing each employee on their skill level relevant to that function and working with the training coordinator to identify three levels of prioritized training needs per person – high, moderate, and low priority on each job function. This process led to a comprehensive view by person of training needs to meet the strategic direction of the company. In addition, as the strategy included the development of a new position of cell leader, leadership competencies were also identified as needing to be developed such as building effective teams, balancing daily operational needs, coaching and developing others, maintaining high ethical standards, taking a systems perspective to problems, and being an advocate for change and continuous improvement. A 360° feedback process was used to identify developmental needs of each cell leader tied to specific courses of action for development.

TABLE 3.9   Training Needs Analysis for Enhancing Teamwork for Astronaut Crews and Flight Controllers

Category	Training Needs Gaps	Recommendations	Next Steps
Training Content	Too few opportunities to develop teamwork skills in monitoring and responding appropriately to others Too few opportunities to develop competencies for working in multi-team systems	More teamwork training in groups living over extended time periods in isolated and confided spaces More multi-team collaboration training into teamwork curricula	Design training to include group living with long periods of monotonous cohabitation Script training for greater astronaut crew autonomy over time with controllers
Training Consistency	Teamwork concepts and definitions vary across specific training programs for astronauts and flight controllers Availability and content of specific astronaut and flight controller training has varied curriculum so that members do not receive equivalent teamwork training	Ensure that all members are provided with opportunities for the same or maximally equivalent teamwork training Select and employ a single teamwork competency model across all training Emphasize how current teamwork focus is related to previous and future teamwork related training activities	Training cycles are lengthy so creating single teamwork model needs to begin without delay New task-related curriculum must include directing developers to better link teamwork activities across trainings to ensure consistency across teamwork activities
Training Method	Online training methods are underutilized	Incorporate online training to prepare members for face to face training and to provide just in time/booster sessions	Create an online training architecture to deliver online training of various types
Amount of Training	Too little time for practice and feedback on teamwork behaviors and too little mentoring between sessions. Too few performance aides and training guides to refer to and use for subsequent training or during mission activities	Extend current teamwork training to allow additional time for practice and feedback. Have coaches provide learning opportunities for practice. Incorporate more job aids and training guides into technical training around teamwork	Develop low fidelity team task to provide opportunities for practice. Create online mentoring system Job aids and guides reference teamwork competency model

Source: Adapted from Smith-Jentsch, K. A., Sierra, M. J., Weaver, S. J., Bedwell, W. L., Dietz, A. S., Carter-Berenson, D., Oglesby, J., Fiore, S. M., & Salas, E. (2015). *Training "The Right Stuff": An assessment of team training needs for long-duration spaceflight crews.* Report International food policy research Institute, Washington DC. http://hdl.handle.net/00568/2089.

CONCLUSIONS

This chapter described the various components of needs assessment, including organizational, work, and person analysis. The key to a successful organizational analysis is taking a systematic approach to planning. It is necessary to consider the variety of methods that can provide useful information and to determine which questions need to be asked. For the needs assessment to be successful, this planning process should be strategic and comprehensive to target the efforts around work and person analysis. The work and person analysis provide critical input for the design of the learning activity or can point to other interventions that are needed to meet the need. The process of going from the work and person analyses to systematic identification of the behaviors to be learned remains one of the more difficult phases in the design of learning interventions. The checklist below presents ten best practice guidelines based on the research reviewed in this chapter. Regardless of what type of learning opportunity – training, guided instruction, developmental job experience, or self-directed – learning needs to take into account learning objectives and a learning plan. These issues are discussed in the next chapter.

Chapter 3: Best Practice Guidelines

- Conduct a systematic learning needs assessment by completing an organizational, work, and person analysis.
- For an organization-wide analysis, conduct a "learning audit" for the company including current organizational learning needs as well as an analysis of future needs.
- Be proactive in identifying learning needs when developing the strategic goals of the organization.
- Identify what tasks, knowledge, skills, and capabilities are required for individual jobs and for working in teams.
- Investigate the organizational factors that can inhibit learning such as resource constraints and a climate that does not support learning.
- Collect quantitative data such as ratings of importance for task clusters, tasks, and knowledge and skills.
- Use cognitive task analysis with job experts to understand the mental aspects (goals, strategies, decision processes) underlying performance to identify areas for accelerating the development of newcomers and job incumbents.
- Gather stories through critical incidents to identify what differentiates the job behaviors of effective from less effective job incumbents.
- Identify specific gaps between what the current level of performance is for employees against the desired level and determine if learning and development is the best solution for enhancing the contribution of the employee to individual, team and organizational effectiveness.
- Determine which type of learning approach is best for each identified learning need.

References

Air Force Handbook (2002). *Information for designers of instructional systems: Guide to needs assessment.* AFH 36-2235, Vol. 6, pp. 1–124.

Bartram, D. (2005). The Great Eight competencies: A criterion-centric approach to validation. *Journal of Applied Psychology*, 90, 1185–1203. doi.org/10.1037/0021-9010.90.6.1185

Beatty, S. E., Ogilvie, J., Northington, W. M., Harrison, M. P., Holloway, B. B., & Wang, S. (2016). Frontline service employee compliance with customer special requests. *Journal of Service Research*, 19(2), 158–173. doi.org/10.1177/1094670515624978

Brannick, M. T., Cadie, A., & Levine, E. L. (2012). Job analysis for knowledge, skills, abilities, and other characteristics, predictor measures, and performance outcomes. In N. Schmitt (Ed.), *The Oxford handbook of personnel assessment and selection.* New York: Oxford University Press.

Butterfield, L. D., Borgen, W. A., Amundson, N. E., & Maglio, A. S. T. (2005). Fifty years of the critical incident technique: 1954–2004 and beyond. *Qualitative Research*, 5(4), 475–497. doi.org/10.1177/1468794105056924

Campbell, J. P., & Wiernik, B. M. (2015). The modeling and assessment of work performance. *Annual Review of Organizational Psychology and Organizational Behavior*, 2(1), 47–74. doi.org/10.1146/annurev-orgpsych-032414-111427

Campion, M. A., Fink, A. A., Ruggeberg, B. J., Carr, L., Phillips, G. M., & Odman, R. B. (2011). Doing competencies well: Best practices in competency modeling. *Personnel Psychology*, 64, 225–262. doi.org/10.1111/j.1744-6570.2010.01207.x

Clardy, A. (2014). Legal aspects of HRD. In N. Chalofsky, T. Rocco, & M. Morris (Eds.), *Handbook of human resource development* (pp. 474–491). Hoboken, NJ: Wiley.

Crandall, B., Klein, G., & Hoffman, R. R. (2006). Incident based CTA: Helping practitioners tell stories. In B. Granddall, G. Klein, G. A. Klein, & R. R. Hoffman (Eds.), *Working minds: A practitioner's guide to cognitive task analysis* (pp. 69–90). Cambridge, MA: MIT Press.

Cutcher-Gershenfeld, J., & Ford, K. (2005). *Valuable disconnects in organizational learning systems: Integrating bold visions and harsh realities.* New York: Oxford University Press.

Czaja, S. J., Sharit, J., Charness, N., & Schmidt, A. C. (2015). The implications of changes in job demands for the continued and future employment of older workers. In L. M. Finklestein et al. (Eds.), *Facing the challenges of a multiage workforce: A use inspired approach* (pp. 159–179). New York: Routledge.

Dargue, B., & Biddle, E. (2016). Mining expertise: Learning new tricks form an old dog. In R. A. Sottilare, A. C. Graesser, X. Hu, A. Olney, B. Nye, & A. M. M. Sinatra (Eds.), *Design recommendations for intelligent tutoring systems* Volume 4: *Introduction to domain modeling and GIFT.* Orlando, FL: U.S. Army Research Laboratory.

Flanagan, J. C. (1954). The critical incident technique. *Psychological Bulletin*, 51(4), 327. doi.org/10.1037hoo61470

Ford, J. K., Quiñones, M. A., Sego, D. J., & Sorra, J. S. (1992). Factors affecting the opportunity to perform trained tasks on the job. *Personnel Psychology*, 45(3), 511–527. doi.org/10.1111/j.1744-6570.1992.tb00858.x

Frieden, R. (2002). Adjusting the horizontal and vertical in telecommunications regulation: A comparison of the traditional and a new layered approach. *The Federal Communications Law Journal*, 55, 207.

Gasparini, J. (2014). Hello, congress: The phone's for you: Facilitating the IP transition while moving toward a layers-based regulatory model. *The Federal Communications Law Journal*, 67, 117.

Goldstein, I. L., & Ford, J. K. (2002). *Training in organizations: Needs assessment, development, and evaluation* (4th edition), Belmont, CA: Wadsworth.

Hedge, J. W., & Teachout, M. S. (1986). *Job performance measurement: A systematic program of research and development (No. AFHRL-TP-86-37).* Brooks AFB, TX: Air Force Human Resources Laboratory.

Holton, E. F., Bates, R. A., & Naquin, S. S. (2000). Large-scale performance-driven training needs assessment: A case study. *Public Personnel Management*, 29, 249–267. doi.org/10.1177/009102600002900207

Horng, J. S., & Lin, L. (2013). Training needs assessment in a hotel using 360 degree feedback to develop competency-based training programs. *Journal of Hospitality and Tourism Management*, 20, 61–67. doi.org/10.1016/j.jhtm.2013.06.003

Horng, J. S., Hsuan, H., Chih-Hsing, L., Lin, L., & Chang-Yen, T. (2011). Competency analysis of top managers in the Taiwanese hotel industry. *International Journal of Hospitality Management*, 30(4), 1044–1054. doi.org/10.1016/j.ijhm.2011.03.012

Klein, G., & Borders, J. (2016). The ShadowBox approach to cognitive skills training: An empirical evaluation. *Journal of Cognitive Engineering and Decision Making*, 10(3), 268–280.

Klein, G., Borders, J., Newsome, E., Militello, L., & Klein, H. A. (2018). Cognitive skills training: Lessons learned. *Cognition, Technology & Work*, 20(4), 681–687. doi.org/10.1007/s10111-018-0528-5

Knapp, D. J. (2014). The US joint-service job performance measurement project. In W. Bennett, C. Lance, & D. J. Woehr (Eds.), *Performance measurement* (pp. 131–158). New York: Psychology Press.

Kozlowski, S. W., & Ilgen, D. R. (2006). Enhancing the effectiveness of work groups and teams. *Psychological Science in the Public Interest*, 7(3), 77–124. doi.org/10.1111/j.1529-1006.2006.00030.x

Murphy, K. R. (2018). The legal context of the management of human resources. *Annual Review of Organizational Psychology and Organizational Behavior*, 5, 157–182. doi.org/10.1146/annurev-orgpsych-032117-104435

Naquin, S. S., & Holton III, E. F. (2006). Leadership and managerial competency models: A simplified process and resulting model. *Advances in Developing Human Resources*, 8(2), 144–165. doi.org/10.1177/1523422305286152

Neubert, J. C., Mainert, J., Kretzschmar, A., & Greiff, S. (2015). The assessment of 21st century skills in industrial and organizational psychology: Complex and collaborative problem solving. *Industrial and Organizational Psychology*, 8(2), 238–268. doi.org/10.1017/iop.2015.14

Ployhart, R. E., Schneider, B., & Schmitt, N. (2006). *Staffing organizations: Contemporary practice and research*. Mahwah, NJ: Lawrence Erlbaum.

Reed, J., & Vakola, M. (2006). What role can a training needs analysis play in organisational change? *Journal of Organizational Change Management*, 19(3), 393–407. doi.org/10.1108/09534810610668382

Roos, I. (2002). Methods of investigating critical incidents: A comparative review. *Journal of Service Research*, 4(3), 193–204. doi.org/10.1177/1094670502004003003

Rouiller, J. Z., & Goldstein, I. L. (1993). The relationship between organizational transfer climate and positive transfer of training. *Human Resource Development Quarterly*, 4(4), 377–390. doi.org/10.1002/hrdq.3920040408

Salas, E., Cooke, N. J., & Rosen, M. A. (2008). On teams, teamwork, and team performance: Discoveries and developments. *Human Factors*, 50(3), 540–547. doi.org/10.1518/001872008X288457

Sanchez, J. I., & Levine, E. L. (2009). What is (or should be) the difference between competency modeling and traditional job analysis? *Human Resource Management Review*, 19(2), 53–63. doi.org/10.1016/j.hrmr.2008.10.002

Schaafstal, A., Schraagen, J. M., & van Berl, M. (2000). Cognitive task analysis and innovation of training: The case of structured troubleshooting. *Human Factors*, 42(1), 75–86. doi.org/10.1518/001872000779656570

Smith-Jentsch, K. A., Sierra, M. J., Weaver, S. J., Bedwell, W. L., Dietz, A. S., Carter-Berenson, D., Oglesby, J., Fiore, S. M., & Salas, E. (2015). *Training "The Right Stuff": An assessment of team training needs for long-duration spaceflight crews*. Report International food policy research Institute, Washington DC. http://hdl.handle.net/00568/2089.

Stone, T. H., Webster, B. D., & Schoonover, S. (2013). What do we know about competency modeling? *International Journal of Selection and Assessment*, 21(3), 334–338. doi.org/10.1111/ijsa.12043

Testa, M. R., & Sipe, L. (2012). Service-leadership competencies for hospitality and tourism management. *International Journal of Hospitality Management*, 31, 648–658. doi.org/10.1016/j.ijhm.2011.08.009

Thayer, P., & Teachout, M. (1995). *A climate for transfer model*. Brooks AFB, TX: Human Resources Directorate, Technical Training Research Division.

Thornton III, G. C., & Byham, W. C. (2013). *Assessment centers and managerial performance*. New York: Elsevier.

Tofel-Grehl, C., & Feldon, D. F. (2013). Cognitive task analysis based training: A meta-analysis of studies. *Journal of Cognitive Engineering and Decision Making*, 7, 293–304. doi.org/10.1177/1555343412474821

Voskuijl, O. F. (2017). Job analysis: Current and future perspectives. In A. Evers, N. Anderson, & O. Voskuijl (Eds.), *The Blackwell handbook of personnel selection* (pp. 25–46). Hoboken, NJ: Wiley

Designing a Learning Plan

Questions

✓ What are the components of a well-written learning objective?
✓ How does one ensure consistency within a plan of instruction?
✓ What are key takeaways from motivational frameworks for understanding the motivation to learn?

Identifying learning needs is the foundation for designing a learning plan. Once identified, the next step is to prioritize which learning needs takes precedence over other needs given resource and time constraints. Once prioritized, decisions can be made as to which type of learning approach or combination of approaches (training, guided learning, job experiences, self-directed learning) best address the need. Quality engineers may need skill updating through formal training programs. New supervisors may need to be given more guided learning opportunities. High potential leaders may need to be given more challenging work assignments along with specific coaching help. Individuals affected by new technology may need to be encouraged to engage in self-directed learning by finding certification programs to enhance their range of skills.

Each learning option must be turned into an effective learning plan. A learning plan includes (1) the development of learning objectives of what is to be gained in terms of knowledge, skills, and/or attitudes as a function of the learning intervention; (2) the creation of a plan of instruction that details how and in what sequence the learning content will be delivered, and (3) the incorporation of learner characteristics and pre-learning interventions to maximize the chances that learning will occur. While the issues above are relevant to any learning intervention, the vast majority of recommendations from research and practice have been within the context of formal training programs. Our best evidence to base best practices resides in this research tradition. Therefore, while this chapter is oriented around instructional design for training, the principles are also relevant for the development of a systematic plan for any type of learning approach.

LEARNING OBJECTIVES

Learning is a complex and multidimensional construct (Kraiger, Ford, & Salas, 1993). It consists of cognitive changes in a trainee's knowledge base and the way learners organize and integrate the new content into their existing frameworks. Learning involves skill changes and how well the learner can enact new behaviors and ways of performing. Learning is evidenced through changes in the attitudes and motivation of the learner to engage in additional learning and to continuously improve performance. How to see or measure these changes is a critical issue when setting up a learning plan. The taxonomies presented in Chapter 2 point to indicators so we can "see" the extent to which learning has occurred as a function of the implementation of the learning plan.

Learning Outcomes

A well-known framework organizes learning outcomes into five categories (Gagné et al., 2005). The set of categories of learning outcomes that organizes human performance are as follows:

1. Intellectual skills. These skills include concepts, rules, and procedures. Sometimes this is referred to as procedural knowledge. The rules for mathematical computations are a good example of intellectual skills.
2. Cognitive strategies. This refers to the idea that learners bring to a new task not only intellectual skills and verbal information but also an understanding of how and when to use this information. In a sense, the cognitive strategies form a type of strategic knowledge that enables the learner to know when and how to choose intellectual skills and verbal information.
3. Verbal information. This category is also sometimes called declarative information, and it refers to the ability of the individual to declare or state something. An example could be to state the various kinds of statistical programs and their uses.
4. Attitudes. Trainee preferences for particular activities often reflect differences in attitudes. People learn to have these preferences. They note that the number of different commercial messages by which we are bombarded is evidence of the common belief that attitudes are learned.
5. Motor skills. This skill refers to one of the more obvious examples of human performance. Examples of motor skills include writing, swimming, using tools, and the like.

The five categories make it clear that there are different kinds of performance capabilities that one might be interested in developing in a person.

An effective plan for learning starts with the identification of indicators of what success looks like – as has been well stated by the novelist James Clavell, "All stories have a beginning, a middle, and an ending, and if they're any good, the ending is the beginning" (A–Z Quotes, 2019). Similarly, the management consultant Stephen Covey notes that "we may be very busy, we may be very efficient, but we will also be truly effective only when we begin with the End in Mind" (Covey, 2013, p. 46). Therefore, before jumping into the design of the learning intervention, the initial question is what the learner should know more of, have more skills in, or have stronger attitudes about as a function of any learning approach.

An Integrated Approach to Design

An effective plan requires a systematic approach for thinking about and designing instruction. The model in Figure 4.1 shows an integrated approach to instructional design with the emphasis on the real-world performance and the need for all components in the design process to be aligned. It is titled the "secret" of instructional design as many programs have been developed based on expediency and not based on a systematic approach as shown in the model (Yelon, 2012).

An examination of the model highlights starting with the problem that is linked to "real world performance" – based on the learning needs identified in the assessment process. Real world performance refers to the gaps that need to be filled or what the organization wants to see in terms of performance on the job that helps the organization move towards its strategic goals. This gap informs the learning designer on what learning objective needs to be set to address the problem. The objectives then tie directly to the evaluation to determine if learning has occurred to the level expected as indicated by the objectives. The evaluation of whether the objectives have been met can be based on tests or observations. Once the objectives and evaluation tools are set, then the designers can get to work on making sure the content of the learning event or activity is organized and sequenced in a way to increase the probability that learners will be able to achieve the objectives. Then the activities of instructions (e.g., explanation, demonstration, and practice) that are best for conveying the content to order to facilitate learning must be determined so that they can achieve the chosen objectives.

FIGURE 4.1   The Secret of Instructional Design.

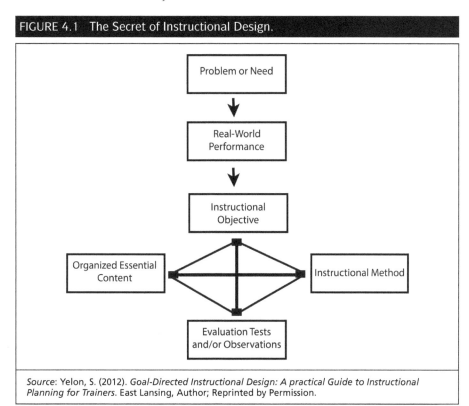

Source: Yelon, S. (2012). *Goal-Directed Instructional Design: A practical Guide to Instructional Planning for Trainers*. East Lansing, Author; Reprinted by Permission.

The components in the model revolve around the learning objectives. Learning objectives constitute the formal description of what a learner should know and/or what they should be able to do that they could not do before the learning intervention. Identifying a comprehensive set of objectives provides a roadmap for planning the learning intervention that targets operationalizing in very specific terms what is to be learned. Well-written objectives provide the basis for the development of the plan of instruction including the framework for developing content, determining the appropriate methods to use and the basis for assessing achievement by the learner.

Creating Learning Objectives

A well-written learning objective includes three characteristics (Mager, 1997). First, an objective includes the capability or desired behavior that demonstrates or shows evidence of learning. The stating of a desired behavior begins with a verb that describes an observable action (e.g., take the temperature of a patient or complete a routine machine set-up). Table 4.1 presents words that can be used to convey capabilities or desired behaviors relevant to each of the five learning outcomes described above. For example, one could be asked to "*identify* the facts in a business case". As one can see, each verb and the action are observable and therefore measurable.

The second step is to specify the conditions under which the behavior is to be performed or demonstrated once the learning phase is completed and the testing or assessment phase begins. Conditions specify (1) what the learner will be provided when asked to perform a learned task, (2) restrictions or limitations imposed on the learner, (3) tools and equipment used, (4) references or other job aids that can be used, and (5) physical and environmental conditions surrounding the task. An example is "with a digital thermometer, take the temperature of a patient." In this case, the condition of performing the task of

TABLE 4.1   Verbs to Describe Behaviors in an Objective

Capability	Verb	Example
Intellectual skill	discriminates	discriminate by matching problems with solution
	identifies	identify the facts in a business case
	classifies	classify problems into routine and nonroutine
Cognitive strategy	adopts	adopt an assertive strategy to deal with an employee
	demonstrates	demonstrate by troubleshooting a problem
Verbal information	states	state orally the questions one cannot ask in an interview
Motor skill	executes	execute by backing up the fork lift
Attitude	chooses	choose to challenge an offensive comment

Source: Adapted from Gagné, R. M., Briggs, L. J., & Wager, W. W. (2005) *Principles of instructional design*, 5th edition. Belmont, CA: Thompson/Wadsworth.

taking the temperature is the learner is given a digital thermometer. Or, in the case of a military task, the learner might be "given an aerial map of the bombing target with resistance pockets identified" (condition) in order to show they can accurately deliver to the target (action) in a simulation game.

The third step is to state the criterion or standard of acceptable performance on the learned task. The criterion specifies how well the learner must be able to perform a learned task. The criterion can consist of minimum standards, time to perform, and the quality and/or quantity of work or service produced. With the military task above, the object might state that the learner must accurately deliver to within 10 feet of the target – within 10 feet being the criterion of interest in the learner achieving by the end of training on a simulator. The criteria or standard might focus on the amount produced within a period of time, quality, accuracy, and the need for assistance.

Table 4.2 provides a summary of the three components making up a learning objective as well as an example of a learning objective with all three components. As can be seen, there are a number of conditions and criteria that can be applied to a learner performing a task so it can be determined if the learner has successfully achieved the objective. In the example in the table, the condition is the standard take-off situation that varies in terms of complexity. The criterion for the objective has two elements of accuracy and level of assistance – placing the airplanes in the correct position and showing one can carry out the task without any assistance from others. For practice, look at the following statement and identify what is the action, condition, and standard: "given access to technical reference material and given one electrical malfunction, be able to troubleshoot the malfunction within 15 minutes." In this case the action or behavior is to troubleshoot a malfunction and the two conditions are the learner has access to reference material when performing the task and is given one electrical malfunction to solve. The criterion is to show one can solve the malfunction correctly within the specified time requirement.

TABLE 4.2   Learning Objective Characteristics and Example

Condition	Behavior	Criterion
Job aids	Observable	Completeness
Equipment	Measurable	Amount
Technical references	Verifiable	Accuracy
Environmental conditions	Actionable	Quality
Problem situations		Time requirements assistance
Example of Aircraft Carrier Flight Launch Assistant:		
Given a standard take-off situations that vary in complexity	Establish contact and direct aircraft to take-off point	Placing three aircraft into the correct position without any assistance

Sources: Adapted from Mager, R. F. (1997). *Preparing instructional objectives* (3rd edition). Center for Effective Performance, Inc. Atlanta, GA; McKimm, J., & Swanwick, T. (2009). Setting learning objectives. *British Journal of Hospital Medicine*, 70(7), 406–409.

Learning objectives are easier to develop for what are called closed skills as opposed to open skills to be trained (Yelon & Ford, 1999). Closed skills are those where workers must respond in one way to complete a task – done in a precise fashion. An auto mechanic changing a turn light bulb on a car has a prescribed process and precise time to complete this task. On the other end of the scale are highly variable open skills – where there is not one single correct or best way to act but rather freedom to perform. With open skills, the objective is generally to learn principles or a set of guidelines for behavior and not concrete, discrete steps. A supervisor attending a training program on how to motivate employees cannot be given a "cookbook" of steps to take. A manager could, however, be shown theories of motivation and be taught how to use different motivational principles to influence employees.

While it is tempting to not specify clear learning objectives for open skills, it can (and should) be done. For example, say there is training for supervisors on knowledge and skills regarding how to resolve conflict situations with employees. At the end of the program, the expectation could be that the knowledge gained should lead to participants being able to state what is meant by work conflict and what distinguishes between conflict and non-conflict situations. In addition, another knowledge objective might state that given ten conflict situations, the supervisors should be able to specify how to resolve each conflict situation presented that meets the criteria of principles around how to create win-win solutions (Jacobs, 2019). Table 4.3 provides a nice example of developing a skill-based objective around this open skill relevant to resolving conflict situations with employees. With this type of precision as to what is expected of the learner from a knowledge and skill perspective by the end of a supervisory training program, the designers can now concentrate on planning out what is the appropriate content, methods, and practice scenarios to use (and time to train) for learners to meet the objective. Breaking down the objective could lead the designer to recognize the need for making sure there is enough time for learners to gain knowledge about what is meant by conflict situations, how to distinguish between conflict and non-conflict situations, and knowing what the components of a

---

TABLE 4.3   Learning Objective for an Open Skill

Resolving supervisory-employee conflict situations
Objective: Given a simulated supervisor–employee conflict situation around the employee's quality of work, be able to demonstrate all the steps in the conflict resolution process to resolve the conflict situation in a manner consistent with company policies
Foundations to Meeting the Skill Objective: 1. Stated the purpose of the meeting concisely at the beginning. 2. Describe specifically what had been seen and why it is a concern. 3. Asked for and listened openly to the employee's explanation for recent behavior. 4. Explained the rationale for why the behavior cannot continue. 5. Asked for ideas from employee on how to address the problem. 6. Discussed options and action steps. 7. Mutually agreed on specific goals and steps to be taken to reach the goals. 8. Offered support in meeting the goals. 9. Planned a specific follow-up date.

conflict resolution process are. From a skill perspective, one would want the learner to practice various conflict situations to gain experience in adapting the resolution process components to fit the types and severity of conflict situations.

Sequencing Objectives

Learning opportunities such as workshops often have multiple objectives. Once they have been identified, the objectives must be sequenced in some way to enhance learning (Gagné et al., 2005). The key to sequencing is to ensure that the prerequisite knowledge and skills have been acquired prior to the introduction of advanced content or skills. Consequently, the instructional sequence chosen may or may not mirror the order in which knowledge and skills are performed on the job. Sequencing for instruction can be done on the basis of (1) logical order – present the least difficult material first and build to the most difficult; (2) problem-centered order – focus on a general problem and develop various ways to solve the problem prior to moving to another problem area; (3) job performance order – order based on the sequence in which a job or task is actually performed; or (4) psychological order – moving from abstract concepts to more concrete examples and hands-on experience.

An example of the sequencing of objectives for on-the-job training of incoming machinists is provided in Table 4.4. The work analysis identified tasks, task clusters, and knowledge and skills including data on difficulty to learn as well as likely errors and the consequence of those errors. As can be seen in the table, the five task clusters of learning need identified through this process included the categories of running production, setting up the machine, completing quality checks with appropriate tools, completing forms and documentation requirements, and interfacing with the machine computer system. The objectives are sequenced around building competence in each of these five task category areas from a novice or introductory level to a competent level where the individual can complete all tasks independently. The objectives are sequenced to build the knowledge and skills necessary to become an independent operator within 12 weeks rather than the six to nine months given the current on-the-job training approach. Material created provided the structure for learning. The expert machinist attended train-the-trainer sessions before conducting the new on-the-job training system. Learners were evaluated and had to pass the assessment criteria (e.g., the novice level objectives) prior to moving on to the next set of objectives (the apprenticeship level objectives).

PLAN OF INSTRUCTION

Effective instruction requires an organized approach from needs assessment to the development of objectives to the creation of a plan of instruction (POI) that includes sequenced content and a detailed plan for conveying the content. For each objective, learning designers can identify the specific facts, concepts, principles, and skills needed to build the knowledge, skills, and capabilities needed in an area. The plan includes the instructional activities and the time needed to accomplish each objective. As noted by Gagné (1996) "the series of events we call instruction need to be designed to activate, support,

TABLE 4.4   Learning Objectives for Machine Operators by Task Cluster

Task Cluster	Novice (2 weeks)	Apprentice (4 weeks)	Partially Proficient (8 weeks)	Independent (12 weeks)
Running Production	Describe the step-by-step procedures	Run production with direct assistance to clear faults	Run production on own and clear common faults	Meet production standards and clear non routine faults
Machine Setup	Name all the parts/accessories and tools for setup	Do the simple parts of the setup tasks under direct supervision	Do all the setup steps for typical setups	Do all parts of setup task for non-routine situations
Quality Checks	State where all quality control tools are located and what each is used for	Properly use gauges, scales, micrometer and square to check for quality	Perform all quality checks accurately with some assistance for difficult parts	Perform all quality checks without any assistance and without error for all types of parts
Forms and Documentation	State what the purpose is of key forms that need to be completed	State what needs to be completed for each part of the work order form for various types of new orders	Complete all paperwork associated with completing a work order	Train new employees on work order and paperwork associated with the job
Computer Interface	Describe basic information displayed on computer screen	Use basic computer controls to run machines	Input part data into computer and set controls	Make adjustments to computer instructions when needed on unique jobs

Source: Ford, J. K., & Olenick, J. (2016). *Training on the B&O Line: Trainer Notes.* Technical Report, Ford & Associates, Williamston, MI.

and maintain a number of internal events that are the processes of learning" (p. 27). He reminds us that any type of instruction must be well designed with focus on how best to support learning. This support can be related to "helping events" that facilitate learning or the elaborate aspects of practice or cues that help retrieval or feedback that confirms learning has taken place.

Components of a Plan

A POI provides a detailed roadmap for designing a learning opportunity to meet learning objectives. Two examples are presented to highlight components that could be incorporated into a POI.

Table 4.5 details a POI for training aerospace ground equipment specialists in the air force that includes 15 blocks of instruction over the course of 87 days. Each block of instruction has a number of learning objectives that are broken down into individual lesson plans within each module. Each lesson plan has material on how to introduce the lesson, how to present the core of the lesson and how to conclude the lesson. The table presents a component within one of the modules of troubleshooting and correcting malfunctions that forms the basis for creating a detailed lesson plan. The objectives, instructional approaches and the time for training for this skill are presented. Instructional activities are divided into lecture/discussion, performance and feedback, and self-study. Thus, some activities are delivered by an instructor in a classroom setting and part of the training is delivered in a simulated work setting.

Similarly, for the machinist on-the-job training described above, after the objectives had been sequenced, then the content and activities for the on-the-job training were articulated in a written plan of instruction. A setup objective for novices (from Table 4.4) is to be able to state the components of the machine (e.g., air compressor, bundle loader, feeder clamps) and simple facts about each component in terms of what it does. Based on this objective, the content of the training required the learner to identify all the components and to provide a written description of the purpose of each component. The trainers were asked to use this content and in a room away from the shop floor to explain what each component does and its location on the machine with the pictures taken to provide a visual. Then the trainer took the newcomer out to the machine and walked along (from left to right) pointing out the components and again explaining what each component did. For the next step, the learner completed a simple setup of the machine talking about the components being worked in in each step. After watching production, the learner was asked to walk around the machine from beginning to end and point to, name, and describe all aspects of the components. The trainer used a checklist to mark which components were named and described correctly. After more discussion and practice, the learner was officially assessed to determine if the objective of successfully naming and describing all components had been met. For this one objective, the learning activities included time for explanation, visuals, demonstration, practice, and feedback. A similar process was created for the other objectives. For skill-based objectives such as use of measurement tools, the final learning assessment requires the learner to show they can perform the task to the level of success expected. For example, the learner would need to run required quality control checks to determine if the same measurements were taken as from a job expert.

TABLE 4.5 Plan of Instruction Example for Air Force Aerospace Ground Equipment Specialists

---

Hydraulic Test Stands

Troubleshooting and Correcting Malfunctions
a. Using a hydraulic test stand, technical order, workbook, electrical diagrams, test equipment and AFTO Form 349, troubleshoot malfunction.
b. Using a hydraulic test stand, technical order, electrical diagrams, and test equipment, correct one malfunction.

Training Equipment
Hydraulic Test Stand (3)
Multimeter (1)
Ear Protectors (1)

Training Methods
Lecture/discussion (0.5 hours)
Performance and Feedback (9.5 hours)
Self-Study (4 hours)

Instructional Guidance
The instructor will issue applicable programmed text, workbooks, multimeters, and technical orders, and conduct a briefing on safety hazards and precautions. Ensure students wear proper ear protection during operational checks to verify malfunctions. The first problem will be a demonstration problem that the students will follow in the workbook. After completion of the demonstration problem, students will practice troubleshooting additional problems, stating the proper corrective action to be taken to the instructor. The instructor will give individual assistance as required. Upon completion of practice troubleshooting, each student will be administered a progress check. Each student will troubleshoot three problems and complete an AFTO Form 349 in the workbook for each problem to document work performed. For safety, only one unit will be operated to identify problems. After identifying a problem, the students will isolate the problem on another non-operating unit. After satisfactory completion of progress change, the instructor will annotate the criterion checklist. After troubleshooting, the students will correct one malfunction on the test stand as designated by the instructor. Two instructors are required for ten hours of student demonstration/performance on the Hydraulic Test Stand when class size exceeds six students.

Source: From the Apprentice Aerospace Ground Equipment Mechanic, Plan of Instruction, Chanute Technical Training Center (POI C3A BR42335 000), 1987.

A Problem-Centered Approach

The examples above highlight the importance of creating a POI that aligns with the learning objectives, content, learning activities, and assessments around the knowledge and skills required to be learned. A useful framework from Merrill (2012) identifies five phases that should be incorporated into a POI. First, the foundation of effective instruction (as noted above in Figure 4.1) is the extent to which the POI is problem centered and targets authentic real-world problems. With a problem-centered approach, tasks to be learned are identified and broken down into steps and the knowledge and skills needed to be mastered for each step are identified. For each step, the trainee can either be expected to remember information or use information to accomplish the task. Second, the POI should specify how to activate relevant previous knowledge from the learners to help them be ready to learn the facts, concepts, procedures, rules, and principles required. With activation, the questions revolve around how the POI links the new instruction to prior knowledge and relevant experience as well as shows the relevance of acquiring the new knowledge and skills. The third phase is demonstration. Demonstration is showing the steps that need to be learned rather than just providing information. From this perspective, learning is enhanced when learners can observe the instructor or expert carry out a task and explain what each step is when performing. While demonstration is typically thought of as relevant for skill building (the how to do procedures), it is also relevant for enhancing knowledge. For knowledge of rules and principles, one could demonstrate what examples fit the rule and those that do not fit the rule. The fourth phase is application. The POI can be examined for the opportunity to practice the new acquired knowledge and skills that are consistent with the learning objectives. Practice must be followed by constructive feedback and guidance during the learning phase that can be reduced over time as the learner gains more skills. Finally, the POI can be examined for the extent to which there is time for the learner to integrate the new knowledge and skills before moving on to other training objectives. The learner can be guided to summarize what they have learned and how the new knowledge and skills relate to prior knowledge. There can also be time devoted to reflection on the learning and how the learner intends to implement or adapt the knowledge and skills back on the job (more about setting goals in the next chapter).

Merrill notes that many POIs he has examined have limited time devoted to activation, demonstration, practice, and integration strategies in the instructional design due to the pressure to cover content. Specifically, many POIs have inadequate time for practice to build the level of knowledge and skills required to meet learning objectives and enhance the probability that the knowledge and skills are implemented immediately on the job. Skills difficult to learn and where the expectation is for skill levels to be much higher than the current level require much effort devoted to demonstration, practice, and feedback.

Based on this framework, Table 4.6 presents a best practice checklist that should be used to evaluate and then improve the quality of a learning plan. For example, the checklist notes that to activate relevant prior knowledge the POI should have learners describe relevant past experience that are foundational for new knowledge, provide relevant experience from experts, and help learners form appropriate structures for organizing the new knowledge.

THE LEARNER

There needs to be an understanding of the learner when planning out a learning opportunity. Learners do not just fall out of the sky but have long and varied experiences within an organization that creates differences in goals, expectations, needs, and attitudes towards a learning opportunity (Campbell, 1989). Consequently, learners differ in terms of their motivation to learn relevant to any learning intervention. This section examines the concept of motivation to learn and presents theories of motivation that have direct implications for developing strategies for enhancing learner motivation. This section ends with a description of interventions for enhancing learner readiness and preparedness to learn prior to the beginning of the learning event or opportunity.

TABLE 4.6 Lesson Plan Checklist

1. Targets real world problems?
   a) Shown the task they will be able to do or the problem they will be able to solve?
   b) Engaged with the problem or task and not just told about it?
   c) Given a sequenced progression of problems rather than given a single problem?
2. Activates relevant prior knowledge or experience?
   a) Have learners describe relevant past experience that are foundational for new knowledge?
   b) Provide relevant experience from experts?
   c) Help learners form appropriate structures for organizing the new knowledge?
3. Demonstrates (shows examples of) what is to be learned?
   a) Demonstrations (examples) consistent with the content being taught?
      i)   Examples and non-examples for concepts provided?
      ii) Demonstrations for procedures and modeling for behavior?
   b) Learner-guidance techniques employed?
      i)   Learners are directed to relevant information.
      ii) Multiple representations are used and multiple demonstrations compared?
   c) Media relevant to the content and used to enhance learning?
4. Opportunity to practice and apply newly acquired knowledge or skill?
   a) Are the application (practice) and the post-test consistent with objectives?
      i)   *"Information-about"* practice requires learners to recall or recognize information.
      ii)   *"Parts-of"* practice requires the learners to locate, name, and/or describe each part.
      iii) *"Kinds-of"* practice requires learners to identify new examples of each kind.
      iv)   *"How-to"* practice requires learners to do the procedure.
      v)   *"What-happens"* practice requires learners to predict a consequence of a process.
   b) Solve a varied sequence of problems and receive constructive feedback?
   c) Access to help or guidance when having difficulty with the instructional materials?
5. Provide techniques for learners to integrate the new knowledge or skill into their job?
   a) Opportunity for learners to publicly demonstrate their new knowledge or skill?
   b) Opportunity for learners to reflect on, discuss, and defend their new knowledge or skill?
   c) Opportunity for learners to create, invent or explore ways to use new knowledge or skill?

Source: Adapted from Merrill, M. D. (2012). *First principles of instruction.* John Wiley & Sons; Merrill, M. D. (in press). *First principles of instruction* (2nd edition). Association for Educational Communications and Technology. Reprinted by permission.

Motivation to Learn

Learners must have some level of motivation to learn so as to be energized to gain benefit from a learning experience. Motivation involves psychological processes around the arousal, direction, intensity, and persistence of behavior (Kanfer, Frese, & Johnson, 2017). Arousal and persistence is about the time and effort that an individual invests, and direction and intensity refer to the behaviors in which the investment of time and effort are made. In that sense, motivation is reflected both in the choice of behaviors that individuals decide to engage in and the amount of effort devoted to those choices. Four motivational theories that are particularly relevant to learning in the workplace are described next. A summary of the key components of each approach to motivation is presented in Table 4.7.

EXPECTANCY THEORY   Expectancy theory explains how behavior is energized and sustained (Eccles & Wigfield, 2002). The theory is based on cognitive expectancies of the possible risks and benefits of directing efforts in a particular direction. Therefore, the expectancy model is future oriented by examining where individuals choose to direct their efforts. The expectancy model consists of three factors. One factor is the expectation by the learner that if they put forth effort in a task such as learning a new skill that a certain level of proficiency (e.g., learning level) can be obtained. This expectancy addresses how ready the learner feels – that is, whether the learner believes they have

TABLE 4.7 Motivational Frameworks				
	Expectancy	**Social Learning**	**Goal Setting**	**Self Determination**
Key Concepts	Expectancy Instrumentalities Valence	Agency Vicarious learning	Goal level Goal commitment Goal orientation	Intrinsic motivation Controlled motivation
Motivational Force	Effort is seen as leading to high levels of learning Amount of learning is seen as leading to valued outcomes	Interactions lead to high levels of self-efficacy	Set specific, challenging goals Gain commitment to goals	Enhance perceptions of autonomy, competence, and relatedness
Enhancing Motivation to Learn	Eliminate obstacles to learning Ensure valued learning outcomes are obtainable and supported	Sequence learning to build efficacy Show mastery models and provide sufficient practice time	Set goals with supervisor prior to learning Provide a mastery goal orientation frame	Learner given some choice on how to achieve learning goals Learner encouraged to develop strategy for accomplishing a learning task

the capabilities (experience, knowledge, skills) to gain from the new learning experience.

A second factor called instrumentality concerns the learner perceptions that if a certain level of proficiency is achieved, what do they see are the likely consequences? To illustrate instrumentality, a learner may feel that even if a high level of knowledge and skill are obtained from a learning experience that ultimately there will be no opportunity on the job to enact the new skill. One could see that if this is the main consequence that the learner motivation levels for acquiring the new knowledge and skill would be low.

The third factor is the value or valence the learner places on the various outcomes that are likely to occur. Possible outcomes can have a high or low valence value. For a continuous learning-oriented person, gaining new knowledge would have a high value regardless of the support the person feels on the job for applying a new knowledge or skill. For someone with high achievement goals, gaining skills that have immediate payoffs on the job would have high value.

The expectancy model contends that the motivational level of an individual is therefore based on a combination of the expectancies, instrumentalities, and valence of the possible outcomes to the individual. For motivation to be at a high level going into a learning opportunity, a person must believe they have the capability to learn and see that the learning would lead to valued outcomes. The model is also cyclical (although not often studied this way) in that a person can learn how well the predictions of expectancies and instrumentalities have come true on the job. Therefore, learning and job experiences can lead to a revision of the learners' expectancies, instrumentalities, and even valence. A job incumbent may come to see that a learning event has helped build capacity leading to a positive cycle in which future learning opportunities are seen even more positively in helping the person towards higher levels of performance. Similarly, poorer performance on a learning task or perceptions that the positive outcomes for learning are limited could lead to lower motivation to continue to learn in that domain.

The theory implies that it is necessary to build up a learner's confidence or expectancy before or early on in a learning opportunity to lead to a successful level of learning. In addition, discussions with supervisors of how gaining the knowledge and skills leads to positive work outcomes can be motivating. Describing how the learning objectives have been carefully based on the needs assessment and are job relevant could booster instrumentalities. Programs that appear unrelated to valued future outcomes will probably not lead to the learner meeting the desired learning objectives.

SOCIAL LEARNING THEORY   Social learning theory contends that behavior stems from decisions made by the learner based on the processing of information. From this perspective, the learner forms structures, or schema, in memory that preserve and organize information about what has been learned. Motivation arises out of the reciprocal interactions of person factors such as beliefs, expectancies, attitudes, behavioral, and contextual factors. This approach conceives of the learner as being a proactive participant in the process of learning rather than being a passive recipient of information (Bandura, 1977).

A key aspect of this theory relevant to learning is the contention that people process and weigh information concerning their capabilities relevant to the learning situation. The motivation to achieve a level of learning is greater to the extent that the learners believe they are capable of mastering the material. This perception of competency is called self-efficacy. The theory contends that when perceived self-efficacy is high, individuals set higher learning goals and have firmer commitments to attaining those goals. The goals provide a sense of purpose and direction. The attainment of goals enhances efficacy when new learning situations emerge. Thus, a learner's beliefs about efficacy are strengthened through mastery and success experiences.

The theory contends that these mastery experiences are more likely when the learner is exposed to "mastery modeling" (Bandura, 1986). The theory notes that if a learner only learns through direct experiences, development is limited. Instead, individuals learn by watching others take action in response to a situational context. Vicarious learning occurs when the observer watches a person and the learned behaviors from those observations become part of the observer's repertoire of potential behavior in similar situations. Vicarious learning is acquired through the learner translating the actions into a mental representation linked to past experiences. Watching a model enhances the observers' beliefs about their own capabilities to perform in a similar way. Modeling also provides clear direction to learner effort – to try and replicate what the person has demonstrated. Learning is an active process of acquiring, storing, and retrieving what was modeled. Learning is enhanced by mental rehearsal of what was modeled as well as physically carrying out the steps modeled. Social learning theory provides an important foundation for a training technique known as behavioral role modeling, which is discussed in Chapter 10.

GOAL SETTING   Goal theory states that goals affect task performance by directing energy and attention, mobilizing effort, and helping individuals persist in that mobilization of effort to meet the goals. Goals also lead to strategy development to better attain the goals (Locke & Latham, 2019). Goals are inherently a process of self-regulation in which individuals determine what goals to strive for (or are given goals by others), evaluate progress towards goals, and make choices as to whether to persist or even abandon goal pursuit (Kanfer, Frese, & Johnson, 2017). More specifically, the theory posits the following propositions:

1. Individuals given hard or challenging goals perform better than those given easy or do your best goals (or no goals at all).
2. Goals have stronger effects when they are given in specific terms rather than as a vague set of intentions.
3. The goals must be matched to the ability of the individual such that the person is likely to achieve the goal if the appropriate level of effort is expended.
4. For goal setting to be effective, the individual must accept the goal that is assigned or set.
5. Feedback concerning the degree to which the goal is being achieved is necessary for goal setting to have its optimal effect.

The setting of specific, challenging goals around acquiring knowledge and skills that are matched to the ability of the individual, followed by feedback on degree of goal achievement, provides a solid foundation for learning design. An underlying assumption is the development of goals not only allows a person to measure one's capabilities against standards but also increases the sense of self-efficacy and feelings of achievement once specific and difficult goals are achieved. Goals can also help in directing future efforts to apply what was gained during a learning opportunity or to persist in enhancing new knowledge and skills.

An additional perspective to goals especially relevant to learning revolves around the underlying approach individuals take relevant to a learning opportunity. In particular, the goal orientation of the learner when placed in a learning situation is posited as a critical factor linked to learning (Pintrich, 2000). Mastery-oriented individuals believe that their efforts can lead to improved learning and retention. Individuals with a mastery orientation view capability as something that is malleable. They focus on developing new skills, attempt to understand their tasks, and define their success in terms of challenging self-referenced standards. In contrast, performance-oriented individuals believe that capability is demonstrated by performing better than others, even during learning trials and practice drills. Moreover, they define success in terms of normative-based standards. These individuals tend to look to ability limitations and attribute any failures to lack of ability rather than the need to put in more effort into the learning task. Mastery and performance orientations thus represent fundamentally different ideas of success and the reasons for engaging in learning thus focusing on different motivational approaches to a learning task. Performance orientation is related to the belief that success requires high ability while mastery orientation is related to the belief that success requires interest, effort, and collaboration. Regarding learning opportunities in the workplace, Sitzmann and Weinhardt (2018) add a third type of goal orientation called a completion goal. A completion goal is the desire to complete a learning event to receive credit (e.g., certification) for its completion. Such an orientation leads to desiring to spend the least amount of time possible on the learning task with the minimum effort needed to pass the course. On-line certification programs that have easy-to-pass assessments can enable this type of goal orientation. Clearly, what type of goal orientation a person brings to a learning opportunity can have major effects on subsequent efforts to learn as well as the amount of new knowledge and skill retained and then applied.

SELF-DETERMINATION THEORY   Self-determination theory describes the energy derived from internal psychological processes when performing tasks or learning new things. It distinguishes between autonomous or intrinsic motivation and controlled motivation (Gagné & Deci, 2005). According to this theory, a major driver of intrinsic motivation is the extent to which choice and strategy to accomplish a learning task is seen as determined or chosen by the individual rather than an outside source. One proposition is that when given this opportunity, people pursue learning tasks that they find inherently enjoyable with motivation coming from one's interest in that activity. Individuals will be most creative, learning focused, and productive when they find the task to be learned as intrinsically interesting and therefore motivating (Liu, Chen, & Yao, 2011).

Controlled motivation is about attempted regulation of one's activities like being told what to do and how to do it from sources external to the individual. The theory posits that strong external pressures to regulate actions can lead people to see that they are only performing or learning a task to meet the external pressure rather than from any internalize need or desire to learn. Thus, when the external pressure is gone, the motivation to continue with the task or acquiring knowledge and skills from a learning opportunity diminishes.

The level of intrinsic motivation that a person has is a function of how well three types of needs are being met – autonomy, competence, and relatedness. Autonomy is enhanced through allowing the individual choice and decision-making power regarding what and how to learn. Competence (or, as we see above, self-efficacy) is about desiring somewhat challenging tasks as they help build up feelings of accomplishment. Relatedness involves feelings of psychological safety in situations such as being able to learn from mistakes rather than being punished. Optimal levels of motivation are linked to the extent to which all three needs are being met during a learning opportunity. Over time, even with some level of external pressures for achievement, job incumbents can come to see the pressure as a reasonable part of their own internal motivation to become highly skilled. In this way, the goal of being a continuous learner becomes part of their own self-identity.

A meta-analysis of the research in the workplace on autonomous and controlled motivation has found that intrinsic motivation predicts task performance – with the influence somewhat higher for the quality of one's performance than the quantity of performance (Cerasoli, Nicklin, & Ford, 2014). This effect is stronger for complex rather than more routine or mundane tasks and remains high when considering the strength of external motiving factors such as work incentives. They also found that the relationship of intrinsic motivation to performance is stronger when the link between the extrinsic motivating factors to performance is indirect rather than directly salient to the individual. While the meta-analysis investigated task performance and not learning per se, the findings suggest that giving learners some choice during the learning process, framing learning as challenging and interesting, and having learners focus on how they want to adapt the learning to best meet needs for improvement in the workplace should lead to greater motivation to learn.

FACTORS LINKED TO MOTIVATION TO LEARN   Motivation to learn can be affected by individual differences in learners, situational factors at work and the strength and effectiveness of the learning intervention itself. To provide an integrative summary of what we know about these issues, Colquitt, LePine, and Noe (2000) completed a meta-analysis of over 100 studies that have examined the link of individual characteristics such as personality traits and situational characteristics on the motivation to learn. The study results are presented followed by more recent studies on motivation to learn.

Personality can be defined as an individual's characteristic patterns of thought, emotion, and behavior along with the underlying psychological mechanisms that are behind those observable patterns (Funder, 2012). The major taxonomy is what has been called the Big Five including traits of conscientiousness, openness to experience, emotional stability, agreeableness, and extroversion. Other traits of interest include locus of control, which refers to the degree to which an individual is likely to make internal or external attributions about outcomes. Internals believe that events occurring at work are based on their own behavior and are therefore under their own control. Externals believe that work outcomes are beyond their personal control.

Externals attribute work outcomes to factors like luck or the actions of others while internals are more likely to focus on their effort levels, accept feedback, and take action to correct performance problems.

The meta-analysis found that personality type variables did indeed affect motivation to learn. For example, they found a strong relationship between locus of control with motivation to learn with internals showing higher motivation levels. Findings also support that higher levels of conscientiousness are correlated with higher levels of motivation – individuals high on this factor are more likely to place energy and direct their attention to the learning opportunity. In addition, anxiety is related to motivation with highly anxious learners being less motivated to learn and also having lower levels of self-efficacy. While a full-blown expectancy theory model was not able to be analyzed in the meta-analysis due to few studies, the analysis did reveal that valence placed on continuous improvement was strongly related to motivation to learn. Not surprisingly and in support of the social learning theory, pre-training self-efficacy also had a strong relationship to motivation to learn. An individual's level of organizational commitment, job involvement, and career orientation was also found to be related to motivation levels going into a learning opportunity. In terms of situational factors, supervisory and peer support were both found related to motivation to learn. In addition, a positive climate for learning within the organization was related to an individual's motivation to learn. These findings highlight that an individual's perceptions of these situational factors do have an impact.

Since that initial meta-analysis, additional studies have reinforced these findings and added additional factors to consider. Klein, Noe, and Wang (2006) found support that those with higher levels of mastery orientation are more motivated to learn. Steele-Johnson et al. (2010) found support for the link of mastery goal orientation to self-efficacy and the link for social support to motivation to learn with a sample of people mandated to go to training. A meta-analysis found support that mastery-oriented learners have higher levels of self-efficacy, are more proactive in developing learning strategies, and more likely to seek feedback from others (Payne, Youngcourt, & Beaubien, 2007).

For some types of learning interventions such as sales and marketing training, individuals high on extroversion are more motivated to learn than those who are introverted. There is support for this perspective as those who are rated as higher on extroversion and agreeableness also were found to have higher levels of motivation to learn from a call center training program (Rowold, 2007). Bell and Ford (2007) found that justice or fairness perceptions based on a pre-training assessment of driving behavior affected truck driver motivation to learn from a defensive driving course. Interestingly, there is emerging evidence in the job development literature that mastery goal orientation and self-efficacy beliefs can buffer learners from the stresses associated with performing assigned and challenging developmental job experiences (Courtright et al., 2014).

There is also strong support for the initial finding by Colquitt and Noe that situational factors affect motivation to learn. When the job situation and leadership are viewed as supportive and enabling success (adequate resources, equipment, opportunities), individuals had higher levels of motivation than when learners perceive obstacles and barriers to applying learning to the job (Klein, Noe, & Wang, 2006).

Readiness and Preparedness

The intent of effective learning experiences is to change how learners perceive, think, plan, and behave. Ultimately, the decision to learn is in the hands of the learner. The learner makes personal decisions on what to attend to during a learning experience and what not to consider (remember discussion in Chapter 2 on what is NOT learning). Therefore, a learning plan needs to consider strategies to enact prior to the learning experience that can increase the probability that the learner benefits from a learning intervention (Ford & Oswald, 2003). This section describes the issue of readiness and presents strategies to better prepare individuals prior to when the learning opportunity begins.

READINESS Before benefiting from any learning method, people must be ready to acquire, store, and retrieve the information from the learning opportunity when needed. Readiness includes having the prerequisites (level of knowledge, skills, and abilities) necessary to gain from the learning content and the way the learning opportunity is designed. Learning programs will fail if the prerequisite knowledge and skills necessary to perform successfully are not considered. Without the experience level needed and the prerequisite knowledge and skill to learn a new computer programming language, learners can have difficulty determining what information to attend to, how to link the new information to current knowledge, or how to apply the new programming codes to the appropriate situations. Low readiness also leads to low self-efficacy or confidence, which reduces the motivation to learn.

To improve the readiness of learners before a learning opportunity, there needs to be an understanding of the capabilities (knowledge and skills) of the learner. In the last chapter, the point was stressed that the needs assessment can provide the information necessary for who needs to be the focus of a learning opportunity to enhance knowledge and skills. Measuring learners on what they know or what skill level they currently are before they begin a learning experience provides valuable information. In addition, there is a need to consider strategies to enhance the preparedness of the learner for the instruction that is to come.

SELECTING AND PREPARING LEARNERS The issue of readiness has led to research on how to select people to increase the likelihood of meeting learning objectives or better preparing the learner for the upcoming learning opportunity. Four preparation strategies beyond selection are also described.

The selection approach to readiness involves finding measures that can predict who will gain the most from a learning opportunity like training. These trainability assessments have been found through initial studies (Robertson & Downs, 1989) and a recent meta-analytic review (Roth, Buster, & Bobko, 2011) to predict later learning success. Trainability assessments are, in essence, a short version or sample of the larger learning program. The sample of tasks reflects more basic aspects of the required knowledge and skills that are then expanded upon in the complete and more complex learning program. Research has demonstrated that work sample tests predict training success in a large number of jobs including carpentry, welding, sewing, forklift operating, dentistry, and bricklaying (Aramburu-Zabala Higuera & Casals Riera, 2004). In the medical field, researchers have found support for using simple simulations as way of determining who would benefit most from a training course on more complex surgical issues (Gardner et al., 2016). In addition, some studies have found that people who performed poorly on the trainability assessments are less likely to turn up for the actual training program and were more likely to leave their job within the first month. This points to the potential benefits of trainability assessments as part of the hiring process to give people a more realistic preview of the job.

Another approach is to incorporate activities or information prior to a learning opportunity with the goal of enhancing the preparation of the learner (Mesmer-Magnus & Viswesvaran, 2010). One strategy is to provide individuals with pre-work or preparatory information. The pre-work could be basic material needed before moving to more complex material, a case study to analyze prior to learning such as how experts would analyze such a case, or problems to be solved to prepare learners to benefit most from the learning experience. Pre-work can help build self-efficacy such that individuals are more likely to believe they have the capabilities to succeed in the learning opportunity. Preparatory information can also help individual set realistic expectations about the learning event to come (Cannon-Bowers et al., 1998).

A second preparation strategy is to provide an underlying set of rules and procedures that will facilitate learning (Foster & Macan, 2002). Learners can be given advice about how to gain the most from the upcoming training by attending to the underlying aspects of a problem and given suggestions on how to self-regulate their own learning. Meta-cognitive strategy training can be applied to give learners skills in how to plan, monitor, and self-reflect about their learning and learning progress so they can adjust their strategies over time to progress towards the learning goals. For example, an intervention can encourage learners to more frequently monitor their progress during learning, be accurate in not overestimating the amount of learning that has occurred, and to reflect on how they could enhance their progress. A study using this intervention found that the meta cognitive prompts prior to a training program led to more meta-cognitive activity and higher levels of self-efficacy as well as greater declarative knowledge and higher levels of skill attainment (Schmidt & Ford, 2003).

A third strategy is to give a pre-learning test to gauge where the learner's knowledge or skill level currently is in relation to what they need to know to be successful in the learning situation. In this case, a pre-test is not being used for selection but instead serves the purpose of providing information about the level of preparedness of the learner to the coach or trainer conducting the instruction. The coach can then tailor the instruction to better match the learner needs. A pre-test is also beneficial as the results can be compared to a posttest to have a strong indicator of how far the learner has advanced over time. The use of a pre-test is consistent with the value of showing learners the learning objectives prior to taking part in a learning activity. In this way, the learner can prepare for the experience and has advanced warning as to learning expectations.

Finally, for teams an additional strategy to enhance preparedness is to conduct pre-briefs before a learning event. During pre-briefs, team performance expectations can be determined and roles and responsibilities of team members reviewed. In addition, any difficulties the team may face during the learning opportunity can be discussed and lead to the development of team consensus on strategies to use if the difficulties arise. This can also lead to higher levels of team self-efficacy and a confident attitude going into the learning opportunity. The issue of pre- and post-briefs is discussed in more detail in Chapter 9 on team learning.

ENHANCING THE DESIRE TO LEARN   There are a number of strategies for enhancing the desire to learn prior to participating in a learning opportunity. Earlier work focused on participation and showed that individuals given some choice in attending a learning activity had a stronger desire to learn if given their first choice – those not given their first choice for training were less excited about the upcoming learning activity (Baldwin, Ford, & Naquin, 2000).

Past experiences with learning events also have a major impact on the desire to learn from new opportunities. Dysvik and Kuvaas (2008) found that in a Norwegian service organization that perceptions of satisfaction with and usefulness of past training opportunities was related to motivation to learn from new opportunities. Hurtz and Williams (2009) examined ongoing participation in employee development activities such as developmental job experiences, formal courses and programs, and professional relationships. They found that reactions to prior developmental experiences as well as perceptions of past support levels (e.g., degree to which participation is recognized and rewarded) within the organization affected learner attitudes of expected usefulness and value of future developmental activities. These perceptions of usefulness and value affected their intentions to participate in future developmental activities. Intentions were also found to be strongly related to later participation in developmental activities. This shows that organizations must focus on providing worthwhile, job relevant learning opportunities – highlighting again the importance of a strong needs assessment process to target relevant skills to ensure learners see the value of the learning opportunity prior to attending. While this seems obvious, the important point is that just throwing together a learning event without much thought has more ramifications than just that the learners did not learn much from it. Once reputations are formed in a learner's mind they are likely to remain!

Other research has shown the benefits of intentionally intervening to frame the upcoming learning opportunity in a way to create a positive learning state on the part of the learner prior to a learning opportunity. In one study, learners were encouraged to take a mastery orientation rather than a performance goal orientation when completing training (Kozlowski & Bell, 2006). A mastery orientation is a focus on learning and improving rather than not making mistakes and performing well during the learning session. Encouraging a mastery orientation increased subsequent measures of motivation to learn during the learning opportunity and enhanced learning outcomes of skill acquisition in a simulation training program. Weissbein et al. (2011) incorporated a pre-training intervention in which the importance of effort and strategy use was emphasized as critical for becoming a more skilled negotiator. They found that those given this framing (compared to a control group) led to higher levels of motivation to and time spent practicing negotiation skills after training was completed. Another study investigated a defensive driving course for truck drivers focused on framing accidents as avoidable. This framing intervention led to driver perceptions that safe driving behaviors are more under their internal control and therefore avoidable due to conscientious effort

rather than as a function of pure luck. This change in internal control perceptions was found to be related to an increase in safe driving behaviors (Huang
& Ford, 2012).

CONCLUSIONS

A plan of instruction provides the blueprint for the design of the upcoming
learning opportunity. A learning plan includes the development of learning
objectives so as to specifically state the goal that the plan is to achieve. The
plan of instruction details how and in what sequence the learning content
will be delivered. A comprehensive plan also takes into consideration learner
characteristics to ensure that learners are ready and motivated to learn. The
motivational theories also have implications for what needs to happen during the learning event to facilitate learning such as setting learning goals,
demonstrating effective behavior, and enhancing self-efficacy. The checklist below presents ten best practice guidelines when developing a plan of
instruction.

Acquiring knowledge and skills that are ultimately not used to improve
job behaviors and performance is not of much value to an organization. The
next chapter examines a variety of factors that can enhance or inhibit learning
and the transfer of learning to the job. These factors include characteristics of
the work environment and the learning principles incorporated into the learning opportunity. Research evidence of which learning principles best facilitate
learning and application are highlighted to drive best practice.

Chapter 4: Best Practice Guidelines

- Take a problem-centered approach to instruction that targets real world performance.
- Identify learning outcomes desired from the learning approach to meet learning needs.
- Translate learning outcomes into learning objectives.
- Write objectives to describe the performance expected, conditions surrounding performance, and standards of success to be achieved by the learner.
- Sequence learning objectives in a way to facilitate the building of knowledge, skills and self-efficacy.
- Ensure consistency in instructional design across objectives, evalu-ation, content, and methods.
- Apply the "Lesson Plan Checklist" from Table 4.6 when developing and evaluating the plan of instruction.
- Incorporate strategies (Table 4.7) that enhance learner motivation to learn.
- Develop strategies to enact prior to the learning experience (e.g., prerequisites) to increase the probability that the learner will benefit from the learning approach.
- Create a positive learning state for the learner by focusing on mastery goals.

References

Aramburu-Zabala Higuera, L., & Casals Riera, M. (2004). Validation of a trainability test for young apprentices. *European Psychologist*, 9(1), 56–63. doi.org/10.1027/1016-9040.9.1.56

A-Z Quotes. (2019). Top 25 quotes by James Clavell | A-Z Quotes. [online]. https://www.azquotes.com/author/2958-James_Clavell [Accessed 5 November 2019].

Baldwin, T. T., Ford, J. K., & Naquin, S. S. (2000). Managing transfer before learning begins: Enhancing the motivation to improve work through learning. *Advances in Developing Human Resources*, 8, 23–35.

Bandura, A. (1977). *Social learning theory*. Englewood Cliffs, NJ: Prentice Hall.

Bandura, A. (1986). Human agency in social cognitive theory. *American Psychologist*, 44, 1175–1184. doi.org/10.1037/0003-066X.44.9.1175

Bell, B. S., & Ford, J. K. (2007). Reactions to skill assessment: The forgotten factor in explaining motivation to learn. *Human Resource Development Quarterly*, 18(1), 33–62. doi.org/10.1002/hrdq.1191

Campbell, J. P. (1989). The agenda for training theory and research. In I. L. Goldstein (Ed.), *Training and development in organizations*. San Francisco: Jossey-Bass.

Cannon-Bowers, J. A., Rhodenizer, L., Salas, E., & Bowers, C. A. (1998). A framework for understanding pre-practice conditions and their impact on learning. *Personnel Psychology*, 51(2), 291–320. doi.org/10.1111/j.1744-6570.1998.tb00727.x

Cerasoli, C. P., Nicklin, J. M., & Ford, M. T. (2014). Intrinsic motivation and extrinsic incentives jointly predict performance: A 40-year meta-analysis. *Psychological Bulletin*, 140, 980–1008. doi.org/10.1037/a0035661

Colquitt, J. A., LePine, J. A., & Noe, R. A. (2000). Toward an integrative theory of training motivation: A meta-analytic path analysis of 20 years of research. *Journal of Applied Psychology*, 85(5), 678–707. doi.org/10.1037/0021-9010.85.5.678

Courtright, S. H., Colbert, A. E., & Choi, D. (2014). Fired up or burned out? How developmental challenge differentially impacts leader behavior. *Journal of Applied Psychology*, 99(4), 681–696. doi.org/10.1037/a0035790

Covey, S. R. (2013). *The 7 habits of highly effective people: Powerful lessons in personal change*. New York: Simon and Schuster.

Dysvik, A., & Kuvaas, B. (2008). The relationship between perceived training opportunities, work motivation and employee outcomes. *International Journal of Training and Development*, 12(3), 138–157. doi.org/10.1111/j.1468-2419.2008.00301.x

Eccles, J. S., & Wigfield, A. (2002). Motivational beliefs, values, and goals. *Annual Review of Psychology*, 53(1), 109–132. doi.org/10.1146/annurev.psych.53.100901.135153

Ford, J. K., & Olenick, J. (2016). Training on the B&O Line: Trainer Notes. Technical Report, Ford & Associates, Williamston, MI.

Ford, J. K., & Oswald, F. L. (2003). Understanding the dynamic learner: Linking personality traits, learning situations, and individual behavior. In M. R. Barrick & A. M. Ryan (Eds.), *Personality and work: Reconsidering the role of personality in organizations* (pp. 229–261). San Francisco: Jossey-Bass.

Foster, J., & Hoff Macan, T. (2002). Attentional advice: Effects on immediate, delayed, and transfer task performance. *Human Performance*, 15(4), 367–380. doi.org/10.1207/S15327043HUP1504_04

Funder, D. C. (2012). Accurate personality judgment. *Current Directions in Psychological Science*, 21(3), 177–182. doi.org/10.1177/0963721412445309

Gagné, M., & Deci, E. L. (2005). Self-determination theory and work motivation. *Journal of Organizational Behavior*, 26(4), 331–362. doi.org/10.1002/job.322

Gagné, R. M. (1996). Learning processes and instruction. *Training Research Journal*, 1, 17–28.

Gagné, R. M., Wager, W. W., Golas, K., & Keller, J. M. (2005). *Principles of instructional design* (5th edition). Belmont, CA: Thompson/Wadsworth.

Gardner, A. K., Ritter, E. M., Paige, J. T., Ahmed, R. A., Fernandez, G., & Dunkin, B. J. (2016). Simulation-based selection of surgical trainees: Considerations, challenges, and opportunities. *Journal of the American College of Surgeons*, 223(3), 530–536. doi.org/10.1016/j.jamcollsurg.2016.05.021

Huang, J. L., & Ford, J. K. (2012). Driving locus of control and driving behaviors: Inducing change through driver training. *Transportation Research Part F: Traffic Psychology and Behaviour*, 15(3), 358–368. doi.org/10.1016/j.trf.2011.09.002

Hurtz, G. M., & Williams, K. J. (2009). Attitudinal and motivational antecedents of participation in voluntary employee development activities. *Journal of Applied Psychology*, 94(3), 635. doi.org/10.1037/a0014580

Jacobs, R. L. (2019). Task statements and training design. In *Work analysis in the knowledge economy* (pp. 197–203). Cham: Palgrave Macmillan. doi.org/10.1007/978-3-319-94448-7_13

Kanfer, R., Frese, M., & Johnson, R. E. (2017). Motivation related to work: A century of progress. *Journal of Applied Psychology*, 102(3), 338. doi.org/10.1037/apl0000133

Klein, H. J., Noe, R. A., & Wang, C. (2006). Motivation to learn and course outcomes: The impact of delivery mode, learning goal orientation, and perceived barriers and enablers. *Personnel Psychology*, 59(3), 665–702. doi.org/10.1111/j.1744-6570.2006.00050.x

Kozlowski, S. W. J., & Bell, B. S. (2006). Disentangling achievement orientation and goal setting: Effects on self-regulatory processes. *Journal of Applied Psychology*, 91(4), 900–916. doi.org/10.1037/0021-9010.91.4.900

Kraiger, K., Ford, J. K., & Salas, E. (1993). Application of cognitive, skill-based, and affective theories of learning outcomes to new methods of training evaluation. *Journal of Applied Psychology*, 78(2), 311. doi.org/10.1037/0021-9010.78.2.311

Liu, D., Chen, X. P., & Yao, X. (2011). From autonomy to creativity: A multilevel investigation of the mediating role of harmonious passion. *Journal of Applied Psychology*, 96(2), 294. doi.org/10.1037/a0021294

Locke, E. A., & Latham, G. P. (2019). The development of goal setting theory: A half century retrospective. *Motivation Science*, 5, 93–105. doi.org/10.1037/mot0000127

Mager, R. F. (1997). *Preparing instructional objectives: A critical tool in the development of effective instruction* (3rd edition). Atlanta, GA: The Center for Effective Performance, Inc.

McKimm, J., & Swanwick, T. (2009). Setting learning objectives. *British Journal of Hospital Medicine*, 70(7), 406–409.

Merrill, M. D. (2007). A task-centered instructional strategy. *Journal of Research on Technology in Education*, 40(1), 5–22. doi.org/10.1080/15391523.2007.10782493

Merrill, M. D. (2012). *First principles of instruction*. New York: John Wiley & Sons.

Merrill, M. D. (in press). *First principles of instruction* (2nd edition). Bloomington, IN: Association for Educational Communications and Technology.

Mesmer-Magnus, J., & Viswesvaran, C. (2010). The role of pre-training interventions in learning: A meta-analysis and integrative review. *Human Resource Management Review*, 20(4), 261–282. doi.org/10.1016/j.hrmr.2010.05.001

Payne, S. C., Youngcourt, S. S., & Beaubien, J. M. (2007). A meta-analytic examination of the goal orientation nomological net. *Journal of Applied Psychology*, 92(1), 128–150. doi.org/10.1037/0021-9010.92.1.128

Pintrich, P. R. (2000). The role of goal orientation in self-regulated learning. In M. Boekaerts, P. R. Pintrich, & M. Zeidner (Eds.), *Handbook of self-regulation* (pp. 451–502). San Diego, CA: Academic Press. https://doi.org/10.1016/B978-012109890-2/50043-3

Robertson, I. T., & Downs, S. (1989). Work-sample tests of trainability: A meta-analysis. *Journal of Applied Psychology*, 74(3), 402. doi.org/10.1037/0021-9010.74.3.402

Roth, P. L., Buster, M. A., & Bobko, P. (2011). Updating the trainability tests literature on Black–White subgroup differences and reconsidering criterion-related validity. *Journal of Applied Psychology*, 96(1), 34. doi.org/10.1037/a0020923

Rowold, J. (2007). The impact of personality on training-related aspects of motivation: Test of a longitudinal model. *Human Resource Development Quarterly*, 18(1), 9–31. doi.org/10.1002/hrdq.1190

Schmidt, A. M., & Ford, J. K. (2003). Learning within a learner control training environment: The interactive effects of goal orientation and metacognitive instruction on learning outcomes. *Personnel Psychology*, 56(2), 405–429. doi.org/10.1111/j.1744-6570.2003.tb00156.x

Sitzmann, T., & Weinhardt, J. M. (2018). Training engagement theory: A multilevel perspective on the effectiveness of work-related training. *Journal of Management*, 44(2), 732–756. doi.org/10.1177/0149206315574596

Steele-Johnson, D., Narayan, A., Delgado, K. M., & Cole, P. (2010). Pretraining influences and readiness to change dimensions: A focus on static versus dynamic issues. *The Journal of Applied Behavioral Science*, 46(2), 245–274. doi.org/10.1177/0021886310365058

Weissbein, D. A., Huang, J. L., Ford, J. K., & Schmidt, A. M. (2011). Influencing learning states to enhance trainee motivation and improve training transfer. *Journal of Business and Psychology*, 26(4), 423–435. doi.org/10.1007/s10869-010-9198-x

Yelon, S. (2012). *Goal-directed instructional design: A practical guide to instructional planning for trainers*. East Lansing: Author.

Yelon, S. L., & Ford, J. K. (1999). Pursuing a multidimensional view of transfer. *Performance Improvement Quarterly*, 12(3), 58–78. doi.org/10.1111/j.1937-8327.1999.tb00138.x

Learning Transfer

Questions

✓ What is meant by learning transfer and what are the conditions of transfer?
✓ What learning principles have been found to be effective in facilitating learning transfer?
✓ What strategies and interventions have been found to enhance the probability of learning transfer?

The acquisition of knowledge, skill and/or attitudes as a function of a learning opportunity is obviously important – and as noted in Chapter 4 needs to be directed towards meeting learning objectives. Nevertheless, the ultimate goal of any learning endeavor is what happens after it has been completed. One needs to think of learning with "transfer" of the learning in mind. This kind of thinking leads to defining what is meant by transfer and determining the indicators of transfer. The next step is to understand the factors that can impact the extent to which the knowledge, skill and attitude gain during learning relevant activities have permanence that can be observed (remember the definition of learning from Chapter 2!). Transfer is an important issue for all type of learning situations including training, one-on-one guided instruction and coaching, developmental job experiences, and informal self-guided learning. For example, one can ask if the knowledge and skill gained from completing a challenging assignment is transferred to another assignment. Or, one could ask if the transmission of knowledge from a job expert to a more junior employee is transferred to appropriate situations when the coach is not present.

A survey by the Corporate Leadership Council of senior managers across 50 companies noted that they were generally dissatisfied with the outcomes of learning and development activities in their organizations (Beer, Finnstrom, & Schrader, 2016). Yet, much research has been conducted to examine the extent to which learning initiatives lead to transfer to the job

(Ford, Yelon, & Billington, 2011). This chapter on learning transfer examines three issues. First, frameworks for understanding the concept of transfer are provided and a model for understanding the factors that can impact transfer is described. Second, there has been many efforts to understand how to design learning environments to facilitate learning and transfer. These efforts have led to the development of learning principles. Third, the person and work situational factors that facilitate transfer are described followed by a discussion of planned interventions that can facilitate transfer and enhance learning impact on the job. The majority of the research on learning transfer and transfer enhancing interventions have been conducted with formal training programs. Nevertheless, the concepts and findings from this research certainly have implications for enhancing the effectiveness of the other learning approaches.

TRANSFER FRAMEWORKS

The commonsense notion of transfer is that learners effectively use the knowledge and skills gained through a learning experience in settings beyond where the learning occurred. The application must have some impact on behaviors and performance if the learning is to be considered to have some permanence and hence value for the learner and the organization. While this provides a general definition of transfer, it belies a deeper understanding and appreciation for the complexities underlying transfer. This section describes the characteristics or conditions of transfer relevant to measuring the extent of transfer and provides a model of the factors that affect the extent of learning transfer.

Conditions of Transfer

Learning transfer involves many things that are often unstated. This can lead to comparing apples to oranges when looking at the results of studies that state they have measured the extent to which learning has transferred (Barnett & Ceci, 2002). Three conditions of transfer revolve around the situations or context one expects to see transfer, the actions one would expect from the learner in those situations, and the timing of those actions. First, a learning opportunity to enhance knowledge and skills can only address certain situations or types of person interactions that might be relevant to the application of those knowledge and skills to the job. This means that transfer involves the generalization of knowledge and skills acquired during learning to the variety of situations and issues found on the job. The second aspect is the extent to which the knowledge and skills gained during the initial learning are used or maintained over an extended period of time. The third aspect goes beyond the application of the new knowledge and skills to behaviors on the job to include the performance effectiveness of the job behaviors exhibited after a learning opportunity. These three issues are detailed next.

The generalization of what is learned from the learning event to the job can be minimal or quite extensive. The direct application of learning outcomes refers to the transfer of the knowledge, skills, attitudes, and behaviors to the exact (or very similar) types of situations, settings, and people depicted in the learning activity. For example, a managerial development program may target improving supervisory skills such as problem analysis, listening skills, and action planning or goal setting. The direct application of transfer occurs if the learner demonstrates effective supervisory skills in situations and settings that are very similar to those used in the skills training program (e.g., how to handle an employee who is constantly late for work). Beyond direct application, one could be more interested in the extent to which a learner is able to take the acquired knowledge and skills and apply them to a variety of appropriate job situations and settings. This issue of generalization or adaptation requires the instructor or coach to clearly identify how often and in what situations and settings one could reasonability expect the learner to demonstrate effective application of knowledge, skills or attitudes to behaviors. If a high level of generalization is an important goal, then direct application without attempts to use the knowledge, skills, or attitudes acquired in other appropriate situations would be considered a transfer problem. To illustrate, after a workshop for improving sales, a salesperson could be expected to transfer a new selling technique to a variety of sales situations – even those not covered in the training – by closely following the learning points from the workshop. In other situations, the learner might have to adapt or customize what has been learned to meet less routine situations and contexts after the original learning has occurred. In this case, the salesperson may see the value in only using a few of the learning points from the workshop to better increase the potential for a sale.

For acquired knowledge and skills to be transferred, they must be retained by the learner over time. This issue of maintenance is important as learners who exhibit similar levels of skill proficiency soon after a program can differ substantially on long-term maintenance due to a variety of factors. Even when knowledge and skills are maintained on the job, another issue is the extent to which continuing educational experiences (workshops, coaching, challenging jobs) are needed to ensure continued use of the knowledge, skills, and attitudes obtained through the initial learning experience. In addition, some acquired skills might not be activated for use for considerable time periods – this lack of opportunity and disuse leads to skill deterioration, which might mean that a skill is no longer functional when needed. Interestingly, how long it takes a learner to rebound or to relearn to the expected level of success can be used as a good index of the successful transfer of the original educational experience in the face of no opportunities to use the skills in the transfer setting.

The extent of generalization and maintenance is seen through the observable behaviors exhibited in the transfer settings. Job behaviors exhibited over time are indicators of performance effectiveness. Performance effectiveness is the level of expertise that the behaviors demonstrate relevant to the goals of the learning experiences (Campbell & Wiernik, 2015). An individual going through training on a manufacturing process might be expected to transfer the knowledge and skills and follow the steps outlined in training to be more efficient and to reduce waste. In this case, one can examine if the learner's behavior is consistent with doing the steps as outlined and practiced in the training program. Performance effectiveness asks the additional question tied to the value or utility of the accumulated learner behaviors. In this case, one might be interested in the extent to which the speed of production increased as a function of the learner following the trained steps. Or, one might want to evaluate whether the learner's behavior leads to reducing waste and improving the quality of the finished products. One can certainly be interested in whether a learner exhibits the expected behaviors on the job but ultimately organizations are often more concerned about the level of effectiveness of the performance indicated by those behaviors.

Transfer Model

Much research has been conducted on the factors that can impact learning transfer. Figure 5.1 presents a model for organizing this large literature on factors that are important to consider for their impact on the conditions of transfer. The model depicts the linkages of instructional design, learner characteristics, and work characteristics to learning and transfer outcomes. Working backwards in the model, transfer addresses the expected outcomes on the job as a function of learning that occurs. As noted above, three aspects of transfer include generalization, maintenance, and performance effectiveness.

Learning outcomes that occur as a function of a learning opportunity have a direct effect on the conditions of transfer (Linkage 6). As defined in Chapter 2, learning is a relatively permanent change in knowledge, skill, and affect produced by some type of experience. Encoding or attending to new information, consolidating and integrating that new information with what is already in long-term memory, and retrieval or pulling the integrated information from long-term memory are key aspects of making learning relatively permanent. While learning implies that the change is relatively permanent, it does not assume that all changes lead to improvements in behavior or performance in the transfer setting. Clearly, people can apply a newly gained knowledge

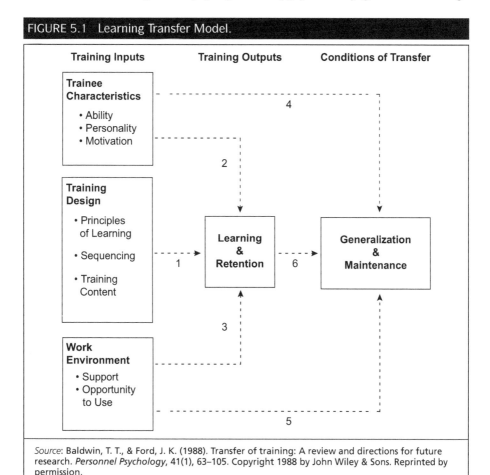

FIGURE 5.1 Learning Transfer Model.

Source: Baldwin, T. T., & Ford, J. K. (1988). Transfer of training: A review and directions for future research. *Personnel Psychology*, 41(1), 63–105. Copyright 1988 by John Wiley & Sons. Reprinted by permission.

in an inappropriate or appropriate way. Learning is operationalized in terms of knowledge, skill, and affective outcomes that hopefully are aligned with the learning objectives. Learning consists of cognitive changes in the learner knowledge base and the way the learner organizes and integrates the new knowledge into an existing framework. Learning also involves skill changes in terms of how well a trainee can enact new behaviors and ways of performing such as being able to perform a task more efficiently or with fewer mistakes. Learning can also be indicated though changes in the attitudes and motivation of the learner to proactively change their behavior to be consistent with a change in attitude (e.g., engaging in safe behaviors on the job) and motivated to continuously improve performance improvement in the domain that was part of the learning experience.

One approach for enhancing learning outcomes is the development of an effective design and plan for learning (Linkage 1). As noted in the previous chapter, needs assessment information identifies gaps that are transformed into learning objectives and a plan to meet those objectives. The plan includes sequencing the learning and systematically providing the content and practice required. In addition to these steps, there is a need to incorporate best practices around learning principles that can maximize the probability that the expected level of learning occurs. As can be seen in the model, instructional design characteristics have an indirect effect on transfer outcomes through their direct impact on the knowledge, skill, and affective outcomes that occur during the delivery of the learning intervention.

The second issue involves an understanding of how learner characteristics can influence learning (Linkage 2) and transfer (Linkage 4). As noted in Chapter 4, learners are not just blank slates when new learning opportunities arise but have different personality characteristics and varying levels of abilities and skills that may or may not lead to a readiness and motivation to learn. The level of motivation to learn is clearly related to learning. The motivation to transfer that learning to the job also should have an impact on the conditions of transfer.

The third issue concerns an understanding of the work environment or contextual factors that can impact the extent to which a learner gains the expected level of learning (Linkage 3) as well as applies what has been learned and retained to job situations in the transfer setting (Linkage 5). Work environmental characteristics can have an influence on transfer by impacting the extent to which the learning that occurs during training is used on the job to improve performance. A well-learned skill may not be applied or maintained on the job due to limited opportunity. To transfer the knowledge and skills, learners must be given opportunities, or the learners must proactively seek ways to apply them to the job setting. In addition, there must also be a climate within the organization that demonstrates to the learner that the knowledge and skills acquired and the subsequent expected behavioral changes are valued. In a positive learning climate, supervisors and peers show support for the knowledge and skills gained, provide the resources needed for successful transfer and minimize obstacles or constraints to the successful transfer of the new knowledge, skills, and attitudes to the job.

There has now developed a strong set of research studies on all three major factors and the six linkages presented in Figure 5.1. The following sections provide what we know from the evidence that can help drive best practices.

DESIGN AND LEARNING PRINCIPLES

The fields of cognitive, educational, and organizational psychology have now produced extensive evidence leading to the identification of learning principles that can enhance learning, retention and transfer. The principles can be incorporated throughout the learning process from early on to the end of the instruction or coaching. However, it is important to remember that the usefulness of any principle of learning is dependent upon the type of task and the learning outcomes expected. How well these principles are incorporated into a program is critical.

Cases are presented below that ask you to consider which of two types of interventions or strategies is likely to lead to more effective learning, retention, and transfer (see Brown, Roediger, & McDaniel, 2014 for various examples). The first set of three cases target knowledge acquisition. A second set of cases focus on skill acquisition and retention. Read the cases and based on what we have already discussed in terms of learning, reflect on why Group A or Group B learned, retained, or showed higher levels of transfer. Push your thinking by coming up with reasons why each strategy could possibly be the better approach before making your final choice. The answers to the cases are embedded in the appropriate learning principles described below each set of cases!

Case 1: Learning Concepts (Gingerich et al., 2014)

The learning goal is for the learners to be able to recall key concepts from a class. Both Group A and Group B were given the same instruction on the same key concepts. Group A is prompted to generate an original example or asked to apply the concept to a real-world situation. Group B is given instructor generated examples of the concepts or applications of the concept to real-world situations. Which group retained the knowledge better as indicated on a later examination in the course and why?

Case 2: Similarities and Differences (Kornell & Bjork, 2008b; Kang & Pashler, 2012)

The learning goal is for participants is to correctly attribute paintings to famous artists who created them. Group A studies one artist at a time and is given multiple examples of painting by that artist before moving on to another artist. Group B studies one painting by an artist and then a painting by a different artist and so on. Both Group A and Group B ended up seeing the same number of total paintings (120) by the same number of famous artists (10). Which group did better at matching painter names to NEW examples (never seen during practice) of their work later after the learning sessions and why?

> ## Case 3:   Preparation (Larsen, Butler, & Roediger, 2009)
>
> The learning goal is to aid medical residents to be able to recall knowledge on a final test. Group A is given three quizzes over the course of learning sessions that do not count towards evaluation and were given feedback. Group B was not quizzed during the classes but was given study sheets on the key concepts covered by the instructor. Group A did not receive the review sheets. Which group did better at later recalling the material on a subsequent test and why?

Prepare Learners for New Knowledge

As discussed in Chapter 4, learners need to be ready to learn – in terms of having the prerequisite skills and motivation to learn. One strategy to aid preparation is incorporating a learning principle of advanced organizer prior to new knowledge being presented. An advanced organizer can be any type of cue – including verbal, quantitative, or graphic cues – that is used to introduce a knowledge or skill by taking advantage of the existing knowledge of the learner. Advanced organizers can include outlines, diagrams, and graphs that provide the learner with a structure for the information that will be provided during the core instruction.

In a series of studies, Mayer and his colleagues (Mayer & Bromage, 1980) used a simplified diagram of the functional structure of a computer and found this advance organizer greatly enhanced learning of the technical terms and rules in a college course on computer programming. The organizer employed familiar language such as shopping lists and ticket windows in the diagrams. These organizers helped improve learning for several reasons. First, they focused attention on the important components and relationships that the subsequent instruction followed. Second, they helped the learner be prepared to organize the incoming information in a systematic way. Finally, the approach aided the learner in linking incoming new information with existing relevant knowledge sparked by the advance organizer.

More recently, learners have been presented with a concept map showing how experts see the interrelationships among key concepts to be learned prior to a module on engineering principles. The group receiving the concept maps were found to have a better understanding of the relationships between topics than those without this exposure (Moore, Venters, & Carbonetto, 2017). In an interesting study of using a game as an advanced organizer, learners who played a digital game to teach algebraic concepts *before* receiving instruction showed significant improvement over those playing the game after instruction (Denham, 2018). In addition, encouraging older adults prior to a training module to make use of cognitive learning strategies led to greater use of those strategies during the learning phase which resulted in improved training performance over those not provided with this advice (Dunlosky & Hertzog, 2001). Another active cognitive organizing strategy is the use of mnemonics to draw attention to new knowledge and help consolidate that knowledge with existing knowledge to facilitate the retrieval of knowledge when needed. One of my colleagues has used a mnemonic to introduce effective instructional design elements to trainers (Yelon, 2012). The word OOMPA was used with each let-ter representing how a trainer should introduce a learning module. OOMPA stands for Overview, Orientation, Motivation, Prerequisites, and Agenda. A visual of the Oompa Loompas from Willey Wonka and the Chocolate Factory helps solidify the mnemonic in the learner's memory. Interviews with medi-cal fellows up to ten years after this training showed that many highlighted the OOMPA as not only memorable but still being part of their own design strategy – now that is training impact (Yelon, Ford, & Golden, 2013). While the overall effect of advanced organizers and mnemonics on learning and transfer are not as large of other learning principles below, it is often strong enough to suggest that its use in workplace learning has been underappreciated.

Make Connections

The underlying conceptual framework for this learning principle is based on generative learning theory. This theory of learning recognizes that the learner is not a passive recipient of knowledge but makes decisions as to whether to attend to and actively construct meaning and understanding of new informa-tion. To increase active learning, a critical linkage needs to be made between new information and the learner's prior knowledge. The learning strategy is to help learners integrate and elaborate on new knowledge by making con-nections between the new knowledge with their existing knowledge base. Learning is not only about encoding but consolidating or mentally reorga-nizing and integrating new information into one's prior knowledge enabling learners to apply what they have learned to new situations (Wittrock, 1990).

Case 1 provides an example of such an integration strategy to make connections in which Group A is prompted to generate their own personal examples of a concept defined by the instructor while Group B is given the examples by the instructor (Gingerich et al., 2014). Group A retained more of the information as the prompts for personal examples helped learners integrate the new concepts with their existing knowledge base thus making it easier to access from memory. Other strategies that can be used to help learners actively make connections include having the learner paraphrase new material in their own words, create analogies, or develop metaphors to aid understanding of a concept (Grabowski, 2004). One can also help learners elaborate on a concept or set of concepts by analyzing the ideas through visual representations of mental images such as creating concept maps of how concepts are connected. Learners can be asked to "play" with the concept to develop new ways of thinking about and applying the concept. Learners can also be asked to predict relationships based on their prior knowledge and then after the presentation of new information refine or revise the original predictions. All these strategies take seriously the notion of an active rather than passive learner and taking steps to facilitate the learner making connections that aid learning and retention.

Provide Contrasts

One aspect of knowledge acquisition is whether learning and transfer is facili-tated more by focusing on similarities or differences. Case 2 presents this issue quite clearly as Group A is assigned to study paintings by one artist before moving to the next which orients the learner towards the similarities within an artist's style. Group B is given a painting by one artist and then a second painting by a different artist and so on which orients the learner to the differences across artists. Interestingly, participants in Group A stated that they like the focus on similarities and felt that they learned more from this approach. Nevertheless, the results show the opposite effect as participants in Group B did much better on a subsequent transfer test of identifying the correct artist when given new examples of their work (Kornell & Bjork, 2008b; Kang & Pashler, 2012). This phenomenon experienced by Group A participants has been labelled the "illusion of knowing" where learners have assumptions about the amount of knowledge gain that is incorrect (Brown, Roediger, & McDaniel, 2014).

The underlying learning principle has been called interleaved practice, which is defined as implementing an approach that mixes different types of material (like the artist studies), types of problems, or types of skills within a learning module. Such an approach requires learners to identify the critical differences across the material, problems, or skills. This discrimination-contrast approach to learning is perceived by learners as being harder as it requires more attentional resources to track differences and to continually retrieve information in memory when a new example is provided. This finding leads to the advice for instructors and educators to not be afraid to enhance "desirable difficulty" into a plan of instruction (Bjork & Bjork, 2011b). Such a plan starts with one problem and then mixes in additional types of a problem followed by a refresher of the initial type of problem with the expectation of the instruction targeting understanding the differences across problem sets (Birnbaum et al., 2013).

The issue of contrast effects has been applied to an interpersonal skills training workshop on how to be more assertive (Baldwin, 1992). In the study, all the participants were given the key behaviors to being assertive and the same instructional content and lectures. The experimental design varied the number of scenarios practiced after instruction (one or two practice opportunities) and whether the demonstration of behavior before practice was positive (the model used the key behaviors in a particular situation calling for assertiveness) or whether the learner was exposed to both a positive and negative (the model did not use the key behaviors appropriately) model. Participants were randomly assigned to one of the four experimental conditions (one situation and positive model, two situations both with a positive model, one situation with both a positive and negative model or two situations both showing a positive and negative model). After practicing the key behaviors, participants were given a final practice role play to measure learning. After the workshop as a participant was walking down a hall, the participant was approached by a trained rater who asked the participant to buy a subscription to various magazines to help the person go the college. The "salesperson" was pushy and after the incident rated the participant on how well the learner had enacted the key learning principles on how to be assertive. The salesperson was unaware of what condition the person was assigned to during training so as not be biased in anyway. The results indicated that being exposed to both positive and negative models led to higher levels of performance on the final practice role play and more importantly higher use of assertiveness tactics during the salesperson exchange after the training.

The groups that saw two different situations role played showed higher level of performance on the final role play than those only seeing one situation, but the number of scenarios was not related to performance on the transfer measure with the salesperson.

The findings support the importance of designing in discriminability skills during learning. In the example above, the contrast provoked by seeing both a positive and negative model led to higher levels of learning and transfer. Seeing both types of models resulted in higher levels of concentration and a richer understanding of the distinction of effective and less effective behaviors. With this more organized mental model, the learner could better perform the learning behaviors around being assertive.

Retrieve Information from Memory

Traditional approaches tout the benefits of restudying material in order to retain information. Restudying can help the learner encode and consolidate information into memory. Research evidence, though, points to the power of retrieval practice rather than restudying as a key learning principle for enhancing learning and transfer. Retrieval practice usually takes the form of having learners tested as they are learning. This testing effect can aid learning and retention by forcing the learner to search long-term memory. This leads to effortful information processing that creates multiple pathways in the brain that facilitate later access of that information (Dunlosky et al., 2013). Learners who actively recall information that is now consolidated in long-term memory strengthen the connections in memory and illuminate more clearly what they need to know better, which leads to a more focused and productive restudy (Roediger, Putnam, & Smith, 2011).

There is a large volume of research examining retrieval practice versus repeated studying prior to a test. Figure 5.2 presents findings from one study that is an exemplar of the typical findings in which having learners retrieve information from memory through practice testing leads to greater retention of that material than when individuals simply restudy the material. The assessment of retention is typically given weeks after the initial practice testing and includes items not on the initial assessment. The findings show that retention is almost doubled with retrieval practice with findings generalizable for both learning facts and learning concepts.

Case 3 above is an example of this type of approach to aid learning and transfer. In this case of medical residents learning new concepts, Group A, which was given short quizzes three times (once every two weeks), retained the information better (13% higher) on the final examination given six months after the instruction than those in Group B who had review study guides to prepare for the final exam (Larsen, Butler, & Roediger, 2009). A follow-up study supported the power of retrieval testing over repeated studying with simulation testing (rather than written tests) with a standardized patient (actors who use a script to portray particular symptoms in a clinical setting).

Other research has found that more frequent repeated testing (higher dosage level) leads to higher levels of retention and generalization to new exemplars beyond those discussed in the learning phase (Roediger & Butler,

FIGURE 5.2   Accuracy on Final Test Performance (from Butler, 2010).

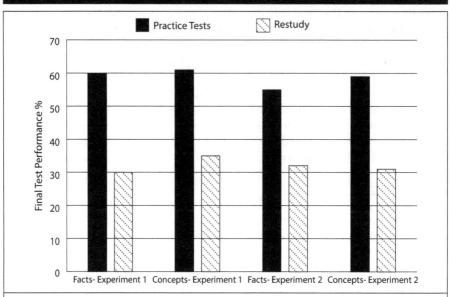

Source: Dunlosky, J., Rawson, K. A., Marsh, E. J., Nathan, M. J., & Willingham, D. T. (2013). Improving students' learning with effective learning techniques: Promising directions from cognitive and educational psychology. *Psychological Science in the Public Interest, 14*(1), 4–58. Copyright 2013 by Sage Publications, Inc. Reprinted by permission.

2011). In fact, there is evidence that these testing effects can be more powerful than generative learning strategies such as creating concept maps, using imagery linked to concepts and self-generated explanations of content (Karpicke & Blunt, 2011). Interestingly, a study found similar effects for the effectiveness of pre-testing before learning the material even though learners are likely to be unsuccessful due to lack of knowledge. Pretesting led to greater accuracy of recall on a subsequent test after instruction was completed than an extended study time condition (Richland, Kornell, & Kao, 2009). This result is consistent with the evidence on advanced organizers described above as the pre-test likely led to more focused attention during the learning phase.

While the impact of retrieval practice has been amply demonstrated, there is evidence that learners do not choose this strategy when offered the choice. In one study, learners were given the opportunity to be repeatedly tested, given time to restudy material, or given the option of removing a tested item from practice after it has been accurately recalled (Karpicke, 2009). In the learner control condition, many learners chose to remove items after initial mastery rather than continue with retrieval practice. This strategy led to lower levels of retention. In addition, it was found that learners tended not to attempt retrieval practice as early or as often as would lead to optimal learning and retention conditions. This finding has important implications for the effectiveness of e-learning and mobile learning (Chapter 7) where the learner often has more control over their own learning process.

Case 4: Practicing a Skill (from Hall, Domingues, & Cavazos, 1994)

The learning goal is for college baseball players to improve their hitting through extra practice sessions. Each batter in Group A and Group B is given 45 pitches two times a week for six weeks. Group A is given 15 of one type (fast balls) and then are given 15 curve balls and 15 change-up pitches. Group B is given the same number of fast balls, curve balls and change up pitches but they are delivered in random order. Which group did better on a later simulation transfer hitting task and why?

Case 5: Timing and Skill Development (from Moulton et al., 2006)

The learning goal is for surgical residents to learn a microsurgery technique on how to reattach tiny blood vessels over the course of four short sessions. Each lesson has some instruction followed by practice. Group A completes all four sessions in a single day, which is the normal in-service schedule. Group B completes the same four lessons but with a week's interval between each session. Which group outperformed the other on the transfer task given at a later time and why?

Perform the Skills to Be Learned

This may sound obvious or simple enough, but many learning opportunities end up with a lot of content and discussion but little in the way of what is termed the "production of a response" or opportunities to practice. This concept of production of response has been developed by cognitive theorists to emphasize having the learner actively produce whatever capability is to be mastered. Gaining knowledge of approaches managers can use with a complaining employee is not the same as having the learner produce the skills by conducting a simulated discussion with the person to resolve a complaint.

One issue relevant to the production of response relates to the size of the unit practiced during a learning session. When whole task procedures are employed during production, the learner practices the task as a single or complete unit. That means that all steps required to perform the task are enacted at one time. The utilization of what is called "part" task procedures breaks the task into action steps that are practiced separately. A learning objective from Chapter 3 noted that giving take-off instructions on an aircraft carrier involves three tasks of establishing contact and identification with the pilot, directing the aircraft to the appropriate take off point, and releasing the aircraft for take-off. A part task approach would target practicing the key knowledge and skills and steps for each of these three tasks and practicing each step separately until they had been learned. For relative novices, cognitive research contends that one should reduce the load on cognitive processing by focusing first on part training to allow the learner to devote the resources needed to learn rather than being overwhelmed with too much information.

In general, the complexity and interrelatedness of the steps (or similarities in types of skills to be learned) determines the usefulness of whole and part learning methods. The examination of the part-whole literature including meta-analytic findings supports the principle that when a task has relatively high similarity across steps (or skills) and relatively low task difficulty or complexity, whole methods are more effective than part methods. When the task steps are complex and the steps require learning a variety of skills, the part method is more effective (Fontana et al., 2009). The use of part methods does raise some concerns related to the eventual performance of the entire task. The job must be analyzed to discover the important components to optimize the part task strategy and to determine the correct sequence for learning the components. During this process, it is useful to ensure that the learner has developed the capabilities necessary to proceed to the next part of the task and that the focus of practice is on the critical steps for the task. An effective approach is where the learner practices one part at the first session. Then, at the next session, a second part is added, and both parts are then practiced together. The addition of parts continues until the whole skill is practiced and learned.

One typically thinks of production of a response as a physical act of behaving in ways consistent with instruction such as practicing a lock-out tag out procedure by a machinist. But what about the role of mental practice of tasks to be performed? Mental rehearsal occurs when learners visualize performing a task that they are attempting to learn or improve. Athletes have been coached to mentally rehearse before a game the physical actions that are to be taken, strategies to be employed in different game situations as well as coping mechanisms to manage anxiety. A tennis player could be coached to think about the mechanics of serving as well as thinking about how to counter the strokes from different types of situations with an opponent on the court (e.g., when to go cross court with a shot and when to do that effectively). Studies usually include comparisons to a control group who do additional physical practice but not additional mental practice. Research in kinesiology supports the effectiveness of athletes completing mental practice over not visualizing tasks and success (Weinberg, 2008). The researcher also cites a longitudinal study of basketball players who improved their free throw percentage when combining physical and mental practice over physical practice alone.

Mental practice helps improve retention as this rehearsal practice effect has been found to positively impact immediate measures of performance (soon after practice) and delayed measures of performance. To illustrate, after skill training on how to perform laparoscopy, one group of trainees was given training on how to mentally practice the task and were asked to visualize and mentally experience performing the procedure. The findings showed that the mental practice group outperformed the group that was given only the physical skill training in a subsequent virtual reality testing situation (Arora et al., 2011). Workplace learning can benefit from taking a more systematic approach to incorporating mental practice into learning opportunities.

Practice Relevant Performance Situations

The principle of practicing relevant performance situations includes the underlying learning principle called identical elements. Identical elements theory contends that transfer is more likely to occur when there are the same task characteristics in the learning and transfer situations. These characteristics include the aims, methods, equipment, and approaches as well as having the opportunity to practice skills on relevant tasks and situations one would face in the transfer setting. An identical element approach goes beyond whether the learning content is job relevant to whether the skills are being produced in the appropriate context. From this perspective, the most positive transfer occurs when the aims, methods, and approaches trained are consistent with the aims, methods, and approaches that are embedded in the job setting. The difficulty of the tasks and the complexity of the situations faced on the job would also be similar to those that are incorporated into the learning opportunity.

Case 4 highlights issues of identical elements. One can certainly hit the ball harder and farther when you are given 15 pitches in a row that are fast balls and then 15 that are curve balls and 15 change ups (Group A) during practice than when the hitter does not know what pitch will be coming during the practice sessions (Group B). Yet, Group B is practicing in a way that replicates the real world of baseball where you do not know what pitch will be thrown (of course, one can have an educated guess depending on the ball and strike count!). The research shows that Group A hit the ball harder in practice than Group B but Group B players did better on the transfer task of hitting in a real-world context. Notice that this baseball example is also consistent with the knowledge principle of orienting the learner to differences during learning with the study of artists. Hitting baseballs without knowing what pitch is coming is enhancing difficulty during learning. Clearly the principles given have ties to enhancing both knowledge and skill acquisition, retention, and transfer.

High levels of identical elements may be easier to achieve for closed skills then open skills (Chapter 4) as the steps to complete the task are much more tangible and prescribed. Nevertheless, there can also be situations within fields that rely on cutting edge technologies where the equipment for training is an older version than that in the field. In addition, instructors may want learners to succeed and therefore provide practice on easy tasks rather than practice the tasks in more complex situations. With open skills it may be difficult to specify or to incorporate the large variety of complexities one could face on the job. Nevertheless, there is evidence that managerial training that includes a higher level of identical elements has been found to lead to more transfer – albeit in a study using self-reported transfer data (van der Locht, Dam, & Chiaburu, 2013). Issue of fidelity of work simulators in Chapter 7 revisits this issue.

Distribute Practice over Time

The underlying issue for the distribution of practice is whether learning occurs in one continuous session (massed learning condition) or over multiple sessions separated by time (spaced learning condition). Case 5 provides a real-life example of a study comparing these two types of practice conditions. One group of surgical medical residents is given one day of training as is typically done to learn four procedures – two hours per procedure. The other group is given one procedure for two hours of training each week for four weeks. Each group receives the exact same amount of training on the exact same material and procedures. So, who did better? A variety of research studies point to the answer.

In a classic study, DeCecco (1968) presents findings that examine massed versus spaced practice on a motor skill task. The learners were required to draw a figure from a mirror image. One group, performing the task under massed-practice conditions, was given 20 trials without any rest periods. The other two groups performed the task under spaced conditions. One group was given short rest periods between trials and the other group one-day rest periods between trials. The findings showed consistent differences between the spaced-practice groups and the massed-practice group, with the spaced-practice groups demonstrating better performance.

Since then, studies show the superiority of spaced over massed practice conditions. Two meta-analytic reviews examining a variety of training methods and types of learners have found that individuals in spaced practice conditions perform much higher than groups in the massed practice conditions (Cepeda et al., 2006; Donovan & Radosevich, 1999). For the specific Case 4 above, the researchers found that both groups showed immediate improvements in surgical skills as a function of the training sessions. More importantly, though, the medical trainees given spaced practice outperformed the traditionally trained surgical residents one month after training ended in terms of less time to complete surgeries, more efficient hand movements during the operation, and higher levels of success at reattaching the served pulsating aortas of live anesthetized rats during the operation (Moulton et al., 2006). The main reason stated for the superiority of spaced practice revolves around the consolidation of new with existing knowledge at each time period leading to the encoding of the steps more deeply into memory. There is also the possibility of more mental rehearsal between sessions.

Despite clear evidence of the superiority of spaced or distributed learning, much face-to-face instruction continues to be consistent with the massed condition. Interestingly, with the advance of e-learning and mobile learning (Chapter 7), designers can incorporate more "chunking" of material into modules that allow for more distributive learning. In addition, the learner often has more control over how much material to focus on at any one time. Based on this research, learners should be encouraged to employ spaced practice rather than massed practice. The design and learner choices around spaced practice may point to reasons why e- and mobile learning can be an effective learning technology.

Provide Appropriate Feedback

A key role for any instructor, facilitator, coach, peer, or supervisor around a learning event is to provide the learner with feedback or what has been termed knowledge of results. Knowledge of results can be about knowledge (items incorrect on a quiz) or skill (steps completed successfully or not within a trained task). For example, a supervisor can provide advice as to how to deal with a particularly difficult situation relevant to a developmental work assignment or a peer in an online workshop can critique a learner's plan of action based on the course instruction. In this way, feedback can have informational value as well as enhancing learner motivation. Feedback can clarify learning expectations, identify what to work on for improvement, and validate one's own self-knowledge regarding development. Meta-analytic evidence across 12 different meta-analytic studies (mostly in educational contexts) provide strong support for the impact of feedback on achievement scores (Hattie & Timperley, 2007). There is little doubt that feedback can be a powerful tool in the toolkit for facilitating learning.

While the importance of feedback for learning is understood, many of those who emphasize its importance simply assume that any form of feedback will accomplish the purpose. This assumption is challenged by reviews that find instances where feedback leads to decreased performance as often as it results in performance improvement (Kluger & DeNisi, 1998). This variability points to the conclusion that not all types of feedback are equal in terms of impact!

What type of feedback has positive informational and motivational outcomes that support enhanced learning and transfer? Feedback during learning needs to be focused on reducing discrepancies between current knowledge and skill level and the desired learning goal. This means that one must have a good understanding of current state and expected future state in order for the feedback to be useful. One suggestion to help in this quest is to ask three types of questions: (1) feed up or what are the learning goals, (2) feedback or how the learner is doing relevant to the learning goal, and (3) feed forward or where does the learner need to go next (Hattie & Timperley, 2007). How well these questions are answered can affect what feedback is given and the extent to which the learner maintains or increases effort to improve or abandons efforts or lowers learning goals.

In order to make good decisions about the incorporation of feedback, one must acknowledge the complexity and multidimensionality underlying the nature of feedback (Massman, 2012): Figure 5.3 presents five different elements of feedback that are described below. The five elements are:

1. Timing of feedback: Feedback can be given immediately after a response by the learner or delayed until sometime after the response.
2. Frequency of feedback: Feedback can be given continuously or quite frequently after learner actions or spread out and only given after a number of responses have been made by the learner.

FIGURE 5.3   Elements of Feedback.

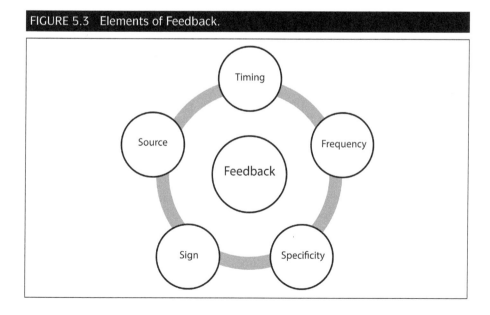

3. Specificity of feedback: Feedback can focus on a high level of specificity around the individual steps taken or more oriented on the overall effectiveness of performance of the learner when producing a response.

4. Sign of feedback: Feedback can be given in a way that focuses on the positive (you completed these steps correctly) or on the negative (you did not complete these steps correctly).

5. The source of feedback: Feedback can be provided by an instructor, coach, supervisor, peer, or by the learner (self-feedback).

The complexity of the nature of feedback is apparent by thinking of each of the five elements of even having just two options (e.g., delayed or immediate feedback) leading to a 2×2×2×2×2 world or 32 cells of feedback! Given this complexity, the research evidence on feedback and learning can point to guidelines, not absolutes.

Typically, one thinks of timely feedback as occurring close to when the learner has acted. This is particularly true for those early in the learning process as the more effective feedback is soon after the production of response and where feedback is fairly frequent so as to keep the learners on track to meeting learning goals. More specific feedback of what behaviors or steps need to be improved or altered is often more useful than overall performance-based feedback. In one study, immediate, task specific feedback during football practice benefited the players more than delayed feedback (Rogers, Rousseau, & Fisk, 1999). Nevertheless, as a learner progresses, the frequency and often the specificity of feedback can decrease as the learner can connect overall performance feedback to what needs to be done to improve performance. In addition, continuous feedback during the acquisition of a motor skill interferes with rather than supports the rate of learning due to the learner relying too heavily on the feedback and not in developing their own capabilities to self-monitor and self-correct themselves – which is an important skill for later transfer to the job (Schmidt & Wulf, 1997). Others have found that increasing feedback specificity can be valuable for learning what to do when things are going relatively well during the learning opportunity and yet be detrimental to learning when the learner is doing relatively poorly in modeling the steps for effective performance (Goodman, Wood, & Hendrickx, 2004). For feedback about knowledge, a meta-analysis found that elaboration given about why a knowledge statement or principle was incorrect was much more effective for learning than just giving the learner the correct answer (Van der Kleij, Feskens, & Eggen, 2015).

Research supports the provision of positive feedback (you completed these steps consistent with the demonstration model) for enhancing learning and transfer as it can build self-efficacy (Kluger & DeNisi, 1998). On the other hand, conveying negative feedback in terms of the specific aspects of the task that needs to be the focus on improvement in a respectful and constructive manner has also been found to increase effort to meet learning goals (Steelman & Rutkowski, 2004). Chiviacowsky and Wulf (2002) found that giving learners control over when they wanted feedback while learning had a beneficial impact on a transfer task over a group where the instructor decided when to give feedback. A follow-up study found that feedback asked for after a reasonably effective trial led to greater learning than feedback asked for after poorer trials – pointing to motivational effects of positive feedback when learning motor skills (Chiviacowsky & Wulf, 2007). While the research evidence can only lead to some guiding principles, an important situational characteristic is the climate for learning from errors or mistakes during the learning opportunity. A supportive climate for learning can lead to the learner feeling comfortable trying out the behaviors and trust that the feedback provider has their best interests for improvement as the goal. In addition, multiple sources of feedback can often help learners focus on the key issues for improvement.

Go Beyond Initial Mastery

A meta-analytic study of transfer finds significant skill decay with nonuse or nonpractice over time since the original learning opportunity for both motor and cognitive tasks (Wang et al., 2013). The decay becomes steeper the longer the time interval of nonuse. When faced with the possibility of nonuse for a period of time, a key learning principle is overlearning. Overlearning is a situation where the learners are presented with a number of extra practices of the knowledge or skills during the learning opportunity even after they have initially demonstrated the required level of mastery on the task. An early investigation examining psychomotor skills studied the disassembly and assembly of weapons and demonstrated the positive benefits of overlearning (Schendel & Hagman, 1982). They trained soldiers to a criterion of one errorless trial and then gave 100% overtraining. This means that if a particular performer took ten trials to perform one errorless disassembly and assembly of the weapon, then he or she received ten additional trials as part of initial training. Another group of soldiers received overtraining, but in this case each person received the extra trials as a refresher training midway through the eight-week retention period. At the end of the eight-week interval, both the overtrained and the refresher group performed significantly better than a control group that was given just the initial training. The overtrained group was superior to the refresher group in terms of the amount retained. More generally, Driskell, Willis, and Copper (1992) found in a review of over 50 studies that overlearning is not only an effective strategy for retaining motor skills (completing a machine setup) but also for more cognitive tasks (troubleshooting problems) with more repetition or practice over original mastery leading to strong retention results.

A relevant and interesting study examined the effects of overlearning on susceptibility to phishing among university undergraduates. After initial training, the students were sent mock phishing emails over the course of the next 1, 8, and 10 weeks. Those students who received 100% overlearning were less susceptible to phishing attacks and more cautious consumers than those who were not in the overlearning condition (Nguyen, 2018). Also, wind turbine technicians who have limited opportunity to use non-routine trained skills who overlearned tasks had less skill decay than those without this additional amount of practice during training (Lawani, Hare, & Cameron, 2014).

Overlearning is linked to the concept of automaticity discussed as a highest order level of skill development in Chapter 2. Automaticity refers to the idea that the performance of a task can become so routinized that it requires limited attentional capacity to be performed. The automatic processes demand little attentional resources, thus becoming easy to accomplish while being able to switch to performing other tasks more seamlessly. They also make the performance of these automatic tasks very quick and efficient.

Summary of Principles

This discussion shows the variety of learning principles that could be incorporated into any learning opportunity. Decisions need to be made as to which principle or principles can have the most impact on learning and transfer. Table 5.1 provides a summary of the nine principles in terms of key concepts and an illustrative example of how to incorporate the principle to improve knowledge and skills and to enhance the likelihood of transfer. The next section explores work factors relevant to learning and transfer followed by a section on the power of interventions to enhance transfer for impact.

TABLE 5.1	Learning Principles, Core Concepts, and Examples	
Principle	**Core Concepts**	**Examples**
Prepare learners prior to learning new knowledge	Advanced organizer	Cues in the form of outlines, diagrams, graphs and concept maps Games Mnemonics
Make personal connections	Generative learning through integration and elaboration	Case 1: Personal examples of concepts Paraphrase new material in own words, create analogies, metaphors, make predictions, "play" with a concept
Provide contrasts	Interleaved practice Enhancing difficulty during learning	Case 2: Identifying Artists Modeling effective *and* ineffective behaviors
Have learner retrieve knowledge from memory	Retrieval practice Testing effects	Case 3: Low stakes quizzes Pretesting, testing during learning, and testing after learning with feedback
Perform the skill	Production of response	Whole/part learning; Variability of situations Mental practice
Practice relevant performance situations	Identical elements Adaptability	Case 4: Baseball and hitting Aims, methods, and tasks that match performance setting
Distribute practice over time	Spaced practice Massed practice	Case 5: Surgical training Chunking content into multiple learning modules Learner control over pacing and sequencing
Provide appropriate feedback	Knowledge of results Feed-up, feedback, feedforward	Timing, frequency, specificity, sign, source
Go beyond initial mastery	Overlearning/automatization	Repeated practice Refresher training Opportunity to perform on job

BEYOND DESIGN

The transfer model (Figure 5.1) shows links beyond design that include person factors and learning (Link 2), person factors and transfer (Link 4), work environment factors on learning (Link 3) and on transfer (Link 5). Much research has been conducted to understand the person and work environmental factors affecting learning and transfer outcomes. In addition, a number of interventions have been developed to enhance transfer.

Factors Affecting Transfer

Person factors that can affect the motivation to learn were presented in Chapter 4. These factors such as readiness and motivation are clearly important for understanding transfer. In fact, meta-analytic evidence points to self-efficacy, motivation to learn and the level of conscientiousness of the learner as important factors predicting the amount of learning transfer (Blume et al., 2010). In addition, motivation to learn is particularly important when learning an open as opposed to a closed skill.

The social and contextual factors at work can play a powerful role as a facilitator or inhibitor of learner motivation to transfer what they have learned. Learning takes place amid individuals doing their day-to-day jobs with performance expectations, functioning within intact teams or with peers from different units, as well as a host of organizational activities unrelated to learning goals. Factors found to impact transfer outcomes include being given the opportunity to use the knowledge and skills gained on the job, the level of support by peers and supervisors for new knowledge and skills as well as changes in behavior on the job, and the reward and incentive systems in place within the organization (Baldwin, Ford, & Blume, 2009). In fact, meta-analytic evidence found that supervisory support was more important for affecting transfer than peer support. Such support can take the form of encouragement, providing guidance or advice, and providing resources or direct assistance to facilitate transfer (Ford, Baldwin, & Prasad, 2018). In addition, the work climate for learning has a strong relationship with transfer while work constraints have a negative effect on transfer outcomes. The need for a positive learning climate is more important for open as opposed to closed skills – as learners are more encouraged to apply what has been learned.

There is also an understanding of why transfer often does not occur due to some combination of work and person factors. There is evidence that some individuals have tendencies to avoid or postpone decisions (procrastination) and therefore while they might say they have intentions to transfer, in reality they favor inaction or no change from current habits (Anderson, 2003). Personal beliefs that one's current level of performance is more than adequate can lead one not to be motivated to learn or apply new knowledge or skills. Or, this tendency towards inaction is enhanced in workplaces that do not place a high value on learning. Interestingly, Anderson also highlights the issue of anticipation of regret that a learner may feel such as worrying that trying out a new skill may not succeed or make one look like they do not know what they are doing. Individuals who know they are going back to a workplace with limited support for the new knowledge or skills may not want to look foolish for trying to transfer learning. In addition, there is evidence that individuals also tend to weight potential losses with a change in behavior greater than potential gains from trying out new ways of behaving on the job. Thus, there are many reasons why an individual may not transfer what has been gained through a learning experience. On the other hand, there is evidence that the success of initial attempts to transfer has positive implications for the subsequent rate of attempts to apply the training to the job. The findings suggest the need to create a positive spiral with initial successful attempts to transfer helping build self-efficacy leading to future transfer attempts and success (Huang, Ford, & Ryan, 2017).

Strategies for Enhancing Transfer

Given what we know about person and work context factors affecting transfer outcomes, it should come as no surprise that attempts have been made to enhance transfer through direct interventions to affect person factors such as motivation, readiness, and self-efficacy as well as affect the work environment or context such as supervisor support. An obvious intervention would be to provide adequate training for coaches or mentors prior to assuming those roles on coaching others how to empower others, secure resources, and removing obstacles. Or when providing a developmental job assignment, one could ensure the supervisor is skilled at providing appropriate feedback (see above about feedback elements!). This section focuses on recommended strategies for enhancing transfer followed by some specific interventions that can be used after the learning experience to enhance transfer.

A number of strategies for enhancing transfer has been recommended to be taken. Table 5.2 provides a summary of these recommended courses of action. The table shows actions that can be taken prior to the learning event or opportunity, during the learning experience and then after the experience. The strategies to consider prior to a learning event include material we have already covered about assessing developmental needs, developing learning objectives, creating a consistent plan of instruction (including learning principles) to meet the learning goals and enhancing readiness. In addition, there is a need to prepare the instructor or coach to be in a position to effectively guide the learning process as well as having supervisors help set expectations with the learner and state their commitment to the application of the learning to the job context. During the learning event(s), there is a need to communicate to the learner the expectation that the application of the learning to the job is the goal as well as to ensure to create a learning environment that is conducive to learning. Learning content needs to be delivered in a way that learners see is credible, practice and meets a developmental need. Practice needs to be tied directly to authentic work requirements and situations including work-based projects if appropriate. Tools to aid retention and to aid performance on the job are also important.

In terms of the work environment, learners must be given the opportunity to apply the knowledge and skills gained. Opportunity is defined as the extent to which a learner is provided with or actively obtains work experiences relevant to the tasks (and underlying knowledge and skills) learned. Opportunity to apply is a multidimensional construct. This includes the breadth of experience (number of trained tasks used on the job), activity level (the number of times each trained task is performed on the job) and task type

TABLE 5.2 Strategies to Facilitate Transfer

Before	During	After
Conduct appropriate assessment to assess developmental need	Communicate to learners the expectation of application to the job	Check in with learners about progress on application
Create learning objectives and prioritize what is to be learned	Create an environment conducive to learning including a focus on mastery and benefits of errors	Send out reminders about key concepts and strategies for application
Develop a plan of instruction to meet objectives	Provide opportunity for self-management of learning	Schedule refresher session if needed
Incorporate relevant learning principles into design	Deliver learning content in a way that is credible, practical, and where learners see the need to apply learning to the job	Evaluate and revise program based on feedback to better meet learning objectives for next cohort or individual learner
Prepare instructors/ coaches to focus on transfer	Ensure authentic practice and deliver feedback in a constructive way	Have learners meet with supervisor about transfer goals
Inform learners and supervisors of learning objectives	Incorporate a project that is work relevant to reinforce content	Ensure learner has relevant opportunities to apply what was learned to the job
Have learners discuss learning objectives with supervisor	Provide tools to aid retention and application	Have supervisors discuss progress and next steps after initial attempts by learner to apply new knowledge or skills to job
Ensure commitment from supervisors to the application of learning goals to the job	Have learners set implementation goals for transfer	Provide support through encouragement, providing resources, and eliminating obstacles

Sources: Broad, M. L. (1997). Overview of transfer of training: From learning to performance. *Performance Improvement Quarterly*, 10(2), 7–21; Broad, M. L. (2003). Managing the organizational learning transfer system. In E. F. Holton & T. T. Baldwin (Eds.), *Improving learning transfer in organizations* (pp. 97–118), Jossey-Bass, San Francisco, CA; Yelon, S., Sheppard, L., Sleight, D., & Ford, J. K. (2004). Intention to transfer: how do autonomous professionals become motivated to use new ideas? *Performance Improvement Quarterly*, 17(2), 82–103.

(the difficulty or criticality of the trained tasks performed on the job). For example, in a research project with the U.S. Air Force, we found that aerospace ground equipment specialists trained on 33 tasks varied widely in their opportunity to apply those tasks, how often the tasks were performed and whether they were assigned to complete high difficulty or easy tasks. The evidence showed that the aerospace ground specialists with high levels of self-efficacy after training obtained more opportunities to apply the knowledge and skills on the job than those who were lower in self-efficacy. This result points to the learner who is self-efficacious is more proactive in asking to gain those experiences. In addition, the level of supervisory support predicts the amount of opportunities given to the trainees on the job (Ford et al., 1992). The aerospace ground equipment learners who were assigned to a supportive supervisor obtained a greater level of opportunity (across the three dimensions) than other trainees four months after the training program.

These findings highlight the gatekeeper role that supervisors can play. In addition, ongoing support is often needed to help learners transfer skills to the job. Not surprisingly, support (from supervisors or peers) is a multidimensional construct that consists of three dimensions (Ford, Baldwin, & Prasad, 2018). Instrumental support includes the provision of resources or direct behavioral assistance of the support person to aiding the transfer of learning to the job. Informational support involves the extent to which the supervisor or peer provides guidance or advice rather than providing resources or direct behavioral assistance. Finally, a support person can give affective support, which refers to giving encouragement or acting in a way to promote positive feeling and build confidence or self-efficacy. Table 5.3 presents ways in which the supervisor can be supportive across all three dimensions. The level of support across these three dimensions can send a message that the learned skills are valued in the organization. The level of support is related to learner motivation to transfer and their level of persistence in continuing to apply the knowledge and skills to the job (Chiaburu, Dam, & Hutchins, 2010). Therefore, interventions to enhance supervisory skills around support can have a significant impact on the transfer of learning.

Transfer Interventions

The research evidence to drive best practices have typically examined helping the learner be better prepared for the transfer setting. The interventions include the framing prior to learning as well as behavioral self-management strategies and the type of transfer goals set at the end of a learning opportunity.

FRAMING Different strategies for how to frame an upcoming learning opportunity can lead to beneficial transfer outcomes. One approach of error management framing encourages the learner to make errors or mistakes while in learning situations. With error management instruction, learners are asked to actively explore a task to be learned rather than being too concerned about performing the task correctly as soon as possible. Learners are told to be open to making errors and learning from them while actively exploring the task to be learned. They are told that errors are a natural part of the learning process and that errors are informative as to what is still needed to be learned.

A meta-analytic study on error management practices found that transfer outcomes are enhanced when learners are given error management instruction over instructions to avoid mistakes or when learners are in a control condition and not given either instruction (Keith & Frese, 2008). Such a focus on errors help learners to concentrate more on mastery of a skill rather than concerns about looking good to others (a performance orientation). Error management framing also leads to higher levels of metacognitive activity in which the learner is more focused on monitoring their own learning and revising strategies over time (Keith & Frese, 2005).

TABLE 5.3 Types of Supervisory Support

Direct Assistance: Helping behaviors and involvement
1. Helped me prepare to get the most out of the training.
2. Set goals with me around applying what was trained to the job.
3. Helped organize my work or social context to maximize opportunities to apply the training.
4. Gave me feedback on how I was doing with meeting the goals for the training program.
5. Followed up with me to find out whether my initial attempts to apply knowledge or skills from training were successful.
6. Provided me with the necessary time and resources so I could apply the training.

Guidance: Information and advice
1. Explained how the organization would benefit from my applying the training program.
2. Made it clear what was expected of me relevant to the training.
3. Gave me some tips on how to get the most out of the training.
4. Referred me to other sources to get advice for applying the training.
5. Suggested what she/he would do in a similar situation when trying to apply what I learned.
6. Told me the best way to apply training to the job.
7. Shared an experience to help me apply my training.

Personal: Affective responses and empathy
1. Expressed respect for my competency acquired during training.
2. Openly listened to me talk about the challenges in applying the training to the job.
3. Told me how he/she felt in similar situations to the ones that I was facing around applying training.
4. Showed interest in how things were going relevant to applying the training.
5. Gave me encouragement to continue to apply training to the job.
6. Recognized the challenges faced when applying training.

Source: Sherbourne, C. D., & Stewart, A. L. (1991). The MOS social support survey. *Social Science & Medicine, 32*(6), 705–714. Items created from discussions with my colleagues Brian Blume and Jason Huang on developing a measure of supervisory support around these three dimensions.

BEHAVIORAL SELF-MANAGEMENT A second strategy for helping learners retain and transfer skills is through self-management training. Two self-management strategies include relapse prevention and self-guidance instruction. With relapse prevention, learners are encouraged to reflect on what knowledge and skills they have acquired during training and to identify high-risk situations on the job that present obstacles to applying the training. High-risk situations might include things like time pressures and work deadlines, work overload, and lack of support from coworkers. Learners develop plans for how to successfully address those high-risk situations on the job. Relapse prevention training also recognizes that failures to transfer are likely and therefore encourages learners to not get discouraged by initial failures to apply. Coping strategies are provided to use when failures occur. An initial study found that a relapse prevention and goal setting intervention led to greater transfer and higher levels of performance than a goal condition alone (Gist, Bavetta, & Stevens, 1990). Subsequent studies have found some, albeit limited, support for the effectiveness of relapse presentation strategies with the strongest effect in work climates that are not highly supportive of continuous learning (Hutchins & Burke, 2006).

Self-guidance builds a learner's self-efficacy regarding transfer. One creative self-guidance approach is having learners write a self-affirming letter on the content from a training program that is most relevant to their job and documenting the ways they intend to apply the knowledge and skills to the job. In essence, it is a motivational letter to oneself. In one study, IT professionals attended a training program on improving their interviewing skills. At the end of the program, each learner in the self-guidance condition (and not the control condition) wrote a letter about the techniques that were most relevant for the learner to apply and how they intended to use the techniques when conducting job interviews. Five weeks after training, learners read their letters that were written at the end of training and then completed a mock interview. Those in the self-guidance condition had higher levels of self-efficacy going into the mock interview than the control condition and were rated as having much higher interviewing skills by trained raters (Shantz & Latham, 2012).

GOAL SETTING AND IMPLEMENTATION GOALS A third, highly popular approach for facilitating transfer is the learner setting personal goals or action plans around what to apply. The simplest form is to ask learners about their general intentions to apply the acquired knowledge and skills to the job. For example, learners can be asked to set a general intention such as delegating more tasks or providing more effective performance feedback.

A more systematic approach asks learners to set specific behavioral goals. A behavioral goal is more observable and measurable than a general intention goal. An example would be a learner setting a goal that "I will delegate to my management team an average of two important decisions per week" (Marx, 2000, p. 42). In terms of research evidence, general intentions are weakly if at all related to subsequent behaviors on the job. One study of a five-day leadership development program found that specific behavioral goals led to improvement in two of the three skill components embedded in the learning opportunity. Having more than one transfer goal led to more improvement overall than when just one behavioral goal was set (Johnson et al., 2012).

One step beyond setting behavioral goals is having learners set implementation intention goals. An implementation goal has a number of elements. The learner is asked to identify the effective behaviors to target and specifies the desired outcomes. The learner also details what opportunities and situations are relevant for exhibiting the learned behaviors tied to those desired outcomes. The learners are encouraged to find opportunities to apply the knowledge and skills as quickly on the job as possible. This process of creating an action plan including behaviors, expected outcomes, situations, and timing has been found to be effective in helping individuals get started at attempting learning transfer rather than procrastinating after a learning event. To illustrate, rather than having a general intention after wellness training to exercise more or even a more specific goal of exercising three times a week, the learner can create an implementation intention such as "at 7:30 a.m. each Monday, Wednesday, and Friday, I will work out at the gym for 45 minutes using these particular pieces of equipment (list) for the next three months to reach my fitness goal." Figure 5.4 presents the findings of a study on the impact of implementation intentions on exercise frequency. The control group self-set goals for exercise without any other prompting. The motivational group was given materials that described the health benefits of exercise and then were asked to self-set their goal for exercise. For the third condition, the participants were given the motivational material and also set specific implementation intentions. When asked later, 91% of the individuals in the implementation intention condition had exercised in a way consistent with their goals while only 35% of those in the motivation condition and 38% of the control condition had met their self-set goals.

A study directly relevant to learning in organizations investigated the effects of implementation intentions by first line sales supervisors. After training on improving sales interactions with customers, learners identified when,

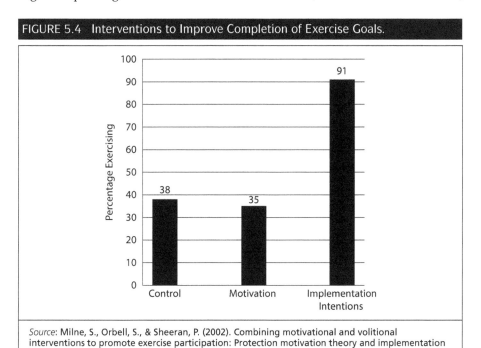

FIGURE 5.4 Interventions to Improve Completion of Exercise Goals.

Source: Milne, S., Orbell, S., & Sheeran, P. (2002). Combining motivational and volitional interventions to promote exercise participation: Protection motivation theory and implementation intentions. *British Journal of Health Psychology*, 7(2), 163–184.

where, and how they intended to apply what they had learned. This included visualizing a future interaction with a customer and writing down a detailed action plan on how to address that and other types of customer situations. In essence, this forces learners to consider if/then propositions in their plan (i.e., situations of an agreeable customer, I would do this while with a more combative customer, I would take this approach). This field study found support for the effectiveness of implementation intentions for enhancing transfer over a control condition whose learners did not create these intentions. Interestingly, transfer was measured by having a mystery shopper rate the learner's performance four weeks after the training providing an objective measure beyond a self-report of behaviors (Friedman & Ronen, 2015).

Meta-analytic evidence for the effectiveness of implementation intentions over more general intentions is strong across a wide variety of domains such as health and well-being, recycling behaviors, and consumer-related behaviors (Gollwitzer & Sheeran, 2006). The meta-analytic evidence also supports the contention that implementation intentions work because they help people remember to act in a way consistent with their self-set goals, lead people to be more proactive in seizing opportunities to meet the goals, and help overcome initial reluctance to act in ways consistent with the implementation intentions.

Setting implementation goals is an effective transfer enhancing strategy with self-management approaches such as relapse prevention and self-guidance as possible adjuncts. What we now need are studies that examine the impact of combining different types of transfer enhancing interventions such as training supervisors on how to be supportive as well as helping the learner set implementation goals. Or, a study could examine the effectiveness of incorporating error-based framing early in a learning situation along with self-guidance after the learning opportunity.

CONCLUSIONS

The bottom line is that organizations typically expend a lot of time, energy and resources to identifying learning needs, planning the instruction, and delivering the instruction. All these aspects around learning are clearly important. The point of Chapter 5, though, is to highlight the need to place a similar amount of time, effort, and resources to enhance transfer. Enhancing the probability of transfer is a function of a comprehensive needs assessment, a thoughtful plan of instruction, and the incorporation of best practices prior to, during, and after the learning opportunity. As a successful middle-distance runner Marty Liquiori once said, "Just remember this: No one ever won the olive wreath with an impressive training diary."

Chapter 5: Best Practice Guidelines
- Identify the conditions of transfer including the situations or context one expects to see transfer, the actions one would expect from the learner in those situations, and the timing of those actions.

- Determine ahead of time what continuing education and learning experiences are needed to ensure retention and continued application of newly acquired knowledge and skills.
- Ensure learners have the opportunity to apply newly acquired knowledge and skills as soon as possible.
- Incorporate a variety of learning principles (Table 5.1) throughout the learning experience to facilitate the acquisition and retention of knowledge.
- Incorporate a variety of learning principles (Table 5.1) throughout the learning experience to facilitate skill acquisition and retention.
- Determine the appropriate level, frequency, and timing of feedback during practice with more feedback given early in a learning process and less feedback over time
- Develop strategies (Table 5.2) to facilitate transfer before, during, and after a learning opportunity.
- Train supervisors on how to give appropriate direct assistance, guidance and personal support to the learner.
- Frame the learning opportunity by encouraging learners to make errors or mistakes during learning as a key to enhancing learning.
- Have learners set specific and measurable implementation goals after a learning opportunity .

References

Anderson, C. J. (2003). The psychology of doing nothing: Forms of decision avoidance result from reason and emotion. *Psychological Bulletin*, 129(1), 139. doi.org/10.1037/0033-2909.129.1.139

Arora, S., Aggarwal, R., Sirimanna, P., Moran, A., Grantcharov, T., Kneebone, R. Sevdalis, N., & Darzi, A. (2011). Mental practice enhances surgical technical skills: A randomized controlled study. *Annals of Surgery*, 253(2), 265–270. doi.org/10.1097/SLA.0b013e318207a789

Baldwin, T. T. (1992). Effects of alternative modeling strategies on outcomes of interpersonal-skills training. *Journal of Applied Psychology*, 77(2), 147. doi.org/10.1037/0021-9010.77.2.147

Baldwin, T. T., & Ford, J. K. (1988). Transfer of training: A review and directions for future research. *Personnel Psychology*, 41(1), 63–105. doi.org/10.1111/j.1744-6570.1988.tb00632.x

Baldwin, T. T., Ford, J. K., & Blume, B. D. (2009). Transfer of training 1988–2008: An updated review and agenda for future research. *International Review of Industrial and Organizational Psychology*, 24(141–70.

Barnett, S. M., & Ceci, S. J. (2002). When and where do we apply what we learn?: A taxonomy for far transfer. *Psychological Bulletin*, 128(4), 612. doi.org/10.1037/0033-2909.128.4.612

Beer, M., Finnstrom, M., & Schrader, D. (2016). *The great training robbery*. Working Paper, 16-121. Harvard Business School.

Birnbaum, M. S., Kornell, N., Bjork, E. L., & Bjork, R. A. (2013). Why interleaving enhances inductive learning: The roles of discrimination and retrieval. *Memory & Cognition*, 41(3), 392–402. doi.org/10.3758/s13421-012-0272-7

Bjork, E. L., & Bjork, R. A. (2011b). Making things hard on yourself, but in a good way: Creating desirable difficulties to enhance learning *Psychology and the Real World: Essays Illustrating Fundamental Contributions Society*, 2, 59–68.

Blume, B. D., Ford, J. K., Baldwin, T. T., & Huang, J. L. (2010). Transfer of training: A meta-analytic review. *Journal of Management*, 36(4), 1065–1105. doi.org/10.1177/0149206309352880

Broad, M. L. (1997). Overview of transfer of training: From learning to performance. *Performance Improvement Quarterly*, 10(2), 7–21. doi.org/10.1111/j.1937-8327.1997.tb00046.x

Broad, M. L. (2003). Managing the organizational learning transfer system. In E. F. Holton & T. T. Baldwin (Eds.), *Improving learning transfer in organizations* (pp. 97–118). San Francisco, CA: Jossey Bass.

Brown, P. G., Roediger, H. L., & McDaniel, M. A. (2014). *Making it stick: The science of successful learning*. Cambridge, MA: Harvard University Press.

Butler, A. C. (2010). Repeated testing produces superior transfer of learning relative to repeated studying. *Journal of Experimental Psychology: Learning, Memory, and Cognition*, 36, 1118–1133. doi.org/10.1037/a0019902

Campbell, J. P., & Wiernik, B. M. (2015). The modeling and assessment of work performance. *Annual Review of Organizational Psychology and Organizational Behavior*, 2, 47–74. doi.org/10.1146/annurev-orgpsych-032414-111427

Cepeda, N. J., Pashler, H., Vul, E., Wixted, J. T., & Rohrer, D. (2006). Distributed practice in verbal recall tasks: A review and quantitative synthesis. *Psychological Bulletin*, 132(3), 354. doi.org/10.1037/0033-2909.132.3.354

Chiaburu, D. S., Van Dam, K., & Hutchins, H. M. (2010). Social support in the workplace and training transfer: A longitudinal analysis. *International Journal of Selection and Assessment*, 18(2), 187–200. doi.org/10.1111/j.1468-2389.2010.00500.x

Chiviacowsky, S., & Wulf, G. (2002). Self-controlled feedback: Does it enhance learning because performers get feedback when they need it? *Research Quarterly for Exercise and Sport*, 73(4), 408–415. doi.org/10.1080/02701367.2002.10609040

Chiviacowsky, S., & Wulf, G. (2007). Feedback after good trials enhances learning. *Research Quarterly for Exercise and Sport*, 78(2), 40–47. doi.org/10.1080/02701367.2007.10599402

Choi, M., & Roulston, K. (2015). Learning transfer in practice: A qualitative study of medical professionals' perspectives. *Human Resource Development Quarterly*, 26(3), 249–273. doi.org/10.1002/hrdq.21209

Denham, A. R. (2018). Using a digital game as an advance organizer. *Educational Technology Research and Development*, 66(1), 1–24. doi.org/10.1007/s11423-017-9537-y

DeCecco, J. P. (1968). *The psychology of learning and instruction: Educational psychology*. Englewood Cliffs, NJ: Prentice Hall.

Donovan, J. J., & Radosevich, D. J. (1999). A meta-analytic review of the distribution of practice effect: Now you see it, now you don't. *Journal of Applied Psychology*, 84(5), 795. doi.org/10.1037/0021-9010.84.5.795

Driskell, J. E., Willis, R. P., & Copper, C. (1992). Effect of overlearning on retention. *Journal of Applied Psychology*, 77(5), 615. doi.org/10.1037/0021-9010.77.5.615

Dunlosky, J., & Hertzog, C. (2001). Measuring strategy production during associative learning: The relative utility of concurrent versus retrospective reports. *Memory & Cognition*, 29(2), 247–253. doi.org/10.3758/BF03194918

Dunlosky, J., Rawson, K. A., Marsh, E. J., Nathan, M. J., & Willingham, D. T. (2013). Improving students' learning with effective learning techniques: Promising directions from cognitive and educational psychology. *Psychological Science in the Public Interest*, 14(1), 4–58. doi.org/10.1177/1529100612453266

Fontana, F. E., Furtado Jr, O., Mazzardo, O., & Gallagher, J. D. (2009). Whole and part practice: A meta-analysis. *Perceptual and Motor Skills*, 109(2), 517–530. doi.org/10.2466/pms.109.2.517-530

Ford, J. K., Baldwin, T. T., & Prasad, J. (2018). Transfer of training: The known and the unknown. *Annual Review of Organizational Psychology and Organizational Behavior*, 5, 201–225. doi.org/10.1146/annurev-orgpsych-032117-104443

Ford, J. K., Quiñones, M. A., Sego, D. J., & Sorra, J. S. (1992). Factors affecting the opportunity to perform trained tasks on the job. *Personnel Psychology*, 45(3), 511–527. doi.org/10.1111/j.1744-6570.1992.tb00858.x

Ford, J. K., Yelon, S. L., & Billington, A. Q. (2011). How much is transferred from training to the job? The 10% delusion as a catalyst for thinking about transfer. *Performance Improvement Quarterly*, 24, 7–24. doi.org/10.1002/piq.20108

Friedman, S., & Ronen, S. (2015). The effect of implementation intentions on transfer of training. *European Journal of Social Psychology*, 45(4), 409–416. doi.org/10.1002/ejsp.2114

Gingerich, K. J., Bugg, J. M., Doe, S. R., Rowland, C. A., Richards, T. L., Tompkins, S. A., & McDaniel, M. A. (2014). Active processing via write-to-learn assignments: Learning and retention benefits in introductory psychology. *Teaching of Psychology*, 41(4), 303–308. doi.org/10.1177/0098628314549701

Gist, M. E., Bavetta, A. G., & Stevens, C. K. (1990). Transfer training method: Its influence on skill generalization, skill repetition, and performance level. *Personnel Psychology*, 43(3), 501–523. doi.org/10.1111/j.1744-6570.1990.tb02394.x

Gollwitzer, P. M., & Sheeran, P. (2006). Implementation intentions and goal achievement: A meta-analysis of effects and processes. *Advances in Experimental Social Psychology*, 38, 69–119. doi.org/10.1016/S0065-2601(06)38002-1

Goodman, J. S., Wood, R. E., & Hendrickx, M. (2004). Feedback specificity, exploration, and learning. *Journal of Applied Psychology*, 89(2), 248. doi.org/10.1037/0021-9010.89.2.248

Grabowski, B. L. (2004). Generative learning contributions to the design of instruction and learning. *Handbook of Research on Educational Communications and Technology*, 2, 719–743.

Hall, K. G., Domingues, D. A., & Cavazos, R. (1994). Contextual interference effects with skilled baseball players. *Perceptual and Motor Skills*, 78(3), 835–841. doi.org/10.1177/003151259407800331

Hattie, J., & Timperley, H. (2007). The power of feedback. *Review of Educational Research*, 77(1), 81–112. doi.org/10.3102/003465430298487

Huang, J. L., Ford, J. K., & Ryan, A. M. (2017). Ignored no more: Within-person variability enables better understanding of training transfer. *Personnel Psychology*, 70(3), 557–596. doi.org/10.1111/peps.12155

Hutchins, H., & Burke, L. A. (2006). Has relapse prevention received a fair shake? – A review and implications for future transfer research. *Human Resource Development Review*, 15, 8–24. doi.org/10.1177/1534484305284316

Johnson, S. K., Garrison, L. L., Hernez-Broome, G., Fleenor, J. W., & Steed, J. L. (2012). Go for the goal (s): Relationship between goal setting and transfer of training following leadership development. *Academy of Management Learning & Education*, 11(4), 555–569. doi.org/10.5465/amle.2010.0149

Kang, S. H., & Pashler, H. (2012). Learning painting styles: Spacing is advantageous when it promotes discriminative contrast. *Applied Cognitive Psychology*, 26(1), 97–103. doi.org/10.1002/acp.1801

Karpicke, J. D. (2009). Metacognitive control and strategy selection: Deciding to practice retrieval during learning. *Journal of Experimental Psychology: General*, 138(4), 469. doi.org/10.1037/a0017341

Karpicke, J. D., & Blunt, J. R. (2011). Retrieval practice produces more learning than elaborative studying with concept mapping. *Science*, 331(6018), 772–775. doi.org/10.1126/science.1199327

Keith, N., & Frese, M. (2005). Self-regulation in error management training: Emotion control and metacognition as mediators of performance effects. *Journal of Applied Psychology*, 90(4), 677. doi.org/10.1037/0021-9010.90.4.677

Keith, N., & Frese, M. (2008). Effectiveness of error management training: A meta-analysis. *Journal of Applied Psychology*, 93(1), 59. doi.org/10.1037/0021-9010.93.1.59

Kluger, A. N., & DeNisi, A. (1998). Feedback interventions: Toward the understanding of a double-edged sword. *Current Directions in Psychological Science*, 7(3), 67–72.

Kornell, N., & Bjork, R. A. (2008b). Learning concepts and categories: Is spacing the "enemy of induction"? *Psychological Science*, 19, 585–592. doi. org/10.1111/j.1467-9280.2008.02127.x

Larsen, D. P., Butler, A. C., & Roediger III, H. L. (2009). Repeated testing improves long-term retention relative to repeated study: A randomised controlled trial. *Medical Education*, 43(12), 1174–1181. doi. org/10.1111/j.1365-2923.2009.03518.x

Larsen, D. P., Butler, A. C., Lawson, A. L., & Roediger, H. L. (2013a). The importance of seeing the patient: Test-enhanced learning with standardized patients and written tests improves clinical application of knowledge. *Advances in Health Sciences Education*, 18(3), 409–425. doi. org/10.1007/s10459-012-9379-7

Larsen, D. P., Butler, A. C., & Roediger III, H. L. (2013b). Comparative effects of test-enhanced learning and self-explanation on long-term retention. *Medical Education*, 47(7), 674–682. doi. org/10.1111/medu.12141

Lawani, K., Hare, B., & Cameron, I. (2014). Skill decay of wind turbine technicians in the use of rescue and evacuation device during emergency. In *Proceedings from CIB W099 international conference achieving sustainable construction health and safety* (pp. 537–553). Lund, Sweden: International Council for Research & Innovation in Building & Construction.

Marx, R. D.(2000). Transfer is personal: Equipping trainees with self-management and relapse prevention strategies. In E. F. Holton, T. T. Baldwin, & S. S. Naquin (Eds.), *Advances in Developing Human Resources*. pp. 36–48). San Francisco, CA: Berrett-Koehler

Massman, A. J. (2012). *Improving third generation learning: The effects of peer feedback training on quality feedback, trainee characteristics, and performance*. Dissertation, Michigan State University, Psychology.

Mayer, R. E. (1979). Can advance organizers influence meaningful learning? *Review of Educational Research*, 49(2), 371–383.

Mayer, R. E., & Bromage, B. K. (1980). Difference recall protocols for technical texts due to advance organizers. *Journal of Educational Psychology*, 72(2), 209. doi. org/10.1037/0022-0663.72.2.209

Milne, S., Orbell, S., & Sheeran, P. (2002). Combining motivational and volitional interventions to promote exercise participation: Protection motivation theory and implementation intentions. *British Journal of Health Psychology*, 7(2), 163–184. doi.org/10.1348/135910702169420

Moore, J. P., Venters, C., & Carbonetto, T. (2017, June). *The retention and usefulness of concept maps as advance organizers*. In *Proceedings of the annual ASEE conference & exposition*, Columbus, OH.

Morgan, G. (2011). Reflections on images of organization and its implications for organization and environment. *Organization & Environment*, 24(4), 459–478. doi.org/10.1177/1086026611434274

Moulton, C. A. E., Dubrowski, A., MacRae, H., Graham, B., Grober, E., & Reznick, R. (2006). Teaching surgical skills: What kind of practice makes perfect?: A randomized, controlled trial. *Annals of Surgery*, 244(3), 400. doi.org/10.1097/01. sla.0000234808.85789.6a

Nguyen, C. (2018). *Learning not to take the bait: An examination of training methods and overlearning on phishing susceptibility*. Dissertation, University of Oklahoma Graduate College.

Richland, L. E., Kornell, N., & Kao, L. S. (2009). The pretesting effect: Do unsuccessful retrieval attempts enhance learning? *Journal of Experimental Psychology: Applied*, 15(3), 243. doi.org/10.1037/a0016496

Rogers, W. A., Rousseau, G. K., & Fisk, A. D. (1999). Applications of attention research. In F. T. Durso, R. S. Nickerson, R. W. Schvaneveldt, S. T. Dumais, D. S. Lindsay, & M. T. H. Chi (Eds.), *Handbook of applied cognition* (pp. 33–55). New York: John Wiley & Sons.

Roediger III, H. L., & Butler, A. C. (2011). The critical role of retrieval practice in long-term retention. *Trends in Cognitive Sciences*, 15(1), 20–27. doi.org/10.1016/j. tics.2010.09.003

Roediger III, H. L., Putnam, A. L., & Smith, M. A. (2011). Ten benefits of testing and their applications to educational practice. In *Psychology of learning and motivation* (Vol. 55, pp. 1–36). Academic Press. doi.org/10.1016/B978-0-12-387691-1.00001-6

Schaefer, P. S., Shadrick, S. B., Beaubien, J., & Crabb, B. T. (2008). *Training effectiveness assessment of Red Cape: Crisis action planning of execution* (Research Report 1885). Arlington, VA: U.S. Army Research Institute for the Behavioral and Social Sciences.

Schendel, J. D., & Hagman, J. D. (1982). On sustaining procedural skills over a prolonged retention interval. *Journal of Applied Psychology*, 67(5), 605. doi. org/10.1037/0021-9010.67.5.605

Schmidt, R. A., & Wulf, G. (1997). Continuous concurrent feedback degrades skill learning: Implications for training and simulation. *Human Factors*, 39(4), 509–525. doi. org/10.1518/001872097778667979

Sherbourne, C. D., & Stewart, A. L. (1991). The MOS social support survey. *Social Science & Medicine*, 32(6), 705–714. doi:10.1016/0277-9536(91)90150-B

Shantz, A., & Latham, G. P. (2012). Transfer of training: Written self-guidance to increase self-efficacy and interviewing performance of job seekers. *Human Resource Management*, 51(5), 733–746. doi.org/10.1002/hrm.21497

Steelman, L. A., & Rutkowski, K. A. (2004). Moderators of employee reactions to negative feedback. *Journal of Managerial Psychology*, 19(1), 6–18. doi. org/10.1108/02683940410520637

Van der Kleij, F. M., Feskens, R. C., & Eggen, T. J. (2015). Effects of feedback in a computer-based learning environment on students' learning outcomes: A meta-analysis. *Review of Educational Research*, 85(4), 475–511. doi. org/10.3102/0034654314564881

van der Locht, M., van Dam, K., & Chiaburu, D. S. (2013). Getting the most of management training: The role of identical elements for training transfer. *Personnel Review*, 42(4), 422–439. doi. org/10.1108/PR-05-2011-0072

Wang, X., Day, E. A., Kowollik, V., Schuelke, M. J., & Hughes, M. G. (2013). Factors influencing knowledge and skill decay after training: A meta-analysis. In W. Arthur Jr., E. A. Day, A. J. Villado, R. M. Glaze, & Schuelke, M. J. (Eds.), *Individual and team skill decay* (pp. 92–140). New York: Routledge.

Weinberg, R. (2008). Does imagery work? Effects on performance and mental skills. *Journal of Imagery Research in Sport and Physical Activity*, 3, 1–21. doi. org/10.2202/1932-0191.1025

Wittrock, M. C. (1990). Generative processes of comprehension. *Educational Psychologist*, 24, 345–376. doi. org/10.1207/s15326985ep2404_2

Yelon, S. L., Ford, J. K., & Anderson, W. A. (2014). Twelve tips for increasing transfer of training from faculty development programs. *Medical Teacher*, 36(11), 945–950. doi.org/10.3109/0142159X.2014.929098

Yelon, S., Sheppard, L., Sleight, D., & Ford, J. K. (2004). Intention to transfer: How do autonomous professionals become motivated to use new ideas? *Performance Improvement Quarterly*, 17(2), 82–103. doi.org/10.1111/j.1937-8327.2004.tb00309.x

Yelon, S. L. (2012). *Goal-directed instructional design.* Author.

Yelon, S. L., Ford, J. K., & Golden, S. (2013). Transfer over time: Stories about transfer years after training. *Performance Improvement Quarterly*, 25(4), 43–66. doi. org/10.1002/piq.21131

Evaluation and Continuous Improvement

■ ■ ■ ■ ■ ■

Questions

✓ What questions should an evaluation plan address?
✓ What are the advantages and disadvantages of different evaluation research designs?
✓ How can evaluation data be used to support the continuous improvement of learning approaches?

As shown in the Learning Systems Model from Chapter 1, after the needs assessment process and the learning needs are determined, an important step is to decide what learning intervention (training, developmental experiences, coaching, autonomous learning) would be most appropriate to meeting the learning need. Once this is determined, the next step is to set learning objectives. Based on those objectives a plan for learning can emerge.

A parallel process with the setting of learning objectives and a learning plan is the development of an evaluation plan. Evaluation is the systematic collection of descriptive and judgmental information necessary to allow for effective decisions related to the selection, adoption, value, and modification of learning interventions. Evaluation can lead to a decision to retain or eliminate a learning opportunity but more likely it provides the information to revise a program to better meet the learning goals for subsequent participants. An evaluation plan should answer three key questions: (1) what is the purpose of the evaluation, (2) what evaluation data needs to be collected to be informative to decision makers, and (3) what is the appropriate intensity or complexity of the evaluation plan? The chapter describes each of these three questions regarding evaluation of being purposeful, informative, and proportionate (PIP!). The final section of the chapter examines evaluation as part of a continuous improvement strategy.

PURPOSEFUL

Evaluation is more than determining if a learning approach "worked" or did not "work." A whole host of questions can be answered between those two extremes. Being purposeful is identifying the evaluation question that needs to be answered. There are five questions that can be addressed by an evaluation plan to understand what is happening relevant to the investment in learning. Table 6.1 presents these questions along with the types of information needed to address the question asked.

Relevance

Job relevancy is the extent to which the learning content covered (tasks, knowledge, skills, behaviors) adequately reflect learner needs given the results of the needs assessment process. While a strong needs assessment should lead to a learning intervention high on job relevancy, it is also possible that there can be a disconnect between what was uncovered during the needs assessment process and what is delivered. Clearly, when a needs assessment is not completed or is inadequate, there is an increase in the possibility that the learning intervention developed might be low on relevancy. In addition, a learning program that starts out high in job relevancy might have become less job relevant over time as the program is modified by different instructors or coaches or does not keep pace with changes in job requirements or technological advances. Two strategies for exploring issues of relevancy are provided next.

TABLE 6.1   Purposes for Evaluation

Purpose	Question	Approach
Relevancy	To what extent is the content of the learning program relevant to job performance?	Content validity (content validity ratio) Ratings of job relevancy
Appropriate Emphasis	To what extent does the learning process have the appropriate degree of emphasis on the different aspects or components to be learned?	Matching technique
Learning Validity	To what extent have the learners met the standards set for the learning objectives?	Knowledge outcomes Skill outcomes Affective outcomes
Transfer Validity	To what extent have the learners applied the knowledge, skill, and affective outcomes on the job?	Use Behavior Performance effectiveness
Organizational Payoff	To what extent have the performance improvements from a learning intervention led to bottom line results for the organization?	Return on investment Success case method

CONTENT VALIDITY One way of measuring job relevancy is through a content validity approach. Content validity is an evaluation of the representativeness or adequacy of sampling the content domain of a job. A visual representation of a content validity approach within the learning space is presented in Figure 6.1. In this figure, the horizontal axis across the top of the figure represents the dimension of importance, or criticality, of the knowledge and skills as determined by a needs assessment. Although the diagram only presents knowledge and skills as being important or not important, it is vital to realize that this is an oversimplification as the dimension has many intermediate points on the scale. The vertical dimension represents whether a knowledge or skill is included in training or other type of learning approach.

This results in the fourfold table with boxes A and C providing support for the content validity of the learning intervention. Knowledge and skills that fall into box A are judged as being important for the job and are included in the learning program while items in box C are judged as not important for the job and are not included. Box B represents knowledge and skills that are included but are not important for the job. This type of content may be "nice to know" but is not essential. Box D represents an error as the knowledge and skills falling into this category are judged as important for the job but are not included in the learning program. From a systems perspective, it is possible that individuals selected for the job are already expected to have knowledge and skills identified in Box D.

The degree of content validity can be quantified. In an examination of a police officer training program, an approach was developed: (1) to determine the extent to which the training content of the existing courses were job related; and (2) to identify needed changes in training content to improve the job relatedness of the program (Ford & Wroten, 1984). These investigators identified

FIGURE 6.1 Relevancy of Learning Content.

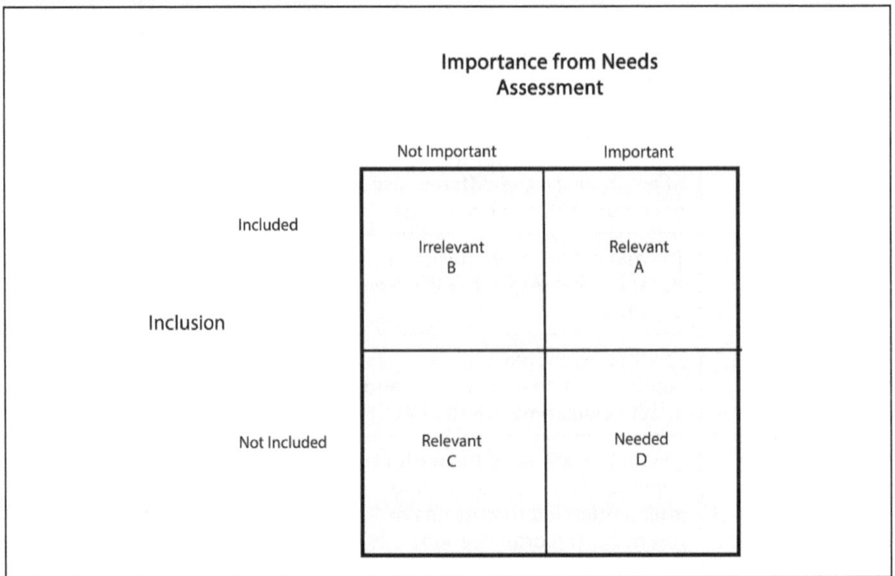

Source: Adapted from Goldstein, I. L., & Ford, J. K. (2002). Training in organizations: Needs assessment, development, and evaluation, 4th ed., Wadsworth, Belmont, CA.

383 knowledge and skills incorporated into a police training program for entry-level officers and an additional 57 knowledge and skills identified as part of the job. They then had 114 experts independently rate the importance of each of the 440 items (383 included in the training program and the additional 57 knowledge and skills). For the first objective of the research, they determined the job relevancy of the trained content. They discovered that 237, or 62%, of the knowledge and skills in the program were rated by experts as being important to cover for initial job performance. Thus, the training program was deemed to have a moderate degree of content validity. To meet the second objective of the project, training designers examined the knowledge and skills that were not seen as important for job performance but were included in the training program to determine whether they should remain in the program. Based on this analysis, some content was eliminated or de-emphasized in the program. In addition, in a separate analysis of the job performance domain, these investigators also examined the 57 knowledge and skills that were part of the job but not included in the training program. A few of those items were judged to be trainable and important, and they were thus added to the program – others were identified as being more appropriate for on-going development on the job through the initial on-the-job coaching and subsequent on-the-job training.

This study shows a systematic approach to examining content validity issues as well as the use of evaluation data to increase its job relevancy. The use of the content validity approach has expanded recently to evaluate the content validity of a team designed training manual (Erdem, 2009). In another case, an assessment instrument for health care providers was used after training to determine the level of knowledge of legal issues and appropriate care responses. The assessment items retained for the instrument were based on expert ratings of the content validity of knowledge questions (Kovacic, 2018).

RATINGS OF JOB RELEVANCE A direct and less expensive (but potentially less robust) strategy is to ask learners directly about the job relevancy of the program that they have just experienced. Learner reactions to a learning event such as training has a long history of study and the ratings are often a critical factor in the continuance of a program. Morgan and Casper (2000) examined the multidimensionality of reaction measures taken from over 9,000 employees of a government agency collected over three years across a variety of training programs including 800 classes for 400 different courses. Statistical analyses revealed six different groupings or dimensions from the ratings of the courses including satisfaction with the instructor, satisfaction with the training management process, testing process, materials used, course structure, and the job relevancy of the program. Another study grouped learner reactions into three categories of learner enjoyment, job relevance, and satisfaction with the technology interface (Brown, 2005). A few sample items for each of these three categories are included in Table 6.2 to gain a feel for what types of participant reaction items make up each grouping.

Evidence indicates that the job relevancy items are most predictive of what is actually learned and transferred to the job. One study found a significant relationship between perceptions of job relevancy and a post-training knowledge test while the learners' enjoyment of the course and their satisfaction with the delivery of content had no relationship with the level of knowledge gained (Brown, 2005). A meta-analytic study examining changes

TABLE 6.2 Categories Reflecting Participant Reactions

Enjoyment
Instructor engaged participants and holds their interest.
Learning this material was fun.
I enjoyed the instruction.

Relevance
The course content was relevant to my job.
The course prepared me to perform my job tasks.
The instructor provided useful examples and illustrations of applications to the job.

Technology Satisfaction
The instructor made effective use of audio and visual aids in the course.
The technology interface was easy to use.
I am satisfied with the how the technology was used to complement the course instruction.

Sources: Adapted from Brown, K. (2005), An examination of the structure and nomological network of trainee reactions: A closer look at "smile sheets". Journal of Applied Psychology, 90, 991–1001; Morgan, R.B. & Casper, W. (2000). Examining the factor structure of participant reactions to training: A multidimensional approach. Human Resources Development Quarterly, 11, pp. 301–317.

in declarative knowledge and procedural knowledge (pre- and post-tests) as a function of training revealed that job relevance ratings were somewhat predictive of learning outcomes (Sitzmann et al., 2008). Ratings of relevancy for specific modules or learning objectives (rather than just overall ratings of relevancy for a complete course) can be quite useful in pointing to potential areas for improvement in the current program.

Emphasis

The analysis of relevancy provides information if the content of the learning program captures the more important knowledge and skills to be learned. One step beyond this is to determine if the learning program provides the appropriate level of emphasis to the knowledge and skills to be learned.

Figure 6.2 presents a conceptual model of a matching technique approach in which the learning emphasis given to tasks, knowledge, and skills in a program is directly compared to the learning needs. The comparison of emphasis with needs leads to the identification of learning content "hits" and "misses." Hits refer to those areas (tasks, knowledge or skills) where the emphasis received in a learning program appropriately reflects their level of importance for job performance. Misses are of two types – deficiencies and excesses. Deficiencies are areas whose level of job importance is not matched by a similar degree of emphasis in the program. Excesses are areas receiving an excessive amount of emphasis in the program relative to their job importance.

An example of this approach is illustrated with a technical training course offered in the U.S. Air Force (Teachout, Sego, & Ford, 1997). They examined the extent to which training time was apportioned consistent with the difficulty of learning. An analysis found that 12 of 33 tasks were considered potentially overtrained (excess) in that more time was being spent than warranted given the difficulty of learning the tasks. Perhaps even more importantly, six of the tasks were considered under-trained (deficiency) as less time was being spent on them than might be expected given their learning difficulty ratings. In

FIGURE 6.2   The Matching Technique and Training Emphasis.

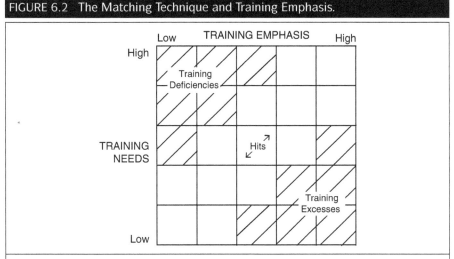

Source: Ford, J. K., & Wroten, S. P. (1984). Introducing new methods for conducting training evaluation and for linking training evaluation to program redesign. *Personnel Psychology*, 37(4), 651–665. Copyright: 1984 by John Wiley and Sons. Reprinted by permission.

addition, for the 12 overtrained tasks, the trainees averaged performing them approximately 18 times over an eight-month period. For the six under-trained tasks, trainees were given the opportunity to perform them only about two times on average over the course of 8 months on the job. Thus, not only was less training time devoted to these tasks, but the trainees had less opportunity to perform them when on the job. These findings suggest that the undertrained tasks were perhaps "nice to know" but not essential for the job. Supervisor rating of the trainee's effectiveness in performing these tasks showed that the highest effectiveness ratings were for those knowledge and skills where training time and transfer opportunities were the highest.

This analysis provides the information necessary to suggest revisions in both the training program itself as well as the design of learning opportunities on the job to produce more positive transfer to the job. Course efficiency can be improved by reducing training time for the overtrained tasks. One option for under-trained tasks would be eliminate them from training and instead make it more of a priority for on-the-job training. A similar type of analysis can also be completed for other learning opportunities such as ensuring that challenging job experiences provide the learner with ample opportunities to apply the knowledge and skills identified as critical to learn. Or, in a coaching situation, one can examine the extent to which the coach and learner interactions prioritize and spend the most time on critical knowledge and skill gaps.

Learning Validity

A program may have high job relevancy and the appropriate emphasis but not lead to the expected level of learning. Learning validity asks the question of whether the expected level of learning has occurred in relation to the standard or criterion of success specified in the learning objectives. Knowledge, skill-based, and affective outcomes can be the focus of an evaluation of learning validity. To have an effective evaluation plan, one must not only identify what to measure

TABLE 6.3 A Classification Scheme for Evaluating Learning		
Learning Constructs	**Measurement**	**Evaluation Methods**
Declarative Knowledge	Facts Concepts	Recognition (multiple choice Free recall
Procedural/Strategic Knowledge	Rules Procedures	Thinking out loud (If/then statements) Probing for strategies
Knowledge Organization	Relatedness of concepts in memory	Cognitive mapping and visualization
Skill Compilation	Speed and fluidity of performance Errors made	ObservationsJob simulations
Skill Expertise	Cognitive resources available Adaptability	Ability to multitask Handling non-routine situations
Attitudes	Attitude direction and strength	Self or other ratings Behavioral choices made
Motivation	Goal setting Self-efficacy	Self or other ratings

Source: Adapted from Applications of cognitive, skill-based, and affective theories of learning outcomes to new methods of training evaluation by K. Kraiger, J.K. Ford, and E. Salas (1993), 78, pp. 311–328. Copyright 1993 by American Psychological Association. Reprinted by permission.

but also how to measure the learning outcomes. Table 6.3 presents the constructs relevant to knowledge, skill, and affective learning outcomes one could be interested and examples of ways to measure each construct to evaluate validity.

The categories of knowledge constructs consist of verbal or declarative knowledge, knowledge organization (or mental maps), procedural knowledge, and cognitive strategies. For measuring declarative knowledge, a multiple-choice test (or free response) around the facts being learned may provide the information desired. If the level of procedural knowledge is what is important to capture in the evaluation, then questions can be asked that are more of a "if-then" basis. One study of a vigilance task evaluated the level of procedural knowledge on a simulation task by asking questions such as "if a target moves in this direction, what does that suggest about the target?" or "If a target characteristics are communication time of 20 seconds and speed of 60 knots, which action should you take" (Bell & Kozlowski, 2002, p. 288). For cognitive strategies, the measurement is around strategic knowledge especially around non-routine situations. Questions can also ask the learner to predict what will happen in different situations.

An evaluation can measure if learners' mental models have gotten stronger and more organized and drawing closer to the expert mental model. The more organized the mental model, the better able a person can describe and explain the what, how, and why surrounding job tasks resulting in higher levels of performance (Smith-Jentsch et al., 2001). Typically, to measure mental models, learners (and experts) complete ratings of how related different concepts or issues to be learned in a program are to one another (e.g., 1 = not related at all to 9 = very related). The relatedness ratings form the basis for generating the cognitive mapping of the concepts in terms of relatedness and those maps can be visualized and compared to capture improvement over time. In one study, the mental models of a skilled players of a computer gaming training program were found to be more organized around the game procedures with the gaming steps viewed in a more connected and streamlined way than those low skill individuals after the training (Day, Arthur, & Gettman, 2001). Figure 6.3 shows differences in models between a skilled player and a less skilled player after three days and nine training sessions with the game. The models were predictive of skill retention after four days of not practicing the skills of the game.

Proficiency is defined as the acquirement of a skill. Levels of skill proficiency can be measured to see progress over time moving from initial trial and error to skill compilation and skill automaticity. Those at the automatic stage can work on multiple task demands at the same time and can handle not only the routine situations but also adapt to nonroutine situations. To examine changes in skill level, one can have a learner complete the task in a simulated setting (hands-on performance) prior to and then at the end of a learning opportunity to gauge the extent of improvement. One study evaluated the acquired skills by surgery residents who had undergone virtual reality training for laparoscopic surgery training. The skill measure included completion time, errors made, and the economy of movement (Stefanidis et al., 2005). A follow-up study measured experts completing the laparoscopic procedure and determined that the experts completed the task within 70 s with no errors. Such information on skill proficiency was then used to compare the performance of the learners to measure their level of improvement over time on that procedure (Stefanidis et al., 2012).

Another component of measuring skill proficiency is the extent to which performance on a task becomes more consistent over time. For team training, one study measured team proficiency in terms of problem solving and task accomplishment. For problem solving, teams were given realistic military scenarios (e.g., solving an enemy code) with explicit time limits that were reduced as the team gained experience through the practice on different scenarios. For the physical tasks, teams were required to develop an action plan and accomplish 14 tasks in the allotted time to be considered meeting the proficiency objectives. Progress was measured in terms of solving problems at the same or higher level of effectiveness as the time limits were decreased over time during the evaluation (Hirschfeld et al., 2006).

Affective outcomes include attitudinal and motivational outcomes such as an individual's (or team) level of efficacy. One can certainly expect that a learning event such as a coaching session with an expert leads the learner to want to learn more about the subject matter addressed. In addition, a learning event such as a training program on safety hopefully leads to learners having more positive attitudes towards being safe that can be seen in the appropriate behavioral choices made once back on the job to reduce the risk of accidents. Another important affective outcome is that the learners perceive they have the capability to enact or apply the learning on the job. Post-training self-efficacy predicts performance in a transfer setting – even when taking into account the knowledge and skill gains made. High levels of self-efficacy help learners to be more resilient in the face of the added complexity and difficulty of the transfer

FIGURE 6.3   Mental Models of High and Low Skilled Trainees.

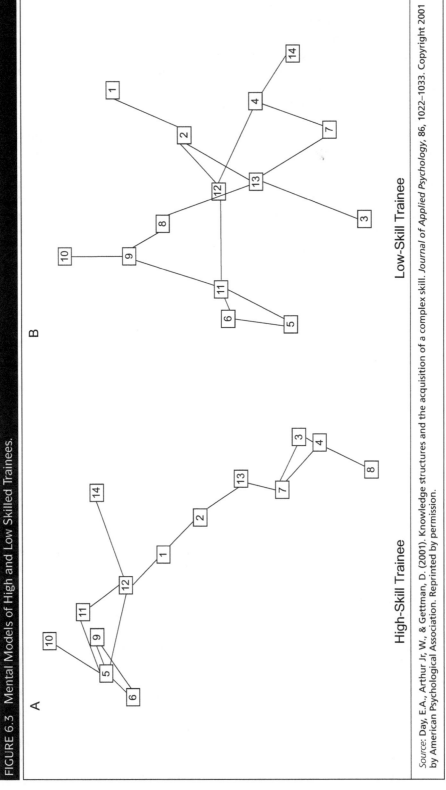

High-Skill Trainee

Low-Skill Trainee

Source: Day, E.A., Arthur Jr, W., & Gettman, D. (2001). Knowledge structures and the acquisition of a complex skill. *Journal of Applied Psychology*, 86, 1022–1033. Copyright 2001 by American Psychological Association. Reprinted by permission.

task (Ford et al., 1998). More generally, meta-analytic findings of over 430 studies show that motivational outcomes such as intentions to learn and the level of self-efficacy have strong effects on learning outcomes (Sitzmann & Ely, 2011).

The bottom line from Table 6.3 is that there are a variety of learning constructs and measurement options to evaluate learning validity. One size does not fit all learning activities. Yet, when I have been called in to help an organization do a better job of evaluating their suite of training programs, it is often the case that the exact same type of measure (e.g., multiple choice knowledge tests) is used regardless of if the focus of training is on open or closed skills or more oriented towards general or highly technical job knowledge. The classification scheme and evaluation measures point to the elements to consider in creating a more effective evaluation plan.

Transfer Validity

Transfer validity asks the question of what the learners are doing differently on the job after a learning event has been completed. There are two types of transfer outcomes that can be assessed. One assessment is to examine what the learner is using on the job now relevant to what is learned. A second level of assessment is the evaluation of performance changes as a function of what is learned. This assessment evaluates to what extent changes in job behavior are leading to improved performance effectiveness (Blume et al., 2010).

APPLICATION/USE   One transfer outcome is the extent to which the learner applies the knowledge and skills obtained to the job. Application or use means that the learner is doing something different while working on job tasks based on what was learned. Application involves more than just mimicking responses to situations presented in the learning intervention – it includes the extent to which learners exhibit new actions on the job in response to settings, people, and situations that may differ from those presented during the learning context. Use can also include less tangible things such as applying an idea or a principle from say a leadership development workshop in order to meet a work goal.

Learners can be asked direct questions about their use of what they learned on the job such as the specific knowledge, skills, tools, or principles taught. As one example, learners could be asked to state how many times in the past month they have used a piece of equipment that was part of a training program to reskill employees. Or learners can be asked to rate the extent to which trained interpersonal skills such as asking appropriate questions were applied "not at all" to "a great deal" on the job. Peers and supervisors can also provide similar types of application ratings about the learner.

The measurement of direct application on the job of what is learned is not a complete picture of use (Yelon, Ford & Bhatia, 2015). Based on structured interviews with learners either early (two years) or later (eight years) after multi-session learning workshops, a taxonomy of five types of use was identified. The five types are presented in Table 6.4. The taxonomy starts with direct use or application a knowledge and skill to the job. A second type of application includes learning from watching others on the job modeling what was taught in the learning experience to further hone one's skills. A third use is to explain ideas to others and encouraging them to adopt a knowledge and skill to their work. A fourth type of use is instructing others on knowledge and skills

TABLE 6.4	Transfer Validity and Types of Use		
Types of Use	**Behavioral and Content Features of Application**	**Relevant Conditions of Application**	**Purposes of Application**
1. Perform desired actions	*Plan and conduct* performance, as taught or adapted based on procedures and principles taught	When there is a need to plan or perform as part of ordinary duties, assigned or chosen	To positively influence the result of the desired performance
2. Assess desired actions	*Evaluate* applications based on taught standards	When deliberately sensing features or outcomes of one's own or other's desired performance	Formative: To discern what to keep, discard, or change in desired performance and to judge the effectiveness of desired performance
3. Explain learned ideas and applications	*Describe*, via conversation or publication, *methods*, principles, and applications based on teachings	When asked a relevant question, when voluntarily explaining one's actions, when advocating for a learned method, when stating relevant work expectations	To generate *understanding of learned methods,* to promote acceptance of *learned* methods, *to motivate* others to learn and use desired methods, to promote meeting performance expectations
3. Instruct to perform as desired	*Teach* how to apply methods and principles as taught or as applied	When asked to meet a work group's or individual's need to improve desired performance within or outside of one's organization	To enable *skilled use* of *desired methods* learned in training, to promote the use of the skill
4. Lead others to apply learned ideas	*Guide others to use* of methods and principles taught, by reminding how to apply, or by requiring application	As a designated leader or member, when at the start or in the *midst* of a relevant work task, or group project	To aid in successful *task completion* of application of the desired performance, changing norms, and improving work processes

Source: Yelon, S., Ford, J.K., & Bhatia, S. (2015). How trainees transfer what they have learned: Toward a taxonomy of use. *Performance Improvement Quarterly*, 27, 27–52. Copyright 2015 by John Wiley & Sons. Reprinted by permission.

gained in an intervention and helping them apply those to their job (a second generalization learning intervention!). A fifth type of use is when learners are in the position to lead teams to adopt a knowledge or skill by changing systems in their organization to be consistent with what was learned. There is empirical evidence supporting the five types of use (Ford, Bhatia, & Yelon, 2019).

JOB PERFORMANCE Performance is defined as behaviors that are evaluated in terms of the level of proficiency or contribution to the goals of the team, unit and organization (Campbell & Wiernik, 2015). Measuring performance requires the identification of which actions to target for evaluation and determining how to measure performance in a way that is an accurate reflection of the learner's level of job performance. As one example, medical professionals attended workshops to learn how to become more effective transmitters of knowledge to medical students and residents. The workshops covered principles of instruction, how to create lesson plans to teach skills, how to design and deliver effective lectures, how to conduct small meaningful group discussions, and how to teach in a clinical setting using variety of specific instructional techniques (Yelon et al., 2015). Performance evaluation requires measuring the extent to which learners are creating more effective lesson plans, delivering more effective lectures, facilitating more effective group discussions, and effectively delivering a "teachable moment" in a clinical setting. This effort requires identifying the performance dimensions to evaluate (e.g., organized lectures), the scaling of performance to use (1 = not effective to 5 highly effective), and implementing a plan for how to evaluate (e.g., student ratings as well as trained observer ratings).

Performance can also be measured through more standardized and objective evaluations. In work with a truck safety commission, my colleagues were asked to evaluate the effectiveness of a driving safety initiative. The program consisted of two main parts. First, truck drivers were given a skill assessment consisting of having a trained observer in the cab and rating the driver who completed a pre-designed route containing seventeen distinct driving segments. These segments were of approximately the same length requiring the driver to perform specific driving tasks (e.g., changing lanes, merging, making a turn). In each of these segments, observers evaluated trainees' performance in four areas: search, speed control, direction control, and overall accident reduction. Trainees were rated as either satisfactory or unsatisfactory based on well-defined performance criteria (Vanosdall, 1993). Observers provided a total of 68 ratings (17 segments × 4 ratings) for each trainee, and these ratings served as the material for the feedback session between the observer and the truck driver. For phase two, the drive attended a daylong defensive driving training program that discussed strategies for reducing the probability of an accident occurring on the road. Issues covered included situational awareness and close calls, how driving tasks and driving behaviors are interrelated, and the connection of search, speed, direction control, and timing. After a few months back on the job, the drivers were assessed by driving the same route with a different observer to determine changes in performance from the initial assessment due to the feedback and training program. The results showed on overall performance improvement gain of 12% across the four dimensions. A stringent criterion of showing satisfactory performance in each area across all of the route segments (all ratings) showed that the number of drivers meeting this high bar improved. For example 35% of drivers met the performance standard for direction and control of the truck prior to the feedback and training program and 57% of the drivers achieved that high level in the subsequent performance assessment.

Organizational Payoff

An important consideration beyond performance in an evaluation plan is the economic impact of changes in performance. Managerial decision makers are often attuned to monetary considerations. When a production manager requests a new piece of equipment or the need for more resources, the request must be supported by showing the projected increases in productivity or decreases in unit cost of production to validate the need for the purchase. In terms of learning, this would require translating learning and transfer validity data into dollar values.

Return on investment (ROI) methods are used to determine how much value a program is providing and whether the learning program is worth the investment. Such an analysis is based on two premises: (1) that the measures of ROI can lead to more rational and productive choices about learning interventions; and (2) the measures can convince others to believe and thus support the conclusions of such an analysis (Boudreau & Ramstad, 2003). Although ROI can be calculated in different ways, it is at its most basic a number (stated as a percentage value) representing how much benefit is gained by having a particular program given the amount of effort put into implementing the program. A common way of calculating ROI is to create a percentage by dividing the benefits of a program by its costs and multiplying by 100 (Phillips, 2011):

$$\text{ROI}(\%) = \frac{\text{Net Program Benefits}}{\text{Program Costs}} \times 100$$

For formal training programs, costs include such things as materials used to deliver the training, amount paid to instructors, money lost due to removing training participants from their jobs, overhead costs, and travel costs to attend training off site. Benefits include performance gains that impact the bottom line. As one case example, a company that conducted a sales training program estimated that the return from the training in terms of increased sales led to a net benefit after costs were covered of $1.95 for every dollar spent on the program (Phillips, 2011). A study of the ROI for workplace wellness programs was found to range from $1.81 to $6.15 for every dollar spent in terms of improved worker health, reduced benefit expense, and enhanced productivity (Cascio, 2007).

Because different types of costs and benefits can be factored into an ROI estimate, there exist many different approaches to measuring ROI. Regardless of the approach, the key criteria are the need for sound practices, simplicity in calculations, and economical ways of measuring relevant variables. Phillips (2011) provides an approach to calculating ROI. The framework encourages conservatism to ensure that ROI estimates remain credible and do not overestimate benefits. The basic steps of the approach are to (1) develop an evaluation plan, (2) measure benefits related to training at different "levels" (i.e., their learning of knowledge and skills, changes in their behavior, and impact of those changes on organizational performance), and (3) estimate ROI based on the data collected. When records cannot be used to calculate exact monetary values for various costs and benefits, expert opinion (if high level of agreement across experts) can be used to derive estimates. One aspect in which this approach is unique is the emphasis on isolating the effects of learning (rather than other factors) for calculating ROI benefits. This is best done thorough research using a control group but can still be accomplished in a credible manner with other research designs including quasi experimental analyses (see below for discussion of research design issues). The measurement can also include indirect costs/benefits and of intangible benefits. Indirect costs include things like the time and money that it takes to develop trainers or coaches for the program. Intangibles are typically things that are difficult to measure or difficult to convert into monetary values such as stress reduction and a reduction in customer complaint. Phillips cautions that ROI studies should be conducted very selectively – perhaps as few as 5% of all learning programs and solutions delivered by an organization can be credibly evaluated in this way. The most logical programs to consider putting in the effort to calculate ROI are those that are strategically focused, expensive, high profile, and controversial where there is the potential to collect the type of data (e.g., reduction in medical errors) that will be seen by key decision makers as highly credible.

The Success Case Method (SCM) is a specific approach for determining whether the changes intended by a program were achieved (Brinkerhoff, 2005). The method attempts to understand how individuals are changing their behavior as a result of what they learned and using this data to estimate the dollar-value of the results achieved from those changes. There are two major steps of this approach. The first is to identify "success cases" among those who have completed a program. Success is based on outcomes that the training program is expected to produce. This step is most often accomplished through surveys but can also be done using records about who is performing well. One can also use the results from this step to estimate how many people are achieving success as a result of the training. The second step is to collect case study information from a select group of people who are identified as successful. Interviews are commonly used to target statements about bottom line impacts of the successful application of the training. The information provides a rich picture about how people are achieving successful results as contrasted with the people who are unsuccessful. A limitation of this methodology is that it is based on "critical incidents" that are self-reports of behavior not actual behavior observed by an unbiased third party. Therefore, success case method depends on the accuracy of people's ability to understand situations and remember their experiences and on the accuracy of their judgements as to the dollar value of improvement reported as a function of the success stories.

INFORMATIVE

Once the purpose of evaluation has been determined, then the appropriate measures can be developed. The data collected must be of high enough quality to be of use to decision makers. Once collected, decision makers can interpret the information and make informed choices regarding program retention, resource allocation, and modifications. This section describes evaluation from the perspective of the various stakeholders interested in the information from evaluation.

Evaluation and Stakeholders

It is important to identify who within the organization is interested in the results from the evaluation and what their expectations are. Perceptions of what data needs to be gathered and how to gather that information can differ among learning designers, trainers, learners, facilitators, learning managers, chief learning officers, and line managers. Some stakeholders may prefer qualitative data such as specific stories of transfer to the job while others may prefer quantitative data from observations, surveys or supervisory ratings. They may also differ in terms of expectations as to what level of knowledge gain and behavioral change is desired for an intervention to be considered successful Decision makers may also want specific recommendations based on the evaluation findings or may want to interpret the findings on their own. In other words, it pays to know what is expected out of the evaluation from key stakeholder groups prior to planning, developing, and implementing an evaluation plan.

To create value in the evaluation process, evaluators must build effective measures that have the potential to answer stakeholders' questions. Data gathered in the evaluation process remains data until it is interpreted and acted upon by decision makers. As noted by Kraiger and Surface (2017) "data does not create value, it's how you use it" (p. 22). Another issue they address is that value is not the same as the return on investment question. Instead, value derives from its importance or worth to the different stakeholder groups. Evaluation needs to be thought of as a transaction process in which the data collected helps decision makers get a better understanding of the expected and actual gains from a learning intervention. They rightfully urge evaluators to develop meaningful questions to address and meet stakeholder needs for timely and relevant information that can lead to actionable insights that create value for the organization. The next section focuses on the importance of having high quality measures as a prerequisite to effectively addressing stakeholder questions.

Quality of Measurement

Logically, we want any learning approach to be planned and delivered to meet learning objectives by developing the knowledge and skills needed to perform successfully on the job. Just as logically, to determine the degree of success in meeting learning goals, the information collected must be reliable and valid.

The fundamental question related to the development of criterion measures (such as measures of learning or transfer effectiveness) is the extent to which each measure captures what it is intended to capture. This is an issue of validity. Figure 6.4 presents a conceptual model of criterion measurement. The top circle in the figure shows what the ultimate or conceptual criterion is – what we are interested in measuring about an outcome from a learning intervention. The bottom circle represents our actual criterion or what the measure that has been created taps into that the evaluator has used. The question of criterion validity is represented by the intersection of the two circles (i.e., where the actual criterion measure captures what we want to capture in the conceptual criterion).

For example, a training program has been developed to enhance an individual's procedural knowledge and skill around troubleshooting electrical

FIGURE 6.4   Constructs of Criterion Validity, Deficiency and Contamination.

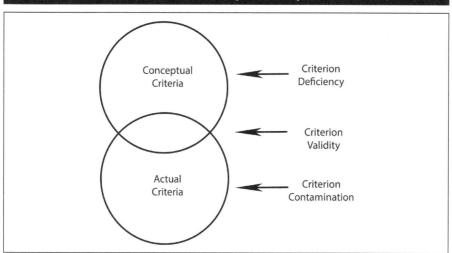

problems. To determine if learners have obtained the expected level or amount of procedural knowledge from the training, the evaluator constructs a test to measure the level of knowledge and skill gained. For the test, learners are given a problem to solve and asked to state out loud how they are solving the problem. A trained observer then rates the extent to which the learner articulates the procedural knowledge (if this happens then I should do…) required to solve the problem. The conceptual criterion is the level of troubleshooting knowledge and skill of the learner – that is, what we want to capture with our measurement. The test with observer ratings of the learner is the actual criterion. We are hoping that the ratings of knowledge is accurately assessing the true level of knowledge gained by the learner as a function of the training – which is the intersection of the conceptual and actual criterion.

While we hope for high levels of validity, the measure that is developed could also be deficient. A deficient measure does not assess all the knowledge or skills that make up the conceptual criteria. In the case of the troubleshooting task above, a deficiency in a learning measure would be if the training plan addressed eight key strategies for troubleshooting but the actual criterion measure used (perhaps due to cost considerations) only targeted four of those strategies in the assessment. If the intent of the training is to ensure that all eight strategies are learned then the current assessment could not tell the stakeholders if the learners had gained the requisite knowledge for the other four strategies.

Information obtained from the criterion measures used can also be affected by some degree of criterion contamination. Criterion contamination occurs when the measure used inaccurately represents the actual level of knowledge and skills of the learner. This can lead to incorrect conclusions as to the effectiveness of the learning approach – either pointing to success that was not actually present or pointing to failure when the approach was actually effective. For example, a supervisor who knows that the subordinates are attending a developmental experience may give them the benefit of the doubt when rating the extent to which they are applying the knowledge and skills gained to the job. This leniency bias may lead to overly optimistic conclusions by stakeholders that the developmental experience has been effectively transferred to the job when that is not the case. In terms of the troubleshooting example, the measure of procedural knowledge may capture other things beside the level of knowledge obtained by learners. Observers may have some biases such as rating older trainees lower than younger trainees. In this case, the ratings of the learner's procedural knowledge include factors not relevant to what we are hoping to measure. Or, observers may not take the ratings seriously and provide all learners with similar scores rather than distinguishing which learners gained the most from the experience resulting in criterion contamination.

It is therefore important as an evaluator to be aware of the potential dangers posed by criterion contamination issues. One way to evaluate the possibility of contamination is to examine the reliability of measurement. Let's assume that in the troubleshooting task that each learner is rated by two observers. If the two observers do not agree on the appropriate rating in terms of how well the person has been able to articulate the procedural knowledge or display the skills trained, we have a situation of low agreement leading to questions about which rater might be providing the more accurate rating. Reliability is a necessary condition – as you need stability in the measurement of a criterion – in order to have a chance for the measure to be valid. Training observers ahead of the evaluation would be helpful in ensuring raters are using the same standards when rating learners on the troubleshooting task. Of course, one could also carefully measure the wrong indicants of success (e.g., both raters have a similar bias) and end up with high reliability but low validity!

PROPORTIONATE

This section discusses the need for the evaluation plan to be realistic given learning needs and the capabilities of the organization to effectively create measures, design studies, analyze data and report findings. Organizations typically have a multitude of learning needs that vary in terms of how important the learning need is to the organization. Therefore, learning solutions should not be treated the same when it comes to the development of an evaluation plan. Organizations have limited budgets and resources that do not allow for extensive testing and evaluation of all learning initiatives. Choices must be made. Therefore, evaluation plans need to be proportionate given the priorities for learning and the available resources available for evaluation.

Choice Points

Evaluation efforts can be simple or complex. Learning priorities identified as critical to future organizational success would suggest a need for a well-designed pilot study that allows for revising the program before launching it to the broader organizational members. Similarly, learning interventions that have highly controversial content likely requires a fairly sophisticated evaluation system in place to determine how the content is being received. Programs to enhance the knowledge and skills of employees around tasks where mistakes or failures could have major consequences for the individual, team, and organization should have a formal evaluation process in place to make sure the targeted employees are transferring the learning to effective behaviors on the job. Learning oriented programs that will be attended by a large number of participants should also be the target of a strong evaluation plan – especially early in the rollout so changes can be made if needed to make the intervention stronger and more effective.

While things like strategic direction, controversy, consequences of error, and number of participants provide input into the seriousness an organization should pay to a strong evaluation plan, the other side of the ledger is the resources available that may constrain what is possible to do relevant to evaluation. Limited budgets often lead to a one-size-fits-all approach to evaluation where all programs are evaluated the same way – as this is highly efficient – but clearly not necessarily an effective way to approach evaluation. Victory is claimed that learning is now being evaluated by multiple choice questions across all programs – regardless if some programs focus more on skills than knowledge or that some programs require more intensive evaluation of learning!

Another issue of resources is the organization's commitment to hire individuals with competencies in evaluation science. Learning groups often have strong administrators, designers, and trainers but the team may have limited background in evaluation approaches, quantitative and qualitative methodologies or research design. This gap in competencies clearly limit what is possible to evaluate.

Collecting data on learning interventions takes a lot of time and energy. In addition, strong evaluations require the collection of timely and often extensive information about the learner and the work situation. If one wants to know if learners are applying certain knowledge and skills on the job after a learning event, people like managers or supervisors or peers must be asked to provide accurate assessments of the learners. Or, efforts must be devoted to obtaining objective job performance data both before and after the learning event to determine if change has occurred. Finally, there needs to be resources available to take appropriate action once evaluation data is collected and analyzed. A formal evaluation that leads to the need to make major changes may only lead to minor tinkering if there are limited resources to make changes in real time before the next groups of learners go through the same program.

People recognize that learning interventions should be evaluated. An awareness of the important factors in implementing an evaluation plan can help decision makers make appropriate choices and thus avoid a useless evaluation. The job of the evaluation team is to choose the most rigorous plan possible balancing the need with given existing constraints and limitations to maximize internal validity. Internal validity asks the basic question, did the intervention make a difference in this particular situation or are there alternative explanations for the results that cannot be ruled out given evaluation choices.

Threats to Internal Validity

Internal validity threats are variables, other than the learning intervention itself, that affect the findings and thus the interpretation of results. The solution is to control these variables by the evaluation design chosen so that they may be cast aside as competing explanations for any learning outcome effects found. Threats to internal validity include the following.

HISTORY History refers to specific events, other than the learning process itself that occurs at a similar time and provides a plausible alternative explanation for results. For instance, an instructional program designed to enhance positive attitudes toward safe practices at work may produce significant behavioral improvements that have no relationship to the program. Instead, a new incentive system put in place at the same time as the training that rewards safe behaviors could have been the major factor leading people to behave more safely. Or, a safety violation might lead to more managerial attention to safety and corrective actions. These actions provide an alternative explanation for the findings of success of a safety training program.

TESTING Testing refers to the influence of an assessment given (often called a pre-test) before the learning approach is started on the later post-learning scores. This is an especially serious problem for instructional programs in which the pre-test can sensitize the participant to the material. Improved performance on the post-test can occur simply by taking the pre-test and through self-study and asking for help without any intervening instructional program. While one might be pleased that people are demonstrating learning it might be inappropriate to assume that the instructional program itself was the cause of the success.

INSTRUMENTATION Instrumentation effects result from changes in measurement standards over time that affect the interpretation of evaluation findings. Observers who know the participants have gone through a learning experience may score the participants more harshly on the post-test than the pre-test observations. In this case, a rating given on the pre-test does not have the same meaning as the exact same rating on the post-test – as the rater's standards have changed. This is particularly a problem if you are asking the coach or on-the-job trainer who is working with the learner to assess skill improvement both before and after coaching experiences. Because rating scales are a commonly employed criterion in learning research, it is important to be sensitive to differences related to changes in the rater as an explanation for positive (or negative) findings rather than actual changes in the learner.

STATISTICAL REGRESSION Participants for additional learning and development opportunities are sometimes chosen on the basis of being seen as high potential. Or, participants with extremely low scores on a skills test are chosen for development. In these cases, a phenomenon known as statistical regression can occur. People who score at the extremes are likely to regress towards the middle of the scoring distribution on a second assessment. Learners with extremely high scores on a pre-test would tend to score somewhat lower on a second test and those with extremely low scores would tend toward higher scores on a second round of testing. This regression occurs because tests are not perfect measures (have some degree of unreliability) of the knowledge and skills that are intended to be measured. There will always be some change in scores from the first to the second testing simply because of this measurement error and has nothing to do with the extent of actual learning that is occurring. Because the first scores are at the extreme ends, the variability must move toward the center or the mean of the entire group with measurement error.

DIFFERENTIAL SELECTION OR LOSS OF PARTICIPANTS   The differential selection effect stems from the way persons are chosen to be part of learning and comparison groups. If volunteers are used in the instruction group and randomly chosen participants are used in the control group, differences could occur between the two groups simply because each group is different before the program began. Those volunteering may be more motivated to learn than the general population in the workplace. This high level of motivation can lead to high levels of knowledge and skill gains. Now if the organization mandates this training for all employees given the success of the first group, one may not find the same level of effect on learning. Loss of participants in the evaluation process also poses challenges to interpretation of results. If only highly motivated participants in the learning group complete a measure on transfer, the findings of successful transfer may not adequately represent the transfer of learning for the group as a whole.

PROGRAM INTEGRITY   Another issue relevant to internal validity is the integrity of the learning process itself. Oftentimes, the designer of a learning plan can be different from the person who delivers the intervention. Due to this, at times, there can be differences between the plan for instruction and the delivery of the content. There can also be differences across instructors as to how the program is implemented. My colleagues and I discovered that knowledge and skills around detective investigations were only being given passing reference for police recruits which was inconsistent with the emphasis given to this topic in the carefully designed plan of instruction. It turned out that over a period of time various trainers had modified the contents of the program and that new instructors based their instruction off of the last instructors' notes rather than going back to the original plan of instruction! Therefore, it is important to collect information about what actually happens during the delivery process and the extent to which the program delivered is consistent with the plan of instruction. In other cases, a program may be found to be delivered in many different ways across a global company making it difficult to determine the effectiveness of the planned intervention.

Evaluation Designs

Evaluation plans can provide answers to two questions: (1) does an evaluation of the various criteria indicate that a change in the learners have occurred; and (2) can the changes found be attributed to the learning intervention? Below we discuss frequently used evaluation designs. For convenience in presenting the designs, T1 represents the pre-test before learning, T2 the post-test, X the treatment or learning program, and R the random selection of participants into the research design groups. The designs presented are organized into several different categories to show the numerous approaches available. The first category includes case study designs that do not have control procedures and thus make it more difficult to specify cause-and-effect relationships. More formal evaluation designs, the second category, have varying degrees of power to control threats to validity. The third category includes quasi-experimental designs that are useful in many evaluation settings where investigators lack the opportunity to exert full control over who is given learning opportunities and who is not given those opportunities.

1. The Learner Post Assessment/Case Study Design:
   Learning Group   X   T2

   In this design, the learners are exposed to the instructional treatment (without a pre-test) and then are tested once at the completion of (or soon after) the learning experience. Without the pre-test, ascertaining any change (question 1) as a result of the learning from before to after the intervention is not possible. Just because learners might do well on a knowledge-based post-test does not mean that the learning plan and delivery led to those high scores (hence an internal validity threat!). This approach, though, can provide useful information. For example, I was asked to help examine a leadership development program that included mentoring from senior executives in between various training workshops. We conducted interviews with the learners three months after the learning intervention was completed and asked questions about transfer. Table 6.5 presents the interview protocol used to assess transfer. Notice that no measure of skills or behaviors was gathered prior to the workshops and thus it is a case study design. Nevertheless, some valuable information and very rich descriptions can stem from this type of an approach to evaluation. Such information provides input for how to modify the current program given participant stories about transfer. It is also important to note that a post-test is all you need for assessment if you are not interested in the degree of change but are solely interested in whether the learner meets the learning objectives or desired performance levels (Sackett & Mullen, 1993).

2. The Learner Pre- and Post-Assessment design:
   Learning Group   T1   X   T2

   When this design is employed, the learners are given a pre-test, presented with the instructional or learning program, and then given a post-test. This design is often used in training settings because it provides a measure of comparison between the same group of trainees before and after a learning opportunity. The design allows one to examine changes within the learner group (question 1). Without a control group (that does not go through the learning experience), it is difficult to clearly establish whether the learning intervention is the prime factor determining any differences that occur between the testing periods. Threats to validity as described above such as history, testing effects or regression to mean are not controlled for in this design.

   It is possible to strengthen this type of design without a control group through taking an internal referencing approach to evaluation (Haccoun & Hamtriaux, 1994). They examined a 45-hour management training program administered over eight weeks on human resources management issues such as communication, power relationships, leadership, and motivation. The course was evaluated in terms of knowledge gained on a multiple-choice test given both prior to and after training. The items written reflected those that were content valid and relevant to the knowledge conveyed in the course and knowledge items that were not covered in the course. The irrelevant

TABLE 6.5 Interview Protocol to Investigate Transfer

Let's first start with a short description of your job and the types of customers you work with before moving on to the discussion of the workshops.

What are your key job responsibilities?

Who are your major clients and how do you interact with them?

Now we will move on to talking about the Development Program and the application of the skills and tools to your job.

1. Pick one of the tools/skills you have found most useful to you on your job. Tell me about a time you used the tool/skill.
   a. Please describe the circumstances and nature of the specific incident.
   b. How did you use the tool/skill? – What specifically did you do in this situation?
   c. What was the outcome?
   d. What did you learn from this attempt to use the skill/tool? Did this experience change or affect how you have approached other similar situations?

2. Tell me about a time you tried to use a tool or skill, and then stopped using it.
   a. Please describe the circumstances and nature of the specific incident.
   b. What was the skill/tool and how did you use the tool/skill? – What specifically did you do in this situation?
   c. What was the outcome?
   d. What did you learn from this attempt to use the skill/tool? Did this experience change how you have approached other similar situations?

3. Tell me about a time where you used only a part of a skill/tool.
   a. Please describe the circumstances and nature of the specific incident.
   b. What was the skill/tool and how did you use the tool/skill? – What specifically did you do in this situation?
   c. What was the outcome?
   d. What did you learn from this attempt to use the skill/tool? Did this experience change how you have approached other similar situations?

4. What tools or skills have you not tried at all, and why?
   a. Please describe a skill/tool you would like to use but have not had the opportunity to use on the job – why have you not had the opportunity and do you foresee an opportunity in the future where you can use the skill/tool?
   b. Please identify a skill/tool where you had an opportunity to use but made a conscious decision not to use in that situation – why did you decide this was not an appropriate skill/tool to apply to that situation and what are the implications for future use?

5. Part of the Development Program included the application of the formal workshop principles between the workshops. How did the application process help you better understand or apply the tools?

   How could the application process be improved?

6. Is there any other information you would like to share about your experiences in the workshops and in applying the skills/tools from the workshop on your job?

items reflected elements that fit the overall theme of the course but simply were not covered. By using this approach, the effectiveness of the training program could be inferred if pre- and post-changes on the relevant items were found to be greater than the changes seen from pre-and post-testing for the irrelevant knowledge items. The outcome of their study is show in Figure 6.5. The increase in scores from the pre- and post-tests for the trained relevant items is much higher than increase in scores for the irrelevant items providing evidence that the training program was successful.

The internal referencing strategy has been used to evaluate the development of skills in a leadership training program (Frese, Beimel, & Schoenborn, 2003). The charismatic leadership program targeted enhancing leader communication skills around a strategic vision and strategy. The learners were videotaped giving a strategy focused message before and after the learning intervention. Trained raters evaluated the videotaped performances on the principles taught in the program and also on items that are relevant to being an effective public speaker but not explicitly taught in the program. The raters did not know whether the videos were completed prior to or after the training program. Two raters rated each video and the level of agreement of the trained raters was found to be strong. Learners showed significant improvement on the 12 principles taught and practiced while most of the irrelevant principles of public speaking did not show any improvement. The findings support the effectiveness of the workshop as well as demonstrating the usefulness of this evaluation approach whether targeting knowledge or skill gains.

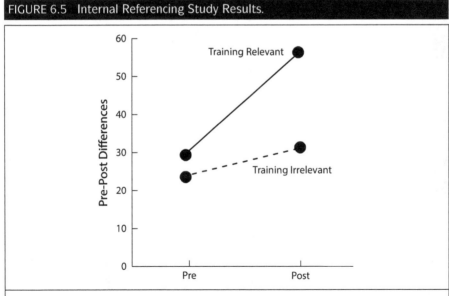

FIGURE 6.5 Internal Referencing Study Results.

Source: Adapted from Haccoun, R., & Hamtriaux, T. (1994). Optimizing knowledge tests for inferring learning acquisition levels in single group training evaluation designs: The internal referencing strategy. *Personnel Psychology*, 47, 593–604. Copyright: 1994 by John Wiley and Sons. Reprinted by permission.

3a. Pre-test/post-test control group design:
   Learning group   T1   X   T2
   Control group   T1   T2

   The specification of changes indicated by pre-measurement and post-measurement does provide useful information relevant to whether change has occurred. This next design adds in a control group, which helps to eliminate some possible explanations for any changes found for the learning group. If scores for the learning group improve from the two time periods but do not improve for the control group, the likely explanation is that the program was successful. Nevertheless, given lack of random assignment to the two types of groups, there could be internal validity threats due to selection of participations and regression to the mean.

3b. Pre-test/post-test control group design:
   Learning group (R)   T1   X   T2
   Control group (R)   T1   X   T2

   In this design, the two groups of participants are chosen at random (R) from the population (e.g., out of all engineers in a department) and assigned randomly to the learning group or control group. Each group is given a pre-test and post-test, but only the learning group is exposed to the learning intervention. This modification to the 3a design leads to a stronger design and reduces the threats to internal validity. Variables like history and pre-testing should affect members of the learning and the control group equally. Randomization to condition is an important component in the evaluation of training impact (Martin, Epitropaki, & O'Broin, 2017).

   In a classic study of evaluating training for building first line supervisory skills, 40 supervisors from a total group of 100 were randomly assigned (Latham & Saari, 1979). Twenty supervisors were assigned to the training condition and the other 20 to a control group. The control group was informed that they would be trained at a later date. At the end of each training session, the trainees were sent back to their jobs with instructions to use the supervisory skills they had just gained. At the next session, the trainees reported their experiences, and for situations where they had experienced difficulties, they re-practiced the desired behavior. The pre- and post-learning measure consisted of a situational knowledge test with 85 questions developed from critical incidents found in the job analysis. An example of one situational question is as follows:

   You have spoken with this worker several times about the fact that he doesn't keep his long hair confined under his hard hat. This constitutes a safety violation. You are walking through the plant and you just noticed that he again does not have his hair properly confined. What would you do?

Trainees were asked how they would handle each situation with a scoring response developed based on expert judgments. The mean score for the training group was significantly higher on the post-test than for the control group. The job performance measure consisted of ratings by the supervisors based on a job analysis that produced critical incidents depicting effective and ineffective supervisory behavior. The investigators found no difference in the performance ratings between the training and control group prior to training but ratings were significantly better for the trained group over the control group months after training was completed. As a final step, the control group was trained. After their training was complete, all differences on the criterion measures between the control group, which was now trained, and the original training group disappeared. This kind of careful implementation and evaluation in a real-work environment serves as a model for what can be accomplished with some thoughtful effort and strong design.

4. Solomon four-group design:

Learning Group (1)	(R)	T1	X	T2
Control (2)	(R)	T1		T2
Learning Group (3)	(R)		X	T2
Control (4)	(R)			T2

The Solomon four-group design represents a highly rigorous design (and thus difficult and time intensive to set up and collect evaluation information) that addresses most of the internal validity threats. This design adds two groups that are not pre-tested. If the participants are randomly assigned to one of the four groups, this design makes it possible to compare the effects of pre-testing as Group 4 provides a control for pre-testing without the instructional treatment. It also permits a comparison of the post-test performance for Group 4, which was not exposed to pre-testing or instructional treatments, to the pre-test scores for Group 1 and Group 2 allowing one to analyze history effects. A Solomon four group design was used when studying the effectiveness of an educational poster campaign around suicide prevention involving staff at emergency and psychiatric departments in the Netherlands. Interestingly, due to high pre-test scores on knowledge in handling these types of cases, the study did not find strong effects of the training intervention (Van Landschoot, Portzky, & Van Heeringen, 2017).

5. A Time Series Quasi-Experimental Design
Learning Group   T1   T2   T3   T4   X   T5   T6   T7   T8

This quasi-experimental design collects a series of measurements before and after the instructional treatment which provides more control than simpler designs. If there are no appreciable changes from pre-tests 1 to 4, it is unlikely that any effects found after the learning intervention can be attributed to testing effects or regression to the mean. The major internal validity difficulty with this design is if the investigator was unfortunate enough to have a major history effect that occurs between T4 and T5.

An ingenious example of the use of a quasi-experimental design is in regards to safety problems in the vehicle maintenance division of a city's department of public works (Komaki, Heinzmann, & Lawson, 1980). A training program, developed based on a needs assessment, depicted unsafe practices, discussed correct safety behaviors, and then demonstrated safe practices. After training, participants were informed about realistic safety goals that were set. Then, randomly timed, daily safety observations were made, and the results were posted on a graph so that the employees could see how they were progressing toward their goals. The first phase, referred to as baseline, consisted of the collection of nine observations before any training or feedback. The second phase of six observations were made immediately after the training program. The third phase added the feedback component followed by nine observation points. Note that all trainees proceeded through the entire sequence of phases and that there are multiple data-collection points in each phase about the number of safety incidents performed safely. Data were collected by trained observers, and there was high-level agreement between the observers. Safety behaviors improved from baseline to after training and then improved more when feedback was added. Before training and feedback, the initial observations showed that the percentage of safe behaviors observed averaged about 45%. With training and feedback, the average percentage of safe behaviors rose to over 60% of the time. The behavior changes observed also led to fewer accidents as injuries were reduced by a factor of seven from the preceding year. Since the observers were present during a relatively small percentage of working hours, it is unlikely that behavioral improvements were confined only to these times. This design allows us to rule out alternative explanations of history and statistical regression effects.

Another example of the use of quasi-experimental design for evaluating the development of "softer" skills investigated the impact of training self-regulatory skills such as goal setting, time management, procrastination, concentration, and self-motivation on changes in self-efficacy, metacognition, stress, and strategy application (Schmitz & Wiese, 2006). Participants keep a daily diary regarding their self-regulated learning behaviors (ratings, and open-ended responses) for five weeks. Training was provided each week on a different topic relevant to building self-regulatory skills such as one week was on issues of procrastination while another week was on time management. Results showed increases for the learning group in terms of self-efficacy and satisfaction with learning results. The study also employed a control group who along with the learning group completed measures of efficacy, motivation and learning strategies at the beginning and end of the study. The investigators found evidence that the learning group made progress from pre- to post-test on efficacy as well as effective handling of distractions over and above the scores of the control group.

CONTINUOUS IMPROVEMENT

The Learning Systems Model shows the various routes that evaluation can have input. These feedback loops can lead decision makers to conclude that the original learning need has been met or that additional learning approaches are required. The feedback can also loop back to reconsidering design, delivery and even evaluation processes such as seeing a need to modify a program to include more practice and feedback. This section describes the feedback loops and ends with recent work on how to speed up or accelerate the evaluation process to allow more timely feedback that is actionable.

Feedback Loops

The evaluation feedback loop needs to be strong to continuously improve the learning enterprise. Three types of information that can be collected to strengthen the feedback loop include evaluation that focuses on summative and formative processes and issues of external validity.

SUMMATIVE AND FORMATIVE EVALUATION   Summative evaluation targets the outcome measures of interest in the evaluation plan such as whether learning objectives have been met (learning validity) or whether performance has improved (transfer validity) as a function of the learning intervention. Thus, summative evaluation examines the overall effectiveness of a learning approach in producing the expected outcomes. Another possible target of summative evaluation is to compare two types of learning interventions that are attempting to address the same learning need and determining which approach leads to better outcomes. For example, one could examine if face-to-face instruction leads to different outcomes than a web-based program relevant to the same set of knowledge objectives. The examination of outcomes can help decision makers determine whether learning needs have been met (if the outcomes show learning and transfer has occurred in the amount expected) and if not, ask the question of whether remedial or additional learning interventions are needed to adequately address the learning need.

A decision-based evaluation system that leads to useful feedback requires not only a focus on outcomes but also an emphasis on understanding why certain outcomes were or were not achieved (Kraiger, 2002). One approach to examine this issue is through formative evaluation. If one does not find high levels of learning validity, information from a formative evaluation can help understand why that might have occurred by gathering information on issues such as comprehensiveness of the learning content in the plan of instruction or the appropriateness of the methods used in learning. How well the learning content was delivered can also be examined as well as the expectations and motivation of the learners coming into the program.

There are different approaches to formative evaluation (Brown & Gerhardt, 2002). One approach is to do a review prior to launching a learning program. This step includes the use of an expert review team who examine the course content, learning objectives and the plan of instruction to locate errors, omissions, or improper emphasis. Another option is to conduct a pilot study with a small group of learners to do a critical review as they are going through the learning experience. In one case, we had learners come into a testing center and go through a web-based course and while going through the course they kept a log of problems with content and delivery. Information can also be gathered from learners or observers about the clarity of learning content, the effectiveness of the technologies used, and the appropriateness of the time given for learners to practice skills.

Table 6.6 presents an example of a formative evaluation process for a new safety training program. The evaluators observed the initial training sessions with a focus on four areas: (1) how well the instructors followed the plan of instruction during the training sessions; (2) how well the instructors linked course content to the training objectives in the course; (3) the extent to which learning principles to aid knowledge and skill acquisition were incorporated

TABLE 6.6 Example of a Formative Evaluation Process

1. *Following the plan of instruction*. Examine: (a) the extent to which the instructors covers the material as intended in the training plan of instruction; (b) the extent to which the material is presented in the order or sequence that was intended; and (c) the extent to which there was adequate pacing of the material relevant to the time allotted.
2. *Linking content back to the training objectives*. Examine: (a) the extent to which the instructors orients the trainees throughout the course as to where they are in the material and how the material is linked to the training objectives for the session; (b) the extent to which the instructors keep the trainees informed of how previous material is linked to what is currently being covered; and (c) the extent to which the instructors provide a clear summary and integration of the material prior to moving to the next part of the session.
3. *Incorporating learning principles into the training content*. Examine: (a) the incorporation of realism or identical elements in the delivery of training (realistic situations and scenarios that learners face on the job), (b) the inclusion of a variety of examples and scenarios so that learners can see the applicability of the training material to the job; and (c) the opportunity for trainees to apply their knowledge through exercises.
4. *Involving trainees in their own learning*. Examine: (a) the extent to which the instructors involve the trainees in their own learning process through strategies to elicit discussion; (b) the extent to which instructors adequately facilitated participation to ensure all learners are involved; and (c) how well the participation levels match those expected in the plan of instruction.

into the program; and (4) the extent to which the trainees were active participants in their own learning. An examination of the observations led to both major and minor revisions to the training program.

Research supports the value of formative evaluation in strengthening learning programs. Brown and Kiernan (2001) examined a health promotion program and conducted multiple focus groups with participants as well as training staff around areas for improvement. The participants recommended changes in lesson format, worksheets, and what content to emphasize more. Changes made based on this feedback led to increases (from previous program) in knowledge gain, positive changes in learner attitudes, and improvements in behavior. Another effort at formative evaluation demonstrated how information was effectively used by teachers to implement new activities to modify instruction to better meet student learning needs. The study also found that changes made with teachers after a formative evaluation process led to improvements in test scores compared to the previous group scores (Andersson & Palm, 2017).

EXTERNAL VALIDITY ISSUES Summative evaluation provides information about the effectiveness of a learning program. External validity refers to the generalizability of these summative evaluation findings to other learning groups and situations. External validity is always a matter of inference and thus can never be specified with complete confidence. External validity points to the importance of conducting multiple studies of the same learning program across different settings, people, and contexts – and subsequent meta-analytic studies to summarize what we know about the program's impact.

Internal validity is a prerequisite for external validity because the learning intervention must be judged effective before there can be concerns over whether the intervention would be effective for other learning groups. If a leadership development intervention is found effective for middle managers in the manufacturing section of an organization, how likely would that same intervention be equally effective with middle managers in the engineering section of the same organization? If an intervention is not as effective in terms of transfer as expected due to lack of supervisor support, how likely would the same intervention be more successful with units that are more supportive? These types of questions target understanding the generalizability of results within a single organization.

Evaluative information should be collected on a new group of learners even if the initial evaluation showed success to determine if the same level of success is obtained (and if not have some data to help understand why different results were found). The examination of these intraorganizational issues of generalizability are particularly important if there have been changes to job duties and required knowledge and skills due to new strategic directions or the development of new technologies for the job. In these cases, one might want to recheck the needs assessment for applicability to estimate the likelihood of generalizing results of an existing program to new learners. Decision makers should at least be provided with some indication of the extent to which a successful learning intervention is likely to generalize to a new group of learners within the organization or be provided recommendations for needed modifications to the intervention to better meet the needs of other learning groups.

As discussed in Chapter 1, organizations often benchmark effective learning approaches and strategies in other organizations. In many cases, the work context in the original organization is different from that of the adopting organization. Therefore, one should be interested in determining if a learning approach found effective in one organization can be as effective in the target organization. This involves the generalizability of findings across organizations or what has been called interorganizational validity. One could be interested in determining if an executive coaching intervention found to be effective in, say, a service sector might be equally effective in an organization in the technology sector. The organizations differ in many ways including the climate of support for learning and the capabilities of the coaches at the different sites as well as the level of production pressure. Given the wide variety of contextual differences across organizations, it is important to understand the key differences so the program can be modified to better fit the new organization. Simply borrowing or mimicking programs of other organizations (even if identified as a best practice as noted in Chapter 1) as a shortcut in the learning process probably does not serve the organization well. Both intra and interorganizational generalizability issues need to be carefully considered.

Rapid Evaluation

The development and implementation of a comprehensive evaluation plan takes a fair amount of time, effort, and resources. Then once the data is generated, it takes additional time to analyze the data, interpret the results, and disseminate to decision makers. Waiting for results is time not spent on improving the intervention or determining if the diagnosed learning needs have been met. In today's fast-paced world, time is of the essence for decision makers. In addition, immediate feedback of how well the learning approach is succeeding or failing helps to make just-in-time corrections through a formative evaluation approach.

Evaluators conducting studies around responses to major ongoing humanitarian emergencies have developed ways to speed up the formative and summative evaluation processes so lessons learned from an intervention can be immediately applied. One such approach called the rapid evaluation and assessment method (REAM) is a set of techniques to achieve a reasonable balance between speed and accuracy of the needs assessment, planning, implementing, and evaluation processes so as to provide decision makers with actionable information in a timely way. The steps in a typical REAM include: (1) real-time evaluations are initiated; (2) multiple evaluators are organized as a cell to systematically collect and review data as the intervention unfolds; (3) evaluators interact and share their observations and recommendations on an ongoing basis with relevant staff to allow operational problems to be immediately corrected; and (4) at the conclusion of the REAM, evaluators hold interactive debriefing sessions with staff and other stakeholder groups about what was learned so as to be better prepared for the next intervention (McNall & Foster-Fishman, 2007).

The typical REAM uses a mixed methods evaluation approach including focus groups, in-depth interviews, and reviews of secondary documentation. The key is to use different data collection methods to rapidly collect, analyze, and report data on targeted outcomes. The goal for the process is to be rapid, participatory (many stakeholder groups), team based (evaluation team working collaboratively on all aspects of the evaluation process), and iterative (data analyzed as it is being collected, preliminary findings guiding decisions about additional data needs, etc.). In an empirical study of a healthcare intervention, McNall et al. (2004) noted that three months after an integrated health care intervention, the evidence was clear that retention of participants (internal validity threat!) in the intervention was a serious problem. An evaluation team examined existing data as well as gathered additional information within a short time frame and quickly developed recommendations for a retention protocol. Results indicated a significant improvement in retention rates for participation in the study.

REAM would seem most appropriate when there is an urgent need for information so that immediate action can be taken such as when an organization is planning on launching a new sales program worldwide. Hayes et al. (2016) provide an example of a rapid evaluation approach to evaluating a multiday leadership academy training program with 24 community coalitions in the U.S. They engaged learners in a structured formative evaluation process as the training was being first conducted to make real-time quality improvements as well as provide input into longer term strategies for improvement. For learning in the workplace, issues such as training on adherence to safety protocols in hospital settings or dealing with emergency conditions would seem to have consequences for error large enough to warrant consideration of using an approach like REAM when a program is first developed and implemented (Hofmann & Mark, 2006). There is a need to integrate this approach into the learning and evaluation plans in organizations.

Chapter 6: Best Practice Guidelines

- Articulate the purpose of the evaluation (Table 6.1) in terms of the question(s) that need to be answered.
- Identify who within the organization is interested in the results from the evaluation and what their expectations are so as to build relevant evaluation measures.
- Take time to create evaluation measures that have high levels of reliability and validity.
- Develop a realistic evaluation plan given the level of learning needs and the capabilities of the organization to effectively create evaluation measures, design evaluation studies, analyze data, and interpret findings.
- Use an evaluation design that minimizes threats to internal validity.
- Where appropriate, use quasi experimental design with multiple time points.
- Use formative evaluation methods (Table 6.6) during a pilot program to improve the quality of instruction prior to launching a learning opportunity.
- Test rather than assume the generalizability of summative evaluation findings to other learning groups within the same organization.
- While benchmarking can be quite useful, do not assume interorganizational validity will be high.
- When appropriate use the rapid evaluation and assessment method to provide decision makers with actionable and timely information.

References

Andersson, C., & Palm, T. (2017). The impact of formative assessment on student achievement: A study of the effects of changes to classroom practice after a comprehensive professional development programme. *Learning and Instruction*, 49, 92–102. doi.org/10.1016/j.learninstruc.2016.12.006

Bell, B. S., & Kozlowski, S. W. (2002). Adaptive guidance: Enhancing self-regulation, knowledge, and performance in technology-based training. *Personnel Psychology*, 55(2), 267–306. doi.org/10.1111/j.1744-6570.2002.tb00111.x

Blume, B. D., Ford, J. K., Baldwin, T. T., & Huang, J. L. (2010). Transfer of training: A meta-analytic review. *Journal of Management*, 36(4), 1065–1105. doi.org/10.1177/0149206309352880

Boudreau, J.W., & Ramstad, P.M. (2003). Strategic industrial and organizational psychology and the role of utility analysis. In W. Borman, D. Ilgen, and R. Klimoski (Eds.), *Handbook of psychology* (Volume 12). New York: John Wiley.

Brinkerhoff, R. O. (2005). The success case method: A strategic evaluation approach to increasing the value and effect of training. *Advances in Developing Human Resources*, 7(1), 86–101. doi.org/10.1177/1523422304272172

Brown, J. L., & Kiernan, N. E. (2001). Assessing the subsequent effect of a formative evaluation on a program. *Evaluation and Program Planning*, 24(2), 129–143. doi.org/10.1016/S0149-7189(01)00004-0

Brown, K. G. (2005). An examination of the structure and nomological network of trainee reactions: A closer look at "smile sheets". *Journal of Applied Psychology*, 90(5), 991–1001. doi.org/10.1037/0021-9010.90.5.991

Brown, K. G., & Gerhardt, M. W. (2002). Formative evaluation: An integrative practice model and case study. *Personnel Psychology*, 55(4), 951–983. doi.org/10.1111/j.1744-6570.2002.tb00137.x

Campbell, J. P., & Wiernik, B. M. (2015). The modeling and assessment of work performance. *Annual Review of Organizational Psychology and Organizational Behavior*, 2(1), 47–74. doi.org/10.1146/annurev-orgpsych-032414-111427

Cascio, W. F. (2007). The costs-and benefits-of human resources. *International Review of Industrial and Organizational Psychology*, 22, 71.

Day, E. A., Arthur Jr, W., & Gettman, D. (2001). Knowledge structures and the acquisition of a complex skill. *Journal of Applied Psychology*, 86(5), 1022–1033. doi.org/10.1037/0021-9010.86.5.1022

Erdem. M. (2009). Effects of learning style profile of team on quality of materials developed in collaborative learning processes, *Active Learning in Higher Education*, 10, 154–171. doi.org/10.1177/1469787409104902

Ford, J. K., Bhatia, S., & Yelon, S. L. (2019). Beyond direct application as an indicator of transfer: A demonstration of five types of use. *Performance Improvement Quarterly*, 32(2), 183–203. doi.org/10.1002/piq.21294

Ford, J. K., Smith, E. M., Weissbein, D. A., Gully, S. M., & Salas, E. (1998). Relationships of goal orientation, metacognitive activity, and practice strategies with learning outcomes and transfer. *Journal of Applied Psychology*, 83(2), 218. doi.org/10.1037/0021-9010.83.2.218

Ford, J. K., & Wroten, S. P. (1984). Introducing new methods for conducting training evaluation and for linking training evaluation to program redesign. *Personnel Psychology*, 37(4), 651–665. doi.org/10.1111/j.1744-6570.1984.tb00531.x

Frese, M., Beimel, S., & Schoenborn, S. (2003). Action training for charismatic leadership: Two evaluations of studies of a commercial training module on inspirational communication of a vision. *Personnel Psychology*, 56(3), 671–698. doi.org/10.1111/j.1744-6570.2003.tb00754.x

Goldstein, I. L., & Ford, J. K. (2002). *Training in organizations: Needs assessment, development, and evaluation* (4th ed.). Belmont, CA: Wadsworth.

Haccoun, R. R., & Hamtriaux, T. (1994). Optimizing knowledge tests for inferring learning acquisition levels in single group training evaluation designs: The internal referencing strategy. *Personnel Psychology*, 47(3), 593–604. doi.org/10.1111/j.1744-6570.1994.tb01739.x

Hayes, H. Scott, V., Abraczinskas, M., Scaccia, J., Stout, S., & Wandersman, A. (2016). A formative multi-method approach to evaluating training. *Evaluation and Program Planning*, 58, 199–2017. doi.org/10.1016/j.evalprogplan.2016.06.012

Hirschfeld, R. R., Jordan, M. H., Feild, H. S., Giles, W. F., & Armenakis, A. A. (2006). Becoming team players: Team members' mastery of teamwork knowledge as a predictor of team task proficiency and observed teamwork effectiveness. *Journal of Applied Psychology*, 91(2), 467. doi.org/10.1037/0021-9010.91.2.467

Hofmann, D.A., & Mark, B. (2006). An investigation of the relationship between safety climate and medication errors as well as other nurse and patient outcomes. *Personnel Psychology*, 59, 847–870. doi.org/10.1111/j.1744-6570.2006.00056.x

Komaki, J., Heinzmann, A. T., & Lawson, L. (1980). Effect of training and feedback: Cmponent analysis of a behavioral safety program. *Journal of Applied Psychology*, 65(3), 261. doi.org/10.1037/0021-9010.65.3.261

Kovacic, D. (2018). Using the content validity index to determine content validity of an instrument assessing health care providers' general knowledge of human trafficking. *Journal of Human Trafficking*, 4(4), 327–335. doi.org/10.1080/23322705.2017.1364905

Kraiger, K. (2002). Decision-based evaluation. In K. Kraiger (Ed.), *Creating, implementing, and maintaining effective training and development: State-of-the-art lessons for practice* (331–375). San Francisco, CA: Jossey-Bass.

Kraiger, K., Ford, J. K., & Salas, E. (1993). Application of cognitive, skill-based,

172 Part II • A Systematic Approach

and affective theories of learning outcomes to new methods of training evaluation. *Journal of Applied Psychology*, 78(2), 311–328. doi.org/10.1037/0021-9010.78.2.311

Kraiger, K., & Surface, E. (2017). Beyond levels: Building value using learning and development data. *Training Industry Magazine*, 21–23.

Martin, R., Epitropaki, O., & O'Broin, L. (2017). Methodological issues in leadership training research: In pursuit of causality. In R. J. Galavan, K. J. Sund, & G. P. Hodgkinson (Eds.), *Methodological challenges and advances in managerial and organizational cognition* (pp. 73–94). Bringley: Emerald Publishing Limited.

McNall, M.A., & Foster-Fishman, P.G. (2007). Methods of rapid evaluation, assessment and reappraisal. *American Journal of Evaluation*, 28, 1151–1168. doi.org/10.1177/1098214007300895

McNall, M.A., Welch, V.E., Ruh, K.L., Mildner, C.A., & Soto, T. (2004). The use of rapid-feedback evaluation methods to improve the retention rates of an HIV/AIDS healthcare intervention. *Evaluation and Program Planning*, 3, 287–294. doi.org/10.1016/j.evalprogplan.2004.04.003

Morgan, R. B., & Casper, W. J. (2000). Examining the factor structure of participant reactions to training: A multidimensional approach. *Human Resource Development Quarterly*, 11(3), 301–317. doi.org/10.1002/1532-1096(200023)11:3<301::AID-HRDQ7>3.0.CO;2-P

Phillips, J. J. (2011). *Return on investment in training and performance improvement programs* (2nd Ed.). New York: Routledge.

Sackett, P. R., & Mullen, E. J. (1993). Beyond formal experimental design: Towards an expanded view of the training evaluation process. *Personnel Psychology*, 46(3), 613–627. doi.org/10.1111/j.1744-6570.1993.tb00887.x

Schmitz, B., & Wiese, B. S. (2006). New perspectives for the evaluation of training sessions in self-regulated learning: Time-series analyses of diary data. *Contemporary Educational Psychology*, 31(1), 64–96. doi.org/10.1016/j.cedpsych.2005.02.002

Sitzmann, T., Brown, K.G., Casper, W.J., Ely, K., & Zimmerman, R. D. (2008). A review and meta-analysis of the nomological network of trainee reactions. *Journal of Applied Psychology*, 93(2), 280. doi.org/10.1037/0021-9010.93.2.280

Sitzmann, T., & Ely, K. (2011). A meta-analysis of self-regulated learning in work-related training and educational attainment: What we know and where we need to go. *Psychological Bulletin*, 137(3), 421. doi.org/10.1037/a0022777

Smith-Jentsch, K. A., Campbell, G. E., Milanovich, D. M., & Reynolds, A. M. (2001). Measuring teamwork mental models to support training needs assessment, development, and evaluation: Two empirical studies. *Journal of Organizational Behavior*, 22(2), 179–194. doi.org/10.1002/job.88

Stefanidis, D., Korndorffer Jr, J. R., Sierra, R., Touchard, C., Dunne, J. B., & Scott, D. J. (2005). Skill retention following proficiency-based laparoscopic simulator training. *Surgery*, 138(2), 165–170. doi.org/10.1016/j.surg.2005.06.002

Stefanidis, D., Scerbo, M. W., Montero, P. N., Acker, C. E., & Smith, W. D. (2012). Simulator training to automaticity leads to improved skill transfer compared with traditional proficiency-based training: a randomized controlled trial. *Annals of Surgery*, 255(1), 30–37. 10.1097/SLA.0b013e318220ef31

Teachout, M. S., Sego, D. J., & Ford, J. K. (1997). An integrated approach to summative evaluation for facilitating training course improvement. *Training Research Journal*, 3, 169–184.

van Landschoot, R., Portzky, G., & van Heeringen, K. (2017). Knowledge, self-confidence and attitudes towards suicidal patients at Emergency and Psychiatric Departments: A randomised controlled trial of the effects of an educational poster campaign. *International Journal of Environmental Research and Public Health*, 14(3), 304. doi.org/10.3390/ijerph14030304

Vanosdall, F.E. (1993). *Identifying truck drivers' training needs*. East Lansing, MI: Michigan State University, Highway Traffic Safety Program.

Yelon, S., Ford, J.K., & Bhatia, S. (2015). How trainees transfer what they have learned: Toward a taxonomy of use. *Performance Improvement Quarterly*, 27, 27–52. doi.org/10.1002/piq.21172

Instructional Approaches and Learning Technologies

Questions

✓ How can trainers and facilitators maximize the benefits of traditional face-to-face instructional methods such as lecture, discussion, case study, and role play?

✓ What are the four types of fidelity that can be incorporated into work simulations?

✓ What is the research evidence for the effectiveness of learning technologies such as virtual reality, serious games, and intelligent tutoring systems?

The previous chapters have examined the assessment, design, and evaluation of learning programs and activities based on the Learning Systems Model. Once the plan of instruction is completed and the evaluation plan is developed, the last step is determining the method of delivery. Learning content material on how to properly fill out accounting forms for automobile leasing agreements could be conveyed by an experienced trainer through the traditional lecture and discussion format. Or, that content could be delivered through a web-based course in which learners can access the information whenever they have the time and need for this training.

This chapter is divided into three sections to show the variety of instructional methods and techniques that can be used. The first section discusses the traditional approach to delivery that is instructor led with learners present in a classroom type setting. The second section describes the use of work simulators where learners practice technical skills. The third section describes delivery platforms that are based on the rapid advances in learning technologies such as virtual reality, serious games and mobile learning.

TRADITIONAL INSTRUCTION

Traditional face-to-face instruction continues to have a major role in the delivery of learning content. More than half of the available learning hours is delivered through traditional classroom instruction and the percentage has not dropped significantly since 2011 (Ho et al., 2016). This section on traditional instruction examines methods of lecture, discussion, demonstration and role play with a discussion of strategies for enhancing their effectiveness.

Lecture and Discussion

The usefulness of the lecture and discussion method has been questioned given the one-way nature that can lead to passivity in learners. Lectures to the "masses" can lead to difficulties in presenting material that is equally cogent to individuals who have wide differences in ability, attitude, and interest and difficulties in providing timely individualized feedback. Interestingly, research does not fully support the poor opinions of the lecture technique as an instrument in the acquisition of knowledge. Limitations of the lecture approach can be overcome to some degree by competent lecturers who make the material meaningful and promote lively discussion and clarification of material.

Research shows that after 10–20 minutes of continuous lecturing that assimilation falls off rapidly (Knowles, Holton, & Swanson, 2015). We also know that attention increases when there is a shift in instructional method from lecture to asking questions or providing examples to engage the learner. This calls for incorporating a variety of engagement strategies throughout a learning experience. To increase engagement, an instructor can ask specific and thought-provoking questions during the lecture to gauge how well learners can organize, apply, analyze, integrate, evaluate, and generate new ways of thinking about an issue (see https://wiki.usask.ca/display/db/Using+Qu estions+to+Stimulate+Thinking; accessed February 20, 2020). Learners can be asked to classify or compare new knowledge or be required to state the evidence that would support a perspective or asked to predict results of a study. The type of questions asked during a learning opportunity tied to learning objectives can be quite effective in facilitating learning.

There are many techniques for engaging learners in their own learning beyond the instructor asking questions (Kroehnert, 2003). One strategy is to have learners record questions they have in their notes as a lecture is presented. Teams can be formed to discuss and present to the instructor one question that they want to be addressed to clarify information from the lecture. As a second strategy, an instructor can use a think/pair/share method. After a lecture on a topic, the learners can be asked to individually create an example consistent with the lecture material (recall the generative learning principle from Chapter 5) and then share that example with, say, two colleagues. The colleagues can then discuss whether the examples fit with the lecture material and then share with the whole group the best example generated. A third example is the four corners technique where the instructor places different content questions in each corner of a room. Small groups go to the different corners and discuss the content and question and write their answer on a flipchart. The groups then move to the next corner and add to, revise, expand or counter the answers from the previous group(s). After the groups have completed each corner the responses can be discussed with the whole group tied to the learning objectives for the day.

A traditional engagement approach is to hold a large-scale discussion with the learners about content covered in the lecture. An effective discussion is relatively original, instructionally functional (consistent with objectives), skillfully planned and created, and is highly productive in terms of being memorable. A good discussion is not just an open ended, anything goes, spontaneous question and answer event. Rather, an instructional discussion is a prepared, controlled dialogue that is implemented in a way to help learners achieve specific learning objectives. This requires that the participants have the information needed to contribute to the discussion around facts and issues rather than just give an opinion. Ground rules for participation in the discussion are provided and ideas generated are recorded in an organized fashion. Rather than ending the discussion abruptly and moving on, the instructor/facilitator should check to make sure all contributions are in, restate the issue or question that initiated the discussion, discuss and evaluate the posted answers, test for consensus, and draw conclusions that are tied to the learning objectives (Yelon, 1996).

The focus on active engagement spotlights the instructor as a facilitator of learning and not just a content expert on a topic. Table 7.1 shows the key competencies, process facilitation approaches and personal characteristics found in effective trainers and instructors. Skill sets include enacting the Learning Systems Model (from Chapter 1) such as conducting needs assessments, setting objectives, developing lessons plans and evaluating outcomes. Effective trainers also facilitate learning through motivating learners, providing constructive feedback, managing the learning environment, and adapting to meet learner needs. Personal characteristics include being responsive, enthusiastic, confident, and professional.

Most learners are looking for reasons to learn and apply what is being taught by the instructor or coach. Research with experienced medical fellows in a yearlong workshop on teaching found that a key decision criteria of learners of their intentions to use an idea or apply a principle or skill revolves around three issues: (1) how credible the information or content of a learning experience is; (2) how practical the skills are to apply; and (3) the extent to which the knowledge or skill is needed (Yelon et al., 2004). Based on this decision criteria, participants intended to apply what was included in the workshop. A qualitative study examined decisions by medical professionals on integrating new learning into their existing clinical practice. There was much variance in how participants defined good practice and this individualized standard led to different implications as to whether the training provided the learner with enough credible research evidence to convince the learner to apply the new approaches to their clinical practice (Choi & Roulston, 2015). Table 7.2 presents ways in which instructors and coaches can enhance learner perceptions of credibility, practicality, and need.

Case Study

Once learners have foundational knowledge of a domain, case studies can be used to advance knowledge in areas of analysis and problem-solving. Typically, the learner receives a report that describes an organizational dilemma or problem. Learners analyze the problem and offer solutions based on a number of factors including people, environment, rules, and physical parameters. The case can be completed individually or within a team. Instructor feedback highlights the key principles embedded in the case so learners gain new insights.

TABLE 7.1	Instructor Roles and Responsibilities
Skill Sets In:	Setting objectives Developing lesson plans Conducting needs assessment Blending learning techniques Involving participants Facilitating discussions and group activities Addressing diversity Evaluating impact Supporting learner needs Demonstrating presentation skills Evaluating learner performance
Facilitating Learning by:	Establishing credibility Providing positive reinforcement Motivating learners Demonstrating effective questioning skills Providing constructive feedback Managing the learning environment Applying facilitation skills Using group process skills Building relationships Adapting to learner needs Showing practicality to job
Personal Characteristics Displayed:	Responsive Enthusiastic Sincere Ethical Confident Ability to listen Helpful Professional Innovative Conscientious Approachable

Source: Adapted from Gauld and Miller, P. (2004). The qualifications and competencies held by effective workplace trainers, *Journal of European Industrial Training*, 28, 8–22; Gauld, D. (2015). The competencies of effective trainers and teachers. K. Kraiger, J. Passmore, N. R. D. Santos, & S. Malvezzi (Eds.), *The Wiley Blackwell Handbook of The psychology of training, development, and Performance Improvement*, 117–135.

One case used in a leadership training program concerns decision-making under uncertainty and time pressure (Brittain & Sitkin, 1989). The case involves the leader of a race-car team who must make a final decision whether to race or not to race. The problem in the case is that the racing team has experienced blown engines in 7 of the 24 races they have raced. One of the mechanics on the team contends that the blown engines are more likely in colder weather and the temperature for this morning's race is in the 40s. While this gut reaction suggests not racing, the current race is important to the racing team as a major sponsorship is riding on the team being about to finish in the top five in the race. Another blown gasket would lead the sponsor to seek other racing teams as well as leave the team in debt for the racing season. Racing and doing well would lead to a key sponsorship and the ability to compete the following year in the top racing venues. The members of the pit crew are excited

TABLE 7.2   Ways to Demonstrate that Ideas, Principles, and Skills are Credible, Practical, and Needed
Credible
Tell stories about successes in application
Show how trainers and supervisors use the ideas, principles, or skills at work
Stated varied cases to remind learners of the good and poor work they have seen
Offer realistic practice exercises to see beneficial results
Repeat the application to various job contexts and situations
Present logical and empirical evidence of effectiveness
Practical
Model the approach "thinking" outload as it is demonstrated
Arrange for application activities that can be practiced outside of the training
Provide well-structured materials for learners to use and relearn
Teach ideas, principles, and skills that require minimal prerequisites
Design skills so there are few steps to recall for each part practiced
Provide a memorable framework
Needed
Have learners describe ways they can improve prior to instruction
Teach cues so learners can recognize when the idea, principle or skill is appropriate
Tell application stories that include conditions that are like the ones learners face
Show where and when the ideas, principle, or skill can be used through stories
Give complete, considerate, but honest feedback during application practice
Clearly provide steps needed to improve
Source: Yelon, S., Sheppard, L., Sleight, D., & Ford, J. K. (2004). Intention to transfer: How do autonomous professionals become motivated to use new ideas?. *Performance Improvement Quarterly*, 17(2), 82–103. Copyright 2004 by John Wiley & Sons. Reprinted by permission.

about the opportunity and consider the race car sound. Another member of the racing team presents data that seems to indicate no relationship between air temperature and the frequency of blown gaskets and encourages the leader to race. Table 7.3 presents one part of the three parts in this case.

Learners read each part of the case and at each point consider whether to race or not leading to a final decision. The rational decision-making approach includes (1) defining the problem, (2) determining the overall objective, (3) weighing the criteria, (4) generating alternative courses of action, (5) weighting alternatives, and coming to a decision. The reasons for or against racing are captured by the instructor. The instructor then probes for more in-depth analysis of the case and the reasons for or against racing.

TABLE 7.3 Carter Racing Case Example

"What should we do?"

John Carter was not sure, but his brother and partner, Fred Carter, was on the phone and needed a decision. Should they run in the race or not? It had been a successful season so far, but the Pocono race was important because of the prize money and TV exposure it promised. This first year had been hard because the team was trying to make a name for itself. They had run a lot of small races to get this shot at the bigtime. A successful outing could mean more sponsors, a chance to start making some profits for a change, and the luxury of racing only the major events. But if they suffered another engine failure on national television ...

Just thinking about the team's engine problems made John wince. They had blown an engine 7 times in 24 outings this season with various degrees of damage to the engine and car. No one could figure out why. It took a lot of sponsor money to replace a $20,000 racing engine, and the wasted entry fees were no small matter either. John and Fred had everything they owned riding on Carter Racing. This season had to be a success.

Paul Edwards, the engine mechanic, was guessing the engine problem was related to ambient air temperature. He argued that when it was cold the different expansion rates for the head and block were damaging the head gasket and causing the engine failures. It was below freezing last night, which meant a cold morning for starting the race.

Tom Burns, the chief mechanic, did not agree with Paul's "gut feeling" and had data to support his position (see Exhibit 1). He pointed out that gasket failures had occurred at all temperatures, which meant temperature was not the issue. Tom had raced for 20 years and believed that luck was an important element in success. He had argued this view when he and John discussed the problem last week: "In racing, you are pushing the limits of what is known. You cannot expect to have everything under control. If you want to win, you have to take risks. Everybody in racing knows it. The drivers have their lives on the line, I have a career that hangs on every race, and you guys have got every dime tied up in the business. That's the thrill, beating the odds and winning." Last night over dinner he had added to this argument forcefully with what he called Burns' First Law of Racing: "Nobody ever won a race sitting in the pits."

John, Fred and Tom had discussed Carter Racing's situation the previous evening. This first season was a success from a racing standpoint, with the team's car finishing in the top five in 12 of the 15 races it completed. As a result, the sponsorship offers critical to the team's business success were starting to come in. A big break had come 2 weeks ago after the Dunham race, where the team scored its fourth first-place finish. Goodstone Tire had finally decided Carter Racing deserved its sponsorship at Pocono – worth a much needed $40,000 – and was considering a full season contract for next year if the team's car finished in the top five in this race. The Goodstone sponsorship was for a million a year, plus incentives. John and Fred had gotten a favorable response from Goodstone's racing program director last week when they presented their plans for next season, but it was clear that the director's support depended on the visibility they generated in this race.

"John, we only have another hour to decide," Fred said over the phone. "If we withdraw now, we can get back half the $15,000 entry and try to recoup some of our losses next season. We will lose Goodstone, they'll want $25,000 of their money back, and we end up the season $50,000 in the hole. If we run and finish in the top five, we have Goodstone in our pocket and can add another car next season. You know as well as I do, however, that if we run and lose another engine, we are back at square one next season. We will lose the tire sponsorship and a blown engine is going to lose us the oil contract. No oil company wants a national TV audience to see a smoker being dragged off the track with their name plastered all over it. The oil sponsorship is $500,000 that we cannot live without. Think about it-call Paul and Tom if you want – but I need a decision in an hour."

John hung up the phone and looked out the window at the crisp, fall sky. The temperature sign across the street flashed "40 DEGREES AT 9:23 AM."

Note from Tom Burns

John, I got the data on the gasket failures from Paul. We have run 24 races this season with temperatures at race time ranging from 53 to 82 degrees. Paul had a good idea in suggesting we look into this, but as you can see, this is not our problem. I tested the data for a correlation between temperature and gasket failures and found no relationship.

In comparison with some of the other teams, we have done extremely well this season. We have finished 62.5% of the races, and when we finished we were in the top five 80% of the time. I am not happy with the engine problems, but I will take the four first-place finishes and 50% rate of finishing in the money over seven engines any day. If we continue to run like this, we will have our pick of sponsors.

– Tom

Relationship between Temperatures and Gasket Failures

(Continued)

TABLE 7.3 (Continued)   Carter Racing Case Example

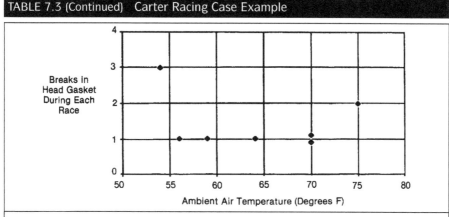

Source: Brittain, J., & Sitkin, S. (1989). Facts, figures, and organizational decisions: Carter Racing and quantitative analysis in the organizational behavior classroom. *The Organizational Behavior Teaching Review*, 1989, 14, pp. 62–81. Copyright by Sage Publications. Reprinted by permission.

In presenting this case to experienced managers, almost all the teams opt to race – a common sentiment is "nothing ventured, nothing gained." Once the decisions have been made and the rationales obtained, the instructor reveals that the car-racing example has many of the same contextual and motivational factors included that led to the decision to launch the ill-fated space shuttle "Challenger". For example, there were tremendous pressures to launch despite warnings from some engineers who feared a relationship between ambient temperature and O ring leakage. This leads to a discussion about the underlying principles of leadership decision-making that this case (and the Challenger explosion) highlights. These principles include the reality of making decisions with limited or partial information, the importance of asking the right questions to obtain the best data before making a decision, the need to listen to negative information rather than downplaying the source of the information, and the need to avoid escalating commitment due to a focus on meeting planned deadlines.

Proponents of the case study method contend that the development of diagnostic skills through self-discovery is likely to lead to longer retention of the underlying principles than if the principles are directly provided to the learners (Rees, & Porter, 2002). A case like Carter Racing can help unfreeze current beliefs and open the learners to learning more about themselves, which can result in a willingness to attend to and more deeply process the principles from the case. Learners can develop their own stories from past experiences and highlight how the principles in the case were or were not incorporated in their own decision-making process. In addition, learners can be asked to think of a decision that will have to be made in the near future and address how the principles learned from the case study can be directly applied to this everyday situation on the job to result in higher quality decisions.

Critics of this approach contend that the case method can be detrimental for learning the underlying principles. Participants can become entangled in the large amount of information presented and never find the basic issue. Or, learners can become so engrossed in the case study that they never see the relevance of the principles to everyday life on the job. Argyris (2002) provides a detailed criticism of the case-study method based on an analysis of two types of learning. One type involves the detection and correction of error called single-loop learning. The second and more powerful form of learning is double-loop learning, which involves changes and corrections to underlying assumptions, and goals of the learner. Argyris's concern is that the delivery of the case method may unintentionally undermine double-loop learning, which can have broader generalizability and impact on learning transfer than single loop learning.

There is some evidence that the case study method can be effective. One study examined the transfer of knowledge gained from case studies to subsequent face-to-face negotiation tasks (Thompson et al., 2009). They found that participants who derived negotiation principles from comparing two case studies were three times more likely to transfer the negotiation principle to the bargaining situation than participants in a control condition who only read the cases and thought about what advice they would give the main persons in the cases. A subsequent study on teams showed the same result as teams who compared two cases were more likely to transfer an important strategy to face-to-face negotiation situations than teams that just read each case without attempts to understanding underlying principles (Loewenstein, Thompson, & Gentner, 2003). These studies illustrate the potential power of using cases and the important role of an instructor in making sure that deep-level processing is occurring for the learners.

Demonstration and Role Play

To show learners how to effectively complete the steps in a task, an instructor or facilitator can model the steps to take. Then, the learner can be asked to imitate the instructor with the goal of the learner gaining the knowledge and skills needed quickly. A four-step approach to effective demonstration involves: (1) telling the learner they will have to perform what is about to be modeled; (2) before demonstrating telling the learner what specific things to observe; (3) stating each step in the process of completing a task as each step is being demonstrated; and (4) asking learners to mentally rehearse the steps and commit the steps to memory before they begin practicing the steps (Yelon, 1996). In this way, the learners can maximize their readiness to practice and learn from that practice.

Principles can also be demonstrated to give the learner direction before role playing a situation. For example, lawyers can be asked to practice providing an opening statement to a case before a "judge" and be given feedback as to their approach. Role playing can also be used to practice interpersonal skills such as how to give employees performance feedback or how to deal with difficult customers. This technique gives learners an opportunity to experience a variety of on-the-job problems in a safe environment to try out new behaviors.

One concern about using role playing is that participants might behave in a manner that is socially acceptable at the time but not be committed to any behavioral changes outside the role-playing environment. Clearly, the success of the method depends on the participants' willingness to adopt the roles and to react as if they are in the work environment. What is equally important is the quality of feedback provided and the opportunities to have multiple practice sessions. Feedback can come from the instructor or fellow learners.

Another impactful feedback process is called *self-confrontation.* In this proce-dure, a videotape replay of the role play is shown to the learner. While viewing the video, the learner describes effective and ineffective behaviors and how to do better the next time it is practiced. This self-assessment can be reinforced by a verbal critique of the performance by the instructor and peers. In an ini-tial study of this technique on cross-cultural skills training, King (1966) gave trainees information about one culture and the desired behaviors within that culture. Then, the learner played the role of an adviser in another country. The results showed that learners who participated in self-confrontation performed consistently better over time than another group of learners who had spent an equivalent amount of time studying the behavioral requirements of an effec-tive role play. Retention tests given two weeks later also showed that the self-confrontation group maintained their skills.

Other studies support the use of role play as an effective way of build-ing skills. A review of medical training studies showed that the use of role play improved communication skills of health care practitioners when talking to patients (Lane & Rollnick, 2007). A more recent review indicated that role playing helped build communication skills in nursing education programs (MacLean et al., 2017).

Cautionary Tale about Learning Styles

A strongly stated and commonly held belief to improve traditional instruc-tion is to alter learning content and processes to match the individual's learn-ing style. From this perspective, some learners gain more from visual or spatial presentations of images and pictures while others may benefit more from auditory or verbal presentations. Other learning styles noted include a preference for learning with others or kinesthetic learners who prefer to be hands-on or figuring things out by working with objects. A popular inventory based on Kolb's (1984b) learning styles contends that learners differ in terms of being concrete or abstract learners as well as active experimenters or reflective observer leading to four categories of styles: divergers, assimilators, converg-ers, and accommodators.

This belief would be supported if the learning style of the individual dic-tates the instructional form needed to lead to superior levels of learning and retention. This conclusion requires evidence that one learning style leads to more effective learning when given an instructional method that differs from the method leading to greater learning for those with a different learning style. The research evidence from rigorous designs has shown this belief is more myth than fact. Customizing learning to match learning styles has *not* been found to lead to more effective learning. In one study with multiple experi-ments, adult learners were assessed for their preferences on how to receive instruction and found that the differences in learning style did not predict learning outcomes (Messa & Mayer, 2006). As can be seen in Figure 7.1, all learners (whether visualizers or verbalizers) benefited more from pictorial help than verbal help.

Going beyond this individual study, a meta-analysis has come to a similar conclusion. While leaners can state their learning preferences and believe that they learn better when learning matches their preferences (recall discussion of the illusion of knowing), these preferences have limited or no

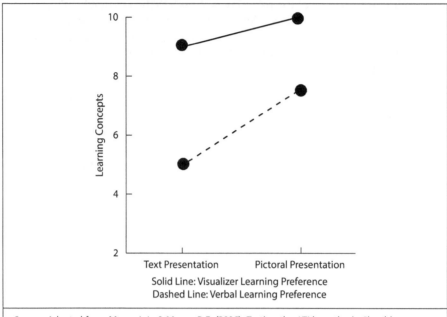

FIGURE 7.1   Learning Styles, Presentation Mode and Learning Performance.

Solid Line: Visualizer Learning Preference
Dashed Line: Verbal Learning Preference

Source: Adapted from Messa, L.J., & Mayer, R.E. (2006). Testing the ATI hypothesis: Should multimedia instruction accommodate verbalizervisualizer cognitive styles?. *Learning and Individual Differences*, 16, 321–336.

impact on the learning process such as task attention or learning outcomes (Pashler et al. 2009). This conclusion from this evaluation of learning style studies is consistent with earlier attempts to find consistent aptitude-treatment interactions effects on learning. From this perspective, higher-ability learners may benefit from a different instructional approach than lower ability learners. A study by Snow and Lohman (1984) found some evidence that low-ability students more from highly structured instructional programs. The opposite was true of high-ability students as they benefited more from low-structure and high-complexity instruction. Unfortunately, few consistent aptitude-treatment interactions have been found despite numerous attempts.

The bottom line is that efforts at improving learning and retention are best placed on systematic instruction design based on a strong needs assessment. Strong design includes the incorporation of learning principles that have been found to lead to greater learning and retention for all learners. This emphasis will better meet learner needs than hoping that matching learning styles will be an effective strategy for personalizing the learning tasks and generating more active learning (Willingham, Hughes, & Dobolyi, 2015). With advances in artificial intelligence and machine learning, perhaps instruction can become more targeted and personalized to better meet learner needs regardless of preferred learning styles.

TRAINING SIMULATORS

Simulators are designed to replicate the essential characteristics of the real world in terms of the equipment and capabilities of the system that are necessary to perform job tasks. They can be used to train newcomers, upgrade skills of more experienced incumbents, provide refresher training, and allow for practicing non routine emergency procedures. From initial work with airline pilots, work simulators have been expanded to improve skills in a variety of domains such as maritime commanders, medical personnel, bus and truck drivers, and emergency preparedness personnel. A variety of simulators have been designed for specific purposes of developing task relevant skills while also building decision-making and problem-solving skills. In this section, simulators designed for technical skill development are discussed. Simulations designed for training interpersonal and team skills are discussed in Chapter 9 and the use of business game simulations for building management and leadership skills are discussed in Chapter 10.

Using Simulators

An early example of a simple but effective simulation was provided in a study on teaching medical students suturing techniques (Salvendy & Pilitsis, 1980). The investigators found that simulator training improved performance beyond the traditional training methods and reduced stress while completing the task when in a real job context. From these early attempts, the use of simulators for training technical skills has risen markedly. Military and commercial aviation use complex simulations to train a variety of tasks. One of the most striking examples of a simulator designed to produce a dangerous safety event is the wind shear simulator. A wind shear is a sudden shift of wind that can cause a plane to go out of control leading to deadly accidents. Airlines have training centers that produce the effects of a wind shear including hydraulic stilts that mimic every bump and roll, aircraft sounds, rain pelting the windshield, and thunder. For example, the steep climb at take-off can push the pilots back in their seats. Then the instrument panels convey and the pilots feel the plane starting to sink due to a wind shear. As warnings of a stall and the strong vibration of the control stick indicate, the pilots have little time to determine and implement a course of action to avoid a crash. As noted in a news article called terror at zero feet, the training comes across as so real that the "cold sweat, fast heartbeat and weak knees were not simulated" (Philips, 1991).

The maritime industry provides training on simulators for tasks such as towing and anchor handling, offshore operations, and port operations. In fact, the International Maritime Organization that regulates training of mariners requires the use of work simulators to build both technical and team management competencies on the bridge (Wahl, 2019). Figure 7.2 presents a picture of a maritime training simulator while Table 7.4 describes in more detail the training requirements for maritime officers.

Five reasons for the popularity of work simulators include:

1. *Controlled reproducibility.* Simulations permit the steps in a task to be reproduced under controlled conditions so that extraneous factors do not get in the way of learning. The simulation permits the instructor to expand, compress, or repeat time to meet learning objectives.

2. *Safety considerations.* The simulator permits learners to be slowly introduced to the essential task characteristics, without any danger

FIGURE 7.2   Simulator Training of Maritime Officers.

Source: www.Shutterstock.com. Reprinted with permission.

to themselves, their fellow workers, or to the expensive equipment. Simulations also permit the learner to practice emergency techniques before being exposed to hazardous job situations.

3. *Utilization of learning principles.* Because the environment is carefully controlled, instructors can easily introduce feedback, arrange for interleaved practice, use part or whole and spaced practice methods, and other best-known principles of transfer.

4. *Accelerated learning.* Work simulations provide opportunities for targeted and relevant practice. Repeated practice accelerates learning within a condensed time period as opposed to on-the-job instruction.

5. *Cost.* Although simulations can be initially expensive to purchase, they are often an economical alternative to using high-priced, on-the-job equipment. For example, after the nuclear power plant accident at Three Mile Island, there was no hesitation to design a $1 million control-room simulator to avoid such problems in the future.

Research evidence supports the overall effectiveness of work simulations. A meta-analysis of 609 studies in the medical field showed that the use of work simulators in health professional education programs had large effects on a variety of learning outcomes including improved knowledge, skills, and job behaviors (Cook et al., 2011). The usefulness of simulators is related to quality of the instructor, the type of feedback and encouragement provided and the amount and type of practice provided to address skill gaps. In addition, the fidelity of the simulation can also impact its learning potential and is the focus of many research efforts.

TABLE 7.4 Simulator Technology for training Maritime Officers

Simulator training of maritime officers is an important component is building skills that lessen the probability of errors on the job. The simulator is a risk-free environment where individuals can learn how to hand complex and potentially dangerous situations at sea and when docking. Such simulators can mirror real-world conditions with high levels of fidelity. They have been used to certify mariners in areas such as navigation and ship handling under a variety of conditions as well as specific operations such as towing and port operations. Training standards for certification has been published by the International Maritime Organization in the form of an International Convention on Standards, Certification, and Watchkeeping for Seafarers that established an international agreement relevant to the standards of training and what was required to earn the certification. Requirements include both technological proficiency in areas such as ship handling as well as informational skills such as understanding charts and information systems. There is also an emphasis on security-related issues. Newer versions of the convention focus on non-technical skills such as training in leadership and teamwork skills. In order to meet high-quality standards, the convention also includes requirements for the level of training staff qualifications as well as the facilities and equipment needed to meet training objectives. The convention also includes a plan of instruction with course materials, timetable for sequencing the training content and suggestions on the percentage of time devoted to lecture, discussion, practice, and assessment. The assessments to validate learning outcomes include not only written and oral tests but also the demonstration of technical and team management skills in authentic conditions through simulation that requiring addressing problem based performance tasks. As seen above, the simulators are what is called full mission ship bridge simulators that have similar physical layout as an actual bridge of a ship with similar types of equipment and instrumentation. The large virtual viewing area allows for replicating routine and nonroutine situations that arise around the ship such as adverse weather conditions making it hard to see what is out there. A qualitative review of 18 studies of maritime simulator training found some evidence that the training improved trainees' ability to analyze a complex situation such as entering a port. Yet, the empirical base on the effectiveness of the simulators is quite small and there are concerns that while the requirements are set, that the implementation of the training is less than optimal.

Sources: International Convention on Standards of Training, Certification and Watchkeeping for Seafarers, 1978: http://www.imo.org/en/OurWork/HumanElement/TrainingCertification/Pages/STCW-Convention.aspx; accessed February 28, 2020; Sellberg, C. (2017). Simulators in bridge operations training and assessment: a systematic review and qualitative synthesis. *WMU Journal of Maritime Affairs*, 16(2), 247–263. Wahl, A. M. (2019). Expanding the concept of simulator fidelity: The use of technology and collaborative activities in training maritime officers. *Cognition, Technology & Work*, 22, 209–222; doi.org/10.10007/s10111-019-00549-4

Fidelity Issues

Simulators are best used when the required skills are explicit and the task behaviors needed on the job can be identified and measured objectively. The work simulators can then be an accurate representation of the operational system, equipment, and environmental context (Thompson et al., 2009). This issue of accuracy of representation concerns the fidelity of the simulator and the fidelity of the simulations.

Fidelity is a multidimensional construct that includes four types of fidelity (Marlow et al., 2018; Wahl, 2019). One type is physical fidelity, which is the extent to which the simulator mirrors the exact equipment used on the job (e.g., knobs and dials are in the same place as on the equipment on the job). For example, I was at a training session for navy personnel at an onshore facility where inside there was a complete replica of the ship and the ship decision-making center.

Physical fidelity can also include auditory, tactile, and movement that mirrors the real world such as forces affecting the roll of the vehicle when taking a sharp turn while driving in a truck simulator. A second issue is one of functional fidelity in which the kind of tasks performed in the simulator are those one would face on the job. These tasks can include routine tasks as well as non-routine tasks where the consequence of errors could be large. A simulation with high functional fidelity not only has job relevant tasks but also has a realistic unfolding of events as the learner completes the steps in a task and makes decisions over time that have consequences. A third type of fidelity is psychological or the extent to which the simulator places the learner into situations that incorporate what it feels like when completing the task on the job. Tasks requiring action under time pressures and challenging scenarios (like the wind shear example) can be designed to produce stress levels that would have to be faced on the job. A fourth issue is one of social fidelity that addresses the extent to which the collaborative nature for tasks on the job is mirrored in the work simulator. A simulator with high social fidelity would simulate the communication, problem-solving and decision-making tasks with other members that is required on the job to get the task accomplished. In the navy example above, there were many people in the simulation who monitored the environment for the presence of enemy submarines, planes, or ships and communicated with each other to ensure accurate understanding of the situation just as would be needed on the job.

An important question is the cost versus benefit of work simulators as a function of the level of fidelity (across the four types) that designers incorporate into the simulations. The design of training simulators can be quite expensive when designers attempt to be completely accurate in terms of four fidelity factors. Costs are high for comprehensive, full mission, simulations that deal with large-scale operations such as those designed to coordinate actions across multiple crews on an air craft carrier.

Another option is to create part-simulations that are often less expensive to design and deliver. Part simulations replicate a critical or difficult portion of the task without attempting to provide full levels of fidelity. Simulation efforts can also use relatively inexpensive personal computers with software programs that provide practice on critical skills and important processes (functional fidelity) that are required for task performance. These so-called low fidelity simulators are often realistic in terms of the types of tasks, issues or problems that need to be practiced prior to going back on the job. The key is to ensure that the tasks performed in the simulator provide the learner the opportunity to reproduce behaviors to perform effectively on the job. An airline pilot can use a joy stick with a computer game to practice landings rather than be in a full-scale simulator with motion – the issue is whether the skills being learned in each type of setting provide the level of fidelity needed to facilitate learning and subsequent seamless job transfer.

The quest for more physically realistic simulation should not come at a cost of losing sight of the true goal of using a training device that has the level of functional, psychological, and social fidelity to impact learning and transfer. In the medical field, evidence supports the conclusion that functional fidelity is often more important than physical fidelity along with the quality of feedback, engagement of the learner, repetitive practice, and having a range of scenarios that vary in terms of difficulty (Hamstra et al., 2014).

The research question that is often examined, then, is how high a level of fidelity is necessary to build necessary skills. For example, is a full motion simulator a needed aspect of military pilot training? Research has provided some answers to the balancing of these fidelity issues. Much research effort has focused on low fidelity simulators and their impact on learning.

Early work supported the conclusion that personal computer-based simulations with low physical fidelity (but high on other types) can be effective relevant to learning (Jentsch & Bowers, 1998). Thompson, Carroll, and Deaton (2009) provide a summary of studies done on lower fidelity flight simulators to counter the argument these types of simulators have more in common with video games than actual work tasks. They examined ten years of research and found that participants rate the content validity of these lower fidelity simulators as quite high and agree that behaviors elicited in the simulations are important for effective on-the-job performance such as coordination behaviors among aircrew. Similarly, research in Europe with maritime training supports the use of low fidelity simulators on ship safety leading to effective learning and more resilient crews when on the job (Dahlstrom et al., 2009). As a final example, Wahl (2019) examined how learning emerges in a desktop full mission ship bridge simulator in the training of mariners that embedded collaborative (high social fidelity) activities. The case analysis shows the value of high social fidelity embedded in the simulation scenarios (e.g., gathering information from various team members) in leading learners to perceive the simulation training to be of high quality as well as realistic. Worldwide confidence in the usefulness of simulators is seen in the acceptance of licenses, certifications, and qualification standards tied to successful performance in simulators (Thompson et al., 2009).

A meta-analysis in the medical field that did compare high and lower fidelity simulators found no significant advantage for the high physical fidelity on learning surgical techniques and cardiac resuscitation tasks (Norman, Dore, & Grierson, 2012). These findings point to the need to pay particular attention to functional, psychological, and social fidelity issues. Best practice implications from this stream of research include: (1) maximize functional and psychological fidelity such that the scenarios emulate the task characteristics and demands required on the job; (2) ensure that the scenarios evoke the appropriate type of practice to build the competencies required and if working with teams that the scenarios incorporate high levels of social fidelity to build teamwork competencies; (3) implement systematic and detailed feedback and debriefing sessions that focus on strategies for meeting the learning objectives; (4) train observers to provide reliable, effective and timely feedback on behaviors observed during the scenarios; and (5) incorporate deliberate and repetitive practice to build core competencies (Marlow et al., 2018).

What still is unknown is the tradeoffs of physical, functional, psychosocial and social fidelity from a cost/benefit perspective across a variety of different types of skills. We also have limited information on the relative benefits of work simulations over more traditional approaches to training. Interestingly, one study showed no significant benefit for simulation training over a traditional case-based approach (people randomly assigned to condition) in terms of knowledge acquisition or comfort in patient assessment (Kerr et al., 2013). These unknowns are avenues for future research.

LEARNING TECHNOLOGIES

Organizations continue to look to alternative delivery methods and learning technologies for facilitating learning. A State of the Industry report from the Association of Talent Development (Ho et al., 2016) showed that 41% of learning hours across organizations are being delivered by mobile and technology-based methods which is 15% higher than what was reported in 2003. Computer enabled technologies such as virtual reality, serious games, and intelligent learning systems have been created to better individualize instruction and to meet increasingly challenging learning objectives such as building complex technical skills and enhancing adaptability skills for a wide variety of jobs (Ritterfeld, Cody, & Vorderer, 2009). In addition, there has been an explosion of e-learning and mobile learning options that have been implemented that can free learners from time boundaries leading to just-in-time learning (Brown, Charlier, & Pierotti 2012).

This section describes these learning technology and delivery mechanisms as well as presenting research findings on their effectiveness. These advances are exciting and changing the nature of learning in the workplace. Nevertheless, technology by itself will not, and cannot be "the answer" to learning in the workplace. As noted by Clark (2010),

> with each new technology wave, enthusiasts ride the crest with claims that finally we have the tools to really revolutionize training. Yet, in just a few years, today's latest media hype will fade, yielding to the inexorable evolution of technology and a fresh spate of technological hyperbole. (p. 12)

Virtual Reality

With virtual reality (VR) (and augmented reality), learners view a 3D world of situations they face on the job with objects in this simulated world that can be touched, looked at, and repositioned. VR has been advocated as a highly motivating, interesting, and effective learning tool as it capitalizes on visual learning and experiential engagement without the physical space requirements of full-scale work simulators. A single VR system can simulate many different types of situations and learning events within a short time frame providing ample opportunities for practice. VR systems also have capabilities to zoom in and out that allow for the study of various levels of detail as well as the ability to control time (faster, slower, reverse, halt). VR modules can be easily updated, integrated, and reused making it flexible tool.

The National Aeronautics and Space Administration in the United States has been involved in virtual reality training since the early 1990s to help prepare international crews for space travel. An interesting early application of successful VR training was the preparation of astronauts for fixing the Hubble Telescope. Over 100 flight controllers experienced simulated extravehicular activities designed to familiarize them with the location, appearance, and operability of the telescope's components and the maintenance components of the space shuttle cargo bay, to verify and improve procedures, and to create contingency plans. The VR technology allowed Bernard Harris, an astronaut from the U.S. stationed in Houston, to enter a virtual environment and interact with astronaut Ulf Merbold who was physically located in Germany. They

FIGURE 7.3 Virtual Reality for Learning how to Weld a Steel Pipe.

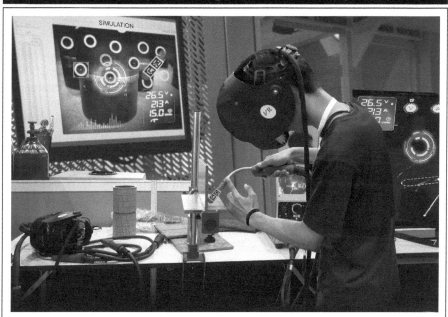

Source: www.Shutterstock.com. Reprinted with permission.

spent over 30 minutes performing the procedures for replacing the damaged lens and communicating with each other. At the conclusion of the procedure, the two astronauts shook hands and waved goodbye in this virtual world (Loftin, 1996).

VR training is being implemented for manufacturing jobs as well as building skills in more traditional skilled trades. One application is construction safety training where hazards can arise on construction sites that lead to predictable problems. Workers in the virtual environment address risks in order to understand the magnitude of these risks. As an example, Figure 7.3 shows an employee wearing VR glasses to "see" while welding a steel pipe while in training.

One study randomly assigned relative newcomers to traditional classroom training with visual examples while the other half were engaged with a 3D immersive VR system (Sacks, Perlman, & Barak, 2013). The system simulated 21 situations that were selected based on frequency of accidents and typical hazards for construction workers such as working at heights and working with tools and equipment. The traditional classroom with visuals went over the same situations and content including safety steps to take. A knowledge test was given before the training and then immediately after the training followed by a third test one month after training. The test included behavioral questions such as presenting an image of a construction scene with a specific hazard (e.g., working under a crane) and the learners were tasked with describing what steps they would take in those situations. While learners in both groups saw the situations depicted as realistic, those in the VR system reported higher levels of attention and greater intentions to adopt the safety steps once on the job. The results provide some evidence of the effectiveness of the VR over traditional classroom instruction relevant to hazard identification and prevention skills that remained over time to the third testing period.

Similarly, Motorola has VR training for gaining skills for operating machines on the manufacturing assembly lines (Ausburn & Ausburn, 2004). Learners can start, run, and stop machines, as well as troubleshoot problems. When they operate buttons and switches, audio and visual reactions of the machine are mimicked. Each course can be completed in 8–12 hours, with specific coursework included, activities scored, and feedback given. Results indicate that workers are more comfortable with this training than traditional approaches and that the VR training accelerates learning during on-the-job training. Verizon has created a digital apprenticeship program where new field technicians use a wearable headset to access information while working hands-free on a virtual utility pole. A post-survey found that a large majority of participants stated that the training improved their job function, helped them complete tasks quicker and reduced the potential for accidents on the job (Castellano, 2019).

As a final example, many VR systems have been developed to train doctors on various surgical procedures such as microsurgical vascular anastomosis (surgical joining of two blood vessels to allow blood flow from one to the other). The tools used in the VR systems create lifelike resistance when the surgeon moves the instruments and the visual image moves as the surgeon moves providing a realistic, safe, predictable, and reproducible setting. Helping train medical students, we now have avatar-mediated technology in which trainees provide bad news to a patient avatar in a three-dimensional simulated clinic (Andrade et al., 2010). Harders (2008) notes the advantages of VR over mock-ups and non-interactive PC-based tools where there is no tactile information, limited interactivity, and no immersion.

Meta-analytic findings on the effectiveness of VR systems are quite encouraging. As an early example, Haque and Srinivasan (2006) examined the evidence across 16 studies of surgical simulators and found that the training lessened the time taken to complete a given surgical task in the operating room over the more traditional clinical training. They also found no differences in error rates on the job between the two training conditions. Larson et al. (2009) examined studies on training for laparoscopic surgery through randomized controlled trials and found that virtual reality training led to the equivalence of the experienced gained from 25 surgeries! In addition, medical doctors trained via virtual reality completed operations in half the time (12–24 minutes) from those trained through the traditional clinical method. More recently, the results of 31 randomized control experiments found that VR simulation of laparoscopic surgery was significantly more effective for those with limited and those with more extensive experience than video trainers on reducing time to complete the task and error counts (Alaker, Wynn, & Arulampalam, 2016). Similar improvements have been found in technical skills for orthopedic surgery outcomes (Aim et al., 2016). The evidence for best practice from these studies is that VR systems need to be targeted, focused, and provide ample time for deliberate practice of specific skills identified as critical to success on the job.

Serious Games

Games have been proposed as one strategy to facilitate active learning by constructing a smaller and more simplified version of real-world issues and problems facing individuals and teams on the job. What has been called serious games (rather than games for entertainment) allow for the development of "what if" scenarios in which participants are embedded into a work-related problem so as to gain valuable knowledge and skills around some goal-driven learning outcome of interest. Serious games are being incorporated into work oriented professional fields such as health and safety as well as the military. Such serious games have the potential to promote deep learning by (1) providing a safe environment to make mistakes and see the consequences of actions, (2) presenting scenarios that stimulate senses and tap into emotions, (3) incorporating interactivity and cause and effect linkages, (4) including a cycle of judgments, behaviors and feedback, and (5) incorporating psychological and functional fidelity (O'Connor & Menaker, 2008).

An early example of incorporating "what if" scenarios into board games is provided by The American Red Cross (1999) who developed a game simulation for training staff in emergency operations. While a manager may only work in one area of operations, there are 23 areas or functions that must coordinate action during an emergency operation. Scenarios require participants to make decisions and take actions (such as opening facilities and placing volunteers) that have identifiable consequences. Embedded into the game are opportunities to practice and gain skills in more effective information sharing, better coordination of limited resources, and smoother transitions form a localized response to a nationwide network of emergency response resources. Formal debriefing and the generation of lessons learned that can be applied back on the job provide another layer of learning in action.

Since then, there has been an ongoing push to build in more interconnectivity such as multiple goals across participants with individual decisions impacting others and more realistic dynamics such as rate of change and degree of feedback delays. There are now numerous design strategies such as branching stories, interactive spreadsheets, interactive diagrams, and practiceware (Aldrich, 2009). The U.S. Department of Defense contracted out movie companies to incorporate compelling storytelling techniques into complex battle simulations to improve their effectiveness (Luppa & Borst, 2007). The games typically are structured to include progressive problem-solving complexity and allow for scaffolding learning and learning from mistakes by repeating scenarios to allow for learners to pursue different strategies to see the outcomes.

More recent serious games have incorporated the use of online animated coaches and avatars to help the learner navigate the game and to aid their progress. As an early example, Rickel and Johnson (2000) describe how an on-screen agent supports learning how to maintain gas turbine engines on a navy ship. Twenty years later, Johnson and Lester (2016) reflected on the dramatic changes that have occurred to serious gaming for learning in the workplace due to the use of animated pedagogical agents. These agents can demonstrate how to perform a manufacturing task, explain the how and why for specific tasks, and work together with the learner to practice the tasks (called learning companions). The pedagogical agents have also been programmed to lead learners around a complex gaming situation to make sure the participants do not get lost in the game, draw attention of the learner to different aspects of the task, and give nonverbal feedback such as head nodding, shaking the head, and facial expressions that show "emotions." Most impressively, agents can through artificial intelligence developments now be more adaptive and timely in their reactions in relation to the actions of the learner. This includes an agent responding differentially given the specific decisions or action steps the learner takes during their turn. Agents can be created to be teachable agents who require learners to explain their rational for steps taken leading hopefully to deeper levels of thinking and learning. The agent as mentor and guide is seen as more engaging than when the agent comes across as an expert. Research evidence shows that the agent as mentor leads to enhanced self-efficacy, motivation, and learning (Kim & Baylor, 2016). This supports the notion of guided discovery learning that will be talked about in the next section of the chapter.

Progress is being made on programming agents to recognize the affective reactions of the learner so that the agent can respond in supportive ways to continue to motivate the learner to continue in the game. In addition, advances in natural language processing and speech recognition software is leading to more natural conversations between the learner and the animated agent. A meta-analysis of 43 studies (mostly in school environments) found that animated agents do enhance learning in comparison to instruction that does not feature such agents (Schroeder, Adesope, & Gilbert, 2013).

A good example of the creative use of agents is the development of the Virtual Cultural Awareness Trainers (VCAT) where learners acquire knowledge of other cultures through simulated encounters with others (Johnson & Lester, 2016). The interactive multimedia and game-based simulation includes a virtual coach to provide guidance and feedback as well as agents embedded into the role plays around culture exchanges. The game was initially developed for training military service personnel to acquire some basic level of intercultural competence before being deployed. The training helps learner gain intercultural knowledge by having them immersed in simulated mission scenarios so the learners can practice and refine their skills (Johnson et al., 2011). A key objective is to build competencies around perspective-taking and how to develop rapport and common ground. The U.S military has implemented a skill-oriented role playing scenario of service personnel discussing issues with Afghan leaders through an interpreter. The learner selects a course of action for their avatar to perform and continues to select actions to take given reactions from the other characters in the scenario – hopefully in a way to resolve the interaction through meeting both local cultural norms and satisfying military mission goals.

Multiplayer, interactive serious games are also being used to build team skills such as coordination and cooperation as well as honing team skills in strategy and tactics. McGowan and Pecheux (2007) describe a game in which learners act as either hazardous materials technicians or the incident commander responding to the release of chlorine gas in a store. The learner can call up different scenarios to practice and can alter the difficulty levels as well as options around shared communication needs so they can experience how various factors impact outcomes.

A systematic review of 61 studies on the effects of games on learning has been completed (Connolly et al., 2012). When looking at high-quality studies using rigorous research designs such as quasi-experimental designs, the researchers found support for the impact of serious games on knowledge acquisition and cognitive skills. While there is much to learn about how to enhance the effectiveness of serious games on learning and transfer, it is clear that serious gaming will continue to grow as a learning method for building knowledge and skills at the individual and team levels.

Intelligent Tutoring Systems

Intelligent tutoring systems (ITS) are computer-based programs that customize the learning experience for individual participants. Through various methods including artificial intelligence, there is a diagnosis of the learner's current level of understanding or performance and the selection of the appropriate next step based on an expert model that can advance a learner toward higher levels of performance.

Pioneering work on ITS was conducted by Carbonell (1970) with the development of a system called SCHOLAR. The system provides training on the geography of different countries. The SCHOLAR program presents information to the student, asks questions, assesses the answers, corrects mistakes and answers student questions like a human tutor. Since then, research and development activity on ITS has expanded greatly. The research activity has focused on how to best meet the goals of diagnosing the types of errors learners make when solving problems and to react to these errors with targeted tutoring.

Figure 7.4 presents a visual of the four attributes within an intelligent tutoring system that includes the development of learner, expert, instruction, and generative models (McCarthy, 2008). The learner model captures the current state of the learner's knowledge and skills as well as the coaching that

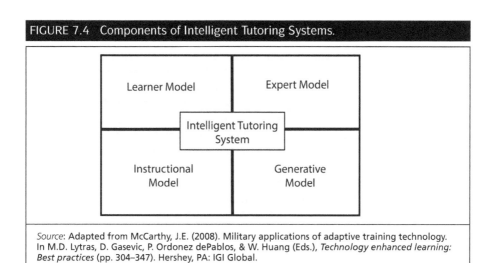

FIGURE 7.4 Components of Intelligent Tutoring Systems.

Source: Adapted from McCarthy, J.E. (2008). Military applications of adaptive training technology. In M.D. Lytras, D. Gasevic, P. Ordonez dePablos, & W. Huang (Eds.), *Technology enhanced learning: Best practices* (pp. 304–347). Hershey, PA: IGI Global.

the learner has received. The expert model represents the knowledge, skill, and performance steps of experts in the content domain. This is often gathered through a detailed cognitive task analysis (see Chapter 3) such as experts 'thinking aloud" as they progress through a task or problem with software developed to capture their competency. The instructional model involves building the capacity of the learning system to make pedagogical inferences and make decisions such as when and how to intervene with the learner based on their responses. The final generative model concerns the capacity of the system to generate appropriate instructional interactions based on learner progress from data gathered through the other models. Together, the four models are linked to ensure the appropriate difficulty of the material is presented to the learner and that decisions by the learner updates the learner model to determine what questions to ask next.

As these systems have become more sophisticated, developers have increased capacity to develop meta-strategies based on a history of the participant's progress. These meta-strategies guide the selection of more specific teaching strategies (next topic, detail level, instructor action) based on the results of tests given at various points in the lessons. The system itself also can learn over time as it tutors many learners through machine learning algorithms that store information about suggestions that were particularly helpful to learners and those suggestions that do not help. By comparing models of the learner's behaviors and cognition with expert content and instructional models, the system selects learning goals and example types, provides tailored feedback, and makes decisions about when to stay at a particular module, when and where to advance and when and where to remediate. Feedback can also be hierarchically structured so that at first, vague hints are given, then direct analogies, and finally explicit instructions given if needed. Learners can also ask questions of the system. These high-end systems respond adaptively to both learning level by making judgments about knowledge level and depth and learning needs. The rapid improvements to artificial intelligence (e.g., voice recognition, natural language processing, avatars) are making it easier to build and implement complex ITS.

The value of ITS has been confirmed by the evidence. As one example, SHERLOCK was developed in the early 1990s to improve troubleshooting skills for jet avionics. Research showed that 25 hours of practice in the ITS environment had the impact on performance of about four years of on-the-job training (Corbett & Koedinger, 1997). As another example, an ITS for training how to deploy a multiple launch rocket system resulted in a 35% improvement in performance compared with the traditional training approach.

Not surprisingly, meta-analytic evidence supports the conclusion of improved learning outcomes over traditional learning methods. A meta-analysis in educational settings found that ITS is more effective than face-to-face large group instruction and non-ITS computer-based instruction for enhancing the acquisition of declarative and procedural knowledge. Interestingly, similar effects are found for the use of one-on-one human tutors as for using ITS (Ma, Adesop, Nesbit, & Liu, 2014). A meta-analysis by Kulik and Fletcher (2016) also found that ITS is an effective instructional tool as participants in ITS outperformed those in the typical classroom instruction in 92% of the 50 controlled evaluations in the meta-analysis. The overall effect was equivalent of improving test performance from the 50th percentile to the 75th!

Learning from a Distance

Technological enhancements have increased the capacity to bring learning opportunities directly to the learner. An initial learning platform that allowed for training across multiple sites at one time was distance learning. Through audio and data links, learners from various sites could access and interact with an instructor from a distant location. A second learning platform was the use of CD-ROM technology to create multimedia training programs. The integration of these various media formats such as video, animation, graphics, and audio permitted more diverse content to be easily accessed by users in multiple ways. The growth of the World Wide Web triggered the third platform around web-based delivery of learning content via the internet or corporate intranet. This platform allows for learning opportunities to be easily updated and be more accessible for just in time learning as well as allowing learners more control over their own learning through the use of hyperlinks to additional material, practice exercises, and feedback.

Learning and Web 2.0 have advanced rapidly to include the facilitation of shared learning and social networking. Technological innovations have now moved e-learning to what has been termed mobile or m-learning. Estimates of delivery methods that organizations plan on using to deliver learning content shows that 82% plan on using e-learning with 35% planning on using mobile apps, 32% using podcasts, 19% using messaging or chat bots and 19% applying microlearning through microsharing (Association for Talent Development, 2019).

E-LEARNING E-learning is a broad array of applications and processes that share a common feature of relying on some type of computer technology (internet, intranet, satellite broadcasts, Massive Open Online Courses or MOOCS) to convey learning content (Brown, Charlier, & Pierotti, 2012). E-learning experiences can vary in terms of their level of interactivity (high or low) as well as instructional focus (on developing skills or more for informational purposes of easy access, storage and use).

Meta-analytic evidence shows e-learning has similar effects on learning as more traditional face-to-face instruction. One of the first meta-analytic reviews (Sitzmann et al., 2006) found that web-based instruction was 6% more effective for the acquisition of declarative knowledge and equally effective for procedural knowledge than traditional classroom instruction. The researchers also found that web-based instruction was 19% more effective for the acquisition of declarative knowledge when learners were provided with some degree of learner control, allowed more time to practice the material, and where learners received diagnostic feedback during the training.

Means et al. (2009) examined 51 studies in higher education, medical schools, and K-12 programs and found that blended instruction of traditional classroom supplemented by web-based instruction was superior to either classroom instruction or e-learning alone. However, an examination of the blended instruction showed that learners in this condition had, on the average, more learning time under this delivery system and were provided with additional instructional elements than the traditional classroom instruction method. The researchers concluded that the positive effected associated with blended learning cannot be solely attributed to the delivery mechanism. Bernard et al. (2009)

examined 74 studies of educational programs and found that student-to-student interaction led to higher achievement scores and better attitudes towards learning than with student to teacher interactions. Yet, they also found that the level of the interactivity was a key driver of increased achievement scores. The bottom line is that research comparing the effectiveness of e-learning compared to traditional classroom instruction must be interpreted with caution as the results may be more a function of the interactivity and focus of the learning experience rather than the technology and delivery mode.

One benefit touted for e-learning is that individual learning can be enhanced by taking advantage of the dynamic capabilities that allow for a more personalized or customized learning experience. Adding in intelligent tutoring systems capabilities into e-learning offers the opportunity to customize learning paths by sequencing of content based on the testing responses of the learner throughout the learning activity. Personalized learning path guidance has been found to lead to higher levels of learning than the "freely browsing" learning mode (Chen, 2008). Liu and Yu (2011) present a strategy to identify aberrant learning patterns early in e-learning (though item response theory models) so that a computer tutoring agent can notify and encourage the learner to try a different approach.

Learner control and exploratory learning have been suggested as important ways for encouraging active learning when delivering content through e-learning. Learner control gives the participant some degree of instructional and scheduling control. Instructional control includes the pace, sequencing, content, amount of guidance and feedback, and how information is presented to the learner (Karim & Behrend, 2014). Scheduling control focuses on the timeframe for completing the learning tasks as well as the location when working on the tasks. Research findings on allowing for learner control of instructional and scheduling has been mixed. For example, too much learner control can lead to more off-task attention as the learner tries to make decisions on what to do next. Studies have found that high levels of learner control may only be effective for those high on personality characteristics such as openness to experience and extraversion (Orvis et al., 2010). A recent meta-analysis found only a small impact of instructional control for gaining specific skills that dissipated over time (Carolan, Hutchins, & Wickens, 2014). Learner control of scheduling, though, has been found to lead to better learning outcomes and would then be more valuable to incorporate into best practices (Karim & Behrend, 2014).

A reason why instructional control is not an effective strategy is that learners tend to make decisions that are not optimal for learning (Kraiger, 2008). Learners may feel they do not need additional practice or do not see the need for more feedback given due to an illusion of knowing (Chapter 5). High levels of learner control can also place a heavy attentional load that distracts the learner as they are trying to acquire new knowledge and skills.

More encouraging findings concern discovery learning with adaptive guidance for the learner. In discovery learning, individuals explore a task or situation to infer and learn the underlying rules, principles, and strategies for effective performance. This active engagement with guidance results in better consolidation and integration as learners reflect more and spend more time monitoring their progress (Bell & Kozlowski, 2008). There are several ways to

TABLE 7.5. Learner Guidance: To What Extent Does your Learning Program …
Help learners maintain a sense of mission/purpose? Provide a model for the inquiry process and instruction s to assist learners with questions or problems? Specify the expected learning outcomes as various times during the program? Give advice on how to approach the learning task such as where to begin, what to focus on and where to go next? Provide advice as to ways to learn effectively and how to retain the information? Emphasize the importance of using feedback to help learners progress? Prompt learners through self-check questions to monitor their comprehension and to consider alternative strategies for learning? Remind learners of the help that is available on how to navigate, access, and practice within the program? Provide extra guidance when learners go off track in the program? Show learners where they have been compared to what they have now accomplished throughout the program? Help learners set goals, select practice exercises, and decide when learning is done?
Sources: Brown, K., Milner, K., & Ford, J.K. (1998). Design of Asynchronous Distance Learning Courses. *Instructional Design Handbook for Distance Learning.* National Center for Manufacturing Sciences. Ann Arbor, MI.; Orvis, K. A., Brusso, R. C., Wasserman, M. E., & Fisher, S. L. (2010). E-nabled for e-learning? The moderating role of personality in determining the optimal degree of learner control in an e-learning environment. *Human Performance,* 24(1), 60–78. Wasserman, & Fisher, (2018). One (lesson) for the road? What we know (and don't know) about mobile learning. K. Brown (Ed.), *The Cambridge Handbook of Workplace Training and Employee Development.* p. 293. Cambridge University Press.

implement a guided discovery approach to e-learning. Guidance can include the following types: having an expert/mentor who gives partial answers to problems, provides leading questions or hints to the learners (from an ITS or human tutor), varies the size of steps in instruction (part versus whole learning), and provides prompts without giving solutions. Guidance can be given to learners on how to form hypotheses and test out these ideas in more effective ways (Mayer, 2004). Learners can be presented with case studies of job situations and asked to draw inferences about effective and ineffective responses to these situations. From these specific incidents, general principles of effective responses can be generated, discussed, and feedback provided. A checklist based on evidence for best practices to consider when incorporating learner guidance is provided in Table 7.5.

From a social networking perspective, e-learning communities can also be set up to share information and best practices. As noted by Boiros (2011), social learning requires three elements to be successful – the right technology platform, a vibrant community of learners and engaging content. Social learning is the exchange among learners to extract meaning in the workplace through completing projects socially and providing feedback, support, and encouragement. Effective social learning requires clear goals and objectives, defined norms for participating in the social networking system, and strategies for dealing with interpersonal issues that might arise (Kraiger, 2008). In addition, social learning rests on the skills and motivations of the community members' ability and willingness to provide accurate information and diagnostic feedback to others to help facilitate the learning process (Bedwell & Salas, 2008).

MOBILE LEARNING Mobile or m-learning goes beyond e-learning by providing learning opportunities through wireless and handheld mobile technologies such as smart phones with web capabilities that can transmit multimedia learning content. This is coming at a time when it is estimated that soon mobile phone connections worldwide will reach 12 billion (Bruck, Motiwalla, & Foerster, 2012)! Advances in mobile technologies allows learners easy access to the learning content required for a job as well as allow for quick access to performance aids. Mobile technologies (like earlier technologies) also allow for collaborative peer-to-peer learning activities (Jeng et al., 2010). M-learning is also touted for its potential to allow learning content to be customized to better meet learner needs.

Wasserman and Fisher (2018) have identified four broad characteristics relevant to m-learning. One characteristic is that the device used by the learner is portable and web-enabled. A second characteristics is that m-learning allows for flexibility in terms of time and place. The learner can access learning opportunities anyplace and at any time. A third characteristic is the social dimension whereby mobile learning can be configured to include communication tools such as weblogs, wikis, podcasts, and apps that support user generated interaction and collaboration through sharing of content, discussion posts, and best practices. They also note the fourth issue of situational connectedness in which the "learner can be taught or shown material based on exactly what she or he is seeing at the very moment and be connected with peers who can offer expertise at the moment that expertise is needed to enhance learning" (p. 297).

The move to micro content for learning given mobile technology advances requires precise planning to hone in on what is essential content that is simple but immediately impactful rather than the nice to know. Learners can now gain competencies by constructing their own learning environments and experiences by selecting learning content and making decisions about the sequencing of material by pursuing material on the web around a specific or narrow task presented in small chunks (Kerres, 2007). Of course, concerns raised about learner control with e-learning also has relevance for m-learning. In addition, m-learning can increase one's level of distractibility whereby an individual's attention shifts from tasks to be performed on the job to learning opportunities and back again. We know that distractions reduce learning and retention. While the benefits of m-learning are touted, one must also recognize this potential downside of how easy accessibility and interconnectivity around learning opportunities affect job performance (Wasserman & Fisher, 2018). In fact, focus groups for professionals in construction (Germany) and health care (UK) discovered concerns raised about an increase in information load for middle management as more digital artifacts are produced and shared requiring more time to determine what to pay attention to and what to ignore (Schäper & Thalmann, 2014).

The rapid growth of m-learning capabilities in the workplace is clear. For example, 75% of the 45 BEST award-winning companies for 2017 from the Association for Talent Development offer mobile learning and 80% give employees access to social networking tools to promote learning (Castellano et al., 2018). Research evidence leading to best practices regarding how to enhance the effectiveness of m-learning has been outpaced by its popularity.

The limited research has mostly focused on usage data and participant satisfaction. For example, Bruck et al. (2012) reported use data for a Knowledge-Pulse mobile platform that included 71 different learning cards available for access through smart phones. The study with governmental employees in the Arab Gulf Emirate found that usage rates were only about 50% but that those who accessed the learning content reported high levels of satisfaction in terms of ease of use and value to learning.

A meta-analysis has found evidence that learners appreciate the collaborative opportunities and the anytime and place for learning. The study also found that an expectation of learners is that the content is relevant and presented in a user-friendly way (Alrasheedi & Capretz, 2013). There is some evidence that micro learning health quizzes provide relevant information and led to improvements in healthy behaviors (Simons et al., 2015). In addition, a recent study of high school students found that in comparison to a control group that received conventional paper based homework, the mobile learning group reported greater learning satisfaction with micro learning homework tasks and also had higher exam performance in terms of factual knowledge (Nikou & Economides, 2018). More research on innovative applications of micro and mobile learning are sure to follow.

CONCLUDING COMMENTS

The delivery options for workplace learning are rapidly expanding as a function of technologies that allow for much more sophisticated learning platforms. A majority of the research that has compared the effectiveness of these computer-based instruction platforms to more traditional classroom instruction has found similar and at times higher levels of learning for the technology-mediated instruction. It must be noted, though, that these results may say as much about the efforts put into learning design with the introduction of new technology as it does about the instructional medium.

Organizations that invest the money to build these new learning platforms are more likely to make sure that the Learning Systems Model is followed carefully in the development of the learning opportunities. Instructional designers may go to great lengths to include instructional principles such as gaining learner attention at the beginning of the learning experience, making sure prerequisites are met by learners, having learning aids embedded into the experience and varying the instructional stimuli to motivate learners.

Learning technologies are becoming more blended in terms of delivery. Web-based programs are no longer standalone systems. Instead, the learner can progress through the content of a program and hyperlink to websites to gain additional information, address case studies, additional examples, or connect with an expert. In addition, programs have been developed where learners can switch from a virtual reality world where they can touch and manipulate objects to more conventional multimedia programs to gain more declarative and procedural knowledge. As one example of blended instruction, a mass casualty training called the Virtual Civilian Aeromedical Evacuation Sustainment Training provides ITS guided instruction for a team of learners in a VR world of an area struck by an earthquake. The team comes across six victims at various levels of need and must make decisions on how to proceed.

Interestingly, the researchers found no differences in learning outcomes (knowledge measures) and transfer indices between a live action training simulation (seen as the gold standard) and the ITS within VR civilian evacuation training (Shubeck, Craig, & Hu, 2016).

Finally, although emerging learning technologies offer significant potential for improving teaching and learning, they also complicate learning design. The challenge is to develop designs that utilize the potential advantages of the technologies rather than simply providing another means of training delivery. How technological capabilities are used in creative ways to facilitate learning is more critical than the technical capabilities themselves. Managing this creativity to develop effective learning is the difficult part. The important aspect here is to use the power of the technology with learning and performance as the key outcomes. Designers must be aware of the cognitive demands their learning systems place on learners. The design must thoughtfully apply techniques that support, not interfere with, learner effort and skill development. As noted by Krendl et al. (1996), it is far easier to create something with great cosmetic appeal that an *integrated learning system* that is consistent with available research and theory.

Chapter 7: Best Practice Guidelines

- Develop appropriate skill sets for instructors including strategies to use that facilitate learning (Table 7.1).
- To increase engagement in face-to-face instruction incorporate specific questions challenging learners to organize, apply, analyze, integrate, evaluatie, and generate new ways of thinking about the learning domain.
- Ensure that instruction comes across to the learner as credible, practical, and needed (Table 7.2).
- Use case studies where learners must use diagnostic skills to uncover the underlying principles in the case(s).
- When demonstrating a skill, tell the learner what specific things to observe, state each step as it is being demonstrated, and ask learners to mentally rehearse the steps and commit the steps to memory before they begin practicing the steps.
- Focus design efforts on the incorporation of learning principles rather than trying to match instruction to learner styles.
- Make sure the appropriate level of functional, psychological, and social fidelity are incorporated into work simulations rather than relying solely on physical fidelity.
- Virtual reality systems need to be targeted, focused, and provide ample time for deliberate practice of specific skills identified as critical to success on the job.
- Provide learners control over scheduling and timeline for completing from distance learning technologies.
- With distance learning technologies, incorporate strategies (Table 7.3) for providing learner guidance; use animated agents to help guide learners through serious games.

References

Aïm, F., Lonjon, G., Hannouche, D., & Nizard, R. (2016). Effectiveness of virtual reality training in orthopaedic surgery. *Arthroscopy: The Journal of Arthroscopic & Related Surgery*, 32(1), 224–232. doi.org/10.1016/j.arthro.2015.07.023

Alaker, M., Wynn, G. R., & Arulampalam, T. (2016). Virtual reality training in laparoscopic surgery: a systematic review & meta-analysis. *International Journal of Surgery*, 29, 85–94. doi.org/10.1016/j.ijsu.2016.03.034

Aldrich, C. (2009). *The complete guide to simulations & serious games*. San Francisco, CA: Pfeiffer/Wiley.

Alrasheedi, M., & Capretz, L. F. (2013, August). A meta-analysis of critical success factors affecting mobile learning. In *Proceedings of 2013 IEEE international conference on teaching, assessment and learning for engineering* (pp. 262–267). Colhoun: Austin, TX: Cognitive Science Society. IEEE. 10.1109/TALE.2013.6654443

Andrade, A. D., Bagri, A., Zaw, K., Roos, B. A., & Ruiz, J. G. (2010). Avatar-mediated training in the delivery of bad news in a virtual world. *Journal of Palliative Medicine*, 13(12), 1415–1419.

American Red Cross. (1999). *Building leadership skills through a board game-based simulation to create shared mental models of the organization's critical systems*. Alexandria, VA: American Red Cross Disaster Services.

Argyris, C. (2002). Double-loop learning, teaching, and research. *Academy of Management Learning & Education*, 1(2), 206–218. doi.org/10.5465/amle.2002.8509400

Association for Talent Development (2019) *Microlearning: Delivering bite-sized knowledge*. Alexandria, VA: ATD Research.

Ausburn, L. J., & Ausburn, F. B. (2004). Desktop virtual reality: A powerful new technology for teaching and research in industrial teacher education. *Journal of Industrial Teacher Education*, 41(4), 1–16

Bedwell, W. L., & Salas, E. (2008). If you build it, will they interact? The importance of the instructor. *Industrial and Organizational Psychology*, 1(4), 491–493.

Bell, B. S., & Kozlowski, S. W. (2008). Active learning: effects of core training design elements on self-regulatory processes, learning, and adaptability. *Journal of Applied Psychology*, 93(2), 296. doi.org/10.1037/0021-9010.93.2.296

Bernard, R. M., Abrami, P. C., Borokhovski, E., Wade, C. A., Tamim, R. M., Surkes, M. A., & Bethel, E. C. (2009). A meta-analysis of three types of interaction treatments in distance education. *Review of Educational Research*, 79(3), 1243–1289.

Boiros, P. (2011). Fundamentals of social media support for learning. *Learning Solutions Magazine*. Retrieved from www.learningsolutionsmag.com/articles/831/fundamentals-of-social-media-support-for-learning

Brittain, J., & Sitkin, S. (1989). Facts, figures, and organizational decisions: Carter racing and quantitative analysis in the organizational behavior classroom. *The Organizational Behavior Teaching Review*, 14, 62–81.

Brown, K. G., Charlier, S. D., & Pierotti, A. (2012). E-learning at work: Contributions of past research and suggestions for the future. In *International review of industrial and organizational psychology*. Oxford: Wiley-Blackwell.

Brown, K., Milner, K., & Ford, J.K. (1998). Design of asynchronous distance learning courses. In *Instructional design handbook for distance learning*. Ann Arbor, MI: National Center for Manufacturing Sciences.

Bruck, P. A., Motiwalla, L., & Foerster, F. (2012). Mobile Learning with Microcontent: A Framework and Evaluation. *Bled eConference*, Bled, Slovenia, 25, 527–543.

Carbonell, J. R. (1970). AI in CAI: An artificial intelligence approach to computer-assisted instruction. *IEEE: Transactions on Man-Machine Systems*, 11, 190–202.

Carolan, T. F., Hutchins, S. D., Wickens, C. D., & Cumming, J. M. (2014). Costs and benefits of more learner freedom: Meta-analyses of exploratory and learner control training methods. *Human Factors*, 56(5), 999–1014.

Castellano, S. (2019, October). *Leading through change: Talent development* (pp. 55–56). Alexandria, VA: Association for Talent Development.

Castellano, S., Harris, P., Fyfe-Mills, K., & Bossov, A. (2018). ATD's 2018 BEST award winners revealed. *Talent development* (October), 26-26-60.

Chen, C. M. (2008). Intelligent web-based learning system with personalized learning path guidance. *Computers & Education*, 51(2), 787–814.

Choi, M., & Roulston, K. (2015). Learning transfer in practice: A qualitative study of medical professionals' perspectives. *Human Resource Development Quarterly*, 26(3), 249–273.

Clark, R.C. (2010). *Evidence-based training methods: A guide for training professionals*. Washington, DC: American Society for Training and Development Press.

Connolly, T. M., Boyle, E. A., MacArthur, E., Hainey, T., & Boyle, J. M. (2012). A systematic literature review of empirical evidence on computer games and serious games. *Computers & Education*, 59(2), 661–686.

Cook, D. A., Hatala, R., Brydges, R., Zendejas, B., Szostek, J. H., Wang, A.T., Erwin, P.J., & Hamstra, S.J. (2011). Technology-enhanced simulation for health professions education: a systematic review and meta-analysis. *Journal of the American Medical Association*, 306(9), 978–988. doi:10.1001/jama.2011.1234

Corbett, A. T., Koedinger, K. R., & Anderson, J. R. (1997). Intelligent tutoring systems. In M. Helander, T. K. Landauer, P. Prabhu (Eds), *Handbook of human-computer interaction* (pp. 849–874). New York: Elsevier.

Dahlstrom, N., Dekker, S., Van Winsen, R., & Nyce, J. (2009). Fidelity and validity of simulator training. *Theoretical Issues in Ergonomics Science*, 10(4), 305–314. doi.org/10.1080/14639220802368864

Gauld, D. (2015). The competencies of effective trainers and teachers. In K. Kraiger, J. Passmore, NR d. Santos, & S. Malvezzi (Eds.), *The Wiley Blackwell handbook of the psychology of training, development, and performance improvement* (pp. 117–135). Chichester: John Wiley & Sons.

Gauld, D. and Miller, P. (2004). The qualifications and competencies held by effective workplace trainers. *Journal of European Industrial Training*, 28, 8–22. doi.org/10.1108/03090590410513866

Hamstra, S. J., Brydges, R., Hatala, R., Zendejas, B., & Cook, D. A. (2014). Reconsidering fidelity in simulation-based training. *Academic Medicine*, 89(3), 387–392. doi: 10.1097/ACM.0000000000000130

Haque, S., & Srinivasan, S. (2006). A meta-analysis of the training effectiveness of virtual reality surgical simulators. *IEEE Transactions on Information Technology in Biomedicine*, 10(1), 51–58.

Harders, M. (2008). *Surgical scene generation for virtual reality-based training in medicine*. London UK: Springer Science & Business Media.

Ho, M., Jones, M., Julien, T., & Body, J. (2016). *State of the industry report*. Alexandria, VA: Association for Talent Development.

International Convention on Standards of Training, Certification and Watchkeeping for Seafarers. (1978). Available at: http://www.imo.org/en/OurWork/HumanElement/TrainingCertification/Pages/STCW-Convention.aspx, accessed February 28, 2020.

Jeng, Y. L., Wu, T. T., Huang, Y. M., Tan, Q., & Yang, S. J. (2010). The add-on impact of mobile applications in learning strategies: A review study. *Journal of Educational Technology & Society*, 13(3), 3–11.

Jentsch, F., & Bowers, C. A. (1998). Evidence for the validity of PC-based simulations in studying aircrew coordination. *The International Journal of Aviation Psychology*, 8(3), 243–260. doi.org/10.1207/s15327108ijap0803_5

Johnson, W. L., Friedland, L., Schrider, P., Valente, A., & Sheridan, S. (2011, May). The Virtual Cultural Awareness Trainer (VCAT): Joint Knowledge Online's (JKO's) solution to the individual operational culture and language training gap. In *Proceedings of ITEC*, Clarion Events London, UK.

Johnson, W. L., & Lester, J. C. (2016). Face-to-face interaction with pedagogical agents, twenty years later. *International Journal of Artificial Intelligence in Education*, 26(1), 25–36. doi.org/10.1007/s40593-015-0065-9

Karim, M. N., & Behrend, T. S. (2014). Reexamining the nature of learner control: Dimensionality and effects on learning and training reactions. *Journal of Business and Psychology*, 29(1), 87–99. doi.org/10.1007/s10869-013-9309-6

Kerr, B., Lee-Ann Hawkins, T., Herman, R., Barnes, S., Kaufmann, S., Fraser, K., & Ma, I. W. (2013). Feasibility of scenario-based simulation training versus traditional workshops in continuing medical education: a randomized controlled trial. *Medical Education Online*, 18(1), 21312. doi.org/10.3402/meo.v18i0.21312

Kerres, M. (2007). Microlearning as a challenge for instructional design. In *Didactics of microlearning: Concepts, discourses and examples* (pp. 98–109). Münster: Waxmann.

Kim, Y., & Baylor, A.L. (2016). Research-based design of pedagogical agent roles: A review, progress, and recommendations. *International Journal of Artificial Intelligence in Education*, 26, 160–169. doi.org/10.1007/s40593-015-0055-y

King, P. H. (1966). *A summary of research in training for advisory roles in other cultures by the behavioral sciences laboratory. Final report 1963–1966*. Aerospace Medical Research Labs Wright-Patterson AFB, Ohio.

Knowles, M.S., Holton, E.F., & Swanson, R.A. (2015). *The adult learner* (8th edition). New York: Routledge.

Kolb, D.A. (1984b) *Experiential Learning: experience as the source of learning and development*. Englewood Cliffs, NJ: Prentice-Hall.

Kraiger, K. (2008). Transforming our models of learning and development: Web-based instruction as enabler of third-generation instruction. *Industrial and Organizational Psychology*, 1(4), 454–467.

Krendl, K. A., Ware, W. H., Reid, K. A., & Warren, R. (1996). Learning by any other name: Communication research traditions in learning and media. In D. H. Jonassen (Ed.), *Handbook of research for educational communications and technology* (pp. 93–111). New York: MacMillan.

Kroehnert, G. (2003). *103 additional training games*, San Francisco, CA: McGraw-Hill.

Kulik, J. A., & Fletcher, J. D. (2016). Effectiveness of intelligent tutoring systems: a meta-analytic review. *Review of Educational Research*, 86(1), 42–78.

Lane, C., & Rollnick, S. (2007). The use of simulated patients and role-play in communication skills training: a review of the literature to August 2005. *Patient Education and Counseling*, 67(1-2), 13–20. doi.org/10.1016/j.pec.2007.02.011

Larsen, C. R., Soerensen, J. L., Grantcharov, T. P., Dalsgaard, T., Schouenborg, L., Ottosen, C., ... & Ottesen, B. S. (2009). Effect of virtual reality training on laparoscopic surgery: Randomised controlled trial. *BMJ*, 338, b1802.

Liu, M. T., & Yu, P. T. (2011). Aberrant learning achievement detection based on person-fit statistics in personalized e-learning systems. *Journal of Educational Technology & Society*, 14(1), 107–120.

Loewenstein, J., Thompson, L., & Gentner, D. (2003). Analogical learning in negotiation teams: Comparing cases promotes learning and transfer. *Academy of Management Learning & Education*, 2(2), 119–127. doi.org/10.5465/amle.2003.9901663

Loftin, R.B. (1996). Hands across the Atlantic. *Virtual Reality Special Report* (March/April), 39–42.

Luppa, N., & Borst, T. (2007). *Story and simulations for serious games: Tales from the trenches*. Burlington, MA: Elsevier.

Ma, W., Adesope, O. O., Nesbit, J. C., & Liu, Q. (2014). Intelligent tutoring systems and learning outcomes: A meta-analysis. *Journal of Educational Psychology*, 106(4), 901.

MacLean, S., Kelly, M., Geddes, F., & Della, P. (2017). Use of simulated patients to develop communication skills in nursing education: An integrative review. *Nurse Education Today*, 48, 90–98. doi.org/10.1016/j.nedt.2016.09.018

Marlow, S.L., Lacerenza, C.N., Reyes, D., & Salas, E. (2018). The science and practice of simulation-based training in organizations. In K. Brown (Ed.), *Workplace training and employee development*. New York: Cambridge University Press.

Mayer, R. E. (2004). Should there be a three-strikes rule against pure discovery learning?: The case for guided methods of instruction. *American Psychologist*, 59, 14–19.

McCarthy, J.E. (2008). Military applications of adaptive training technology. In M.D. Lytras, D. Gasevic, P. Ordonez de Pablos, & W. Huang (Eds.), *Technology enhanced learning: Best practices* (pp. 304–347). Hershey, PA: IGI Global.

McGowan, C., & Pecheux, B. (2007). Serious gaming: Advanced computer simulation games help to transform healthcare and disaster preparedness. *Health Management Technology*, 14, 16–23.

Means, B., Toyama, Y., Murphy, R., Bakia, M., & Jones, K. (2009). *Evaluation of evidence-based practices in online learning: A meta-analysis and review of online learning studies*. Washington DC: U.S. Department of Education, Center for Technology in Learning.

Messa, L.J., & Mayer, R.E. (2006). Testing the ATI hypothesis: Should multimedia instruction accommodate verbalizer-visualizer cognitive styles?. *Learning and Individual Differences*, 16, 321–336. doi.org/10.1016/j.lindif.2006.10.001

Nikou, S. A., & Economides, A. A. (2018). Mobile-Based micro-Learning and Assessment: Impact on learning performance and motivation of high school students. *Journal of Computer Assisted Learning*, 34(3), 269–278. doi.org/10.1111/jcal.12240

Norman, G., Dore, K., & Grierson, L. (2012). The minimal relationship between simulation fidelity and transfer of learning. *Medical Education*, 46(7), 636–647. doi.org/10.1111/j.1365-2923.2012.04243.x

O'Connor, D.L., & Menaker, E.S. (2008). Can massively multiplayer online gaming environments support team training? *Performance Improvement Quarterly*, 21, 23–41. doi.org/10.1002/piq.20029

Orvis, K. A., Brusso, R. C., Wasserman, M. E., & Fisher, S. L. (2010). E-nabled for e-learning? The moderating role of personality in determining the optimal degree of learner control in an e-learning environment. *Human Performance*, 24(1), 60–78. doi.org/10.1080/08959285.2010.530633

Pashler, H., McDaniel, M., Rohrer, D., Bjork, R. (2009). Learning styles concepts and evidence. *Psychological Science in the Public Interest*, 9, 105–119. doi.org/10.1111/j.1539-6053.2009.01038.x

Philips, D. (1991); Terror at zero feet: A crew's simulated brush with disaster. *Washington Post*, January 1, A3.

Rees, W. D., & Porter, C. (2002). The use of case studies in management training and development. Part 1. *Industrial and Commercial Training*, 34(1), 5–8. doi.org/10.1108/00197850210414026

Rickel, J., & Johnson, W. L. (2000). Task-oriented collaboration with embodied agents in virtual worlds, In J. Cassell, S. Prevost, E. Churchill and J. Sullivan (eds.), *Embodied Conversational Agents* (pp. 95–122). Cambridge, MA: MIT Press.

Ritterfeld, U., Cody, M., & Vorderer, P. (Eds.). (2009). *Serious games: Mechanisms and effects*. New York: Routledge.

Sacks, R., Perlman, A., & Barak, R. (2013). Construction safety training using immersive virtual reality. *Construction Management and Economics*, 31, 1005–1017. doi.org/10.1080/01446193.2013.828844

Salvendy, G., & Pilitsis, J. (1980). The development and validation of an analytical training program for medical suturing. *Human Factors*, 22(2), 153–170.

Schäper, S., & Thalmann, S. (2014). Technology support for informal learning in mobile work situations. In D. Kundisch, L. Suhl, & Beckmann, L. (Eds.), *MKWI* (pp. 846–854). Paderborn, Germany: Universität Paderborn.

Schroeder, N. L., Adesope, O. O., & Gilbert, R. B. (2013). How effective are pedagogical agents for learning? A meta-analytic review. *Journal of Educational Computing Research*, 49(1), 1–39. doi.org/10.2190/EC.49.1.a

Sellberg, C. (2017). Simulators in bridge operations training and assessment: A systematic review and qualitative synthesis. *WMU Journal of Maritime Affairs*, 16(2), 247–263

Shubeck, K. T., Craig, S. D., & Hu, X. (2016, September). Live-action mass-casualty training and virtual world training: A comparison. In *Proceedings of the human factors and ergonomics society annual meeting* (Vol. 60, No. 1, pp. 2103–2107). Sage CA: Los Angeles, CA: SAGE Publications.

Simons, L. P., Foerster, F., Bruck, P. A., Motiwalla, L., & Jonker, C. M. (2015). Microlearning mApp raises health competence: hybrid service design. *Health and Technology*, 5(1), 35–43. doi. org/10.1007/s12553-015-0095-1

Sitzmann, T., Kraiger, K., Stewart, D., & Wisher, R. (2006). The comparative effectiveness of web-based and classroom instruction: A meta-analysis. *Personnel Psychology*, 59(3), 623–664.

Snow, R. E., & Lohman, D. F. (1984). Toward a theory of cognitive aptitude for learning from instruction. *Journal of Educational Psychology*, 76(3), 347.

Thompson, T. N., Carroll, M. B., & Deaton, J. E. (2009). Justification for use of simulation. In P. Hancock D. Vincenzi, J. Wise, and M. Mouloua (Eds.). *Human factors in simulation and training* (39–48). Boca Raton, FL: CRC Press/Taylor & Francis.

Wahl, A. M. (2019). Expanding the concept of simulator fidelity: The use of technology and collaborative activities in training maritime officers. *Cognition, Technology & Work*, 22, 209–222. doi. org/10.10007/s10111-019-00549-4

Wasserman, & Fisher. (2018). One (lesson) for the road? What we know (and don't know) about mobile learning. In K. Brown (Ed.), *The Cambridge handbook of workplace training and employee development*, (293). Cambridge: Cambridge University Press.

Willingham, D. T., Hughes, E. M., & Dobolyi, D. G. (2015). The scientific status of learning styles theories. *Teaching of Psychology*, 42(3), 266–271. doi. org/10.1177/0098628315589505

Yelon, S.L. (1996). *Powerful principles of instruction*. White Plains, NY: Longman.

Yelon, S., Sheppard, L., Sleight, D., & Ford, J. K. (2004). Intention to transfer: How do autonomous professionals become motivated to use new ideas? *Performance Improvement Quarterly*, 17(2), 82–103. doi.org/10.1111/j.1937-8327.2004. tb00309.x

PART III

Learning Strategies

Building Individual Capabilities

Questions

✓ What are effective strategies for onboarding and socializing new-comers to an organization?

✓ Why are apprenticeship programs expanding?

✓ What can organizations do to encourage informal learning and self-management of careers?

As noted in Chapter 1, work is becoming more knowledge driven and global in scope requiring a deeper combination of information, experience, under-standing and problem-solving skills that can be applied to actions around strategically critical situations. Organizations are dependent on the level of knowledge and skilled expertise of its employees especially in jobs critical for future growth and success. Career development can be studied as a series of movements along three different dimensions: (1) moving up in the hierarchy in an occupation or organization, (2) moving laterally across various subfields or an occupation or functional group, and (3) moving toward the centers of influence in a job function due to the development of a deep level of expertise in that specialization (Schein, 2006).

Learning experiences can have a major impact on what types of career movements are possible and whether the changes involved in each move-ment are made in a smooth and effective manner. Job incumbents increasingly recognize that their knowledge and skills need to be continually updated to remain current with the present job and to prepare for future career goals. Organizational changes lead to rethinking the relevance of the traditional career pyramid with its emphasis on developmental efforts around promo-tion and upward mobility. There are increasing efforts to develop and enhance deep levels of specialization for core jobs in an organization.

Newcomers need to get up to speed quickly on a job for the organiza-tion to get immediate value out of the investment of recruitment, selection, and initial training costs. Longer-term developmental strategies are needed for individuals to progress towards expertise in their jobs. Given that it can take years of training, learning activities, coaching, and work experiences to develop deep specialization, it is important to identify key levers to accelerate individual development over time (Hoffman, 2014). As individuals move from newcomer status to established insider in the organization, employees are asked to enlarge their knowledge and skill base and more fully utilize their talents. The learning experiences employees receive are targeted to improving technical proficiency as well as developing more general competencies that lead to a better-rounded individual who can succeed in the workplace over the course of a career. The overall goal of development is the achievement of consistent, superior performance. This superior performance is a result of experience, training and on-the-job learning activities that have a "developmental punch" (Kraiger & Ford, 2007).

The purpose of this chapter is to examine the intentional learning strategies created to develop individual employees' job proficiency as well as more general competencies that lead to a well-rounded individual who can succeed in the workplace over the course of a career. First, strategies for accelerating learning of newcomers are described followed by the role of learning from on-the-job experiences in furthering knowledge and skill gains. In the second section, intentional efforts for job incumbents to gain knowledge and skills through learning experiences such as job rotation and informal learning are examined. The chapter ends with a discussion of self-development and career management strategies that have been found to help individuals keep pace with the changing realities of the workplace.

NEWCOMER DEVELOPMENT

It is important to get newcomers off to a strong start to increase the probability of job success and reduce the possibility of early turnover. The difference between a weak start and a strong start can be lasting impacts such as the time it takes for the newcomer to become competent in the job as well as the newcomer perceptions of fit with the organization's culture. A strong start for a newcomer is more than any initial orientation but is a process that can last months.

Effective onboarding employs a variety of learning strategies such as individual learning through web-based sources, formal training, and coaching and mentoring. An effective onboarding process is a planned activity implemented consistently over time so the newcomer can transition into the job. Best practices for the planning process for onboarding includes engaging relevant stakeholders in the planning process, developing a comprehensive onboarding plan and creating milestones (e.g., 30, 90 days) and setting expectations. When conducting onboarding, best practices include (1) making the first day on the job special; (2) discussing right away the expectations and milestones; (3) clarifying roles and responsibilities; (4) using a formal orientation program with purposeful application of learning technologies; (5) making onboarding engaging and participatory and (6) then later checking progress on the milestones (Bauer, 2010). Onboarding practices from the initial orientation sessions through formal and informal socialization tactics are important strategies to meet newcomer needs, affect the time to proficiency, and integrate the individual into the workgroup.

Orientation and Initial Training

Onboarding typically begins with orientation sessions to give newcomers a sense of the job and the organization. The orientation introduces the new employee to job duties and expectations, organizational policies and regulations, and the use of resources such as computers. The building blocks of effective orientation sessions revolve around the four "Cs" of: (1) compliance to rules and regulations; (2) clarification of job duties and expectations; (3) cultural norms and values; and (4) connection to the interpersonal and informational networks in the organization (Bauer, 2010). The quality and quantity of these initial learning experiences affect the readiness of the worker in terms of acquiring needed knowledge and skills to be a productive member of the workforce.

Orientation programs also provide the organization with an opportunity to give newcomers a realistic view of what to expect from the organization. If the initial program provides the necessary and accurate information required for the newcomer to perform effectively in the new position, then it is possible that some of the reality shock of entering the new organization can be minimized. A newcomer with exaggerated beliefs and unrealistic expectations is a likely candidate for early turnover. Research describing three case studies with onboarding of software developers in globally distributed projects found that only in one of the three cases were newcomers given a realistic preview of the job (Britto et al., 2018).

Research on the effectiveness of formal orientation programs is limited. More personal, face-to-face sessions have been found to lead to greater commitment and job satisfaction than orientation information delivered through more impersonal sources such as the web (Wesson & Gogus, 2005). This points to the challenges of delivering effective orientation sessions with remote workers (e.g., software developers) that are globally distributed (Steinmacher & colleague, 2015). A study of orientation practices of temporary agencies examined the extent to which the agency provided training on equipment to be used on the job as well as the orientation practices of the client where the temporary worker was placed (e.g., did they provide you with a tour of the company, tell you what the company's work procedures are). The findings indicate that greater efforts at newcomer orientation are rewarded with higher levels of job commitment and satisfaction as well as lower turnover intentions (Slattery, Selvarajan, & Anderson, 2006). Given the move to more temporary workers, this study highlights the importance of orientation by both the temp agency and the client organization.

A nice framework for an effective orientation process emphasizes the need to Inform, Welcome, and Guide newcomers. Table 8.1 presents a list of 30 actions organizations can take around these three concepts to properly orient newcomers to the job, coworkers, and the organization. Informing includes the types of communication to the newcomer, access to the proper resources to succeed, and the initial training to systematically build required capabilities. Welcoming involves intentional activities for newcomers to meet and interact with team members and members in other relevant departments and functions. Guiding focuses on intentional strategies to provide a personal touch in which a person is assigned to help the newcomer during those important first days on the job (Klein & Polin, 2012).

TABLE 8.1   Categories and Activities for Newcomer Orientation

Inform – Communication: Planned efforts to facilitate communication with newcomers. Includes both the provision of one-way messages and opportunities for two-way dialogue
I went to a question and answer session where new hires were able to ask senior leaders questions.
I was invited to meet with a senior leader.
My managers set aside a block of uninterrupted time to spend with me.
I met with a representative from Human Resources.

Inform – Resources: Making materials or assistance available to new hires. These efforts differ from communication in that the new hire has to take the initiative to access them
I was shown how to find things on the company website.
I was given an initial plan that outlined opportunities for my development.
I was given a glossary of abbreviations and buzzwords used in the company.
I was directed to a section of the company website specifically designed for new associates.
I was given a list of names and contact information on important people within the company.
My workspace was ready for me (including all supplies, materials and equipment).

Inform – Training: Planned efforts to facilitate the acquisition of skills, knowledge, and behavior
I was shown a new employee video.
I was encouraged to observe a fellow associate for a period of time.
I received on-the-job training on how to perform my job.
I was given a tour of the facilities.
I attended an orientation program with other new hires.
I completed an on-line orientation program.
I attended a session with presentations by fellow associates who are experts on certain tasks and procedures.

Welcome: Activities that provide opportunities for new hires to socialize and for members to celebrate arrival of newcomers
I received a personalized welcome to the company (phone, email, letter) from a senior leader.
I received a personalized welcome from my manager.
I was given a welcome kit.
I participated in an exercise to get to know my fellow associates.
There was a gathering (meeting, welcome lunch) for me to meet my fellow associates.
A new associate welcome celebration was held.
I was invited to participate in a social event to get to know fellow associates.
My family was invited to attend a social activity held outside of work.
My joining the company was announced in an email on the company website or company newsletter.
Company t-shirts or other items with the company logo was given to me.

Guide: Activities that provide a personal guide for each new hire
Someone at a higher level than my manager was assigned to be my mentor.
I had a single point of contact (e.g., welcome coordinator) that I could reach out to with any questions.
A fellow associate was assigned as my "buddy" to help answer any questions I might have.

Source: Klein, H. J., Polin, B., & Sutton, K.L., (2015). Specific onboarding practices for the socialization of new employees. *International Journal of Selection and Assessment*, 23, 263–283. Copyright 2015 by John Wiley & Sons. Reprinted by Permission.

Using this framework, a study examined the orientation practices of ten organizations and obtained perceptions of the orientation experience from 372 newcomers in those organizations (Klein, Polin, & Sutton, 2015). The top ten onboarding practices across these organizations included practices such as "my manager set aside a block of uninterrupted time to spend with me," "I received on-the-job training on how to perform my job," and I had a single point of contact (welcome coordinator) that I could reach out to with any questions." The ten best practices for aiding the socialization of the newcomers are italicized in Table 8.1. The Informing practices around communication and the Guiding practices typically occurred on the first day of employment while the Welcome practices tended to occur late in the first week of employment. Informing about resources and the initial training occurred early in the second week of employment. The findings illustrate that the higher the number of specific orientation practices offered, the higher the employees rated their level of understanding of how to perform their job duties as well as their understanding of the company's core values. Required activities rather than those that had been encouraged were seen my newcomers as more helpful. Interestingly, newcomers reported experiencing fewer orientation activities around resources than the organization had noted as being offered. More generally, there is clearly room for improvement in this area as that research indicates that best practice orientation tactics are generally underutilized.

Socialization

Once the newcomer has completed the orientation program and activities, another factor influencing how well the individual will fit into and be a productive member of the organization is the subsequent process of socialization. Organizational socialization is the learning and adjustment process by which a person gains a greater (and perhaps more realistic) understanding of the values, norms, and expected behaviors, which helps the person to participate effectively as a member of the organization. Through this process, organizations attempt to shape the efforts of the newcomer around valued organizational outcomes while also facilitating their adjustment to new roles and responsibilities. At the same time, the newcomer can proactively begin to craft the job to better fit their own needs and desires for the job.

Socialization takes place over months after initial entry and orientation process. Socialization processes are also critical when people change jobs within the same organization, move up the hierarchy through promotions and when becoming more central and influential within the organization. Our focus here is on newcomer socialization and what needs to be learned and how best to facilitate that learning.

The goals of socialization are to build on the orientation program so that newcomers acquire the knowledge, skills, behaviors, and attitudes needed to become integrated into the organizational structure and culture. Socialization tactics and practices help newcomers understand task requirements and clarify roles that affect distal outcomes of job satisfaction, commitment, performance, and retention. Organizations use a variety of socialization tactics (Chao, 2012). Some companies have a formal process of progression while others allow the process to unfold in a more informal way by assuming the work team will provide the information, support, and resources the newcomer needs. There can be a set sequence of activities that newcomers go through (e.g., like in the military) or the process can be more open and adaptable to the needs of the newcomer. Newcomers can be formally assigned to a "buddy" to serve as a role model for task performance and worker adjustment. In general, socialization tactics can be categorized as being institutionalized (formal, sequenced, and fixed) or individualized (informal, open, self-directed).

Regardless of the tactics taken, a key issue is what is learned by the newcomer during this process. Investigators have examined what information is delivered as part of the socialization processes to understand this question and to study how that content affects their adjustment. A framework of 12 dimensions of what can be learned during the socialization process is presented in Table 8.2. For example, task proficiency focuses on the extent to which individuals learns to perform the required job tasks. Working relationships target establishing successful and satisfying work relationships with established employees. Politics concerns the individual's success in gaining the

TABLE 8.2 Dimensions of Socialization Content

Dimension	Construct Definition: The extent to which the individual has learned:
Language	the unique technical language, acronyms, slang and jargon
History	the history, traditions, origins, and challenges of the organization
Task Proficiency	the necessary job knowledge and skills needed to successfully perform required tasks
Working Relationships	the necessary information about others to establish effective relationships including learning of work colleague's expectations, needs, and working styles
Social Relationships	the necessary information about others to develop a network of social relationships including personal things about a work colleague (i.e., common interests, family)
Structure	the formal structure including the physical layout and where formal responsibility and authority is assigned
Politics	the informal power structure including where actual control of resources, decision making, and influence over decision resides
Goals and Strategies	the current product/market mix, competitive position and pressures, mission, goals, and strategies
Culture and Values	the customs, myths, rituals, beliefs, and values including guiding principles, symbols, and ideology
Rules and Policies	the formal workplace rules, policies, and procedures
Navigation	the implicit rules, norms, and procedures of the workplace
Inducements	what is offered in exchange for their contributions including pay, development opportunities, benefits, and intangibles

Source: Klein, H.J., & Heuser, A.E. (2008). The learning of socialization content: A framework for researching orientating practices. *Research in Personnel and Human Resources Management, 27,* 279–336. Copyright 2008 by Emerald Group Publishing Limited. Reprinted by Permission.

information about the power structure within the organization so as to understand how things get done. Language describes the proficiency of the newcomer in acquiring the technical job specific language as well as knowledge of organizational acronyms and jargon unique to the organization itself. Goals and values contain the mission, strategy and competitive position of the organization. As a final example, the issue of history conveys an appreciation for the organization's traditions, customers, myths, and rituals that drive action and provide explanations for why certain things occur in the organization.

In a pioneering study of 182 engineers, managers, and professionals, Chao et al. (1994) found that those with a stronger understanding of the organizational goals and values and organizational history showed higher personal income, greater career involvement, and higher levels of job satisfaction. Greater learning during the socialization process also results in higher levels of performance and higher levels of commitment to the organization (Ashforth, Sluss, & Saks, 2007). In addition, from the newcomer perspective, greater learning during the socialization process leads to role clarity, high levels of self-efficacy, and acceptance by respected organizational insiders (Bauer & Erdogan, 2011).

Interestingly, the levels of these psychologically relevant variables can change over time for newcomers. Figure 8.1 shows this variation over time with levels of self-efficacy increasing over the first three months on the job and then decreasing over the next six months. Role clarity decreased during the first three months and then increased while perceived acceptance went down in the first six months and then rose for month nine only to see it go down again by month 12. The shape and consistency of these adjustment curves certainly vary depending on the effectiveness of the onboarding and socialization

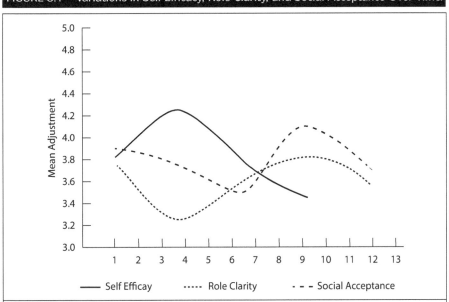

FIGURE 8.1   Variations in Self-Efficacy, Role Clarity, and Social Acceptance Over Time.

—— Self Efficay   ⋯⋯ Role Clarity   - - - Social Acceptance

Source: Bauer, T. N., & Erdogan, B. (2011). Organizational socialization: The effective onboarding of new employees. *APA Handbook of Industrial and Organizational Psychology*, 3, 51–64. Copyright The American Psychological Association. Reprinted by permission.

practices. The importance of having a systematic process of socialization is seen in the findings of a meta-analytic study. More intentional approaches to helping individuals adjust quickly resulted in greater role clarity and higher levels of self-efficacy. Those individuals with greater role clarity and high levels of self-efficacy also had higher levels of job performance, organizational commitment, and intentions to remain in the organization (Bauer et al., 2007).

Some argue that highly structured, institutionalized approaches to socialization can stifle innovation and creativity while others note that newcomers need a more structured approach early in their career. Results of various studies have shown mixed findings around these issues. For example, the more institutionalized approach has been linked to increased newcomer learning including knowledge of one's role and interpersonal resources. The information acquired through these socialization tactics are then linked to enhancing work attitudes of satisfaction and commitment to the organization (Cooper-Thomas & Anderson, 2002). Other studies have not found support for the advantage of an institutionalized approach to socialization (Gruman, Saks, & Zweig, 2006). Clearly, organizations need to take seriously the socialization process – whether following a more institutionalized or individualized approach so as to smooth out this transition period for the newcomer. Monitoring and evaluating the effectiveness of the approaches taken and refining them are critical for organizational effectiveness.

Guided Learning

Organizations often go beyond initial training and pair up newcomers (or people changing job positions) with a trainer/coach who has a major responsibility for building their proficiency level and being a support person. Two major strategies for guided learning through mentoring and coaching include apprenticeships and on-the-job training.

APPRENTICESHIPS Apprenticeships are formal programs used to teach various skilled trades. Typically, the trainee receives both classroom instruction and supervision, training, and coaching from one or more experienced employees on the job. At the end of a specified period of training and experience, the apprentice becomes a journeyman and with more experience and assessment of progress on the job become a certified skill trade's person. This system is employed in a wide variety of skilled trades (e.g., bricklayers, electricians, pipefitters, millwright, carpenters, plumbers) across industries such as construction, advanced manufacturing, healthcare, information technology, and transportation.

Apprenticeship-training programs were formulated in the United States by the National Apprenticeship Act of 1937, which created the Federal Bureau of Apprenticeship and Training (BAT) as part of the Department of Labor. These purposes, which have largely remained unchanged, are to formulate labor standards to safeguard the welfare of apprentices and to extend the application of those standards. Another mission is to bring together employers and labor to develop programs and to cooperate with state agencies in developing performance standards for apprenticeships such as the number of hours needed. In the U.S., the Department of Labor noted that there has been a 56% increase in the number of apprentices over the last 5 years with over 580,000 active apprentices (over 230,000 new apprentices) and over 23,000 active programs in 2018 (www.doleta.gov/oa/data_statistics.cfm). Up to a million more apprentices are estimated to be in programs not monitored by the federal government (Gonzalez, 2011). These numbers continue to rise with equally impressive numbers in other countries such as over one million individuals registered in the National Apprenticeship Training Scheme (NATS) in India (http://mhrdnats.gov.in/).

European countries have long had vocational training for a variety of occupations. In Austria, Denmark, Germany and Switzerland, 45%–70% of 16 to 19-year-olds participate in some form of apprenticeship programs as part of their educational system. Switzerland alone offers training in 240 different occupations with programs in specialized areas in banking, public administration, human resources, insurance, transportation and logistics, and international trade (Fuller & Sigelman, 2017).

As one example within a global company, Dow Corporate has a variety of apprenticeship programs offered in many European countries (https://corporate.dow.com/en-us/careers). The purpose of the apprenticeships is to create a sustainable talent pipeline to address an aging workforce around technical positions in the company. In France, one issue is that 54% of Dow employees in certain manufacturing and engineering technical positions are older than 45. Thus, the apprenticeship programs in occupational groups such as maintenance technician, automation engineering, and lab technician have been intensified to address the impending talent gap. The program includes attending a school two days a week to learn the relevant background information about the chosen field and three days in the company. Graduation is possible after one to three years depending on the type of program and successful completion of written and hands-on examinations. In Belgium, the focus is on smoothing out succession planning at the manufacturing site with occupations such as quality assurance technician. The program includes half time learning in the classroom and half time on the job for up to 12 months with some subsidies paid for by regional Belgium authorities. Research shows that, in Europe, apprenticeship programs have led to higher levels of income and lower levels of inequalities in income between non-college graduates of the program and college graduates (Lerman, 2012).

As a recent non-traditional approach to apprenticeships, Table 8.3 presents the elements in a newly formed winemaking program that has recently begin in Michigan in the U.S. The program includes technical instruction and on-the-job learning by pairing the apprentice with a mentor. Those in registered apprenticeships with the grape and wine industry can obtain a nationally recognized certificate upon completion that guarantees to employers that the person is fully qualified for the job.

There is evidence that firms benefit from investing in apprenticeship programs. Muehlemann et al. (2010) examined companies in Germany and Switzerland who adopted apprenticeship programs in areas such as mechanics and IT technicians and compared them to companies that did not employ apprenticeship programs. The costs include the wages of the apprentices and the training personnel while potential benefits revolve around enhanced productivity levels over time as the apprentice gains more skills. Results indicate that productivity levels increase rapidly and that the majority of companies in Switzerland recoup their costs within three years. In Germany, recouping

TABLE 8.3 A Registered Apprenticeship for the Grape and Wine Industry

The Registered Apprenticeship program has five components that are essential to success for the employer and the apprentice.

1. Business Involvement – Employers are the foundation of every Registered Apprenticeship program.
2. Structured On-the-Job Learning (OJL) – Apprentices receive job-specific training from an experienced Mentor for typically not less than one year.
3. Related Technical Instruction (RTI) – Apprenticeships combine OJL with RTI at two-year colleges. RTI could be provided at a college, on-line, or at the job site.
4. Reward for Skills Gain – Apprentices receive increases in wages as they gain higher level skills.
5. National Occupational Credential – Registered apprenticeship programs result in a nationally recognized certificate – a 100% guarantee to employers that apprentices are fully qualified for the job.

Employer is the One Who
- Determines the type of occupations, length of RA programs, and education and competencies needed
- Determines qualifications for apprentices, wages, and hiring/firing conditions
- Identifies sources of education and specific requirements for Related Technical Instruction
- Hires the Apprentice
- Awards credit for relevant prior education and experience
- Provides On-the-Job Learning by pairing an Apprentice with a Mentor
- Oversees progress of the On-the-Job Learning and Related Technical Instruction

Apprentice is a Full-time Employee Who
- Participates in On-the-Job Learning – 2000 h of work annually
- Participates in a recommended minimum of 144 h of Related Technical Instruction
- Receives wage increases commensurate with achieving competencies
- Receives a nationally-recognized Certificate from the U.S. Department of Labor upon completion of a Registered Apprenticeship.

Source: www.vesta-usa.org/Professionals-Entrepreneurs/Registered-Apprenticeships. VESTA National Center, Springfield, Missouri. Reprinted by permission.

costs is a function of high retention rates for those completing apprenticeship programs. The evidence is strong as to the benefits of apprenticeship programs relevant to recouping costs. There is also evidence that the investment in apprenticeship programs leads to higher rates of innovative activities within those organizations (Bauernschuster, Falck, & Heblich, 2009; Lerman, 2014).

Given the expense and time-consuming nature of apprenticeship programs, two important criteria are how likely individuals are to drop out of the program (attrition rates) and if they remain whether the individual successfully completes the program in a timely way. Across a variety of apprenticeship programs, jointly sponsored programs (e.g., union-management jointly sponsored programs) lead to less attribution than programs that are set up unilaterally by an organization (Kuehn, 2019). Other research supports this conclusion but also finds evidence that women are less likely to complete the programs than men (Berik, Bilginsoy, & Williams, 2011). More attention to understanding the factors affecting retention and completion is clearly needed.

Apprenticeship programs are becoming more prevalent in non-skilled trades occupations including those that have traditionally been called white collar occupations. For example, The Harford, an insurance company, plans on hiring 200 apprentices as claims operators (Gurchiek, 2017). Apprentices attend a two-year program and complete 2,400 hours of paid on-the-job training. This movement to nontraditional apprenticeships is consistent with existing models in Europe to fast track the development of skills in a variety of valued white collar jobs in careers such as information technology, cybersecurity, and even entry level apprentice managers in a public relations agency (Krupnick, 2016). Clearly, there is high growth potential for expanding the apprenticeship model to additional occupational groups that require college level degrees as well as those that do not require such a degree. A skills analysis of job postings over the course of one year identified 54 additional occupations where such a model would make sense. If apprenticeship programs are created in those areas this would lead to eight times the number of apprentices than currently seen with skilled trades (Fuller & Sigelman, 2017). Many of the occupational groups such as machine tooling programmers, medical technologists, cabinet makers, and graphic designers are in areas where it is often hard to find the talent level needed for the open positions. The need for this expansion in apprenticeship programs is seen in the IT field as there are almost three million tech job postings in the U.S., which far outpace the number of computer science and engineering degrees from four-year colleges each year (Ellis, 2019).

These new types of apprenticeship jobs help people earn a reasonable wage while gaining valuable skills, which can turn into full time jobs. Companies can use these opportunities to help fill the talent gaps, bring in a diverse set of apprentice workers, and be able to have time to see how they do on the job. For example, the consulting company AON has developed the Chicago Apprenticeship Network to help large employers explore and create new apprenticeship opportunities linked to city colleges within Chicago to enhance the diversity of the apprenticeship pool. This movement is leading to partnerships between business and educational institutions to co-develop and shape the curriculum around these new apprenticeship opportunities.

ON THE JOB TRAINING AND LEARNING On-the-job training and learning (OJTL) assigns incumbents to jobs and encourages or mandating them to observe and learn from an experienced job incumbent. What distinguishes OJTL from other instructional methods is that it is carried out at the workplace, delivered while the learner is engaged in performing work tasks, and conducted often as a one-on-one guided learning experience. Typically, an experienced employee who has the same job as the learner is the coach and instructor. Prior to OJTL, formal off the job instruction might be created so that the learner is better prepared for OJTL. In one organization I worked with, a new machine operator first completed a variety of on-line courses on issues like basic measurement devises, understanding mechanical systems, issues with metal manufacturing, personal protective equipment and safety requirements prior to moving to the shop floor.

An example of a formal OJTL is found in most police organizations. After selection into a police force, new recruits attend a formal training academy to learn the basic knowledge and skills to become an effective police officer. Through lectures, discussions, demonstration, and practice, recruits acquire knowledge about issues such as the legal system, techniques such as investigation and observation, and skills such as firearms and driving skills. This initial training may take anywhere from three to six months. The recruits are then assigned to a field-training officer for an extended time to learn "on the job." The role of the field training officer is to model appropriate actions, provide opportunities for the new officer to practice the skills obtained in training, and provide feedback to the new officer on how to improve.

The typical OJTL experience is a more informal procedure in which an experienced worker is given a new person to train without much of a systematic plan. This informal OJTL is seen with new waitstaff told to follow an experienced waitstaff person to "learn the ropes." In one situation, a manufacturing company asked me to help improve their informal approach to OJTL as it was taking far too long for a learner to become a completely independent operator. This approach with an employee who has not received any training on how to train and coach others reflects the main argument against the use of OJTL. Too often, practicality is the main reason that this unstructured and informal form of training is chosen; it is cheap and easy to implement with no planning at all. The simple instruction to "help the newcomer learn the job," does not make for an effective process. The entire instructional process is placed in the hands of an individual who may consider the training of others as an imposition. Under these conditions, OJTL can take second place to the trainer's own performance of the job. It may not be possible to slow the pace of work, appraise the responses, and supply constructive feedback to the learner in a job setting where the pressure for performance overwhelms any attempt to create a learning environment for building proficiency.

On the other hand, a carefully designed structured OJTL instructional system, supported by management, should be as successful as other learning approaches. The success of the program demands that the objectives and the instructional environment be carefully planned before implemented. Given these proper conditions, there are certain advantages to on-the-job training. The transfer problem becomes less a factor as the individual is being trained in the exact physical and social environment in which he or she is expected to perform. There is also an opportunity to practice the required behaviors and to receive immediate feedback on to the effectiveness of the steps taken.

The best practice for structured OJTL is to follow the issues already described including a comprehensive needs assessment to identify what the knowledge and skills are that must be developed and the creation of learning objectives that are sequenced to build capabilities in a systematic and timely way. Then there can be the development of a plan of instruction that includes effective learning strategies. Coaches then need to be trained on how to follow the instructional plan and how to put the learner at ease as well as how to give constructive feedback that builds rather than destroys confidence and motivation to learn. Coaches also need to be trained on how to clarify performance standards, how to demonstrate effective performance steps and how to allow for and correct errors (Rothwell & Kazanas, 2004). Table 8.4 presents what on the job coaches should *not* do when training a newcomer on the job. As one example, coaches should not assume the learner understands how to do the task just by watching someone do it! The content on the list should be part of any train the trainer program.

If you recall, the list of sequenced objectives provided in Chapter 4 was developed for a manufacturing company OJTL program to reduce the time to proficiency. In this case, the training for the trainer is organized around seven

TABLE 8.4   Things That On the Job Trainers/Coaches Should NOT DO
1. *Assume* the learner is familiar with the basic terms, tools, and processes relevant to the job.
2. Speak or act in ways that *add* stress/anxiety for the learner concerning the task or the learning process.
3. Demonstrate how to do the task to the learner – *without* first explaining what will be done.
4. *Assume* the learner understands how to do the task, just by watching you do it.
5. Have the learner practice the task *without* your direct supervision.
6. Focus *only* on what the learner did wrong.
7. Assume that if the learner can correctly state a factor or knowledge principle needed to perform a task, they will not need any additional reminders or refresher training.
8. *Assume* that a one-time correct demonstration of the task means that the appropriate level of mastery has been achieved by the learner.
Source: Ford, J.K., & Olenick, J. (2016). *Training on the B&O Line: Trainer Notes.* Technical Report, Ford & Associates, Williamston, MI.

steps. First the trainer shows the newcomer how to do the steps on the checklist. Second, the trainer tells the newcomer what the steps are and why they need to be followed in the proper sequence. Third, the trainer demonstrates the steps again. Fourth, the trainer allows the newcomer to try out the simple parts of the steps in the task. Fifth, the trainer allows the trainee to complete the whole set of steps in a task. Sixth, feedback to the trainee is given by comparing the trainee's performance to the checklist and identifying ways in which the trainee could improve. Finally, the trainer has the trainee complete the set of tasks again until all the steps in the task are completed accurately and efficiently and the newcomer could do the tasks independently. Specific training instructions for the trainer also emphasized that doing these steps effectively requires having organized, essential content, checking for understanding through asking good questions, and providing a cycle of practice and feedback (see Table 8.5).

Evidence suggests that companies with effective OJTL programs can realize a return on their investment. A structured OJTL in a large truck assembly plant had twice the financial benefits and much higher levels of efficiency in the work of newcomers compared to unstructured OJTL (Jacob, Jones, & Neil, 1992). A more recent study provided evidence that a structured approach led to increased confidence by the newcomers and decreased time to proficiency of newly hired engineers in Kuwait (Jacobs & Bu-Rahmah, 2012). Additional evidence is needed as, unfortunately, a recent review paper found that most of the 56 papers on OJTL were on the importance of OJTL or the planning and delivery of OJT – few efforts have been placed on actually evaluating the effectiveness of OJTL compared to other forms of learning and instruction (Ahadi & Jacobs, 2017).

ENHANCING CAPABILITIES

Developing an individual's capabilities to be productive at work requires intentional approaches to enhance learning after the initial efforts. A survey of human resource professionals finds that over 54% of respondents note that

TABLE 8.5 Train the Trainer Instructions

A good trainer keeps in mind a number of core "principles" that help a trainee learn:
Organized, Essential Content

- Prepare the trainee for learning by showing them the objective, asking general questions about what they already know and encourage them to do their best.
- Explain how you will give them the information they need relevant to each objective and that you will demonstrate each step and then ask them to do it.
- Explain that you will give them feedback so they can improve.
- Provide new information in small chunks so as not to overwhelm the trainee.

Examine Trainee Understanding Through Asking Good Questions

- Ask questions directly relevant to the objective. The questions you ask help your trainee see what issues you consider important for that objective.
- Ask one question at a time and wait for a response, even if it feels uncomfortable. This increases the likelihood that your question will generate an answer.
- Use questions that start with how, what, why that help probe understanding rather than simple 'yes or no' questions. Ask follow up questions to encourage trainees to expand, clarify, or justify their answers.

Cycle of Practice and Feedback

- Explain what you are doing next and why this is being done now.
- Make sure trainee understands what the key issue/names are before moving to demonstration.
- Provide a demonstration by talking as you are doing a task.
- Have trainee practice one thing at a time.
- Have trainee talk about what they are doing as they are doing it to check for understanding.
- Have trainee say what the next step is before doing it so you can see if they understand the process.
- Provide feedback on whether what they are going to do next is correct or not and redirect is incorrect.
- Watch trainee perform a step and then ask how it went and if they feel if there was anything they would do differently next time.
- Give specific feedback as to how well the trainee did and encourage on how to do it better (e.g., next time, try doing this…).
- Have trainee practice the same thing again regardless of whether they did it correctly the first time or not.
- Provide feedback and if have done it correctly at least two times in a row, move on.

Source: Ford, J.K., & Olenick, J. (2016). *Training on the B&O line: Trainer notes.* Technical Report, Ford & Associates, Williamston, MI.

they emphasize various on the job learning activities and continual training to a "very high extent" or a "high extent" (Association for Talent Development, 2019).

Learning can come from working on job activities by expanding the number of tasks an individual performs on the job, providing more opportunities to perform developmental tasks, and assigning individuals to work on more complex or difficult situations and tasks (Ford et al., 1992). A meta-analytic review found that work experience is related to enhanced performance. The more tasks assigned, the more times a task is performed, and the more complex the tasks assigned, the greater the progress of the individual relevant to job performance (Quiñones, Ford, & Teachout, 1995). The intensity of work experiences as well as its timing affects the learning potential of work activity. The timing dimension refers to "when a work experience occurs relative to a longer sequence of successive experiences such as those that character-ize a career" (Tesluk & Jacobs, 1998; p. 329). Having a mentor who observes and immediately provides detailed feedback on how to improve performance following a challenging assignment is a timely and intensive experience that facilitates learning. Two intentional job activity experiences are job rotations and individual efforts at self-directed or informal learning to build knowl-edge and skills viewed as important to improve by the individual and/or the supervisor.

Job Rotation

Job rotation is where workers are moved between different jobs through an intentional and planned approach. Surveys of manufacturers indicate that job rotation is used by 42% of the companies surveyed (Jorgensen et al., 2005) while across all industries the percentage was 17% (Association for Talent Development, 2016). With highly repetitive jobs in manufacturing, job rotation is seen as a way or reducing repetitive stress injuries, although the evidence across studies for its effectiveness is weak (Padula et al., 2017). Job rotation has also been touted as leading to higher levels of motivation and job satisfaction as well as providing skill variety and enrichment (Kaymaz, 2010).

For our purposes, job rotation is examined for its role in exposing employ-ees to different work experiences that widen the variety of skills gained, enhance versatility, and opens career options. Eriksson and Ortega (2006) examined factors in Danish firms that led to the use of job rotation as a learn-ing strategy. The results show that job rotation is more likely in larger firms with more levels in the hierarchy, companies with shorter firm tenure and companies with high growth potential. Another discovery is that firms invest-ing more resources and money towards formal training are also more likely to employ job rotation assignments than companies that invest less money on training. In the Hay group survey of 1,279 companies, the strategy of offering rotational programs for high potential employees ranks among top five HR strategies for workforce development (Su & Berardocco, 2018). Interestingly, evidence suggests that high job performers benefit more from job rotation than lower performing individuals (Kampkötter, Harbring, & Sliwka, 2018).

One strategic effort around job rotation is to expose employees to not only new job knowledge but to intentionally consider job rotation as a way of ensuring the transfer of knowledge from experts to job incumbents. This rotation strategy is a mechanism for unlocking the knowhow, experience and creative insights that come from high performers with a reservoir of experi-ence and who are the go-to people when there are major issues or challeng-ing problems. In this way, important and often tacit knowledge about tasks, jobs, and strategies for success are shared with others. This would be espe-cially important when experts are planning on leaving for retirement. Lu and Yang (2015) describe a framework for thinking about job rotation as a way of transferring this less tangible tacit knowledge of experts to others starting with identifying (similar to a needs assessment) the goals of such a job rotation program in terms of the knowledge that needs to be transferred, who needs to be the recipient of that knowledge transfer and who has the right capabilities or expertise to be the sender of that knowledge to the employee for particular high value jobs. This framework provides the starting point to consider how to conduct this knowledge transfer analysis and how to evaluate the effectiveness of interventions targeted to enhance this transfer.

An extension to the traditional job rotation strategy is the project-to-project rotation employed by many software organizations where individuals experience different challenges with multiple projects but typically remain in the same role across projects. One interesting aspect is the possibility of the rotation occurring while a project is in progress and not just a logical conclusion after a project is completed. The touted benefits of intentional project-to-project rotation are increasing the employees understanding of the organizational strategies while working with many different people, across different methodologies and tasks. A recent paper provided a synthesis of what is known about the benefits and limitations of these rotation programs (Santos et al., 2016). Based on the evidence available, key benefits include learning opportunities that lead to knowledge acquisition, skill variety, and knowledge exchange across employees. Possible limitations include learning costs, time requirements, disruption of workflow, and lack of satisfaction around completion of an individual project. As a cautionary tale, an analysis of an in-depth case found that the benefits of versatility and individual learning did not outweigh the limitations and so in this instance the company abandoned the project-to-project job rotation program for future software development projects (Faegri, Dyba, & Dingsoyr, 2010).

Informal Learning

Individuals certainly develop knowledge and skills from formal training programs, one-on-one guided instruction and from simply repeating the performance of the same task. These efforts typically lead to individuals learning how to be more efficient and effective on job relevant tasks. Individuals also enhance knowledge and skills through self-directed, informal learning. Informal learning is defined as "non-curricular activities pursued in service of knowledge and skill acquisition that take place outside formally-designated learning contexts. Such activities are predominately self-directed, intentional, and field-based" (Cerasoli et al., 2018; p. 204). This definition highlights that informal learning is highly experiential in the sense that the individual is trying something out intentionally in the hopes that it will lead to learning gains. This can include choosing a respected employee to observe and to learn a new way of approaching a task. It consists of intentionally practicing a new strategy or approach when performing a task to see if it is more effective than the normal approach. Therefore, informal learning is self-initiated and under the control of the learner. The learner determines when to start and when to stop trying something new. The learner also makes decisions whether to adopt a new approach or strategy in order to obtain the self-set learning goals.

The intentional focus on mastery was talked about in Chapter 2 regarding the road to expertise and the importance of deliberate practice. With deliberate practice, an employee creates structured activities to increase their mastery of targeted knowledge and skills to enhance performance. Systematic attempts to gain mastery (or reduce the potential for skill obsolescence) is particularly relevant for problems in highly technical jobs. Product development engineers for the auto industry or power plant operators are faced with many ill-defined and varied situations and problems posing challenges for developing deep specialization of knowledge and skills. These types of jobs require complex learning within dynamic situations that often require employees to learn on their own how to generalize information and strategies from one type of problem situation to new, unpredictable problems.

Four strategies that can be used to build capabilities in these more ill-defined tasks while performing routine day-to-day work activities include estimation, experimentation, extrapolation, and explanation (Fadde & Klein, 2010). Estimation involves weighing what is known about a task or project and reflecting on how it might be related to other tasks or projects, as well as how it could be affected by factors in the work context. Supervisors can help the learner by asking the person (or could do this on their own) to approximate the amount of time and resources needed to complete a task prior to working on the task. An engineer could be prompted to estimate the amount of time and effort that would be needed to troubleshoot an electrical problem and then be asked to reflect after completing the task on why or why not the prediction was accurate. Experimentation is intentionally placing an individual into a situation and encouraging the person to try out different strategies for accomplishing a task. As the learner works on the task, adjustments are made based on whether the original strategy is successful or not. This situation pushes the learner to consider alternative strategies and to try them out and reflect, often with a mentor, on what strategies works best and why. Extrapolation is using a prior task that was completed successfully or unsuccessfully (whether through direct experience or the experience of others) as a reference point for the learner to think about why success is achieved or how things might have been done differently to prevent a negative outcome. This is part of the power of debriefs that will be talked about in the next chapter about teams. Explanation involves having the learner discuss the steps taken on a project, explain why things were done the way they were, justify the order of the steps taken and explain what cues prompted different responses and why. Explaining actions helps the learner make better sense of those actions, the situation, and the feedback loop in order to identify more effective strategies, understand the bottlenecks in the system and make improvements.

One successful instance of incorporating these types of strategies for learning into the workplace is described by Sonnentag and Kleine (2000). The study investigated systematic attempts at deliberate practice by insurance agents during work while regularly performing key tasks with the aim of upgrading their competence. The more time agents spent on deliberate practice on cases, the higher their rated performance. Overall, mental stimulation such as imagining difficult situations with a client and mentally exploring what to do as well as asking for feedback were determined to be the main aspects practiced in a deliberate way while working on the job. The most difficult part of deliberate practice is to make sense of the feedback received in the workplace environment. By estimating and experimenting on-the-job learners make inferences about their environment, consider strategies to test those inferences on their own or with colleagues, and receive feedback from their environment on the success of those strategies. Clearly, supervisors can facilitate this learning from these experiences by providing opportunities to work on challenging tasks and encouraging the use of the four strategies above.

Another example comes from the medical field and the examination of how medical professionals engage in activities during work to continue their professional development while on the job. Semi-structured interviews completed with residents and internist find that discussions with colleague and getting feedback on the approach taken with patients are valued as key learning opportunities around improving patient care (Van de Wiel et al., 2011). Respondents also report learning more from challenging and difficult cases. In addition, some learning became clearer when trying to give explanations to others of what one was thinking about and strategies being considered for a patient. As one participant states, "you also learn things yourself while explaining as you may discover gaps" (p. 88). The study also shows, though, the difficulty of doing deliberate practice when the demands of the job for patient care is seen as requiring full attention throughout the day. This leads to questions of how to incorporate and manage learning opportunities at regular times to aid an individual's own self-regulated learning that is closely tied to the activities of the job.

One approach to facilitate informal learning is the use of technology and equipment and embedding structured learning experiences while on the job. Controlled exercises or vignettes can be called up and worked on by employees who are operating the various equipment relevant to the task at hand. These controlled exercises allow the learner to practice skills in a variety of situations to help build automaticity around routine activities as well as to practice skills relevant to situations that do not occur very often on the job but are critical to perform.

A meta-analysis on factors affecting informal learning behaviors and the outcomes of those behaviors shows that the level of support from leaders and other team members and the investment in learning resources are critical factors affecting the extent to which individuals engage in informal learning behaviors. Individuals in jobs with high autonomy are also more likely to exhibit more informal learning behaviors. Higher levels of informal learning behaviors are related to job performance, promotions, and project effectiveness. The researchers note that those who engage in high levels of informal learning averaged 32% higher job performance than those with low levels of informal learning behaviors (Cerasoli et al., 2018).

Clearly, organizations need to consider how to support informal learning through intentionally encouraging continuous learning and improvement as a core value rather than leaving this up to chance. Figure 8.2 presents four components that form the cornerstone for encouraging and supporting informal learning. The four elements include leadership, culture, resources, and employees forming learning networks. These four elements point to way towards evaluating an organization's focus on incorporating best practice.

A large-scale qualitative study through intensive interviews of lower, middle, and senior levels in an organization examined the leadership factors influencing the extent of informal learning on the job (Ellinger, 2005). The findings support the dominant role supervisors and managers play in affecting the amount of informal learning occurring. The leader support efforts include creating the opportunities for informal learning, serving as role models around spending time for informal learning and growth as a leader, and instilling the importance of encouraging and modeling the sharing of knowledge as well as the importance of developing others.

FIGURE 8.2 Positive Organizational Context Factors Affecting Informal Learning Behaviors.

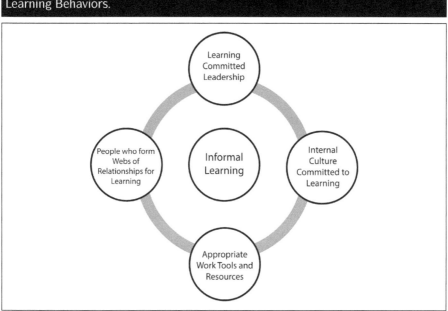

CAREER DEVELOPMENT

Fields like information technology, computer science, engineering, and bio-medical science are advancing in knowledge, applicable methodologies, and accelerating what is known about best practices. The estimates of the half-life of knowledge and skills gained through formal education (the time it tasks for half the knowledge gained is no longer best practice) in a career field like, say, computer science could be quite short. This issue is illustrated by examples such as when a newly graduated computer scientist with a master's degree joins a company and is asked to help on a coding project. The newcomer is handed what has been started by a more work experienced person in the orga-nization – perhaps even his/her supervisor who graduated as computer sci-entist years earlier. The newcomer looks at the coding and wonders why such an "old" version of a coding system is being used as there are now much more efficient ways to coding for this project that the person just learned in school while doing a project for a capstone course.

One innovative way of gaining insight into the issue of half-life is by looking at what software engineering ideas were being discussed with under-graduates in 1998 and seeing which of those ideas were still relevant in 2008 or looking at what was taught in 2008 and see what is still relevant in 2018. This type of approach led a researcher to estimate five years for the half-life of ideas in the software engineering domain (Kruchten, 2008). One wonders what the half-life in this career field will be ten years from now given the accelerat-ing pace of change! Clearly, these types of estimates are just that – estimates (remember the 10,000-hour rule!) – nevertheless, the implication cannot be denied that job incumbents need to keep an eye on these advancements or risk skill obsolescence sooner than they may want to admit. Therefore, individu-als at a more midlevel career stage need to maintain or enhance skills as well as adjust to these changing realities. In this section, the first issue to explore is how organizations help individuals obtain the knowledge and skills to stay current given this reality of advancement. The second issue is how individuals can self-manage their career to stay ahead of the wave of change or move to other career options.

Skill Updating

Mid to later-career issues include keeping current with the needed skills and knowledge or learning new skills for a career change (Beier, Torres, & Gilberto, 2017). A survey in England around product marketing strategies identified a wide range of job and generic skills such as problem-solving that needed updating for those in a mid-career stage (Mason & Constable, 2011). This calls attention to the needs assessment process and identifying skill updating needs across job domains and building learning strategies for advancing key knowledge and skills for established job incumbents.

A sobering report on the impact of artificial intelligence and automation on people and places contends that 25% of the U.S employment (about 36 million jobs in 2016) face a high probability of being substituted by automation – especially those jobs that perform routine and predicable tasks (Muro, Maxim, & Whiton, 2019). This continual demand for updating technical skills or learning new skills for a change in career can be quite stressful for individuals facing the possibly of being replaced.

There are a variety of options for organizations to facilitate skill updating of employees including the traditional route of face-to-face workplace training or blended learning approaches that include both face-to-face training opportunities with on-line offerings such as pod casts and technical videos that provide the employee (and supervisors) with more flexibility. Other approaches include tuition assistance programs for advanced degrees or certifications. How successful these attempts are have rarely been studied making it difficult to provide some best practice advice. The importance of skill updating is discussed further in Chapter 11 around societal issues and learning.

Microlearning is a relatively new approach for learning on demand to meet the need for continuous learning and improvement. Microlearning is the provision of short bits of information on a single topic area that can be easily integrated into daily work activities. The psychology behind microlearning is that people learn more effectively (think of the part-whole learning principle from Chapter 5) when the content is broken down into small and manageable chunks. Microlearning is different from the more traditional training model around issues such as content creation, content retrieval, the learning cycle, and the learner role. It uses flexible technologies such as micro learning apps that facilitate mobile learning so that learners can acquire new knowledge quickly and easily or access information when it is most needed (Kolodny, 2016). Microlearning also has the potential to customize delivery for better meeting individual needs as well as allowing employees to co-create and distribute content (Buchem & Hamelmann, 2010). Microlearning approaches can also be used to assist learners who are dealing with real-time problems and seeking ways of approaching and solving the problem. For example, a technician facing a new type of equipment issue does not have to return to the workplace to find relevant information in a technical manual but can retrieve relevant information and visuals by scanning the serial number of the device.

A survey of users of microlearning approaches found that usage level was high and learners were satisfied with this approach to learning (Bruck, Motiwalla, & Foerster, 2012). Another study examined the use of gamification with microlearning over a seven-month period and analyzed the impact on the learning behavior of 175 employees. The findings indicated that the gamification aspect raised user engagement. On the other hand, due to the engagement quality, employees began to access the microlearning away from their job when they could more carefully attend to the learning content of the games – in a sense defeating the purpose of moving to microlearning (Göschlberger & Bruck, 2017)! Going beyond this descriptive type of research, there is a clear need to examine the effects of various types of microlearning strategies on upgrading skills, impacting job performance, and facilitating lifelong learning.

Self-Management

The changing nature of the workplace and workforce has had an impact on career development issues. The process has changed from employees assuming they would stay with one organization for a long time to achieve deep specialization or to move up in the organization. Increasingly, career development is being described as including a strong self-directed activity component to increase one's career options within and across organizations. Many Fortune 100 companies provide career self-management workshops to help individuals identify their strengths and weaknesses and set up sessions for mentoring and coaching to enhance strengths and minimize weaknesses. The goal of self-management strategies is for employees to take more control over their own career direction by being more proactive in regularly gathering information and planning for career decision-making and being better prepared for job mobility.

A study of a career self-management workshop finds mixed results on its success (Kossek et al., 1998). The objectives of the program are to foster career empowerment, provide strategies for networking, and identify options for career change opportunities. In one study, six to eight months after the workshop, a phone interview was conducted with participants asking about the extent to which they sought developmental feedback and efforts at job mobility preparedness. The findings show that participants in the workshop (as opposed to a control group not going through the workshop) are *less* likely to have engaged in the two self-management behaviors of feedback seeking and career preparedness. The researchers suggest that the expectations about taking more control over one's career is not being supported back in the workplace leading to unmet expectations – a classic case of the transfer of training problem. This is another example of the need for an organization to have a more holistic strategy around behavioral change rather than relying on a single training event.

In Belgium, the government subsidizes external career counseling services for adult employees. The counseling intervention includes taking information about the individual concerns about their career direction and exploring options. Counseling can be as short as three sessions over three weeks or a longer number of sessions and timeframe. A study on the success of this type of counseling intervention examined over 200 individuals across the age spectrum who came to counseling due to being dissatisfied with their current employment situation (Verbruggen & Sels, 2008). Measures of career self-awareness and career adaptability were given at the intake and then six months after the career counseling. Results indicated that perceptions of career adaptability (perceived competence and motivation to adapt to changing employment conditions) changed as a function of the intervention. In addition, 37% of participants had started career related training in pursuit of the goals set during the counseling sessions and 35% had changed employers. The findings provide some support that career self-management is in part malleable through interventions such as this. Nevertheless, given the lack of a control group, it is difficult to know how much an improvement in career self-directness is captured by this intervention. In general, there is quite limited evidence of the efficacy of training or counseling on career self-management outcomes (Whiston, 2011).

A tactical approach to career progress and/or adjustment that has emerged is through digital badging and mini certifications. There are a number of self-directed learning opportunities available to individuals to grow in targeted knowledge and skills. Digital badges or microcredentials provide a mechanism by which achievements in these types of self-directed learning opportunities are recognized. With badging, learners complete a course around skills that can then be validated. Later, an employer can click on the digital badge in a person's portfolio that links skills to the issuer of the badge, the badge's description and what was required to earn the badge and what activities that went into earning the badge (Finkelstein, Knight, & Manning, 2013). As one example, IBM has partnered with Coursera to provide learning paths for individuals that can make a difference by helping individual learners build their personal brand in order to advance their desired career direction (www.ibm.com/blogs/ibm-training/ibm-badges-coursera/). Individuals can take any IBM course on this platform and once passing an assessment at the end of the course earn a digital badge that consists of verifiable data on the skills embedded in the course that was passed. Courses can be completed to upgrade existing skills or help launch a new career direction in areas with job growth such as data science and cybersecurity. Since 2015 over 500,000 badges in over 175 countries have been issued with a large majority of participants noting they are more engaged with their company as a result (Cupples, 2017, November 14; https://medium.com/propellerhead/recognising-employee-skills-with-a-digital-badging-system-c021ddf41190). Findings from Samsung Electronics in the UK and Ireland show that on-line course completions are much more likely when linked to a badge system. In addition, Booz Allen Hamilton report that the move to digital badging has helped incentivize taking additional skill development programs beyond those mandated (Freifeld, 2018; https://trainingmag.com/trgmag-article/badge-benefits/). Badges for military veterans can be particularly useful in helping transition personnel into civilian jobs by directly linking the skills acquired in the military to duties performed in civilian jobs (Finkelstein, Knight, & Manning, 2013).

Chapter 8: Best Practice Guidelines

- The planning process for onboarding should include engaging relevant stakeholders in the planning process, developing a comprehensive onboarding plan and creating milestones (e.g., 30, 90 days) and setting expectations.
- Make the first day on the job special by discussing the expectations and milestones and clarifying roles and responsibilities.
- Use a formal orientation program with purposeful application of learning technologies to make onboarding engaging and participatory.
- Have orientation sessions revolve around the four "Cs" of compliance to rules and regulations, clarification of job duties and expectations; cultural norms and values; and connection to the interpersonal and informational networks in the organization.
- Provide robust newcomer orientation sessions by taking the steps (Table 8.1) of informing, welcoming, and guiding the newcomer.
- Ensure that socialization processes are intentional around the 12 dimensions provided in Table 8.2 to help newcomer adjustment and foster organizational commitment.
- Train on-the-job trainers on how to deliver organized, essential content, demonstrate job steps effectively, clarify performance standards, evaluate trainee understanding through asking good questions, and create a cycle of practice and feedback for continuous improvement.
- Be intentional about creating a positive context (Figure 8.2) that encourages and supports informal and self-directed learning.
- Hold leaders accountable for providing opportunities for informal learning, serving as a role models around spending time for personal growth, and instilling the drive of sharing knowledge and developing others.
- Encourage skill updating and career self-management through a variety of strategies including tuition reimbursement, developing microlearning applications, and facilitating the attainment of certifications through digital badging or other means.

References

Ahadi, S., & Jacobs, R. L. (2017). A review of the literature on structured on-the-job training and directions for future research. *Human Resource Development Review*, 16(4), 323–349. doi.org/10.1177/1534484317725945

Ashforth, B. E., Sluss, D. M., & Saks, A. M. (2007). Socialization tactics, proactive behavior, and newcomer learning: Integrating socialization models. *Journal of Vocational Behavior*, 70(3), 447–462. doi.org/10.1016/j.jvb.2007.02.001

Association for Talent Development. (2016). *2016 state of the industry*. Alexandria, VA: ATD Press.

Association for Talent Development. (2019). *2019 State of the industry*. Alexandria, VA: ATD Press.

Bauer, T. N. (2010). Onboarding new employees: Maximizing success. *SHRM*

Foundation's effective practice guideline series, 7, Alexandria, VA: Society of Human Resource Management.

Bauer, T. N., & Erdogan, B. (2011). Organizational socialization: The effective onboarding of new employees. *APA Handbook of Industrial and Organizational Psychology*, 3, 51–64.

Bauer, T. N., Bodner, T., Erdogan, B., Truxillo, D. M., & Tucker, J. S. (2007). Newcomer adjustment during organizational socialization: A meta-analytic review of antecedents, outcomes, and methods. *Journal of Applied Psychology*, 92(3), 707. doi. org/10.1037/0021-9010.92.3.707

Bauernschuster, S., Falck, O., & Heblich, S. (2009). Training and innovation. *Journal of Human Capital*, 3(4), 323–353. doi.org/10.1086/653713

Beier, M. E., Torres, W. J., & Gilberto, J. M. (2017). Continuous development throughout a career: A lifespan perspective on autonomous learning. In *Autonomous learning in the workplace* (pp. 179–200). Routledge.

Berik, G., Bilginsoy, C., & Williams, L.S. (2011) Gender and racial training gaps in Oregon apprenticeship programs. *Labor Studies Journal*, 36, 221–244. doi. org/10.1177/0160449X10396377

Britto, R., Cruzes, D. S., Smite, D., & Sablis, A. (2018). Onboarding software developers and teams in three globally distributed legacy projects: A multi-case study. *Journal of Software: Evolution and Process*, 30(4), e1921. doi.org/10.1002/smr.1921

Bruck, P. A., Motiwalla, L., & Foerster, F. (2012). Mobile learning with micro-content: A framework and evaluation. *Bled eConference*, 25, 527–543. https://aisel.aisnet.org/bled2012/2

Buchem, I., & Hamelmann, H. (2010). Microlearning: A strategy for ongoing professional development. *eLearning Papers*, 21(7), 1–15.

Cerasoli, C. P., Alliger, G. M., Donsbach, J. S., Mathieu, J. E., Tannenbaum, S. I., & Orvis, K. A. (2018). Antecedents and outcomes of informal learning behaviors: A meta-analysis. *Journal of*

Business Psychology, 33, 203–230. doi. org/10.1007/s10869-017-9492-y

Chao, G. T. (2012). Organizational socialization: Background, basics, and a blueprint for adjustment at work. In S. W. J. Kozlowski (Ed.), *Oxford library of psychology. The Oxford handbook of organizational psychology, Vol. 1* (pp. 579–614). New York: Oxford University Press.

Chao, G. T., O'Leary-Kelly, A. M., Wolf, S., Klein, H. J., & Gardner, P. D. (1994). Organizational socialization: Its content and consequences. *Journal of Applied Psychology*, 79(5), 730. doi. org/10.1037/0021-9010.79.5.730

Cooper-Thomas, H., & Anderson, N. (2002). Newcomer adjustment: The relationship between organizational socialization tactics, information acquisition and attitudes. *Journal of Occupational and Organizational Psychology*, 75(4), 423–437. doi.org/10.1348/096317902321119583

Cupples, J. (2017, Novmenber 14). Recognising employee skills with our own digital badging sytesm. *Properllerhead NZ*. Available at: https://medium.com/propellerhead/recognising-employee-skills-with-a-digital-badging-system-c021ddf41190

Ellinger, A. D. (2005). Contextual factors influencing informal learning in a workplace setting: The case of "reinventing itself company". *Human Resource Development Quarterly*, 16(3), 389–415. doi.org/10.1002/hrdq.1145

Ellis, R. (2019, November). Primed for apprentices. *Talent Development*, November, 28–33.

Eriksson, T., & Ortega, J. (2006). The adoption of job rotation: Testing the theories. *ILR Review*, 59(4), 653–666. doi.org/10.1177/001979390605900407

Fadde, P. J., & Klein, G. A. (2010). Deliberate performance: Accelerating expertise in natural settings. *Performance Improvement*, 49(9), 5–14. doi.org/10.1002/pfi.20175

Fægri, T. E., Dybå, T., & Dingsøyr, T. (2010). Introducing knowledge redundancy practice in software development: Experiences with job rotation in support work. *Information and Software*

Technology, 52(10), 1118–1132. doi.org/10.1016/j.infsof.2010.06.002

Finkelstein, J., Knight, E., & Manning, S. (2013). *The Potential and Value of Using Digital Badges for Adult Learners Final Report*. American Institutes for Research, 16.

Ford, J.K., & Olenick, J. (2016). *Training on the B&O Line: Trainer Notes*. Technical Report. Williamston, MI: Ford & Associates.

Ford, J. K., Quiñones, M. A., Sego, D. J., & Sorra, J. S. (1992). Factors affecting the opportunity to perform trained tasks on the job. *Personnel Psychology*, 45(3), 511–527. doi.org/10.1111/j.1744-6570.1992.tb00858.x

Freifeld, L. (2018). How organizations can use badging to encourage learning and generate results. *Training*. Available at: https://trainingmag.com/trgmag-article/badge-benefits/

Fuller, J. B., & Sigelman, M. (2017). *Room to grow: Identifying new frontiers for apprenticeships*. Report, November 2017. Published by Burning Glass Technologies and Harvard Business School, Managing the Future of Work.

Gonzalez, J. (2011). Apprenticeship programs expand with help of community colleges. *The Education Digest*, 76(6), 19.

Göschlberger, B., & Bruck, P. A. (2017, December). Gamification in mobile and workplace integrated microlearning. In *Proceedings of the 19th international conference on information integration and web-based applications & services* (pp. 545–552). Salzburg, Austria: ACM.

Gruman, J. A., Saks, A. M., & Zweig, D. I. (2006). Organizational socialization tactics and newcomer proactive behaviors: An integrative study. *Journal of Vocational Behavior*, 69(1), 90–104. doi.org/10.1016/j.jvb.2006.03.001

Gurchiek, K. (2017, June 1). Employers unlocking the potential of apprenticeship for white-collar jobs. *Society of Human Resource Management newsletter*. Available at: www.shrm.org/resourcesandtools/hr-topics/organizational-and-employee-development/pages/employers-unlocking-the-potential-of-apprenticeship-for-white-collar-jobs.aspx, accessed May 2019.

Hoffman, R.R. (2014). *The psychology of expertise: Cognitive research and empirical AI*. New York: Springer-Verlag.

Jacobs, R. L., Jones, M. J., & Neil, S. (1992). A case study in forecasting the financial benefits of unstructured and structured on-the-job training. *Human Resource Development Quarterly*, 3(2), 133–139. doi.org/10.1002/hrdq.3920030205

Jacobs, R. L., & Jaseem Bu-Rahmah, M. (2012). Developing employee expertise through structured on-the-job training (S-OJT): An introduction to this training approach and the KNPC experience. *Industrial and Commercial Training*, 44(2), 75–84. doi.org/10.1108/00197851211202902

Jorgensen, M., Davis, K., Kotowski, S., Aedla, P., & Dunning, K. (2005). Characteristics of job rotation in the Midwest US manufacturing sector. *Ergonomics*, 48(15), 1721–1733.

Kampkötter, P., Harbring, C., & Sliwka, D. (2018). Job rotation and employee performance–evidence from a longitudinal study in the financial services industry. *The International Journal of Human Resource Management*, 29(10), 1709–1735. doi.org/10.1080/09585192.2016.1209227

Kaymaz, K. (2010). The effects of job rotation practices on motivation: A research on managers in the automotive organizations. *Business and Economics Research Journal*, 1, 69–85.

Klein, H.J., & Heuser, A.E. (2008). The learning of socialization content: A framework for researching orientating practices. *Research in Personnel and Human Resources Management*, 27, 279–336. doi:10.1016/S0742-7301(08)27007-27006

Klein, H. J., & Polin, B. (2012). Are organizations on board with best practices onboarding. In *The Oxford handbook of organizational socialization* (267–287).

Klein, H. J., Polin, B., & Sutton, K. (2015). Specific onboarding practices for the socialization of new employees. *International Journal of Selection and Assessment*, 23(3), 263–283.

Kolodny, L. (2016, March 13). The latest approach to employee training. *The Wall Street Journal*. Retrieved from www.wsj.com/articles/the-latest-approach-to-employee-training-1457921560 (on June 1, 2018)

Kossek, E. E., Roberts, K., Fisher, S., & DeMarr, B. (1998). Career self-management: A quasi-experimental assessment of the effects of a training intervention. *Personnel Psychology*, 51(4), 935–960. doi.org/10.1111/j.1744-6570.1998.tb00746.x

Kraiger, K., & Ford, J. K. (2007). The expanding role of workplace training: Themes and trends influencing training research and practice. In L. L. Koppes (Ed.), *Historical perspectives in industrial and organizational psychology* (281–309). Mahwah, NJ: Lawrence Erlbaum Associates.

Krupnick, M. (2016, September 27). U.S. quietly works to expand apprenticeships to fill white-collar jobs. *Higher Education, The Hechinger Report*. Available at: https://hechingerreport.org/u-s-quietly-works-to-expand-apprenticeships-to-fill-white-collar-jobs/

Kruchten, P. (2008). The biological half-life of software engineering ideas. *IEEE Software*, 25(5), 10–11. doi: 10.1109/MS.2008.127

Kuehn, D. (2019). Registered apprenticeship and career advance for low-wage service workers. *Economic Development Quarterly*, 1–17. doi.org/10.1177/0891242419838605

Lerman, R. I. (2012). *Can the United States expand apprenticeship? Lessons from experience* (No. 46). IZA Policy Paper.

Lerman, R. (2014). Do firms benefit from apprenticeship investments?. *IZA World of Labor*. doi: 10.15185/izawol.55.v2

Lu, H., & Yang, C. (2015). Job rotation: An effective tool to transfer the tacit knowledge within an enterprise. *Journal of Human Resource and Sustainability Studies*, 3(01), 34. doi: 10.4236/jhrss.2015.31005

Mason, G., & Constable, S. (2011). *Product strategies, skills shortages and skill updating needs in England: New evidence from the National Employer Skills Survey, 2009*. UK Commission for Employment and Skills, Evidence Report 30.

Muehlemann, S., Pfeifer, H., Walden, G., Wenzelmann, F., & Wolter, S. C. (2010). The financing of apprenticeship training in the light of labor market regulations. *Labour Economics*, 17(5), 799–809. doi.org/10.1016/j.labeco.2010.04.006

Muro, M., Maxim, R., & Whiton, J. (2019). *Automation and artificial intelligence: How machines are affecting people and places*. Washington, DC: Brookings Institute

Padula, R. S., Comper, M. L. C., Sparer, E. H., & Dennerlein, J. T. (2017). Job rotation designed to prevent musculoskeletal disorders and control risk in manufacturing industries: A systematic review. *Applied Ergonomics*, 58, 386–397. doi.org/10.1016/j.apergo.2016.07.018

Quiñones, M. A., Ford, J. K., & Teachout, M. S. (1995). The relationship between work experience and job performance: A conceptual and meta-analytic review. *Personnel Psychology*, 48(4), 887–910. doi.org/10.1111/j.1744-6570.1995.tb01785.x

Rothwell, W.J., & Kazanas, H.C. (2004). *Improving on-the-job training: How to establish and operate a comprehensive OJT program* (2nd edition). San Francisco, CA: Pfeiffer.

Santos, R. E., da Silva, F. Q., & de Magalhães, C. V. (2016, June). Benefits and limitations of job rotation in software organizations: A systematic literature review. In *Proceedings of the 20th international conference on evaluation and assessment in software engineering* (pp. 1–12). doi.org/10.1145/2915970.2915988

Schein, E.H. (2006). *Career anchors*, (3rd edition). San Francisco, CA; Jossey-Bass.

Slattery, J. P., Selvarajan, T. T., & Anderson, J. E. (2006). Influences of new employee development practices on temporary employee work-related attitudes. *Human Resource Development Quarterly*, 17(3), 279–303. doi.org/10.1002/hrdq.1175

Sonnentag, S., & Kleine, B. M. (2000). Deliberate practice at work: A study with insurance agents. *Journal of Occupational and Organizational Psychology*, 73(1), 87–102. doi.org/10.1348/096317900166895

Steinmacher, I., Silva, M. A. G., Gerosa, M. A., & Redmiles, D. F. (2015). A systematic literature review on the barriers faced by newcomers to open source software projects. *Information and Software Technology*, 59, 67–85. doi.org/10.1016/j.infsof.2014.11.001

Su, B & Berardocco, A. (2018). *Are there companies that build business rotations into their HR development strategies?*. Retrieved January 28, 2020 from Cornell University, ILR School site: https://digitalcommons.ilr.cornell.edu/student/201

Tesluk, P. E., & Jacobs, R. R. (1998). Toward an integrated model of work experience. *Personnel Psychology*, 51(2), 321–355. doi.org/10.1111/j.1744-6570.1998.tb00728.x

Verbruggen, M., & Sels, L. (2008). Can career self-directedness be improved through counseling?. *Journal of Vocational Behavior*, 73(2), 318–327. doi.org/10.1016/j.jvb.2008.07.001

Van de Wiel, M. W., Van den Bossche, P., Janssen, S., & Jossberger, H. (2011). Exploring deliberate practice in medicine: How do physicians learn in the workplace?. *Advances in Health Sciences Education*, 16(1), 81–95. doi.org/10.1007/s10459-010-9246-3

Wesson, M. J., & Gogus, C. I. (2005). Shaking hands with a computer: An examination of two methods of organizational newcomer orientation. *Journal of Applied Psychology*, 90(5), 1018. doi.org/10.1037/0021-9010.90.5.1018

Whiston, S. C. (2011). Vocational counseling and interventions: An exploration of future "big" questions. *Journal of Career Assessment*, 19(3), 287–295. doi.org/10.1177/1069072710395535

Team Learning and Development

Questions

✓ What are the underlying knowledge, skills, and attitudes important for building an effective team?
✓ Which team training interventions have been found to be effective?
✓ How do team debriefs or after action reviews facilitate learning and enhance team effectiveness?

Many organizations have adopted team-based work systems as a way of meet the increasing needs for tighter interconnectedness required to tackle the complex issues facing organizations and to develop effective solutions (West, 2017). The teams can be a permanent part of the organizational structure or include project teams whose members come together to complete tasks to meet organizational needs and then are disbanded with members moving to other projects. Teams have become a fundamental learning unit in organizations. A recent survey of trends in the workplace found that the number one global workplace trend was developing effective teamwork (Kaplan et al., 2016).

Teams often have heavy information-processing and decision-making demands as well as the need to respond to rapidly changing conditions that call for team members to adapt work processes (Baard, Rench, & Kozlowski, 2014). This chapter examines what we know about how to build and sustain effective work teams. An organizing framework for the chapter on building team effectiveness is presented in Figure 9.1. The framework shows that team effectiveness is a function of three main factors, which in turn are impacted by three types of learning strategies. The next section describes the three factors in terms of the knowledge, skill, and attitudes that are relevant for team effectiveness. The second section describes a variety of team training strategies that have been implemented to build those knowledge, skills and attitudes. The final two sections describe learning strategies beyond training that help facilitate team learning around job tasks and from team self-management strategies.

FIGURE 9.1 Team Effectiveness.

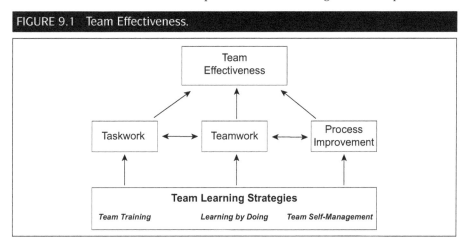

Evidence to support best practices are described as well as challenges that need to be addressed to better understand team development issues.

FOUNDATIONAL ISSUES

Before examining strategies for facilitating team learning, one foundational issue is to clearly define what constitutes a team and what is not a team. With the increasing pressures to have "teams" in the workplace, managers often call a group of people loosely connected a team when, in fact, it may not share characteristics of a real team. A second issue is the assessment of learning needs for building an effective team. Teams require more capabilities than having members with individually strong technical skills.

Defining a Team

A team consists of two or more individuals who exhibit job and task interdependencies. Team members have different roles and responsibilities as well as complementary skills and are committed to a common purpose, goals, and approach for which they hold themselves mutually accountable (Kozlowski & Ilgen, 2006).

More specifically, four dimensions are key to determining the nature of teams. These dimensions include interdependence, shared objectives, reflexivity (or team reflection), and boundedness. Table 9.1 presents the four dimensions that separate out if a group of individuals is a real team or a pseudo team. An intact team requires team members to work in a closely coordinated and timely manner towards common goals and objectives. A pseudo team works alone or in separate dyads towards disparate goals and objectives. With a real team, there are one or more clearly shared objectives that are agreed upon by the members. It is likely that we should not expect similar learning outcomes for teams that are loosely connected relevant to these four dimensions from those that are strongly connected.

Team members hopefully have clearly defined, differentiated roles and responsibilities and have some level of autonomy to get the individual and team tasks done to meet team goals. To perform effectively, team members must therefore develop an understanding of how their actions affect and are affected by others (Kozlowski, 2018).

TABLE 9.1 Distinguishing Real versus Pseudo Teams		
Team tasks require team members to work in a closely coordinated and timely manner towards common goals and objectives	**Interdependence**	Typical tasks require members to work alone or in separate dyads towards disparate goals and objectives
There are one or more clear shared team objectives that team members agree upon	**Shared Objectives**	There are as many different accounts of team objectives as there are team members
Team members systematically review team performance and adopt future objectives and processes accordingly processes accordingly	**Reflexivity**	Team members occasionally meet together to exchange information, often through obligation or habit with no consequent innovation
At any given moment, team members are clear about who is a member of the team and who is not	**Boundedness**	Team boundaries are highly permeable, with team members being unclear about who is part of the team and who is not

Source: From West, M. A., & Lyubovnikova, J. (2012). Real teams or pseudo teams? The changing landscape needs a better map. *Industrial and Organizational Psychology*, 5(1), 25–28. Copyright 2012 by Cambridge University Press. Reprinted with Permission.

Team Effectiveness Factors

Three factors of taskwork, teamwork and team process improvement distinguish effective from less effective teams (Salas et al., 2015). Effective teams have developed strong capabilities in these areas so that they become a self-managed team who holds themselves accountable for meeting team goals.

First, effective teams have members who are highly skilled technically and who can complete various tasks that the team must perform. Individuals must be competent in their role if they are to become effective team players. This development of the technical competencies of individual team members discussed in the last chapter has been called taskwork skills. One company I visited formalized a train the trainer system with the philosophy of first you learn a job in the team, then you apply the skills until you become proficient in the skills of that job, you then teach that skill to others, and evaluate whether that new person is able to learn and become proficient in the skills required. Taskwork skills also include understanding the interdependencies across team members where the work of one person on the team affects the performance of another person on the team. Therefore, with taskwork, one considers the complementariness of skills across members to get the job done (Crawford & LePine, 2013). With this knowledge, team leaders can plan how to best distribute work tasks to accomplish team goals (Fisher, 2014).

Second, effective teams have highly developed teamwork competencies that support working well together to accomplish team goals. The teamwork competencies involve the interaction among team members independent of the taskwork being performed. Figure 9.2 provides a framework identifying the underlying knowledge, skills, and attitudes important for building teamwork.

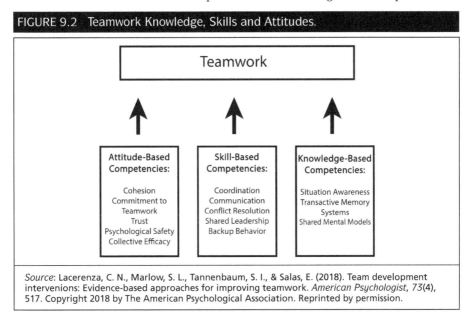

FIGURE 9.2 Teamwork Knowledge, Skills and Attitudes.

The framework is based on years of research to identify the characteristics of effective teams around what has been learned.

Attitude-based teamwork competencies include elements of developing team cohesion and trust as well as creating feelings of psychological safety so members are confident in bringing up difficult or challenging issues to the team leader or other team members. In addition, effective teams have high levels of collective self-efficacy, which is defined as team members' shared beliefs of the team's ability to perform at the level needed to meet expectations. Skill-based teamwork competencies include coordination and communication skills as well as interpersonal skills such as conflict resolution. An important teamwork action step is to recognize when and how to help other team members through back-up behaviors so a task within the team can be accomplished in a timely manner. This requires mutual performance monitoring of team member actions and providing timely and corrective feedback so as to facilitate team progress. Mutual performance monitoring highlights the role of shared leadership in effective teams as all members are committed to helping each other rather than relying on a single designed leader to take action. The knowledge-based competencies include situation awareness, transactive memory systems, and shared mental models. Situation awareness is a having the knowledge depth in members so that the team can perceive and consolidate information relevant to what is happening around the team that can impact team performance. Scanning for and obtaining such information is critical so that team members can interpret the situation in order to be proactive in taking any corrective actions if necessary. Transactive memory systems is defined as the network or shared mental models of uniquely held knowledge across team members (Austin, 2003). Shared mental models are where team members have similar ways of organizing their understanding of the task procedures, strategies, and team roles and responsibilities. A strong transactive team memory system improves team coordination and problem-solving and therefore helps teams to work seamlessly (Mathieu et al., 2000).

Third, effective teams develop process improvement procedures that help team members address constraints on team performance or that provide opportunities for expanding the team's value to the organization. A core competency for process improvement is problem-solving skills. Effective teams have team members who can identify key problems, analyze root causes, develop alternative solutions and then make decisions based on which solution seems best suited to address the problem. Effective problem-solving requires facilitation skills (at least on the part of some team members) so that meetings can be productive. Facilitation skills include how to run effective meetings, how to engage all team members in a discussion, and how to assess team progress to enhance continuous improvement. Rather than being satisfied with maintaining the status quo, effective teams are drivers for change and innovation in an organization. Therefore, effective teams are adaptable and adjust strategies. Such process consultation skills include how to create a sense of urgency for change, build a shared vision for the future, develop a strategic plan, monitor the implementation of the plan and revise plans when necessary to meet the vision.

Targeted team development interventions advance the ability of teams to develop taskwork, teamwork, and process improvement competencies. The building of these competencies can lead to high levels of effectiveness on a day-to-day basis around the routine team tasks. In addition, the development of these types of competencies are critical when the team needs to dynamically adapt to the demands of non-routine situations. Due to the great stress and high workload under which many teams must operate (e.g., emergency response teams, air crews), team success is likely to be heavily influenced by the degree to which team members demonstrate effective task work and teamwork skills. A dramatic example of dealing with a non-routine situation requiring team adaptation involved a three-person crew flying a United Airlines DC-10 flight from Denver to Chicago. The crew, whose members had been provided a variety of team training experiences, faced the disintegration of the center engine, severing lines to the rudder and other mechanisms needed to maneuver the plane. In the 34 minutes before crash landing at the nearest airport, the pilots had to come up with the approach for bringing the plane under better control, assessing the damage and context, finding options and choosing a landing site, and preparing the crew and passengers for the crash. Minute-by-minute analysis of the cockpit conversation revealed intense interactions – 31 communications per minute (one per second at its peak). In these minutes, a fourth pilot who was a passenger was recruited to help prioritize and to divide up their work. The constant communication allowed everyone to be aware of unfolding events and decisions. Junior crew members freely suggested alternatives and the captain responded with appropriate commands. The conversations also included moments of emotional support, enabling the crew to cope with the extreme stress. The coordination and communication among the crew was a key to saving the lives of most of the people on board (Helmreich & Foushee, 1993).

TEAM TRAINING PROGRAMS

Team training is a key strategy for developing people in intact and project-based teams. Not surprising, extensive efforts have been undertaken to examine the effectiveness of team training efforts. In general, the findings across many studies is that team training (across many types of team training interventions) is effective. Hughes et al. (2016) conducted a meta-analysis of 129 studies on team training in health contexts that included a pre- and post-training evaluation design. They found strong evidence for the effectiveness of the training on improvements in learning over those who had not attended the training. They found evidence for the impact of team training on cognitive transfer – cognitive strategies retained and used on the job as well as skill-based transfer – technical skills retained and used on the job. Perhaps more importantly, they also found evidence for bottom line results – in this case the reduction in medical errors. Another meta-analysis examined 72 team training interventions using fairly rigorous experimental designs across a number of domains including aviation, military, academia, and health care. The results show that training interventions lead to higher levels of teamwork behaviors and team performance especially for relatively newly formed teams (McEwan et al., 2017).

The types of team training interventions developed to enhance taskwork, teamwork, and process improvement skills are described below. The methods described exemplify the tremendous variety of training and learning activities that have been created to address the changing reality of organizations towards team-based work systems.

Team Coordination and Cross-Training

Team coordination training is designed so that team members acquire a working knowledge of the job of one's teammates including tasks, roles, responsibilities, expectations, and the interconnections among team members. In this way, the training can lead to the building of a shared mental model among team members as to how the team operates and what type of cooperation and coordination is needed to be an effective team.

Team coordination training can take four different forms that vary in the intensity of the effort: positional clarification, positional modeling, position rotation, and cross-training (Blickensderfer, Cannon-Bowers, & Salas, 1998). The first three forms represent less intensive training methods than cross-training where members are expected to become fully proficient in some or all the jobs within a team. Positional clarification refers to providing members with information-based training on various facets of their teammates' jobs. Positional modeling is a training procedure in which the duties of one's teammates are not just discussed but then are directly observed. Positional rotation is experientially based training, wherein team members for a short period of time actually perform the duties of other team members to get a hands-on perspective of the roles, responsibilities, and coordination requirements of that job (Dierdorff & Ellington, 2017).

The form of team coordination training utilized should correspond to the level of interdependence of the team, with positional clarification being sufficient for teams with minimal interdependence, and positional rotation appropriate for more highly interdependent teams. Studies have provided some empirical support for the utility of the lower intensity team coordination training for enhancing team-effectiveness. Volpe et al. (1996) found that two-member teams operating a PC flight simulator demonstrated greater overall teamwork, more efficient communication strategies, and greater team performance when provided with positional clarification than when trained only on performing their own taskwork duties. Another study found that the benefits of positional clarification training were greatest under high-workload situations, in which demands on team effectiveness are the highest (Cannon-Bowers et al., 1998). Such situations are a common characteristic of the situations in which emergency response teams must operate.

The most intensive coordination approach (and more researched) for increasing the effectiveness of teams is cross-training. Cross-training is about building taskwork skills. The specific goal of cross-training is for individuals on a team to learn two or more of the jobs performed within the team. With cross-training, individuals acquire knowledge and skills so that they can successfully perform the work duties of other members of the work team. Cross-training increases flexibility in staffing positions, helps prevent employee obsolescence, and allows teams to become more self-managed or autonomous. With skill-based pay systems, team members may also receive additional pay for acquiring the knowledge and skills required to do other jobs within the team.

As one example, the work of a manufacturing team might be to transform a piece of steel into gears or sprockets for heavy equipment like farm tractors or large gears for wind turbines. To produce a product, the team tasks include sawing the metal into manageable pieces, making a rough cut of the steel rod with a lathe, drilling holes through the metal, creating the "teeth" of the gear through a hobbing process, and deburring the gear to get rid of excess metal. With cross-training, individuals become proficient in many, if not all, of the tasks to be completed by the team to produce the part. In addition, team members can also become proficient in more generalizable skills such as checking the quality of the parts produced, enhancing the safety of the manufacturing process, maintaining machines, and how to set up the machine to run different types of parts. The more skills an individual learns while on the team, the more efficient the team can be with the routine tasks and be more prepared to handle non-routine situations as they arise.

There is research support for the value of cross-training for affecting team cognition (transactive memory) and behaviors (e.g., backing up behaviors). Marks et al. (2002) found that cross-training enhanced shared mental models and coordination of team members leading to higher levels of team effectiveness. Cross-training also plays an especially important role as job demands increase as it leads to more information dissemination and less tension among members than teams not cross-trained (Ellis and Pearsall, 2011). A study of three-person cross-trained teams on a multi-user computer-based simulated performance task incorporated two extended nonuse intervals to see the impact of skill decay on team performance (Villado et al., 2013). They found that cross-trained teams had less performance reduction with nonuse than those in the individually trained condition. They contend team characteristics such as enhanced task interdependencies may help mitigate skill loss. Similarly, Cooke et al. (2013) studied team members working collaboratively on a reconnaissance mission. They measured team performance decrements as an indicator of team skill retention over 8–10 weeks after simulation training. Even though two of the three team roles showed skill decrements at the individual level, team performance was not affected by the individual skill decay functions. Rather, higher levels of team situation awareness and coordination of the cross-trained group led to a smaller impact of individual decay on over-all team performance.

An interesting view of the future of work concerns cross-training in a manufacturing task to improve the performance of human–robot teams. The learning component occurs in a simulated work setting that involves a collaborative task requiring interdependencies between the robot and human actions to successfully complete the task. The robot is programmed in a way to "learn" how to interact efficiently with human action as the outcome of the robot action is dependent on human action. A study finds that the human–robot teamwork improves with cross-training. Table 9.2 provides a case analysis of this unique, future directed cross-training intervention. Figure 9.3 shows a picture of the cross-training that come from this case of a human and robot learning to work together to perform a set of job tasks.

While cross-training sounds like a wise investment, Abrams and Berge (2011) remind us that the possible complexity, cost, and implementation challenges require some consideration in any decision-making. A case analysis provides insight into difficulties in sustaining a cross-training program once implemented (Cutcher-Gershenfeld & Ford, 2005). They report on a rolled steel manufacturing company that introduced a "craft-combination" training process. Craft combination training focuses on merging skilled trades. For example, the craft-combination training involves broadening a welder's skills to include pipefitting competencies and expanding a pipefitter's competencies

---

TABLE 9.2 The Future of Cross-Training!

An interesting view of the future of work for used cross-training in a manufacturing task to improve the performance of human–robot teams. The learning component occurred in a simulated work setting that involved a collaborative task requiring interdependencies between the robot and human actions to successfully complete the complete task.

The robot is programmed in a way to "learn" how to interact with human action as the outcome of the robot action is dependent on human action. First, the robot completed their assigned "task" in relation with the human actions on the person's assigned task. Second, the roles were switched (cross-trained) with the human doing the robotic task and the robot doing the human part of the task.

Compared to the typical approach (doing the first step above alone), the cross-training intervention led to improvements in performance outcomes. For example, with cross-training, the human operator spent 41% less time idling – interestingly, idle time was also less for the robot! Ratings by the operator showed that the cross-trained group saw the robot as more trustworthy and also reported that the robot perceived accurately what "my preferences are."

Evidence was also found that the robot "mental model" showed evidence of a reduction of uncertainty about the actions of the human when cross-trained leading to more concurrent motion by both robot and human while performing the task. The researchers concluded that the results "provide the first evidence that human–robot teamwork is improved when a human and robot train together by switching roles in a manner similar to that used in effective training practices for human teams" (Nikolaidis, Lasota, Ramakrishnan, & Shah, 2015; p. 1728).

Source: Case derived from study by Nikolaidis, S., Lasota, P., Ramakrishnan, R., & Shah, J. (2015). Improved human–robot team performance through cross-training, an approach inspired by human team training practices. *The International Journal of Robotics Research*, 34(14), 1711–1730.

FIGURE 9.3   Human and Robot Working Together.

Source: Shutterstock.com. Reprinted by permission.

to include welding. Over 900 skilled trade employees went through the training modules with on-the-job experiences. Despite these efforts, a subsequent evaluation of the system found that many supervisors did not allow those who had successfully completed the training to use the skills learned in training. Instead, the supervisors preferred someone who was originally certified and trained as a welder rather than calling a pipefitter who had been cross-trained on welding skills. Thus, the problem was not one of training but of the transfer of training to a work environment where the pressure was to keep production moving and putting out fires as quickly as possible rather than supporting the development of the individuals who had been cross-trained by giving them opportunities to perform on the job.

Team Resource Management Training

Many teams work in high consequence of error types of domains. Training to aid teamwork for intact teams was introduced into the aviation community in 1970 due to the high level of accidents and close calls that, upon review, were based more on team-related human error in the cockpit rather than mechanical factors. Given the initial focus on aviation, the training of teamwork skills was called crew resource management training. Since then, occupations such as medical nuclear power, safety personnel in police and fire, and offshore oil production domains have adopted the teamwork elements underlying this type of training. The team training is relevant for temporary teams that disband and are reconstituted such as air crew and surgical teams as well as more permanent team structures. The sense of urgency for this training is based on a variety of data such as the finding that 75% of more than 7,000 root cause analysis reports on health care errors were found to be due to communication failures among team members (Dunn et al., 2007).

Team resource management training is designed to build skills for interacting effectively around the taskwork of the team, sharing relevant information needed for the team to perform effectively, and enhancing teamwork competencies like coordination, collaboration, communication, and assertiveness. The building of these competencies allows the team to better cope with situational demands that would overwhelm any one individual team member. A major emphasis of the training is to promote team goals of error avoidance, the early detection of errors so teams have time to deal with the situational demands, and the minimization of negative consequences resulting from team errors. The design fosters skills in threat recognition, error management, and team problem-solving and decision-making (Salas et al., 2001).

This direction is captured by the mnemonic STAR – stop, think, act and review (Baldwin, 2008). The STAR system refers to stopping and taking the time to examine what tasks have to be done and thinking about the situation currently being faced (how the situation is similar or different from other situations) and developing options that take into account the risks, possible consequences, and contingency plans as a situations changes. The next step is to act on the option seen as most optimal given the situation with steps taken to avoid errors. After action, there is a review of the procedures followed and the outcomes to determine whether the option selected was appropriate. The process of STAR is restarted if the monitoring of progress suggests that the current path is not leading to expected outcomes or if an error occurs that needs to be addressed.

Program development typically begins with the identification of the team mission requirements and procedures. This is followed by an assessment of the coordination demands (i.e., specific tasks requiring teamwork). These team tasks are then linked to theories of team performance to derive the specific competencies to be trained. Each competency is translated into a training objective and plans of instruction that can be empirically evaluated. Scenarios or exercises are developed to provide trainees opportunities to practice each competency. These exercises also provide a means for assessing whether the targeted behaviors are demonstrated sufficiently by team members. Based upon this assessment, constructive feedback is provided concerning effective and ineffective behaviors. When practicing teamwork skills through simulations or scenarios, team members often are engaged in talking about how to improve their behavior and performance before going into the next practice round.

One training approach called the Team-Oriented Medical Simulation (TOMS) is designed for interdisciplinary team training of surgical teams (Baker et al., 2005). The training consists of three main parts. First, core teamwork concepts such as situational awareness and communication are defined and discussed in relation to team performance. Second, the team creates a plan for a simulated surgery with a focus on pre-planning to enhance teamwork followed by the simulated surgery. Third, the team conducts a post-surgery review and the team members diagnose problematic teamwork behaviors and identify strategies for improvement. The cycle of planning for the next simulated surgery is followed by a review of the videotape over trials to solidify effective teamwork behaviors.

TABLE 9.3 Team Resource Management Training Criteria of Success	
Criteria	**Observations**
Anticipation and Planning	Key decisions are made early Distribute the workload Develop a shared understanding of the situation faced
Team Leadership	Designate leader Mobilize all available resources Aware of their own individual roles and team roles Immediate objectives understood by all Hold members accountable to team goals Help create shared mental model around key tasks
Communication	Communicates needs as issues progress Clear communication among team members Clarify ambiguous information Acknowledgement that message has been received Follow-up among team members
Error Detection and Management	Create norm to speak up about problems that can lead to errors Check prior to use to avoid errors Verbalize procedures that are going to be performed next Think out loud to ensure everyone is on the same page
Prioritization and Adaptability	Makes priorities clear given time limitations Help each other to stay on task and not become distracted Anticipate and address each team member needs Attend to triggers that point to need for changing strategy

Sources: Adapted from Alonso, A., Baker, D.P., Holtzman, A, Day, R., King, H., Toomey, L, & Salas, E. (2006). Reducing medical error in the military health system: How can team training help. *Human Resource Management Review,* 16, 396–415; Mercer, S. J., Howell, M., & Simpson, R. (2010). Simulation training for the frontline-realistic preparation for Role 1 doctors. *BMJ Military Health,* 156(2), 87–89; Midwinter, M. J., Mercer, S., Lambert, A. W., & De Rond, M. J. (2011). Making difficult decisions in major military trauma: A crew resource management perspective. *Journal of the Royal Army Medical Corps,* 157(Suppl 3), S299–S304.

This approach has also been adapted for training astronauts. Spaceflight Resource Management targets the management of human errors during time critical events such as launch and complicated extra vehicular situations in space. The two goals of the training are to establish open communication and a positive team climate for crew members as precursors to error detection and remediation (Rogers, 2010). Table 9.3 provides a more detailed presentation of the steps that are part of resource management training design for a variety of teams such as health care, military, and airline crews. The steps identify criteria that can be used to evaluate team effectiveness around anticipation, leadership, communication, error management, as well as prioritization and adaptability during realistic training scenarios around team resource management.

Evaluations of the effectiveness of team resource management training programs have shown encouraging results. An initial narrative evaluation of crew resource management training programs suggested that there was a 20% increase in effective teamwork behaviors in teams trained under this method (Salas et al., 1999a, 1999b). The researchers also found that the team training led to increases in positive attitudes toward teamwork, knowledge of teamwork principles, and demonstration of teamwork competencies in a simulated mission for relatively new aviators and more experienced ones. An updated review found more mixed results for the impact of the training on behavioral changes. In addition, questions were raised as to the impact of team training on bottom line criteria such as decreasing accidents (O'Connor et al., 2008). A recent meta-analysis of 20 studies in acute care domains across a variety of types of teams (intensive care, operating room personnel, and emergency room personnel) finds that participants react positively to the training and that the training results in more positive attitudes towards working as a team. There is also a large effect on knowledge gains and for changes in team behaviors exhibited by team members from pre- to post-assessment (O'Dea, O'Connor, & Keogh, 2014). Clearly, team resource management training has been adopted by many organizations and team training is better than just assuming that people will work well together. Nevertheless, evidence of comparing changes in the training and non-trained groups on results-oriented return on investment criteria would provide stronger evidence of its effectiveness (Salas et al., 2006a, 2006b).

Team Building

Team building training is used to enhance social relations and improve interpersonal interactions among teammates so that the team can function at a high level (Shuffler, DiazGranados, & Salas, 2011). The team building intervention that is most appropriate depends on the developmental stage of the team.

One well-known team performance developmental model identifies steps that need to be addressed to move to a high team performance (Drexler, Sibbet, & Forrester, 1988). Building an effective team starts with orienting the team as to purpose and team direction. The second phase is trust building such that team members come to appreciate each other's competencies and there is a feeling of mutual regard. The third phase is one of goal clarification in which there is a shared vision and specific goals that team members agree on and that drive behavior. Once the first three phases are resolved at some reasonable level, the team can then move to the fourth phase around building team commitment not only to goals but also about team process such as role clarity, fair distribution of resources, and an understanding of how decisions are made. The fifth phase involves disciplined execution of tasks through a shared understanding of team process and alignment of efforts towards the team goals. Continual efforts at disciplined execution can lead to a high performance team that interact seamlessly, have high energy and surpass expectations. With new members or dynamically changing situation, high performance teams need a period of renewal and rededication and commitment to new goals and processes.

Team building interventions can target any one of these phases such as being designed to build trust, clarify goals, and gain commitment to those team goals. For example, if a team is struggling around role ambiguity, the focus could be on goal clarification and re-assigning roles and allocating resources effectively. A team struggling with relationship issues may lead to team building training around trust, creating a supportive environment, and dealing with conflict.

A a case example from sports looked at a team building intervention of five three-hour team building sessions over three months for an equestrian team. The training was designed to have team members better articulate the roles and responsibilities of the team leaders and to clarify team expectations regarding how individuals treat each other. Some sessions focused on building effective nonverbal and verbal communication skills especially around providing and accepting constructive feedback and how to personally deal with disappointments (e.g., not being chosen for a competition). Exercises were also conducted targeting social support and building collective efficacy including a competitive spirit and spirit de corps for team success. Individual interviews and focus groups conducted pre and post the team building training intervention showed improvement in team harmony and closeness and less reliance on cliques. Team members also reported feeling more support from teammates during competitions. While there were encouraging results, unfortunately, hard data on team performance of success was not gathered (Bloom & Stevens, 2002).

A popular team building training option is outdoor experiential training or adventure learning. This approach to team building is an international industry that involves the use of intact teams exposed to difficult and/or unfamiliar physical and mental challenges in an outdoor environment and tasked with solving the challenges embedded in the activities (Ng, 2001). The goals of these activities are typically for a team of participants to explore strategies for enhancing teamwork, building trust, and developing stronger support networks. The activities can also focus on incorporating risk management strategies into team decision-making. At a personal level, the courses can help team members acquire skills in taking initiative, making quick decisions, and setting personal improvement goals. The interventions include such activities as ropes courses, rock climbing, rappelling, sailing, rafting, and wilderness exploration. Outdoor experiential training provides the opportunity for team members to try new activities, time for individual personal reflection, and a facilitated session with all team members to share insights and ways to improve teamwork back on the job.

Evidence regarding the effectiveness of adventure learning for team building goals is quite limited. In fact, most outdoor training programs do not state specific learning objectives or clearly articulate what behavioral changes on the job should be expected as a function of the training – making formal and systematic evaluation difficult (Williams, Graham, & Baker, 2003). Support for these learning experiences is mainly based on positive reactions from participants ("I really gained a lot from this experience") and from anecdotal evidence that team members feel they will be more effective now. The lack of clarity as to team building objectives is illustrated well by a comment by one participant of a mountain outdoor learning experience who stated "it was a great achievement to walk over the mountain but did I gain anything out of it? Yeah, I gained a nice view" (Jones & Oswick, 2007). Clearly, there is a need for rigorous quantitative studies with learning objectives identified with measures of behavioral changes on the job. In addition, what is needed are studies with actual intact work teams as many of the studies are with college students often in temporarily created teams.

Multiagency Training

While team resource management training focuses on within team competencies, other training approaches target the need for multiagency teams that must coordinate efforts. For example, disasters occur all too frequently taking the form of floods, hurricanes, earthquakes, terrorism, and hazardous

FIGURE 9.4 Multi-Agency Training Drill.

Source: Shutterstock.com. Reprinted by permission.

materials accidents. Effective efforts to minimize the potential for and lessen subsequent impact of disasters requires strong coordination of resources and actions across multiple teams representing different types of organizations and functions. Figure 9.4 is an example of multiagency training around responding to a major earthquake. The picture shows soldiers, paramedics and medical personnel who are rescuing injured people and maintaining order during the simulated drill. The drill is being videotaped to allow for post-training review of the responses by the various personnel across the multi-agency teams.

The learning challenge is to develop not only individual and within team expertise but to build knowledge and skills around multi-team and multi-organization coordination and cooperation. In the public health arena, there has been a call to bring together the variety of agencies who deal with health related issues (hospitals, public health agencies, schools) to join together in a collaborative to have more "collective impact" on public health within a community. The five elements of a collective impact approach is for this newly formed multiagency team to create a common objectives and direction, create and share relevant public health data (e.g., smoking rates, diabetes rates), coordinate activities across the agencies towards the common purpose, increase communication across leaders of the agencies, and designate and adequately resource the supportive infrastructure needed to drive collective impact (Kania & Kramer, 2011). I have been involved in a long-term attempt by a community to create collective impact around public health. The effort required to maintain a collaborative requires building trust among the agencies, integrating activities, and spending time on learning and growing as a multiagency team.

One strategy for developing skills for multi-agency team coordination is through scenario based and serious gaming type interventions (Chapter 7). These training interventions involve the development of a simulation exercise that requires participants across agencies to make decisions and take actions that have identifiable consequences. While a more simplified version of real-world issues and problems facing multiple teams, the games allow for the development of "what if" scenarios in which participants are embedded into a work-related problem requiring coordination of effort. The games often unfold through brief situation reports that participants receive at the beginning of each round. For emergency action teams, a number of tasks are embedded into the game that require participants to complete tasks such as staffing and opening facilities, assisting people, and placing staff and volunteers. The situation is often combined with teaching modules that concentrate on specific issues and skills relevant to successful multi-team performance in regard to communication, strategic planning, interpreting reports from the field and estimating costs. Formal debriefing and generation of lessons learned that can be applied back on the job provide another layer in the learning process.

Scenarios can stimulate the senses, incorporate interactivity, and simulate cause and effect linkages. These embedded aspects allow for a cycle of judgments, behaviors, and feedback with high levels of functional and psychological fidelity (Ford & Meyer, 2013). Multiplayer, interactive serious games can facilitate team effectiveness by building team skills such as coordination and cooperation as well as honing skills in strategy and tactics. Multiplayer games often model events requiring critical decisions. Trainees take on the role of a specific identity often represented in the gaming environment (e.g., America's Army, Counter-Strike) as an avatar. For example, De Kleermaeker and Arentz (2012) report on a team-based serious game called Water Coach for training crisis response in the Netherlands on reacting to storm surges. The teams can call up different scenarios to practice and can alter the difficulty levels and the ways team members can communicate among themselves so participants can experience how these factors influence team process and outcomes. Such multiplayer games have the potential to promote deep learning in teams by (1) providing a safe environment to make mistakes and see the consequences of actions; (2) presenting scenarios that stimulate senses and tap into emotions; (3) incorporating interactivity and cause and effect linkages; (4) including a cycle of judgments, behaviors and feedback; and (5) incorporating psychological and functional fidelity (O'Connor & Menaker, 2008).

Training multi-agency teams has generated positive evaluations. Khoury et al. (2018) created a complex serious game on management of resources that involved multiple stakeholders around flood mitigation in the UK. They found that the team training improved participants' understanding of the problems and helped the teams to improve their coordinated approach/planning for flood risk management. The training also led participants to form new local partnerships to be better prepared in the future. As a cautionary tale about designing for effectiveness, the researchers found no relationship between scenario-based training and an organization resilience measure that focused on improved situational awareness and more adaptive capability of the teams (Ahmad, Johnson, & Storer, 2015).

TEAM LEARNING ACTIVITIES

While formal training interventions help build team effectiveness, learning can also be a focus when teams are on-the-job performing team tasks. Learning interventions on the job can facilitate the transfer as well as can build additional strength of the team around continuous learning.

Action Learning

An action learning approach emphasizes that much learning can occur by dealing directly with and solving complex real-life problems. Table 9.4 presents an example of a problem that was used to take an action learning approach within a manufacturing company that produces gears and sprockets. The recurring quality problem was identified. A team was created that included operators, the quality coordinator, manufacturing engineers, and purchasing. The team was trained in basic problem-solving methods including how to conduct root cause analysis. In addition, the members had already been trained in statistical process control and other methods for analyzing data. For this project, the team utilized a cause-effect analysis that helped the team to identify and organize the factors that led to the recurring quality problem. The team mapped out a list of factors that included quality issues between groups or departments within the company, contextual factors, information and communication impediments relevant to this project, and operator factors. The team generated 29 factors that led to the quality problem and then prioritized the factors in terms of which were the most critical. Internal quality problems included that the tooling on the machine was not designed properly, the metal being used was warped during earlier heat treating of the metal (done off-site), the sequence of operations were difficult and unfamiliar to most operators, the order was not reviewed properly to discover and solve engineering problems prior to giving the job to the operator, and there was a lack of timely recognition that the parts being produced were not complying with the specifications. The team then generated a list of possible solutions including getting more tolerance from the customer, re-sequencing how the job would be completed, training operators on inspection methods, and doing heat treatment within the company to maintain high quality. After coming to consensus on the solutions to implement, the

---

TABLE 9.4 Action Learning

A company quoted and received an order from a new customer. The customer called for two counterbores with unusual dimensions for normal machining operations. The company was under delivery pressure from the customer. Employees proceeded with production per standard operation procedures. During the final inspection, it was discovered that approximately 35% of the parts were nonconforming to the specifications desired by the customer. The poor quality parts were sorted out and those that were marginal were inspected in order to made decisions as to what could be shipped to meet the deadline. The errors were chalked up to machining issues. Two weeks later, when trying to ship for the next scheduled delivery, there was a similar rejection rate. A department leader tried to troubleshoot the job and found it was impossible to do a high-quality job given the type of information given to the operators. Thus far, the company has scrapped several hundred dollars' worth of material and has compromised quality by shipping parts that did not completely meet product specifications. Similar problems have occurred when working with new customers with complex parts. Everybody is frustrated. It is time to create a team to examine this quality problem.

team members divided up the implementation tasks (e.g., one team member focused on simplifying inspection techniques while another created a team to re-sequence the production operations for this part). The next time the part was ordered by the customer, the results showed a dramatic improvement in quality and on time delivery.

The problem was addressed by the team and learning did occur in this action learning process. Throughout this process, team members were encouraged to discuss lessons learned from this experience and how to generalize this learning to other new product situations and other more common product situations. Team members also focused on how well they were working together as a team (e.g., engineering and sales had rarely worked with operators on the floor). Based on these experiences, a common problem-solving model was adopted by the organization to use in future situations. In addition, new procedures for how to deal with new and complex products were developed that included the creation of product teams to examine the product specifications prior to the job going to the operator. The product team included a diverse set of employees including engineering, operations, quality, and leaders.

As can be seen in the example, the main goal of action learning is the creation of creative ideas and innovative strategies that lead to solving an existing problem. This experience is seen as leading to learning how to work together and how to diffuse the innovation to other parts of the organization. While there is good agreement on what makes for an effective action learning process, the data on the effectiveness of this approach is limited to successful case studies like the one above. Many companies have moved to an action learning approach where training and learning go hand in hand with problem-solving and improved job performance.

Team Debriefs

Team debriefs are team meetings where the members conduct a post-action review to examine and critique team performance as well as summarize lessons learned that can guide improvements in future performance. A central component of this post-action review is the provision of both individual and team-level feedback. Debriefs were first adopted by the military to promote learning from experience after training and have now been expanded into a variety of occupational fields including the medical field, fire service, aviation, and education (Allen et al., 2018). While debriefs are typically completed after a performance episode on the job, debriefs can also be effectively utilized in training simulations. Between practice sessions on the simulation and discussions among trainers, the team participants and observers identify learnings from previous mistakes in order to develop a team plan on how to improve before going back into the simulator for more practice.

In a review of the literature, Tannenbaum and Cerasoli (2013) identify four essential aspects that define debriefs as opposed to other types of team interventions. Table 9.5 presents these four key elements of debriefs: what they are and what they are not. The elements include active self-learning, developmental intent, specific event focused, and having multiple information sources. Debriefs are structured and systematic experiences with a clear

TABLE 9.5	Essential Elements of Debriefs	
Element	**Definition**	**Excludes**
Active self-learning	Participants engage in some form of self-discovery or active involvement and are not merely passive recipients	Passive receipt of feedback; being told how to improve by a coach or facilitator
Developmental intent	A clear, primary intent for improvement or learning that is nonjudgmental and focused on future directions	Performance appraisals or reviews; incidental learning
Specific events	Involves reflection on specific events or performance episodes rather than general performance or competencies	General discussion of a team's or person's overall strengths and weaknesses; 360° feedback about overall competencies
Multiple information sources	Includes input from multiple team members or from a focal participant and at least one external source such as an observer	Personal diary keeping; self-reflection

Source: From Tannenbaum, S. I., & Cerasoli, C. P. (2013). Do team and individual debriefs enhance performance? A meta-analysis. *Human Factors*, 55(1), 231–245. Copyright 2013 by the Human Factors and Ergonomics Society. Reprinted by permission.

intent to analyze what happened during a performance episode (e.g., like a near miss between two aircraft), a discussion of why the problem occurred, an understanding of both positive and negative behaviors and how they impacted the outcomes, and a discussion of how the participants could have worked better together to minimize the problem from occurring again in similar situations.

Are debriefs effective? Tannenbaum and Cerasoli (2013) examined studies comparing debrief interventions (who met the criteria in Table 9.5 of distinguishing a debrief from other team interventions) with control groups where a debrief was not conducted. The typical group size was between five and six team members with the average number of three debriefing sessions of about 20 minutes each per study. Effectiveness measures included objective performance indicators such as simulator results, hospital records and performance ratings by observers. Evidence from the meta-analysis of 46 studies show that debriefs improve team effectiveness at a rate of 25% over the control groups. As a dramatic example of effectiveness, Neily et al. (2010) reports an 18% reduction in annual mortality rates for medical facilities conducting pre- and post-briefs versus a 7% increase in those rates over time for facilities where debriefs are not conducted.

A fundamental characteristic that enhances the effectiveness of debriefs is honest and constructive feedback to focus team members on critical aspects of the task. The effectiveness of post-action reviews is also influenced by the climate of openness and trust in the team. In other words, there needs to be some level of psychological safety so that team members can feel comfortable admitting mistakes and be willing to talk about confusing situations that occurred among team members during performance. One means of building such a climate is for all team members to first provide a self-critique of their own role in affecting team performance early in the post-action review before moving to the team level. The team leader as facilitator of learning plays a critical role in the success of team debriefs. The meta-analysis described above found that facilitated debriefs were three times more effective than unguided debriefs highlighting the importance of someone skilled at leading the discussions. Skilled facilitators and trained leaders can ensure that expectations are set, manage the flow of information and gather multiple points of view and perspective. Actions that have impacted others are explored to help the team generate specific lessons learned with detailed action plans for improvement (Scott et al., 2015).

In addition to team debriefs after an action or experience, teams can also incorporate a pre-brief prior to task practice or team performance during which the team prepares for the upcoming activity. Pre-briefs provide the team leader and members an opportunity to set both individual and team-level goals, discuss strategies, clarify roles and responsibilities, and focus on potential problems to be encountered. They can be used to explicate the linkages between individual roles and those of their team members. Additionally, specific strategies can be developed for a variety of likely contingencies, allowing team members to form common expectations of how each other will respond. A pre-brief begins with an emphasis on the objective to improve team process. Teamwork issues such as how to communicate effectively and how to provide support for others are highlighted and discussed. Team members are reminded of the goals that they have set from previous practice sessions on achieving greater team cooperation and coordination. Then, team members are told that it is their responsibility to share learning experiences and analyze team performance once the performance experience is completed.

In the medical field, pre-briefs have been introduced as an important component before temporary teams work together in an operating room. An evidence-based approach based off of team resource management strategies to reduce medical errors is called Team Strategies and Tools to Enhance Performance and Patient Safety (TeamSTEPPS). The aim of the training design is to implement pre- and post-briefings as well as encouraging higher levels of situational awareness, mutual support and enhanced communication during the operating procedures. Effectiveness data was collected before the TeamSTEPPS intervention and then for similar time post training intervention. Results across 1481 medical cases show that mean time to start the surgery as well as mean surgical time is significantly shorter after teams go through the training intervention. Safety patient issues that could have led to problems also decreased significantly after the training was instituted (Weld et al., 2016).

Coaching and Team Learning

Investigations on coaching effects tend to examine individual knowledge and skill acquisition. Nevertheless, with the increased use of teams in organizations, there is a recognized need to understand the role of coaches and team development. Team coaching is typically seen as a role of leadership in the organization but can also be a role for an external (or internal) consultant. Team leaders have taken on roles to enhance team effectiveness such as structuring tasks and ensuring adequate resources are available to the team. Team leaders are also a critical factor around how to address problems as well as how to exploit opportunities for continuous learning and improvement. Hackman and Wageman (2005) contend that coaching around team strategy facilitates team effectiveness more than efforts at team building around interpersonal relationships.

While the emphasis on coaching has increased in workplaces, the evidence on factors leading to individual and team learning and enhanced team performance is limited (Beattie et al., 2014). There is evidence that coaching efforts are more beneficial for teams that are well structured and supported than those who are not (Wageman, 2001). Hagen and Aguilar (2012) examined team leader coaching expertise within the content of Six Sigma projects in high performance work teams within heavy manufacturing, manufacturing sales, service, and a high technology companies. They found that the level of coaching expertise of team leaders was related to team reported indicators of team learning and enhanced effectiveness.

Three components of effective team coaching are providing developmental feedback to clarify key behaviors, behavioral modeling in which the coach models the way so that team members can learn vicariously, and the setting of challenging but attainable goals. Dahling and colleagues (2016) conducted a study of the coaching skill and frequency of coaching interactions of district managers in a global pharmaceuticals company on the attainment of sales goals by team members. They found that coaching skill (measured by trained observers of the managers during simulated role plays) had a direct positive effect on sales goal attainment. Interestingly, managers who interacted frequently with the sales members who had weak coaching skills led to a negative influence on sales attainment. Those identified as highly skilled coaches were found to influence goal attainment regardless of the frequency of their contact with team members.

A cross-national comparison of data sets from England, USA, and Scotland using the critical incident technique led to the identification of common ineffective coaching behaviors. One key finding is that ineffective coaches go too fast during initial instruction, do not clarify roles, do not recognize the complexity underlying the learning needs of team members, and are not likely to follow up with learners to help with transfer. Effective coaching behaviors relevant to team learning include encouraging employees to think through the issues, providing feedback, identifying developmental needs, using analogies and examples to broaden perspectives, and being an effective role model (Hamlin, Ellinger, & Beattie, 2006).

TEAM SELF-MANAGEMENT AND ADAPTATION

As teams build competencies through training and job experiences, they can become more self-sufficient and autonomous. With a high level of effectiveness, teams can potentially manage their own internal processes such as assigning people to work projects, evaluating team success, taking action to improve team effectiveness, and monitoring their own learning. Evidence suggests many teams do not reach this high level of becoming self-managing and continuously improving. Two strategies for enhancing team learning and improvement are described below.

Learning from Other Teams

Team self-management can be accelerated by learning from other teams. This notion of vicarious learning has typically been applied to individual learning. The old adage of not reinventing the wheel makes as much sense for team learning. Vicarious learning to enhance team efficiency and performance can include just observing and copying what another team is doing well. However, with complex and dynamic team tasks, there is a need to explore what specific aspects to exploit about what other teams have done well and what aspects to not pursue.

Disruptive events, new priorities, or organizational change initiatives along with time pressures can heighten the need to accelerate learning from other teams. Bresman (2013) reports on an extensive qualitative study consisting of interviews over time for a variety of teams in the pharmaceutical industry. The analysis of interviews reveals that teams are active in searching out other teams who have experience in the new priorities for the focal teams. Based on information obtained by the focal team, the team members often have intense discussions of the team strategies observed and whether the strategies should be adopted. The findings also highlight how teams modify what other teams are doing, learn from other team mistakes, recognize the need to challenge underlying assumptions of the tasks assigned to the team, and learn timely lessons about team process and how to work more effectively together. For example, in terms of team process, one team reported that they found that a successful team had worked hard to clarify team goals and roles. This observation led the focal team to have a productive meeting clarifying goals and roles and uncovering discrepancies among members that would have affected the team if it had not been uncovered and dealt with early in the process.

There is evidence that vicariously learned knowledge is more susceptible to decay than knowledge that is from direct team experience (Madsen & Desai, 2010). This illustrates the importance of the team engaging in discussions soon after observations and then spending enough time experimenting and learning how to translate and adopt the lessons learned from other teams. This notion is supported by another study by Bresman (2010) who found that teams that are proactive in vicariously learning from other teams have higher levels of performance only when the teams are also active in discussing, translating, adopting, and testing the strategies from the other team rather than simply adopting them. Another study finds that teams with more identifiable structures such as well-defined goals, roles, and a clearly identified leader are more likely to exhibit vicarious learning from external sources. Team member perceptions of psychological safety is also a critical factor – strong team structure leads to higher levels of perceptions of team psychological safety that in turn results in more attempts to learn from other teams – as well as more attempts to learn from each other within the team (Bresman & Zellmer-Bruhn, 2013).

Team Reflexivity

A second strategy for enhancing team self-management skills is through what has been called team reflexivity. Reflexivity is defined as the extent to which team members set aside time to examine their own performance and how to improve. The discussions can be about the current objectives, strategies, and team decision processes with systematic reflections on how to enhance team effectiveness by adapting strategies to meet current and anticipated circumstances (West, 2000). Team reflexivity is a critical team learning activity in dynamic and complex task situations. Reflexivity is closely related to the concept of meta-cognition for individual learning and performance where the learner reflects on their individual strategy and success on a task. Reflexivity differs from team debriefs in that debriefs target one particular event and how to improve that task when performing it again. Reflexivity is much broader in scope in that the team is examining its overall functioning as a team based on a variety of team tasks and over time. Reflexivity is more likely to occur naturally after some changes in team membership, when milestones are achieved, or where new technology is being adopted (Schippers, Edmondson, & West, 2014).

Teams can reflect on (1) how to manage the boundaries of the team so as to maintain team identity, (2) how to fulfill the team's function or key tasks, and (3) how to build and enhance interpersonal relationships in the team (Schein, 1999). In terms of team identity, members can reflect on whether the team has the right skill mix as well as what additional structures are needed to maintain team identify given changing organizational needs. For team tasks, members can reflect on whether the team has the appropriate goals and, if so, the extent to which the problem identification and decision-making process are effective. For interpersonal management, members can reflect on the level of trust among team members, the appropriateness of how member conflicts are managed, and the extent to which the team has effective norms around team cohesion, diversity, and inclusion. Learning from reflection can then lead to prioritizing the types of issues impacting team effectiveness and determining the appropriate course of action moving forward.

Reflexivity is much more likely when the team proactively decides to experiment with new ways of acting or approaching a task in a novel way (Senge, 2006). This notion is similar to the description of deliberate practice approaches for individuals discussed in Chapter 7. There is evidence that teams who naturally have higher levels of reflexivity also have higher levels of team learning and innovation (Schippers, West, & Dawson, 2015). Other research finds that teams may do initial strategy discussion and planning but tend not to spontaneously change or revise those strategies over time as pressures for task completion and results win out over the desire to learn to improve team processes (Goh, Goodman, & Weingart, 2013).

A typical reflexivity intervention asks teams to reflect on how they have performed on a team task and to discuss what strategies have been enacted and what strategies might be enacted to lead to the improvements that are needed. Then the team is asked to develop a plan around new strategies to meet their goals and to come up with an implementation plan. Teams are encouraged to be ready to adapt as the team is performing the task. Research evidence supports the effectiveness of guided reflexivity on team outcomes. Gutner et al. (2007) used a simulated military simulation and found that guided reflexivity led to more strategy communication, a higher degree of members having a shared team mental model and greater likelihood of implementing strategies, which in turn was related to stronger team performance. Reiter-Palmon et al. (2018) conducted an experiment with 16 rural hospitals to reduce patient falls. They created an intervention to facilitate team reflexivity and over a two-year period found that increasing reflexivity was related to implementation of more innovative ideas as well as having a bottom-line impact on reducing fall rates. In another study, 73 manufacturing production teams were assigned to training on team reflexivity or to a control group who were given team building exercises. For those in the training condition, team reflexivity then occurred on the job site at the end of each shift. The team members reviewed team objectives, discussed what went well in the shift and what facilitated meeting objectives, and discussed what did not go well and why, and then developed steps to take to improve outcomes in the next shift as well as how to measure success and hold each other accountable for improvement. Training in team reflexivity at the end of the shifts led to improvements in team member well-being such as lower levels of emotional exhaustion, cynicism, and feelings of inefficacy (Chen et al., 2018). This example provides further evidence of the limited usefulness of team building exercises over interventions focused directly on improving team task performance. Interestingly, a recent study of the National Health Service in England finds that well-structured and interdependent teams that engage in reflexivity report fewer errors and experience fewer work-related injuries than those reporting loosely connected team members (Lyubovnikova et al., 2015).

CONCLUDING COMMENTS

As noted by Dierdorff and Ellington (2017), the nature of teams is changing along a number of dimensions including "more fluid membership, greater use of technology, more geographic dispersion, and increased team member diversity" (p. 398). The interconnectedness of people and teams at work will only accelerate. The move to teams has positive aspects but also has the potential for increasing stress and tensions. This is particularly relevant as more people become members of multiple teams simultaneously and where teams are faced with strong pressures for immediate outcomes within high levels of time pressures. The push for more and more teaming and collaboration within organizations must be balanced with the need not to stretch people beyond their ability to handle the pressures embedded in these efforts. Team interventions to support learning need to not only target knowledge and skill development but also on the more affective components of working in teams that promote wellness.

Team learning interventions matter. As described in this chapter, there are individual studies and meta-analytic findings that show team interventions lead to more learning and improve team outcomes such as efficiency and effectiveness. Yet, research needs to keep up with the changing realities and explore new approaches for improving team knowledge, skills, and attitudes. In addition, much of team learning research has been completed with limited measures of transfer of training to the job over time. There is also a need for more intensive efforts to study intact teams in work settings. Clearly, leadership is a key aspect of effective taskwork and teamwork. The next chapter addresses the various approaches to developing effective leaders.

Chapter 9: Best Practice Guidelines

- Ensure team members have an appropriate level of taskwork knowledge and skills prior to heavily investing in building teamwork competencies.
- Identify the teamwork attitude, skills, and knowledge competencies that are priorities before team development programs are designed.
- Cross-train team members when job demands and coordination requirements are high and where flexibility is critical to team success.
- Employ positional clarification rather than the more intensive cross-training when the team has low levels of interdependence.
- Design team resource management training to foster skills in threat recognition, error detection and management, and team problem-solving and decision-making.
- Develop the criteria of success as to the effectiveness of team resource management training (Table 9.2) so observers can target areas for improvement.
- Clearly identify team-building learning objectives and ensure activities are selected to meet those objectives.
- Incorporate the five elements of collective impact into multiagency collaboration efforts.
- Conduct team debriefs around specific events or performance episodes of the team that encourages self-discovery, focuses on future directions, and includes input from multiple team members and observers.
- Train leaders on how to hold structured debriefs (and pre-briefs) by ensuring that expectations are set, managing the flow of information, gathering multiple points of view about how actions impacted others, and helping the team generate specific lessons learned with detailed action plans for improvement.

References

Abrams, C., & Berge, Z. (2011). Workforce cross training: A re-emerging trend in tough times. *Journal of Workplace Learning*, 22, 522–529. doi.org/10.1108/13665621011082882

Ahmad, A., Johnson, C. W., & Storer, T. (2015). Impact of scenario-based exercise on organization resilience in critical infrastructure organizations. *Journal of Technology Management and Business*, 2(1). Retrieved from https://publisher.uthm.edu.my/ojs/index.php/jtmb/article/view/1092

Alonso, A., Baker, D. P., Holtzman, A, Day, R., King, H., Toomey, L, & Salas, E. (2006). Reducing medical error in the military health system: How can team training help. *Human Resource Management Review*, 16, 396–415. doi.org/10.1016/j.hrmr.2006.05.006

Allen, J. A., Reiter-Palmon, R., Crowe, J., & Scott, C. (2018). Debriefs: Teams learning from doing in context. *American Psychologist*, 73(4), 504. doi.org/10.1037/amp0000246

Austin, J. R. (2003). Transactive memory in organizational groups: The effects of content, consensus, specialization, and accuracy on group performance. *Journal of Applied Psychology*, 88(5), 866. doi.org/10.1037/0021-9010.88.5.866

Baard, S. K., Rench, T. A., & Kozlowski, S. W. (2014). Performance adaptation: A theoretical integration and review. *Journal of Management*, 40, 48–99. doi: 10.1177/0149206313488210

Baker, D. P., Gustafson, S., Beaubien, J. M., Salas, E., & Barach, P. (2005). Medical team training programs in health care. In K. Henriksen, J. B. Battles, E. S. Marks, & D. Lewin (Eds.), *Advances in patient safety: From research to implementation* (Vol. 4), Programs, tools, and products. Rockville, MD: Agency for Healthcare Research and Quality.

Baldwin, E. (2008). Integrating space flight resource management skills into technical lessons for international space station flight controller training. In *Third International Association for the Advancement of Space Safety Conference*, Noordwijk, the Netherlands.

Beattie, R. S., Kim, S., Hagen, M. S., Egan, T. M., Ellinger, A. D., & Hamlin, R. G. (2014). Managerial coaching: A review of the empirical literature and development of a model to guide future practice. *Advances in Developing Human Resources*, 16, 202–221. doi.org/10.1177/1523422313520476

Blickensderfer, E., Cannon-Bowers, J. A., & Salas, E. (1998). Cross-training and team performance. In J. A. Cannon-Bowers & E. Salas (Eds.), *Making decisions under stress: Implications for individual and team training*. Washington, DC: APA.

Bloom, G. A., & Stevens, D. E. (2002). Case study: A team-building mental skills training program with an intercollegiate equestrian team. *Athletic Insight: The Online Journal of Sport Psychology*, 4(1), 1–16.

Bresman, H. (2013). Changing routines: A process model of vicarious group learning in pharmaceutical R&D. *Academy of Management Journal*, 56(1), 35–61. doi.org/10.5465/amj.2010.0725

Bresman, H. (2010). External learning activities and team performance: A multimethod field study. *Organization Science*, 21(1), 81–96. doi.org/10.1287/orsc.1080.0413

Bresman, H., & Zellmer-Bruhn, M. (2013). The structural context of team learning: Effects of organizational and team structure on internal and external learning. *Organization Science*, 24(4), 1120–1139. doi.org/10.1287/orsc.1120.0783

Cannon-Bowers, J. A., Salas, E., Blickensderfer, E., & Bowers, C. A. (1998). The impact of cross-training and workload on team functioning: A replication and extension of initial findings. *Human Factors*, 40(1), 92–101. doi.org/10.1518/001872098779480550

Chen, J., Bamberger, P. A., Song, Y., & Vashdi, D. R. (2018). The effects of team reflexivity on psychological well-being in manufacturing teams. *Journal of Applied Psychology*, 103(4), 443. doi.org/10.1037/apl0000279

Cooke, N. J., Gorman, J. C., Myers, C. W., & Duran, J. L. (2013). Interactive team cognition. *Cognitive Science*, 37(2), 255–285. doi.org/10.1111/cogs.12009

Crawford, E. R., & LePine, J. A. (2013). A configural theory of team processes: Accounting for the structure of taskwork and teamwork. *Academy of Management Review*, 38(1), 32–48. doi.org/10.5465/amr.2011.0206

Cutcher-Gershenfeld, J., & Ford, K. (2005). *Valuable disconnects in organizational learning systems: Integrating bold visions and harsh realities*. New York: Oxford University Press.

Dahling, J. J., Taylor, S. R., Chau, S. L., & Dwight, S. A. (2016). Does coaching matter? A multilevel model linking managerial coaching skill and frequency to sales goal attainment. *Personnel Psychology*, 69(4), 863–894. doi.org/10.1111/peps.12123

De Kleermaeker, S., & Arentz, L. (2012, April). Serious gaming in training for crisis response. In *Proceedings of the 9th international ISCRAM conference*, Vancouver, BC, Canada (pp. 22–25).

Dierdorff, E. C., & Ellington, J. K. (2017). Team training. In M. D. Coovert & L. F. Thompson (Eds.), *Cambridge handbook of workplace training and employee development* (p. 383). Cambridge: Cambridge University Press.

Drexler, A. B., Sibbet, D., & Forrester, R. H. (1988). The team performance model. In W. B. Ready & K. Jamison (Eds.), *Team building: Blueprints for productivity and satisfaction* (pp. 45–61). Alexandria, VA: NTL Institute for Applied Behavioral Science.

Dunn, E. J., Mills, P. D., Neily, J., Crittenden, M. D., Carmack, A. L., & Bagian, J. P. (2007). Medical team training: Applying crew resource management in the Veterans Health Administration. *Joint Commission Journal on Quality and Patient Safety*, 33(6), 317–325. doi.org/10.1016/S1553-7250(07)33036-5

Ellis, A., & Pearsall, M. J. (2011). Reducing the negative effects of stress in teams through cross-training: A job demands-resources model. *Group Dynamics: Theory, Research, and Practice*, 15, 16–31. doi.org/10.1037/a0021070

Fisher, D. M. (2014). Distinguishing between taskwork and teamwork planning in teams: Relations with coordination and interpersonal processes. *Journal of Applied Psychology*, 99(3), 423. doi.org/10.1037/a0034625

Ford, J. K., & Meyer, T. (2013). Advances in training technology: Meeting the workplace challenges of development, deep specialization, and collaborative learning. In *The psychology of workplace technology*. Society for Industrial and Organizational Psychology Organizational frontiers series (pp. 43–76). London: Taylor & Francis Group.

Goh, K. T., Goodman, P. S., & Weingart, L. R. (2013). Team innovation processes: An examination of activity cycles in creative project teams. *Small Group Research*, 44(2), 159–194. doi.org/10.1177/1046496413483326

Gurtner, A., Tschan, F., Semmer, N. K., & Nägele, C. (2007). Getting groups to develop good strategies: Effects of reflexivity interventions on team process, team performance, and mental models. *Organizational Behavior and Human Decision Processes*, 102, 127–142. doi.org/10.1016/j.obhdp.2006.05.002

Hackman, J. R., & Wageman, R. (2005). A theory of team coaching. *Academy of Management Review*, 30(2), 269–287. doi.org/10.5465/amr.2005.16387885

Hagen, M., & Aguilar, M. G. (2012). The impact of managerial coaching on learning outcomes within the team context: An analysis. *Human Resource Development Quarterly*, 23, 363–388. doi.org/10.1002/hrdq.21140

Hamlin, R. G., Ellinger, A. D., & Beattie, R. S. (2006). Coaching at the heart of managerial effectiveness: A cross-cultural study of managerial behaviours. *Human Resource Development International*, 9(3), 305–331. doi.org/10.1080/13678860600893524

Helmreich, R. L., & Foushee, H. C. (1993). Why crew resource management? Empirical and theoretical bases of human factors training in aviation. In E. Weiner, B. Kanki, & R. Helmreich (Eds.), *Cockpit resource management* (pp. 3–45). San Diego, CA: Academic Press.

Hughes, A. M., Gregory, M. E., Joseph, D. L., Sonesh, S. C., Marlow, S. L., Lacerenza, C. N., Benishek, L. E., King, H. B., & Salas, E. (2016). Saving lives: A meta-analysis of team training in healthcare. *Journal of Applied Psychology*, 101(9), 1266. doi.org/10.1037/apl0000120

Jones, P. J., & Oswick, C. (2007). Inputs and outcomes of outdoor management development: Of design, dogma and dissonance. *British Journal of Management*, 18(4), 327–341. doi.org/10.1111/j.1467-8551.2006.00515.x

Kania, J., & Kramer, M. (2011, Winter). Collective impact. *Stanford Social Innovation Review*, 201, 36–41.

Kaplan, M., Dollar, B., Melian, V., Van Durme, Y., & Wong, J. (2016). Shape culture: Drive strategy. In *Global human capital trends 2016: The new organization: Different by design*. New York: Deloitte. Retrieved from Deloitte Insights: https://www2.deloitte.com/global/en/insights/focus/human-capital-trends/2016/impact-of-culture-on-business-strategy.html

Khoury, M., Gibson, M. J., Savic, D., Chen, A. S., Vamvakeridou-Lyroudia, L., Langford, H., & Wigley, S. (2018). A serious game designed to explore and understand the complexities of flood mitigation options in urban–rural catchments. *Water*, 10(12), 1885. doi.org/10.3390/w10121885

Kozlowski, S. W. (2018). Enhancing the effectiveness of work groups and teams: A reflection. *Perspectives on Psychological Science*, 13(2), 205–212. doi.org/10.1177/1745691617697078

Kozlowski, S. W. J., & Ilgen, D. R. (2006). Enhancing the effectiveness of work groups and teams. *Psychological Science in the Public Interest*, 7, 77–124. doi.org/10.1111/j.1529-1006.2006.00030.x

Lacerenza, C. N., Marlow, S. L., Tannenbaum, S. I., & Salas, E. (2018). Team development interventions: Evidence-based approaches for improving teamwork. *American Psychologist*, 73(4), 517. doi.org/10.1037/amp0000295

Lyubovnikova, J., West, M. A., Dawson, J. F., & Carter, M. R. (2015). 24-Karat or fool's gold? Consequences of real team and co-acting group membership in healthcare organizations. *European Journal of Work and Organizational Psychology*, 24(6), 929–950. doi.org/10.1080/1359432X.2014.992421

Madsen, P. M., & Desai, V. (2010). Failing to learn? The effects of failure and success on organizational learning in the global orbital launch vehicle industry. *Academy of Management Journal*, 53(3), 451–476. doi.org/10.5465/amj.2010.51467631

Marks, M. A., Sabella, M. J., Burke, C. S., & Zaccaro, S. J. (2002). The impact of cross-training on team effectiveness. *Journal of Applied Psychology*, 87(1), 3. doi.org/10.1037/0021-9010.87.1.3

Mathieu, J. E., Heffner, T. S., Goodwin, G. F., Salas, E., & Cannon-Bowers, J. A. (2000). The influence of shared mental models on team process and performance. *Journal of Applied Psychology*, 85(2), 273. doi.org/10.1037/0021-9010.85.2.273

McEwan, D., Ruissen, G. R., Eys, M. A., Zumbo, B. D., & Beauchamp, M. R. (2017). The effectiveness of teamwork training on teamwork behaviors and team performance: A systematic review and meta-analysis of controlled interventions. *PloS One*, 12(1), e0169604. doi:10.1371/journal.pone.0169604

Mercer, S. J., Howell, M., & Simpson, R. (2010). Simulation training for the frontline-realistic preparation for Role 1 doctors. *BMJ Military Health*, 156(2), 87–89.

Midwinter, M. J., Mercer, S., Lambert, A. W., & De Rond, M. J. (2011). Making difficult decisions in major military trauma: A crew resource management perspective. *Journal of the Royal Army Medical Corps*, 157(Suppl. 3), S299–S304. doi.org/10.1136/jramc-157-03s-08

Neily, J., Mills, P. D., Young-Xu, Y., Carney, B. T., West, P., Berger, D. H., Mazzia, L. M., Pauli, D. E., & Bagian, J. P. (2010). Association between implementation of a medical team training program and surgical mortality. *JAMA*, 304(15), 1693–1700. doi:10.1001/jama.2010.1506

Ng, H. A. (2001), Adventure learning: Influence of collectivism on team and organizational attitudinal changes, *Journal of Management Development*, 20(5), 424–440. doi.org/10.1108/02621710110395444

Nikolaidis, S., Lasota, P., Ramakrishnan, R., & Shah, J. (2015). Improved human–robot team performance through cross-training, an approach inspired by human team training practices. *International Journal of Robotics Research*, 34(14), 1711–1730. doi.org/10.1177/0278364915609673

O'Connor, P., Campbell, J., Newon, J., Melton, J., Salas, E., & Wilson, K. A. (2008). Crew resource management training effectiveness: A meta-analysis and some critical needs. *International Journal of Aviation Psychology*, 18(4), 353–368. doi.org/10.1080/10508410802347044

O'Connor, D. L., & Menaker, E. S. (2008). Can massively multiplayer online gaming environments support team training? *Performance Improvement Quarterly*, 21(3), 23–41. doi.org/10.1002/piq.20029

O'Dea, A., O'Connor, P., & Keogh, I. (2014). A meta-analysis of the effectiveness of crew resource management training in acute care domains. *Postgraduate Medical Journal*, 90(1070), 699–708. doi.org/10.1136/postgradmedj-2014-132800

Reiter-Palmon, R., Kennel, V., Allen, J., & Jones, K. J. (2018). Good catch! Using interdisciplinary teams and team reflexivity to improve patient safety. *Group & Organization Management*, 43(3), 414–439. doi.org/10.1177/1059601118768163

Rogers, D. G. (2010). Crew resource management: Spaceflight Resource Management. In B. Kanki, R. Helmreich, & J. Anca (Eds.), *Crew resource management* (2nd ed.). New York: Academic Press.

Salas, E., Burke, C. S., Bowers, C. A., & Wilson, K. A. (2001). Team training in the skies: Does crew resource management (CRM) training work? *Human Factors*, 43(4), 641–674. doi.org/10.1518/001872001775870386

Salas, E., Fowlkes, J. E., Stout, R. J., Milanovich, D. M., & Prince, C. (1999a). Does CRM training improve teamwork skills in the cockpit? Two evaluation studies. *Human Factors*, 41, 326–343. doi.org/10.1518/001872099779591169

Salas, E., Prince, C., Bowers, C. A., Stout, R. J., Oser, R. L., & Cannon-Bowers, J. A. (1999b). A methodology for enhancing crew resource management training. *Human Factors*, 41(1), 161–172. doi.org/10.1518/001872099779577255

Salas, E., Shuffler, M. L., Thayer, A. L., Bedwell, W. L., & Lazzara, E. H. (2015). Understanding and improving teamwork in organizations: A scientifically based practical guide. *Human Resource Management*, 54(4), 599–622. doi.org/10.1002/hrm.21628

Salas, E., Wilson, K. A., Burke, C. S., & Wightman, D. C. (2006a). Does crew resource management training work? An update, an extension, and some critical needs. *Human Factors*, 48(2), 392–412. doi.org/10.1518/001872006777724444

Salas, E., Wilson, K. A., Burke, C. S., Wightman, D. C., & Howse, W. R. (2006b). Crew resource management training research, practice, and lessons learned. *Reviews of Human Factors and Ergonomics*, 2(1), 35–73. doi.org/10.1177/1557234X0600200103

Schein, E. (1999). *Process consultation revisited: Building the helping relationship*. Reading, MA: Addison Wesley.

Schippers, M. C., Edmondson, A. C., & West, M. A. (2014). Team reflexivity as an antidote to team information-processing failures. *Small Group Research*, 45, 731–769. doi.org/10.1177/1046496414553473

Schippers, M. C., West, M. A., & Dawson, J. F. (2015). Team reflexivity and innovation: The moderating role of team context. *Journal of Management*, 41(3), 769–788. doi.org/10.1177/0149206312441210

Scott, C., Dunn, A. M., Williams, E. B., & Allen, J. A. (2015). Implementing after-action review systems in organizations: Key principles and practical considerations. In J. A. Allen, N. Lehmann-Willenbrock, & S. G. Rogelberg (Eds.), *Cambridge handbooks in psychology. The Cambridge handbook of meeting science* (pp. 634–659). New York: Cambridge University Press.

Senge, P. M. (2006). *The fifth discipline: The art and practice of the learning organization*. New York: Doubleday.

Shuffler, M. L., DiazGranados, D., & Salas, E. (2011). There's a science for that: Team development interventions in organizations. *Current Directions in Psychological Science*, 20(6), 365–372. doi.org/10.1177/0963721411422054

Tannenbaum, S. I., & Cerasoli, C. P. (2013). Do team and individual debriefs enhance performance? A meta-analysis. *Human Factors*, 55(1), 231–245. doi.org/10.1177/0018720812448394

Villado, A. J., Day, E. A., Arthur Jr, W., Boatman, P. R., Kowollik, V., Bhupatkar, A., & Bennett Jr, W. (2013). Complex command-and-control simulation task performance following periods of non-use. In *Individual and team skill decay* (pp. 77–91). New York: Routledge.

Volpe, C. E., Cannon-Bowers, J. A., Salas, E., & Spector, P. E. (1996). The impact of cross-training on team functioning: An empirical investigation. *Human Factors*, 38(1), 87–100. doi.org/10.1518/001872096778940741

Wageman, R. (2001). How leaders foster self-managing team effectiveness: Design choices versus hands-on coaching. *Organization Science*, 12(5), 559–577. doi.org/10.1287/orsc.12.5.559.10094

Weld, L. R., Stringer, M. T., Ebertowski, J. S., Baumgartner, T. S., Kasprenski, M. C., Kelley, J. C., Cho, D. S., Tieva, E. A., & Novak, T. E. (2016). TeamSTEPPS improves operating room efficiency and patient safety. *American Journal of*

Medical Quality, 31(5), 408–414. doi. org/10.1177/1062860615583671

West, M. A. (2000). Reflexivity, revolution and innovation in work teams. In M. M. Beyerlein, D. A. Johnson, & S. T. Beyerlein (Eds.), *Product development teams* (Vol. 5, pp. 1–29). Stamford CT: JAI Press.

West, M. A. (2017). The future of teams. In E. Salas, R. Rico, & J. Passmore (Eds.), *The Wiley Blackwell handbook of the psychology of team working and collaborative processes* (pp. 589–596). Malden, MA: Wiley.

West, M. A., & Lyubovnikova, J. (2012). Real teams or pseudo teams? The changing landscape needs a better map. *Industrial and Organizational Psychology*, 5(1), 25–28. doi. org/10.1111/j.1754-9434.2011.01397.x

Williams, S. D., Graham, T. S., & Baker, B. (2003). Evaluating outdoor experiential training for leadership and team building. *Journal of Management Development*, 22(1), 45–59. doi. org/10.1108/02621710310454851

Developing Leaders

Questions

✓ What are ways to improve the effectiveness of leadership development programs?

✓ How can coaches help make challenging job assignments a developmental experience for leaders?

✓ What do we know about developing effective global leadership competencies?

The changing nature of the workplace and workforce highlights the need for effective leadership. Leaders structure activities that enhance engagement, productivity, and well-being. The pace of change, the influx of new technologies, and changing customer expectations place increasing demands for effective leadership. The move to team-based work systems and the changing expectations of employees towards increased responsibility and empowerment place pressures on leaders to be more creative in how human resources are utilized. The Global Human Capital Trends survey found that 80% of respondents placed leadership as a top priority but only 41% of the respondents stated that their organization was prepared to meet current and future leadership needs (Volini et al., 2019).

Leadership development programs and activities have exploded over the last 20 years to become a multibillion-dollar global business (Bersin, 2014). Yet, a recent survey of human resource professionals shows that only 35% of respondents note that they have a systematic program to develop high potentials to create a leadership pipeline. In those organizations that do have systematic leader development programs, only 55% noted that their company attempted to measure the effectiveness of those programs (Mitchell, Ray, & Van Ark, 2017). The first section of this chapter discusses an underlying theory of leader development followed by the identification of key skills and competencies required of leaders. The second section describes a variety of learning interventions including training, job experiences, and coaching that are employed by organizations in developing leaders. The chapter ends with an analysis of global leadership issues including skill and competency challenges, and the effectiveness of learning interventions created to enhance global leadership capabilities.

LEADERSHIP SKILLS AND BEHAVIORS

Leadership development refers to activities to build knowledge, skills, and attitudes that enhance an individual's capacity to effectively enact the roles and responsibilities of whatever leadership position the person is currently holding or positions that the person is aspiring towards obtaining. Understanding a theory of leader development and the various roles leaders play are fundamental to creating leadership development opportunities.

Theory of Leadership Development

A theory of leadership development provides a window into understanding the progression of learners from relative novices leaders to fully competent and expert levels. Table 10.1 presents a useful framework that identifies knowledge, skills, and mindset changes as the learner progresses over time in leadership roles. Each stage of progression describes the qualitative shifts in knowledge, the depth and breadth of skills acquired, and the mindset shifts that occur as learners come to internalize the role of being a leader (Lord & Hall, 2005).

As can be seen in the table, moving from a relative novice leader to the competent or intermediate level requires an increase in efficiency in the way information is processed and the development of tighter connections as knowledge becomes more organized in memory with strategies for dealing with specific situations tied to rules and principles learned from experience. The growth in knowledge from intermediate to expert involves a greater understanding of organizational levels, functions, how things get done, and what is needed to change organizational systems (McCauley et al., 2006). To address constructively the problems and situations leaders face, an expert leader "sees" the interconnectedness of the various functions and levels in an organization and has a firm mental model of cause-effect relationships within the organization.

In terms of skill progression, novices move from basic problem identification and using existing skills to maintain daily operational requirements to an expanded level of interpersonal and business decision-making skills. Job experiences and other learning opportunities broaden the breadth and depth of leadership skills. Competent leaders have grown in their roles and responsibilities and are able to draw out principles that can be generalized across situations and people rather than each situation seeming to be unique. This level of understanding allows the leader to act more decisively and in a timely way to routine and less routine situations. The progression in skills towards high proficiency is where behaviors are based on strongly held internal values, beliefs, and working assumptions based on learning experiences with skills being enacted more autonomously. As an example, in discussing the principles of lean manufacturing, one leader noted that lean is a way of thinking, not just a list of things to do (Cutcher-Gershenfeld & Ford, 2005).

A key mindset issue over time is the progression of learners coming to identify themselves as being a leader. New leaders tend to have an

TABLE 10.1 Differences by Leadership Level			
Competency Level	**Knowledge**	**Skill Set**	**Mindset**
Novice	Reliance on leader orientation, training and mentoring, vicarious learning from observing other leaders, and trial and error to know what is appropriate behavior for different situations	Basic problem identification, problem-solving, and decision-making. Building skills on how to manage others while maintaining daily operational requirements	Individualized focus on being recognized as a leader by others and looking for what is unique that person is bringing to the leadership roles and responsibilities
Competent	Increase in efficiency in processing information as knowledge becomes more organized in memory with rules for dealing with specific situations tied to rules and principles learned from experience	Expanded interpersonal, business and decision-making skills. Given more proceduralized and strategic knowledge given experiences able to act more decisively and in a timely way	Comfortable with roles and responsibilities that go with being a leader. Some job crafting to better address perceived needs for workgroup and organization
Highly proficient	Deep understanding of how various systems in the organization operate and role leaders need to play in helping organization be more efficient and effective as well as roles and responsibilities of leadership to facilitate organizational change and adaptability	Application of skill set to leader behaviors based on internally held values, beliefs, and working assumptions	Self-identity tied to being an effective leader. Collectivist focus on what is best for the workgroup and the organization as a whole

Source: Adapted from Lord, R. G., & Hall, R. J. (2005). Identity, deep structure and the development of leadership skill. *The Leadership Quarterly*, 16(4), 591–615. Copyright 2005 by Elsevier Science and Technology. Reprinted by permission.

individualistic focus on being recognized as a leader and seeking to differentiate one's style from other leaders. With the move to more expert status, individuals have a collective sense of what it takes to be an effective leader by networking with other leaders, peers, and followers. In addition, the change in mindset is for leaders to self-identify as a leader. This self-identification is a more collectivist orientation around what is best for the workgroup and organization. The implication from thinking about the progression of leader development is that systematic learning efforts by organizations need to take into account the sequencing of developmental activities. Leader growth includes paying attention to not only building knowledge and skills but also engaging learners in ways to change mindsets.

Leader Roles

Leadership research has a long history of identifying the roles and behaviors needed for effective leadership. These efforts have gone from the initial work from The Ohio State leadership studies in the 1950s around consideration and initiating structure behaviors to a more modern focus on the broad types of effective leader behaviors around transactional (day-to-day leadership) and transformational (adaptation and change) leadership (Bass & Riggio, 2006).

A review of these various approaches to understanding leadership effectiveness has led to the creation of a taxonomy of leadership roles and behaviors (Yukl, 2012). The taxonomy encompasses 4 major categories and 15 leader behaviors that must be accomplished by leaders in these four types of roles. The four types include the leader roles of being task oriented and relationship oriented as well as the role of being a change leader (transformational) and the role of being externally focused. Table 10.2 provides this hierarchical taxonomy with the 15 behaviors identified and defined relevant to these four major role categories. For example, for the task-oriented role there are four leader behaviors identified including clarifying roles and responsibilities of others, planning and coordinating work, monitoring operations and checking progress, and problem-solving and taking decision actions.

These 15 roles provide a roadmap for targeting leadership development initiatives. A focus on the change leadership role could have the goal of enhancing a leader's understanding of systems thinking so as to be a more effective advocate for change or develop skills to help guide the creation and communication of a vision and a sense of urgency for an organizational change initiative. I was part of a team helping a police agency move to a community policing approach. We discussed systems thinking with key leaders during a five-day training intervention on change leadership. This workshop led to the identification of 23 systems in the police agency that would need to change to align and support the move to community policing. This provided the grounding needed to help the leaders envision the future for themselves, the police officers and staff, and for the community.

There are a variety of learning and development interventions and strategies to build leader knowledge and skills relevant to the roles and behaviors identified in Table 10.2 In general, meta-analytic studies demonstrate the effectiveness of leadership development programs for enhancing knowledge, skill, and behavioral learning outcomes. One study examined formal leadership training programs on human relations and general management principles and found that the success of such programs varied across the 83 studies with the average effect size showing a moderate impact on improving leadership behaviors on the job (Collins & Holton, 2004). The findings are fairly robust across the different types of evaluation designs employed in the studies. Examining a broader array of learning opportunities for leaders, a study investigated the extent to which leadership interventions have their intended impact. Leadership interventions included formal knowledge-based training programs as well as an analysis of various scenario and role-playing training interventions. The results of the meta-analysis of 200 studies showed that the leadership interventions on average have a positive impact on a variety of learning and transfer outcomes. The researchers estimated that across the studies there was a 66% probability of having a positive outcome versus

TABLE 10.2 Taxonomy of Leadership Roles and Behaviors

Roles	Behaviors	Description
Task oriented	Clarifying	Explains roles and responsibilities; sets goals and priorities; explains rules and policies
	Planning	Develops short-term plans for work; schedules and coordinates activities; identifies resource needs to accomplish tasks
	Monitoring operations	Checks on progress and quality of work; evaluates performance in a systematic way
	Problem-solving	Identifies issues that disrupt work, diagnoses and takes decisive action to resolve issues
Relationship oriented	Supporting	Shows concern for needs of employees; provides support and encouragement when needed
	Developing	Gives helpful feedback and coaching for others; provides opportunities for skill development
	Recognizing	Praises effective work performance and recognition for achievements; recommends and/or provides appropriate rewards
	Empowering	Involves members in making important work-related decisions; delegates responsibilities and allows others to resolve problems without prior approval
Change oriented	Advocating change	Identifies emerging opportunities and threats; provides rationale for why there is a sense of urgency for change; pushes for what needs to change
	Envisioning change	Communicates a clear and appealing vision of what the future can hold for an organization; links vision to member values and ideas; is enthusiastic about the future state
	Encouraging innovation	Encourages strategic and creative thinking around new approaches; supports efforts to develop new products, services or processes
	Facilitating collective learning	Uses systematic procedures to understand underlying reasons for success or failures; encourages sharing of new knowledge and best practices
External	Networking	Attends meetings or events and joins professional associations to enhance social relationships so as to increase information flow, idea generation and create possibilities for assistance when needed
	External monitoring	Analyzes information about changes in the external environment so as to identify implications for the organization
	Representing	Seeks resources for unit; promotes and defends the reputation of the work unit; negotiates agreements and coordinates activities with others

Source: Yukl, G. (2012). Effective leadership behavior: What we know and what questions need more attention. *Academy of Management Perspectives*, 26(4), 66–85.

a 34% chance the leaders program would have a limited effect relative to a comparison group not undergoing the training (Avolio et al., 2009). Therefore, there is empirical evidence that leader development interventions are typically effective. The next section goes into detail about the types of leadership development interventions and strategies and what can be done in the design to increase their effectiveness.

LEADER DEVELOPMENT STRATEGIES

To meet leadership development challenges, organizations are not only emphasizing formal training for incumbent leaders but also set up special opportunities for learning and development to enhance the leadership capabilities of high-potential employees. In this section, five types of leadership development interventions are highlighted including behavioral modeling, business simulations, feedback intensive approaches, challenging job assignments, and leadership coaching and mentoring. The learning interventions differ in their emphasis on which leader behaviors or competencies to focus on and the approach taken to leader development.

Behavioral Modeling

A behavioral role modeling approach stresses the importance of modeling, practice and reinforcement as steps for modifying behavior. Goldstein and Sorcher (1974) adapted many of the principles of social learning theory (Chapter 4) into this systematic training approach. Their goal was to improve interpersonal related supervisory skills and behaviors. They argued that training programs typically tell managers that it is important to be good communicators, with which almost everyone agrees along with advice on how to be a better communicator. In contrast, the behavioral modeling approach consists of providing learners with the key behaviors found to be effective in particular situations (e.g., how to be assertive) and then showing the learners models performing those specific behaviors. The participants are then given opportunities to practice the key behaviors demonstrated by a model and receive feedback on the extent to which the behaviors were displayed and what steps can be taken in the next practice trial to further refine skills in displaying the key behaviors.

An exemplar of this approach is the study discussed in Chapter 6 on the use of a pre-post experimental design with random assignment (Latham & Saari, 1979). The training modules for this program targeted a number of supervisory skills around orienting a new employee, correcting poor work habits, handling a complaining employee, and overcoming resistance to change. An example of the key behaviors for the module of handling a difficult employee is presented in Table 10.3. Each session followed the same procedure of introducing the topic and the key behaviors, presenting a demonstration video of a supervisor effectively handling the situation by using the key behaviors, group discussion of the effectiveness of the model in demonstrating desired behaviors, practice in role-playing the desired behaviors, and feedback on the effectiveness of the learner demonstrating desired behaviors. During the role-playing practice sessions, one participant took the role of the supervisor, and another participant took on the role of the employee. During the session, the

TABLE 10.3   Key Behaviors for Reducing Conflicts with an Employee
• Avoid responding with hostility or defensiveness.
• Ask for and listen openly to the employee's complaint.
• Restate the complaint for thorough understanding.
• Recognize and acknowledge his or her viewpoint.
• State your position nondefensively.
• State a specific date for a follow-up meeting.

Source: Adapted from Latham, G. P., & Saari, L. M. (1979). Application of social-learning theory to training supervisors through behavioral modeling. *Journal of Applied Psychology*, 64(3), 239–246. Copyright 1979 by The American Psychological Association. Reprinted by permission.

key behaviors were posted so that the learner could make use of the principles during the role-plays.

Two trainers were present at all sessions, with the first trainer supervising the role-playing practice. The second trainer worked with the group to teach them how to provide constructive feedback that would enhance the confidence of the person receiving feedback. At the end of each session, the trainees were sent back to their jobs with instructions to use the supervisory skills they had gained. At the next session, the supervisors reported their experiences including difficulties they encountered. Then they picked some of the challenging situations to role-play to reinforce the initial training with the peers providing feedback. Managers of the supervisors were also given advice on how to support and reward the newly trained supervisors for their on-the-job behaviors relevant to the training received.

Since that pioneering study, a number of studies have been conducted leading to a meta-analysis of 107 studies on the effectiveness of behavioral modeling training (Taylor, Russ-Eft, & Chan, 2005). The evidence from these studies with manager and peer ratings of performance supports the effectiveness of the training for enhancing interpersonal skills. Subordinate ratings of performance change show smaller levels of improvement. Results for transfer are positive regardless of the study design (studies with or without a control group or with or without random assignment). The impact of behavioral modeling is stronger when the practice sessions are spaced out over time (remember the learning principles from Chapter 5!). Clearly, behavioral modeling with role-playing can be a reasonable approach for leaders to gain the "softer" skills relevant to working with and dealing effectively with others.

Business Simulations and Gamification

Business simulations and gamification allow leaders to become immersed in an experiential learning experience with events from authentic situations. The learning by doing approach allows leaders to experience the complexity of issues and choices embedded in the simulation. From these immersive experiences, learners gain knowledge and skills in linking one's understanding of contexts, situations, and possible strategies and responses by seeing the consequences of decisions make in the simulation (from self and from others) and from feedback provided by experts (Lopes et al., 2013).

Business simulations are a direct outgrowth of the long history behind war games used to train officers in combat techniques. One military war game developed in 1798 used a map with 3,600 squares, each representing a distinctive topographical feature, on which pieces representing troops and cavalry were moved (Raser, 1969). After visiting the Naval War College in 1956, members of the American Management Association developed the first application of war games to business situations for leaders. It is estimated that over 30,000 executives participated in the large number of simulations that were developed in the following five years (Stewart, 1962). The early business games were nearly all designed to teach basic business skills such as how to allocate resources to tasks, how to keep manufacturing costs low, and how to market products.

Since then, leadership simulations have become extremely diverse in terms of the complexity of the issues addressed, the number of participants engaged in the simulation, the types of tasks performed, and the number of organizational levels involved. The simulations help build specific leadership skills such as situational awareness, coordination skills, communication and interpersonal skills, problem-solving, and decision-making. Another main difference today is the immersive nature of incorporating more realism, complexity, and dynamism into the simulations and serious games. Business simulations include financial, political, military, marketing, sustainable development, production, strategic planning, and health-related games. As one example, the consulting firm Booz Allen Hamilton has created a one-day business simulation (within a four-day residential program) where new leaders practice addressing a client opportunity. They also have created a leadership board game to provide new leaders with the opportunity to engage as a team in making decisions such as planning for events and winning procurements. The game allows participants to try out different strategies so as to learn from the outcomes from these experiences (Backus et al., 2010).

A longstanding and carefully developed and implemented leadership development simulation for mid- and upper-level functional managers is Looking Glass, Inc. which has been modified over time since its inception (McCall & Lombardo, 1982). Looking Glass, Inc. is a hypothetical medium-sized glass-manufacturing corporation. Information for participants includes an annual report, plausible financial data, and a variety of glass products with a variety of positions across levels and functions. Together with background information common to all participants, the information provided differs somewhat from division to division, level to level, and position to position. Participants spend the simulation responding to these interlocking sets of communications acting and interacting as they choose. The number of problems exceeds the time available to deal with them. The purpose of this redesigned simulation today is to present participants with situations requiring decisions to be made within a global context. In terms of leader competencies, the simulation captures communication, team dynamics, and problem identification and solving with feedback and coaching provided at the end of the exercise.

Simulations like Looking Glass offer a number of potential advantages including a risk-free experience across a variety of situations. In addition, simulations are dynamic as decisions made by participants have consequences.

This allows participants to see more clearly the linkage between actions and the effects of those actions on others. These characteristics can have a powerful impact on learning.

The military has moved forward with scenario-based training to facilitate leader development of adaptive thinking skills. The training is designed to activate the deliberate practice of thinking skills to enhance problem identification, analysis, and problem-solving so that the learner comes closer to the mental models of (and the methods employed by) experts. Participants respond to complex tasks under changing conditions with ambiguous or missing information. The important elements of adaptive thinking are seeing the big picture, using all assets available, visualizing the battlefield, and considering timing when making decisions (Shadrick, Lussier, & Fultz, 2007). Table 10.4 presents eight behavioral elements that are the focus for building adaptive thinking. Participants are presented with a variety of scenarios or vignettes and are encouraged to incorporate thinking elements into their understanding of the issues and developing possible solutions. Learners discuss and defend

TABLE 10.4   Adaptive Thinking Behaviors
Focus on the Mission and Higher Intent – Commanders must never lose sight of the purpose and results they are directed to achieve – even when unusual and critical events may draw them in a different direction.
Model a Thinking Enemy – Commanders must not forget that the adversaries are reasoning human beings intent on defeating them. It's tempting to simplify the battlefield by treating the enemy as static or simply reactive.
Consider Effects of Terrain – Commanders must not lose sight of the operational effects of the terrain on which they must fight. Every combination of terrain and weather has a significant effect on what can and should be done to accomplish the mission.
Use All Assets Available – Commanders must not lose sight of the synergistic effects of fighting their command as a combined arms team. They consider not only assets under their command, but also those which higher headquarters might bring to bear to assist them.
Consider Timing – Commanders must not lose sight of the time they have available to get things done. Experts have a good sense of how much time it takes to accomplish various battlefield tasks. The proper use of that sense is a vital combat multiplier.
See the Big Picture – Commanders must remain aware of what is happening around them, how it might affect their operations, and how they can affect others' operations. A narrow focus on your own fight can get you or your higher headquarters blind-sided.
Visualize the Battlefield – Commanders must be able to visualize a fluid and dynamic battlefield with some accuracy and use the visualization to their advantage. A commander who develops this difficult skill can reason proactively like no other. "Seeing the battlefield" allows the commander to anticipate and adapt quickly to changing situations.
Consider Contingencies and Remain Flexible – Commanders must never lose sight of the old maxim that "no plan survives the first shot." Flexible plans and well thought out contingencies result in rapid, effective responses under fire.
Source: Shadrick, S. B., Lussier, J. W., & Fultz, C. (2007). *Accelerating the development of adaptive performance: Validating the think like a commander training* (No. ARI-RR-1868). Alexandria, VA: Army Research Institute for the Behavioral and Social Sciences.

what considerations they had for each scenario, are presented with the expert model, and are given individualized feedback. The feedback leads to a discussion about why certain elements were considered and incorporated into the expert model. The time available to make decisions for a vignette is decreased over time to add in time pressure.

Evaluation of the adaptive thinking training has been positive showing increases in the percentage of critical information identified by learners as relevant to the scenario and more rapid analysis of the situations so that performance continued to increase even as the amount of time allowed to respond to the scenario decreased. As can be seen in Figure 10.1, the mean percentage of critical information identified continued to increase over the course of seven vignettes even with a decrease in time to make a decision going from 15 minutes down to 3 minutes by the seventh vignette. Importantly, from a transfer perspective, there is also evidence of higher quality operational orders in the field after participation in the adaptive thinking simulation (Shadrick & Lussier, 2009).

The content validity of many simulations and scenario-based training programs are typically high as the focus of design is to practice leader behavior within realistic situations. Participants typically react quite favorably to how realistic the simulation situations are, how involved they feel in the game, and how well they enjoy the simulation. Participants also note how much they feel they learn and intend to apply the learning to the job. These self-reports, while encouraging, are inadequate to evaluate the effectiveness of the simulations. Unfortunately, there are few high-quality studies that gather more objective measures of improved skills and behaviors as a function of participating in a business stimulation (Anderson & Lawton, 2009). Given the plethora of

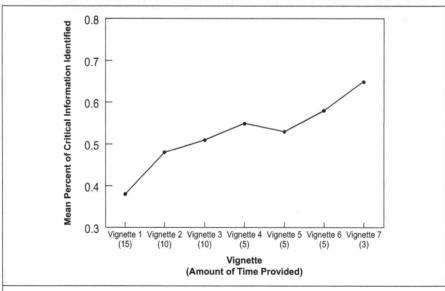

FIGURE 10.1 Assessment of Adaptive Thinking in Terms of Accessing Critical Information.

Source: Shadrick, S. B., Lussier, J. W., & Fultz, C. (2007). *Accelerating the development of adaptive performance: Validating the think like a commander training* (No. ARI-RR-1868). Alexandria, VA: Army Research Institute for the Behavioral and Social Sciences.

leadership competencies that have been identified, evaluation studies are clearly needed that study changes in specific behavioral competencies that are emphasized in the simulation. While clearly promising and engaging, it is difficult to know how to enhance the effectiveness of business simulations without more data on learning and transfer outcomes.

Possible inhibitors to learning and transfer with business simulations have also been identified. First, in some simulated games, participants may become so involved in the excitement and at times competitive aspects of the game that they lose sight of the principles to be learned. Second, business simulations can lead participants to learn solutions to particular problems rather than learning more generalizable underlying principles and concepts. Leaders may then see a similar problem in the workplace and apply the solution implemented in the business game only to find out that the solution has been inappropriately applied. Third, most games are designed to achieve learning related to problem-solving and interpersonal skills, yet the feedback may not provide the level of specificity needed to change behavior. Best practices with business simulations and game design are tied to providing adequate practice, time for self-reflection, feedback from others, individualized coaching, and additional spaced practice in the simulation with different contexts and interaction patterns to reinforce the learning expected.

Assessment Centers and Feedback Intensive Programs

Efforts at leader development have targeted providing leaders with specific and detailed feedback on their behaviors to facilitate self-development. The intensive feedback can come from attending a formal assessment center for leader development purposes. More recent initiatives have combined multi-rater (360°) feedback approaches with other developmental strategies to aid in self-development.

DEVELOPMENTAL ASSESSMENT CENTERS The assessment center is a structured off-the-job approach to measuring the knowledge, skills, and behaviors found to be relevant for leadership effectiveness. The term assessment center refers to a set of simulated activities and testing components that learners are asked to complete under standardized conditions. The assessments can include personality and ability tests, work task simulations such as an in-basket exercise (where learners must deal with a number of work situations), individual interviews, and situational exercises. These situational exercises are usually leaderless group discussions in which learners are asked to work on an issue or problem with other learners without any group structure. From this unstructured setting, one can observe the leadership and organizational skills of the participants as they emerge during the exercise. Trained observers rate the participants on a variety of leadership behaviors that differ depending on the type of exercise completed. Developmental assessment programs often have learners complete a formal presentation, address a real-life problem, and complete case studies than what is required for centers that focus on selecting participations for leadership roles (Thornton & Krause, 2009).

Typically, learners are assessed in groups of six or seven by a highly trained group of assessors. For developmental centers, feedback is typically delivered face-to-face with the learner to review the participant's actions during the exercises and identify behavioral strengths and areas in need of improvement. Action plans on how to improve behaviors on the job are completed by participants after the feedback session. In addition, a formal feedback report might be generated summarizing strengths and areas for improvement across participants as this learning needs assessment can provide valuable insights to drive future leadership interventions to improve leadership skills (Kleinmann & Ingold, 2019).

Table 10.5 presents seven dimensions and their definitions that are often used to evaluate assessment center participants. Participants can be rated on

TABLE 10.5	Assessment Center Dimensions and Definitions	
Dimension	**Definition**	**Examples**
Organizing and planning	Extent to which individual systematically arranges own work and resources for efficient task accomplishment. Anticipates and plans for the future	Administrative ability Recognizing priorities Strategic focus Thoroughness
Problem-solving	Extent to which an individual gathers relevant information, effectively analyzes data and information, generates viable options and selects supportable courses of action. Generates and recognizes creative solutions	Analytical ability Problem detection Judgment and decision making Innovative thinking
Communication	Extent to which an individual conveys information in an effective way. Responds appropriately to questions and challenges	Presentation skills Written communication Oral defense
Consideration/ awareness of others	Extent to which an individual's actions reflect a consideration for the feelings and needs of others. Awareness of the impact of decisions on others	Interpersonal skills Sensitivity Understanding people Building relationships
Drive	Extent to which an individual originates and maintains a high activity level. Sets high performance standards and persists in their achievement	Career orientation Continuous improvement focus Energy level Perseverance
Influencing others	Extent to which an individual persuades others to do something or adopt a point of view to produce desired results. Takes action consistent with one's own convictions	Negotiation and persuasion skills Inspiring trust Self-confidence Results oriented
Tolerance for stress/ambiguity	Extent to which an individual maintains effectiveness in diverse situations under varying degrees of pressure. Handles disappointments and opposition	Adaptability and flexibility Resilience Tolerance for uncertainty Coping skills

Source: Adapted from Arthur Jr, W., Day, E. A., McNelly, T. L., & Edens, P. S. (2003). A meta-analysis of the criterion-related validity of assessment center dimensions. *Personnel Psychology*, 56(1), 125–153. Copyright 2003 by John Wiley & Sons. Reprinted by permission.

a scale such as this dimension is a clear strength to this dimension is clearly a development need. A meta-analytic study finds that ratings of the participants on these seven dimensions during the assessment center are predictive of later job performance indicators, promotions, and salary level (Arthur et al., 2003). In particular, the four dimensions of organizing and planning, problem solving, influencing others, and communication account for the largest improvement in the performance outcomes.

There are some studies that have examined the developmental impact of assessment centers. Jones and Whitmore (1995) examined the extent to which feedback from an assessment center in a large insurance company led managers to take action to develop the knowledge, skills, and abilities identified for managerial success. Results indicated that participants who scored best in the center were more likely to accept the feedback from the center as accurate. Center ratings, though, were found to be unrelated to developmental activity. Nevertheless, the percentage of developmental activities followed by participants were found to be related to subsequent promotions. This result poses a critical challenge in the use of assessment centers for development because poorer performers are the ones for whom following developmental suggestions could lead to the greatest gains in performance. There is evidence that participant self-assessment ratings made before an assessment center become more consistent with the assessor ratings post participation showing enhancement of self-awareness (Halman & Fletcher, 2000).

From a best practice perspective, developmental assessment centers that are followed by an emphasis on more skill training, special assignments, and additional coaching are most effective for improved performance on the job (Thornton & Rupp, 2006). This highlights once again that in order for transfer to occur, organizational support mechanisms must be in place to develop skills identified in the assessment center process as needing improvement.

MULTI-RATER FEEDBACK Many developmental approaches for self-development include feedback-intensive programs such as 360° or multi-rater feedback. Multi-rater feedback interventions have been reported to be used by over 33% of organizations in U.S. and Canada with increasing use in countries such as Argentina, Australia, Slovakia, China, Spain, and the United Kingdom (Brutus et al., 2006). With multi-rater feedback, ratings on core competencies (many of the same dimensions that are evaluated in the assessment center) are gathered from supervisors, peers, and subordinates. Self-ratings and customer ratings also are often obtained.

In one large automobile supplier company, raters provided evaluations of the effectiveness of the leader on specific items relevant to the core dimensions of vision and strategy maker, motivator, change manager, performance manager, coach and guide, communicator, team builder, and relational partner. Each dimension had four to five specific behavioral items to be rated. Feedback reports compared results at the item and core dimension level across rater groups. Perhaps a leader is consistently rated as low on the motivator competency and especially in the item level areas of "celebrating small gains" and "provides me with the freedom to accomplish a project." By being confronted with this reality, the leader may see the need to set in motion developmental efforts in those areas. Rather than being solely a self-directed effort, facilitators are used to help the leader interpret the data from the various rater groups and to aid in the translation of the new insights gained to actionable steps the leader can take to improve behaviors on the job.

There is a reasonable amount of research evidence on the effectiveness of multi-rater feedback for enhancing leader development. An initial study examined subordinate ratings collected for over 200 managers at two points in time six months apart. After the first rating period, the managers received an extensive feedback report including the data and guidelines for interpreting the results of the upward feedback process. Results indicated that managerial behavior improved from the first to the second rating period (Smither et al., 1995). A five-year study of upward feedback with 252 managers found that there were significant improvements in leader behavior ratings. A more detailed analysis discovered that those managers who met with their subordinates to discuss their feedback report were more likely to improve their behaviors than those who did not meet with their subordinates (Walker & Smither, 1999). Bailey and Fletcher (2002) studied the impact of 360° feedback on competency ratings of managers in the United Kingdom. They found improvements in managerial behaviors as rated by self-assessments and from subordinate ratings over one year from the initial assessment.

A meta-analysis of 24 studies finds positive improvements in ratings by all groups but the improvement is small and the effects are smaller when looking beyond 12 months since the initial assessment (Smither, London, & Reilly, 2005). Leader reactions to feedback is a critical factor in improvement attempts. Those leaders who express positive reactions to the process are more likely to improve behavior than those who have a negative emotional reaction to the feedback. Some leader behaviors are more difficult to change than others. Evidence shows that managerial improvement is lower for those leader behaviors that are more difficult to develop than those that are easier to develop pointing to the challenges of leader development (Dai, De Meuse, & Peterson, 2010).

The results suggest that the 360° assessments are more effective when there are coaches to help the individual reflect on the assessment information. The Center for Creative Leadership includes assessments by fellow participants based on the exercises they have worked on together along with the multi-rater assessments the participants brought to the workshop. Classroom instruction around topical leadership issues and the factors impacting leadership effectiveness is often provided for context. Coaches help the individual leader to integrate the feedback from the various sources to set developmental goals and action plans for improvement (King & Santana, 2010). It is logical to surmise that consistent information about areas for improvement across a variety of methods and sources as well as having coaching support has a more powerful effect on leader development. Research evidence is needed, though, on behavioral changes as a function of these more comprehensive approaches.

Experience-Centered Learning

Experience-centered learning is based on the assumption that challenges in the job itself can stimulate learning and development of leadership skills and behaviors. As noted in Chapter 1, leaders who have been questioned as to what factors had their greatest impact on developing their managerial competencies often pointed to direct work experience followed by coaching and mentoring by more senior leaders. This section examines the research on job challenge followed by a discussion of coaching and mentoring.

There are two types of learning situations from job experiences: incremental and frame breaking. Incremental learning situations are those that provide opportunities to address more routine task-oriented leadership roles of clarifying, planning, and monitoring. Frame-breaking learning experiences place individuals in more difficult and less routine positions. Such situations require the acquisition of a large number of new skills such as adaptability in order to be successful. Frame-breaking experiences require individual investment with high potential for learning, but also high risk for failure (Sessa & London, 2015). Frame-breaking experiences provide the opportunity for a leader to break free of inappropriate assumptions, and increase problem-solving skills. Intentionally placing individuals into situations that require the leader to change their preferred approach or strategy can lead to a new insights and skills about how to lead (Nelson, Zaccaro, & Herman, 2010). Frame-breaking situations that have been found to accelerate learning include features such as having to handle responsibilities that are much broader than previous ones, fixing problems created by others, developing new directions for a workgroup, and handling pressures from external stakeholder groups. Table 10.6 presents examples of these types of job challenges.

Tools to help leaders get the most out of their job experiences focus on how leaders can (1) take advantage of the learning opportunities in their current job; and (2) make job assignments part of a development planning process. The Center for Creative Leadership has created the Developmental Challenge Profile questionnaire that asks leaders to report the extent to which their current job provides challenges in areas presented in Table 10.6. Leaders can compare their learning challenges to a normative database of leaders who have approached similar challenges to investigate how to enhance learning opportunities while on challenging job assignments. The leader and facilitator can examine areas of low challenge in their current job and create a developmental plan to increase job challenges. For example, if the developmental focus is on starting something new or making strategic changes, the action plan can include reshaping the job by taking on a new project, building a five-year business scenario for one's unit or taking on a temporary assignment such as joining a project team that is moving the organization in a new direction such as opening a new market. In addition to individual development, the data can be examined across leaders in an organization to more systematically evaluate what types of challenges leaders are or are not obtaining. The research challenge is the need to investigate the extent to which these developmental tools change what developmental job assignments are sought and whether there is an increase in on-the-job learning that leads to improved leadership effectiveness (McCauley, 2006).

Evidence supports the effectiveness of challenging job assignments especially for relatively new leaders. For early career managers, the quality of managerial assignments and the learning orientation of the manager (mastery focused versus performance focused) results in a higher level of development of leadership skill that cannot be explained simply by the

TABLE 10.6 Components of a Developmental Experience	
Experiencing a Job Transition	
Unfamiliar responsibilities	Handle responsibilities that are new or very different from previous ones
Creating Change	
New directions	Responsible for starting something new in the organization or making strategic changes in the business
Inherited problems	Fix problems created by a predecessor or exiting when you took the job
Employee problems	Employees lack adequate experience, are incompetent, or are resistant to change
Managing at High Levels of Responsibility	
High stakes	Clear deadlines, pressure from senior managers, high visibility and responsibility for key decisions make success or failure clearly evident
Scope and scale	Sheer size of job tasks are large and responsible for multiple functions, teams, products and/or services
Managing Boundaries	
External pressure	Manage the interface with important teams outside the organization such as customers, unions, or governmental agencies
Influence without authority	Doing the job requires influencing peers, higher management, or other key people over whom you have no direct authority
Addressing Diversity	
Working across cultures	Work with people from different cultures or with institutions in other countries
Workgroup diversity	Responsible for the work of a diverse group of people

Source: Adapted from McCauley, C. D., Ruderman, M. N., Ohlott, P. J., & Morrow, J. E. (1994). Assessing the developmental components of managerial jobs. *Journal of Applied Psychology*, 79(4), 544. Copyright 1994 by the American Psychological Association. Reprinted by permission.

number of years in the organization (Dragoni et al., 2009). On the other hand, when leaders feel over challenged, the acquisition of leadership skills shows diminishing returns unless there is systematic and helpful feedback from others available to aid work on the challenging assignment (DeRue & Wellman, 2009). Interestingly, a study of managers in an international furniture retailer found that for mid-career managers high levels of job challenge had diminishing returns for job performance while for early career managers the inverse was found – higher job challenge led to higher levels of job performance (Carette, Anseel, & Lievens, 2013). More generally, the extent to which individuals successfully complete challenging job assignments is related to supervisory evaluations of their promotability over and above current job performance ratings (De Pater et al., 2009). Self-efficacy mediates the relationship between developmental challenging assignments and ratings of promotability – supporting the notion that the job assignments must lead to the individual believing they had developed the capabilities to succeed as a leader (Seibert et al., 2017).

Executive Coaching and Leader Mentoring

Individuals can gain leadership skills and improve leader behaviors from experiences with learning partners. These coaches and mentors are often at an organizational level above the focal leader but are not their direct supervisor. The goal of the coaching and mentoring process is to enhance leader self-awareness and to build skills in a targeted manner so as to shorten the time it takes to become proficient while avoiding costly trial and error approaches to learning. Zenger and Stinnett (2006) note that 70% of organizations with formal leadership programs also use coaching as a component in the development of leaders. Organizations use coaching for a variety of purposes including the socialization of new managers, preparation of leaders identified as high potential as well as the development of underrepresented groups in management. While coaching clearly can occur for individuals at any level of management, much recent attention has examined executive level coaching.

Coaches typically fill three roles. One role is to create a supportive social and emotional environment where the protégé feels comfortable talking about work related issues or problems. The coach can help the learner to not become discouraged when dealing with difficult situations. Coaches can also provide insights, encouragement, and recognition for successes in order to build the learner's sense of competence. A second role is one of being improvement oriented. By providing feedback, the coach helps the learner target efforts in areas like collaborating, goal setting, and problem-solving to improve job performance. A third role is around career progression including giving advice as well as increasing the protégé's exposure and visibility to top management. In this way, the coach helps the protégé to be better prepared to handle future promotions and assignments (D'Abate, Eddy, & Tannenbaum, 2003).

Some coaches are more effective than others. A qualitative study from interview data of best practices of coaches in Asia and Europe found a reasonable amount of agreement that effective coaches: (1) create strong relationships with the focal leader by building rapport and a feeling of psychological safety, (2) use a structured approach through setting a schedule, agenda, and plan for development that includes objectives and indicators of success, (3) provide direct support through advice giving and emotional support, (4) challenge protégés to go beyond what they are comfortable talking about and implementing, (5) gather systematic data though assessments, observations, discussions with stakeholders so as to give data-driven constructive feedback, and (6) are willing to continually develop or improve their own coaching skills through feedback from the learner, other coaches, and through self-reflection (Gentry et al., 2013).

As with most studies about learning and developmental efforts, participants generally report that they enjoy having a coach and find the experience useful. There are now a number of meta-analytic studies with the conclusion being that coaching is effective for developmental outcomes such as skill improvement, wellbeing, and successful completion of goal-directed activities (Theeboom, Beersma, & Van Vianen, 2014). As one caveat, many of the studies in the meta-analyses use self-reports of the outcomes from coaching so one must be cautious in interpreting those results. De Meuse, Dai, and Lee (2009) evaluated the effectiveness of executive coaching studies that included pre and post coaching data. This meta-analytic study found that the size of the improvement gain was much higher when using self-reports than when examining improvement ratings gathered from others (e.g., peers). In addition, meta-analytic studies have noted stronger improvements for affective and relationship type outcomes like working together more effectively than goal-directed outcomes around task performance (Sonesh et al., 2015).

The bottom line is that coaching can be an effective method for enhancing learning and performance on the job. Research supports the conventional wisdom of linking individuals with coaches who are interested in developing others and have the coaching skills needed to facilitate the development of others. Quality mentoring relations facilitate career advancement and job satisfaction of protégés. This relationship can also have a positive impact on the coaches who learn new skills or competencies from the experience about helping others.

GLOBAL LEADERSHIP

As noted in Chapter 1, the workforce is becoming more diverse and international competition is becoming increasingly intense. More organizations are crossing international lines. Enhanced technologies allow virtual, international teams to be formed to deal with global organizational issues such as how to standardize work processes across multiple organizational units within the same multinational firm. The teams may be made up of employees located anywhere in the world. Given these realities, it is not surprising that a survey of over 1,400 organizations found that 48% of the companies see developing global leadership capabilities as a high or a very high priority. In addition, few organizations report having a selection process in place to fill future global assignments and many organizations do not have a dedicated or distinct global leadership development strategy (Davis, 2015). Other survey reports indicate that there is a gap between the need for effective global leadership and the reality of today. In one report, executives note that a major concern is that their leaders do not have an adequate global perspective and that this limits the extent to which the organization can meet its future strategic goals (Deloitte Consulting, 2013).

This section of the chapter is divided into three parts. First, the reality of global roles and responsibilities of leadership are described. Second, the types of leader development strategies to meet learning needs relevant to those roles and responsibilities are discussed. Finally, the specific topic of developing leaders selected for international assignments through service learning projects is described.

Roles and Responsibilities

The world is becoming a smaller place as the marketplace becomes increasing global in scope. A global organization is defined as one where the elements of production are dispersed across many nations. Effective global management is a key competitive advantage for firms as they enter the international markets.

The characteristics of effective global leaders include the same behavioral competencies that one would look for from any effective leader. These competencies include great communication and relationship skills along with a high level of business knowledge, high ability levels for cognitive complexity, and high levels of emotional energy and drive. In addition, the role demands for leaders in a global organization are multifaceted. These roles include motivating multicultural teams, managing information across multiple time zones, maintaining a variety of relationships (alliances, joint ventures, and licensing arrangements) across countries that have different laws and standards, finding ways to customize products to meet the needs of a variety of markets and customers, and negotiating in different business environments and cultures. This has led organizations to develop a separate competency framework around talent management for those going to or currently in global leadership positions. The global leadership competency frameworks are based on job analysis information, the key skills needed, the cultural and contextual factors underlying global leadership positions, and the identification of critical incidents separating effective from less effective global leader behaviors.

One study identified 160 global leadership competency terms found in the research literature and categorized the competencies into three main groupings presented in Table 10.7. The three areas are business and organizational acumen, managing people and relationships, and managing oneself. Business acumen includes understanding the practical realities of how to get work done efficiently and effectively within multicultural teams or in leading global initiatives. Relationship-oriented skills focus on the ability to contextualize one's communication and interpersonal relationships in culturally appropriate ways. Managing oneself involves issues such as the ability to cope with the additional stresses of global leadership roles and responsibilities such as multiple time zones, large distance, a variety of cultural norms, and differing rules, regulations, and political realities across the globe (Bird, 2013).

TABLE 10.7 Framework of Global Leadership Competencies

Business and Organizational Acumen	Managing People and Relationships	Managing Self
Vision and strategic thinking Leading change Business savvy Organizational savvy Managing communities	Valuing people Cross-cultural communication Interpersonal skills Teaming skills Empowering others	Inquisitiveness Global mindset Flexibility Integrity and maturity Conscientiousness Resilience

Source: Bird, A. (2013). Mapping the content of global leadership competencies. In M. Mendenhall & Associates (Eds.), *Global leadership: Research, practice, and development* (2nd ed., pp. 80–96). New York: Routledge. Copyright 2013 by Routledge. Reprinted by permission.

While expanding skill sets are important, there is also the challenging task of shifting mindsets by stretching one's mental map of the world:

> *A domestic leader need only put his/her mind around one country, limited cultural paradigms, one political system and one set of labor laws. A global leader must stretch his/her mind to encompass the entire worlds with hundreds of countries, cultures, and business contexts (Black & Gregersen, 2000; p. 174).*

The authors highlight the need for global leader development approaches that help the leader redraw their mental map. They contend that a first step is to direct attention and awareness by challenging the way one has learned how to lead others. Given this awareness, the second step is for the leader to confront the contrasts that have been identified through this challenge. As a third step, leaders need help and guidance developing a revised mental model of what it means to be an effective leader in a global leadership position.

A case analysis of this process of self-awareness, contrast, and replacement is described by Oddou and Mendenhall (2013). The case describes a purchasing agent from Germany who is doing business in Malaysia. The agent has to deal with the inconsistencies in communication with the Malaysian supplier, which is in sharp contrast to the efficiency focus and expectation of the purchasing agent. One expectation is that people respond quickly to emails and to other forms of communication. The agent is challenged to confront this mindset. Out of this confrontation process, the agent begins to question why the agent expects the suppler to work in the same way. Now the agent is freed up to think about and come to a greater understanding of Malaysian culture. A key value in the culture is an emphasis on high personal contact in order to form strong interpersonal relationships as the first step to working together effectively. This realization leads to a mindset change about what work effectiveness means. This perspective of change highlights the need to be systematic and intentional in developing global leadership skills and capabilities. These efforts have to be at depth so that the developmental programs, activities, and support have lasting impact on enhancing global leader effectiveness.

An understanding of the important role of context in the development of effective global leaders has been demonstrated from a more than 20-year study of cultural differences across countries. The implications of those differences for effective leadership is called appropriately enough Global Leadership and Organizational Behavior Effectiveness or GLOBE (Dorfman et al., 2012). Over 200 researchers across the world have helped out during this project and 62 cultures from 59 nations have been investigated and ranked on eight cultural dimensions. The project has identified 6 leadership dimensions (and 21 underlying leadership behaviors). These leadership dimensions include: (1) charismatic and value based; (2) team oriented, (3) self-protective (i.e., status conscious); (4) participative; (5) humane oriented; and (6) autonomous.

There are a number of important findings from this massive research effort. First, some leadership behaviors are universally seen as either effective or ineffective. For example, being trustworthy, having foresight, being positive, dynamic and encouraging, and being communicative are universal behaviors of leadership effectiveness. Being a loner, being non-cooperative, and being dictatorial is universally seen as an impediment to leader effectiveness.

Second, there are culturally contingent leader attributes such as being individualistic or autonomous, being status conscious, and being a risk taker. For example, Brazilian managers dislike leaders who are individualistic, autonomous, and independent (Javidan et al., 2006). This means that a leader from a different cultural context who is working with or is assigned to work in Brazil should be concerned that actions and decisions are not seen as or interpreted as being individualistic. Third, when leader behaviors are congruent with cultural expectations, the leader is perceived to be more effective. Results show that participative leadership is expected in countries such as Brazil, the United States, and Germany and is linked to perceptions of effectiveness. A participative leadership style is not seen as a fit for countries such as Egypt and Russia. The findings from GLOBE certainly have relevance to addressing the issue of mindset shifts (Table 10.1) so as to facilitate the redrawing of mental models during leader development activities that are based on these cultural contingent characteristics.

In addition to the cultural contextualization of leadership effectiveness, a typology that identifies types of global leadership roles has been developed (Reiche et al., 2017). The typology of the four different roles is based on whether the situation facing the global leader is one with low or high levels of relationship complexity paired with low or high levels of task complexity (see Figure 10.2). These four types of global leadership roles have implications for the specific knowledge and skills to develop to be consistent with the global leadership role. For the incremental global leadership role, there are low levels of variety and flux in the tasks for this job (low task complexity) and few types of boundaries to negotiate in terms of the number and types of relationships with low levels of interdependence (low relationship). The major role for this type of global leader is primarily based on a high degree of technical specialization with limited type and scope of interactions with global partners. These

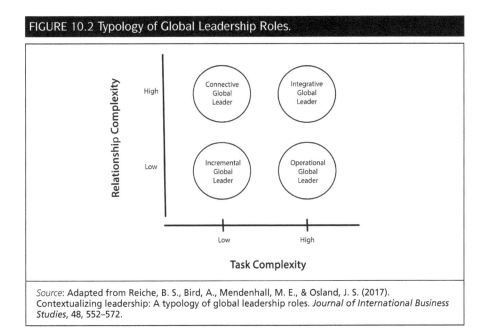

FIGURE 10.2 Typology of Global Leadership Roles.

Source: Adapted from Reiche, B. S., Bird, A., Mendenhall, M. E., & Osland, J. S. (2017). Contextualizing leadership: A typology of global leadership roles. *Journal of International Business Studies*, 48, 552–572.

types of leaders may need a developmental focus on gaining specific types of business acumen to help continuously improve the organization through technical innovation. In contrast, the integrative global leadership role (high task complexity and high relationship complexity) involves many different types of cultural boundaries with a high need for interdependence across those boundaries. These leaders are faced with variable and often rapidly changing conditions (at least at some locations) that require the leaders to adapt and make adjustments as well as being flexible given the collaborative needs across varied members of the multinational teams. This leader role requires a much more extensive effort on building skills of collaboration and developing synergistic solutions to complex problems. This typology, therefore, provides much needed nuance to the generic calls for enhancing the development of global leadership within organizations.

Developing Global Leaders

More leaders are being asked to complete assignments in other countries to become internationally centered rather than targeting parochial interests. The traditional approach is for a leader to go to another country for a long period of time such as from one to five years. Unfortunately, failure rates of leaders coming back earlier than expected are estimated to be fairly high with each failure costing upwards to $500,000 per executive (Doherty & Dickmann, 2012). Part of this failure rate has been attributed to the minimal amount of training and preparation given to leaders and families prior to departing to the host country. In addition, there is evidence that the level of support for a returning international assignees is often limited making the transition back to the host country and home office more challenging and frustrating for the returnees especially if they stay for a long period of time (Bailey & Dragoni, 2013).

Given changes in communication technology and ease of travel, organizations are employing alternative forms of international assignments. These alternatives include shorter-term assignments of less than one year. Other options include international business travel ("experience assignments") that involve short but frequent trips to meet the evolving needs of project team members in other countries. Or, one can be given "commuter assignments," which means frequent travel from home to foreign location with work responsibilities in both countries (Collings & Isichei, 2018).

Strategies and interventions to develop global leadership capabilities can certainly be based on the developmental interventions that have already been discussed above. Leaders can learn how to provide performance feedback to individuals from different cultural contexts through behavioral modeling programs. Individuals already in a global leadership position can be assessed though a feedback intensive program with an emphasis on global leadership dimensions leading to an action plan for improvement. Assessment centers can assess skill levels and provide developmental feedback around global leadership competencies such as adaptability, cross-cultural sensitivity, and cross-cultural team influence through role-plays, situational interviews, leaderless group discussions and case study analysis (Herd, Alagaraja, & Cumberland, 2016). Newly selected global leaders can be assigned to a coach who has extensive international experience. A leader in a multinational firm could be given a challenging job assignment such as leading an internationally diverse project team and developing a long-term approach for taking a new product throughout the business cycle from design to production to marketing. This section examines three strategies for the development of global leaders that are targeted specifically on building global leadership capabilities.

HIGH CONTACT LEARNING EXPERIENCES One argument is that the highest level of learning comes from intensive cross-cultural interactions. Figure 10.3 presents a framework consistent with this idea showing developmental strategies along a continuum from low to high on cultural contact experiences. This schematic contends that high contact experiences linked with numerous feedback opportunities (including self-feedback) have the best potential to not only build skills but also lead to the mental model remapping discussed above that is needed to enhance global leadership effectiveness.

A study of over 300 leaders in a large United Kingdom-based diversified firm finds that high contact experiences (as well as high levels of extroversion) are related to leader effectiveness in global leadership positions (Caligiuri & Tarique, 2009). Consistent with high contact experiences, the accumulation of work experiences by leaders in terms of varying roles and responsibilities predict higher levels of strategic thinking in U.S. executives (Dragoni et al., 2011). Taking this notion to an international context, Dragoni et al. (2014) examined the effect of the accumulated global work experiences

FIGURE 10.3 Global Leadership Developmental Potential.

Source: Adapted from Oddou, G. R., & Mendenhall, M. E. (2013). Global leadership development. In M. E. Mendenhall & Associates (Eds.), *Global leadership: Research, practice, and development* (pp. 215–239). New York: Routledge. Copyright 2013 by Routledge. Reprinted by permission.

for 231 leaders on their level of strategic thinking. They measured strategic thinking skills through a systematic assessment center evaluation of the leaders. Trained assessors (who did not know where the leader had been place globally or for how long) rated each leader on innovative thinking, analytic business judgment, and the ability to think strategically from behavioral interview and four simulated business exercises. They found that leaders who had high contact experiences in cultures that were quite different from their own home cultural norms and expectations exhibited higher levels of strategic thinking.

To give some needed balance to this perspective, it has been posited that too much international experience may build skills and change mindsets but may also delay the career advancement of leaders to executive level positions. A study of 163 CEOs from firms headquartered in four European countries found support for a curvilinear relationship of a variety of high contact international experiences and time it took executives to reach the top of the organization. The bottom line is there are benefits with a moderate amount of international experience but some risks with a large amount of experience – at least in regards to promotions in the firm (Georgakakis, Dauth, & Ruigrok, 2016).

CROSS-CULTURAL TRAINING Only 40% of US firms report offering pre-departure cross-cultural training and the training is often of a short nature. This is in stark contrast to a much higher percentage for European and Japanese firms who have more intensive training experience (Black & Morrison, 2014). For firms that do embrace training as a strategy in preparing the international assignee, a variety of intercultural training interventions have been developed. The goals of these programs are to help participants reduce culture shock, establish good interpersonal relationships with others and to improve task effectiveness when working in other cultures.

Training content in these programs typically describe the stages of adjustment that one will go through as well as identify the challenges that will have to be faced overseas at each stage of adjustment. In addition, programs often discuss why people behave the way they do in another culture with the assumption that understanding the why will help with adjustment and integration. Participants are encouraged to suspend judgments early in an overseas job assignment so that additional information can be obtained about the people and situations so the leader can form a more nuanced understanding of the cultural norms. Training can also address the participants' cultural awareness with the trainer leading a discussion that challenges participants to question their own cultural assumptions. Programs sometimes have a more experiential component including demonstrations, role-plays, and feedback as well as completing simulation exercises.

One example of a long-standing training program is the use of a cultural assimilator (Triandis, 2006). The assimilator helps people learn to make attributions similar to those made by individuals in the host culture. Scenarios are created based on data from critical incidents gathered of effective and ineffective intercultural interactions. The incidents highlight cultural difference in the host culture from those of the leader's cultural context. Participants are asked to read each scenario, reflect on the source of misunderstanding, and choose the attribution from the various alternatives in that situation. The answers lead to a complete analysis of cultural differences and why particular behaviors are or are not appropriate in a given situation.

Initial evidence provided support that cross-cultural training interventions such as the cultural assimilator *can* be effective in affecting participant's perceptions of the host culture, impacting behavior in the host country, and reducing failure rates. Nevertheless, Bhawuk and Brislin (2000) critically note that there is a strong need to use more varied criteria beyond the often used self-report of participants (back to Chapter 6 and evaluation criteria!). Subsequent reviews have found mixed findings. For example, one study examined 28 evaluation studies that used some type of reasonably rigorous experimental design to study the effectiveness of cross cultural training program and found support that leader knowledge about the host culture – including differences with their own culture – was enhanced with training (Mendenhall et al., 2004). Yet, in terms of behaviors (e.g., problem-solving and ability to deal with cross-cultural misunderstandings), the majority of studies reported limited improvement. There is also mixed findings on the impact of the training on attitudes such as cultural interest, attitudes towards members of other cultures as well as a reduction in stereotyping of others. A study of 339 expatriates from 20 German multinational organizations found little impact of cross-cultural training on leader adjustment to the host country. Interestingly, they did find that the level of foreign language skills was related to perceptions of adjustment showing the importance of building hard skills such as language acquisition prior to going to the host country (Puck, Kittler, & Wright, 2008).

Positive results have been reported for interventions that build what has been termed cultural intelligence (CI) or the capacity to function effectively in an intercultural context (Raver & Van Dyne, 2017). CI is viewed as a malleable form of intelligence affected by high contact experiences with other cultures, travel, and cross-cultural training. A cultural intelligence scale has been developed to measure the extent to which leaders have gained CI from these types of cross-cultural experiences. The items include measures of changes in cognition (I know the cultural values and religious beliefs of other cultures), motivation (I am confident that I can socialize with locals in a culture that is unfamiliar to me), behavior (I change my verbal behaviors, e.g., accent, tone when a cross-cultural interaction requires it), and metacognition (I adjust my cultural knowledge as I interact with people form a culture that is unfamiliar to me) (Ang et al., 2007). Studies show that that intensive developmental experiences are related to positive changes in CI. CI is also related to more distal outcomes such as adjustment to cultural challenges (not necessarily adjustment to work) and to some extent performance dimensions such as communication effectiveness (Ott & Michailova, 2018). Nevertheless, it must be noted that a majority of studies on the impact of changes of CI on key outcomes have focused on college or graduate students so generalization of these studies to the complex roles and responsibilities around developing global leadership await more research.

International Service-Learning Projects

Many organizations are promoting the cause of corporate social responsibility (CRS). CSR is a label around being a good corporate citizen including supporting community efforts and an emphasis on sustainable development that can benefit a variety of external stakeholders. Examples of practices include reducing environmental impacts, participating in fair trade, integrating social concerns into business operations, and volunteering in the community. Perceived benefits of CRS include attracting and retaining top talent and enhancing relationships with communities affected by business activities or who can be helped by actions taken to address issues within a community (Dahlsrud, 2008).

The move to CSR highlights the perceived need to balance the traditional focus on economic and legal domains with the ethical (and philanthropic) domain (Schwartz & Carroll, 2003). Economic issues include maintaining profits and enhancing the shared value to stockholders while legal issues include compliance, avoidance of risk, and anticipating changes in law. These continue to be important areas of concern for leaders. A CRS approach emphasizes that a similar level of importance needs to be given to the ethical domain, which involves a consideration of one's duty or obligation to societal issues relevant to moral rights, fairness, and justice. Clearly there can be overlap among these three domains. For example, corporate giving to causes can be strategically focused to improve one's public image in order to help sustain profitability in the long run.

In terms of global leadership development, organizations have created personal growth opportunities to build leader competencies around diversity, self-management, and the CSR business model. In particular, some organizations have begun to incorporate international service learning assignments in their global leadership development portfolio to increase leader awareness of social, environmental, and fairness issues throughout the world. These high-intensity experiences, often in developing countries, are viewed as enhancing CI as well as building skills around teamwork and collaboration. There is also an orientation towards building an ethical mindset around socially responsible leadership that goes beyond the traditional leader concerns about economic and legal issues.

PriceWaterhouseCoopers has created an international service-learning approach called the Ulysses Program that sends teams of three or four leaders to countries to work in collaboration with nongovernmental organizations to address critical local issues. For this service learning program, there is a two-month preparation phase, a two-month field assignment phase and an eight-day debriefing phase. The overall stated goal is to develop responsible leaders who can assume senior global leadership roles. The multinational teams of leaders are sent to help with issues such as fighting poverty, reducing the spread of disease or improving access to clean water. Leaders are prepared for the experience ahead of time and learning events are built into the service-learning assignments. Assessments such as 360° feedback, coaching, and reflection exercise are used to help solidify learning by increasing self-awareness and self-management skills. Teambuilding exercises are used once the team is formed and before beginning the work assigned. Coaches help the team to develop team goals and a plan of action. After participation in the service learning project, there is a debriefing process in which team members reflect on key learnings that have occurred as a function of the experience. Participants are encouraged to share stories on the transforming nature of the experiences relevant to the assignment. This can also include one-on-one coaching debriefs where the emphasis is on how to take what has been learned back to the job and to help the leaders envision their organizational role into the future. Alumni gatherings are also held to support each other's continual global leadership development (Pless, Maak, & Stahl, 2011).

Empirical evidence of the effectiveness of international service learning assignments on global leadership behaviors is limited. One study conducted an extensive and systematic interview and survey approach for 70 participants from 23 teams to identify global responsible leadership behaviors that participants believe are enhanced by the experience as well as the learning mechanisms facilitating those improvements. The interview data was categorized into major themes around learning outcomes. The major themes identified included the development of a more responsible mindset on the role of organizations in society as well as enhanced moral literacy around issues of justice. Participants also noted more self-awareness around cultural issues such as norms and customs as well as the virtue of being more nonjudgmental. Tighter connections were reported about the need for a global mindset. Skill development areas listed as improved included engaging stakeholders and building relationships as well as improvements in communication and interpersonal skills. In terms of learning mechanisms, the responses were categorized into cognitive (activities that helped built intellectual awareness), affective (activities that enhanced emotional awareness), and behavioral (activities that built skills and changed one's approach to a situation). Survey responses show strong evidence that the service-learning experience is perceived to lead to positive changes in tolerance and open mindedness, sensitivity to local concerns, ethical and moral reflection, and self-awareness of own strengths and limitations relevant to socially responsible leadership (Pless, Maak, & Stahl, 2012).

An interesting comparative analysis of six international service learning programs (including companies like PriceWaterhouseCoopers, IBM, Intel, and Pifizer) in three industries of health, technology, and accounting that differed in their focus on individual leadership development, broader organizational development, or community development was recently completed (Pless & Borecká, 2014). This study shows that programs differed in terms of participants (senior executives, high potential leaders) placement length (from 2 to 24 weeks), the nature of the assignment (creating a framework for good governance, optimizing supply chains, and business functions), and the learning methods used (extensive coaching, training, 360° feedback, team building).

Given the relative newness of this approach to global leadership development and the relatively small number of leaders who participate each year, it is difficult to generate a list of best practices for the design and implementation of such programs. Clearly, the programs based on learning processes already discussed in this book such as feedback intensive activities and the use of debriefing sessions would likely have similar levels of success. Nevertheless, research evidence is sorely needed on the transfer issue relevant to these programs. To what extent does this experience translate into new leadership behaviors and approaches that are more effective than those exhibited prior to this developmental experience? Pre-post experimental designs with transfer outcomes beyond self-report are needed.

CONCLUSIONS

This chapter has highlighted the leadership knowledge, skills, behaviors, and competencies that could be part of a developmental experience. It has also touched upon the tremendous variety of learning activities that are available to impart those knowledge, skills, and attitudes to learners. The methods range from formally structured training opportunities, developmental job assignment experiences and more informal, less structured learning experiences. The methods described also show the blurring of the distinction of what is considered "training" as opposed to "performance" enhancement.

The review of the evidence shows the exciting opportunities available to those interested in leadership development in work organizations. Organizations are taking leadership development more seriously as a key to competitive advantage. There is some way to go, though, in evaluating the effectiveness of various training methods and learning activities. Some methods such as behavioral modeling have reasonable evidence supporting their effectiveness, some methods such as cross cultural training has showed mixed results and for some approaches such as international service learning we have limited data on effectiveness. Best practice guidelines are provided below.

The last chapter of this book expands our notions of learning beyond individuals, teams, and leaders to viewing learning from a broader organizational systems perspective. This includes an emphasis on building continuous learning organizations. From this perspective, the development of an organization's human resources is viewed as a key to competitive advantage in our increasingly global economy. In addition, the chapter presents global attempts to deal with today's serious social problems such as skill obsolescence, training the unemployed, and helping those who have been affected by organizational downsizing or advances in technology.

Chapter 10: Best Practice Guidelines

- Create a leadership development system that incorporates the building of knowledge and skills for all the leadership roles (Table 10.2).
- Use behavioral modeling training for building interpersonal skills with participant input into the learning points, demonstration of learning points with both positive (effective) and negative (ineffective) models, a variety of role-play practice scenarios and feedback from multiple sources (other learners, facilitator and self-feedback).
- Ensure that business simulations and game design include adequate initial practice, time for self-reflection and feedback from others, individualized coaching, and additional, spaced practice with a variety of different contexts and interaction patterns.
- Use developmental assessment centers and feedback-intensive interventions to identify areas for leadership growth and provide additional skill training, special job assignments, and additional coaching on the job after the developmental intervention.
- Train facilitators to help leaders interpret the data and gain insights from feedback intensive interventions so as to generate actionable steps to improve behaviors on the job.
- Provide developmental job experiences (Table 10.6) for leaders that are intentionally created to accelerate learning by placing leaders into situations that challenge their current approaches combined with appropriate coaching and mentoring.

- Have coaches create a structured learning approach with a schedule, agenda, and plan for development that includes objectives and indicators of success as well as gathering systematic data (though assessments, observations, discussions with stakeholders) so as to give data-driven constructive feedback to the learner.
- Ensure that global leadership development efforts include issues of business and organizational acumen, managing people and relationships, and managing oneself.
- Identify the global leadership role required (Figure 10.2) and tailor developmental efforts to meet the specific knowledge, skills, and attitudes relevant to each global role.
- Provide high contact learning experiences to facilitate the development of cultural intelligence.

References

Anderson, P. H., & Lawton, L. (2009). Business simulations and cognitive learning: Developments, desires, and future directions. *Simulation & Gaming*, 40(2), 193–216. doi.org/10.1177/1046878108321624

Ang, S., Van Dyne, L., Koh, C., Ng, K. Y., Templer, K. J., Tay, C., & Chandrasekar, N. A. (2007). Cultural intelligence: Its measurement and effects on cultural judgment and decision making, cultural adaptation and task performance. *Management and Organization Review*, 3(3), 335–371. doi.org/10.1111/j.1740-8784.2007.00082.x

Arthur Jr, W., Day, E. A., McNelly, T. L., & Edens, P. S. (2003). A meta-analysis of the criterion-related validity of assessment center dimensions. *Personnel Psychology*, 56(1), 125–153. doi.org/10.1111/j.1744-6570.2003.tb00146.x

Avolio, B. J., Reichard, R. J., Hannah, S. T., Walumbwa, F. O., & Chan, A. (2009). A meta-analytic review of leadership impact research: Experimental and quasi-experimental studies. *The Leadership Quarterly*, 20(5), 764–784. doi.org/10.1016/j.leaqua.2009.06.006

Backus, C., Keegan, K., Gluck, C., & Gulick, L. M. (2010). Accelerating leadership development via immersive learning and cognitive apprenticeship. *International Journal of Training and Development*, 14(2), 144–148. doi.org/10.1111/j.1468-2419.2010.00347.x

Bailey, C., & Fletcher, C. (2002). The impact of multiple source feedback on management development: Findings from a longitudinal study. *Journal of Organizational Behavior*, 23(7), 853–867. doi.org/10.1002/job.167

Bailey, C., & Dragoni, L. (2013). Repatriation after global assignments: Current HR practices and suggestions for ensuring successful repatriation. *People and Strategy*, 36(1), 48.

Bass, B. M., & Riggio, R. E. (2006). *Transformational leadership*. New York: Psychology Press.

Bersin, J. (2014). Deloitte's new leadership development factbook 2014: Benchmarks and trends in U.S. leadership development. Bersin & Associates Factbook Report, 1–96. Retrieved from http://marketing.bersin.com/ corporate-learning-factbook-2014.html

Bhawuk, D., & Brislin, R. (2000). Cross-cultural training: A review. *Applied Psychology*, 49(1), 162–191. doi.org/10.1111/1464-0597.00009

Bird, A. (2013). Mapping the content domain of global leadership competencies. In M. Mendenhall, J. Osland, A. Bird, G. Oddou, M. Maznevski, M. Stevens, & G. Stahl (Eds.), *Global leadership 2e* (pp. 80–96). New York: Routledge.

Black, J. S., & Gregersen, H. B. (2000). High impact training: Forging leaders for the global frontier. *Human Resource Management*, 39(2–3), 173–184. doi.org/10.1002/1099-050X(200022/23)39:2/3<173::AID-HRM7>3.0.CO;2-W

Black, J. S., & Morrison, A. J. (2014). *The global leadership challenge* (2nd ed.). New York: Routledge.

Brutus, S., Derayeh, M., Fletcher, C., Bailey, C., Velazquez, P., Shi, K., Simon, C., & Labath, V. (2006). Internationalization of multi-source feedback systems: A six-country exploratory analysis of 360-degree feedback. *The International Journal of Human Resource Management*, 17(11), 1888–1906. doi.org/10.1080/09585190601000071

Caligiuri, P., & Tarique, I. (2009). Predicting effectiveness in global leadership activities. *Journal of World Business*, 44(3), 336–346. doi.org/10.1016/j.jwb.2008.11.005

Carette, B., Anseel, F., & Lievens, F. (2013). Does career timing of challenging job assignments influence the relationship with in-role job performance? *Journal of Vocational Behavior*, 83(1), 61–67. doi.org/10.1016/j.jvb.2013.03.001

Collins, D. B., & Holton III, E. F. (2004). The effectiveness of managerial leadership development programs: A meta-analysis of studies from 1982 to 2001. *Human Resource Development Quarterly*, 15(2), 217–248. doi.org/10.1002/hrdq.1099

Collings, D. G., & Isichei, M. (2018). The shifting boundaries of global staffing: Integrating global talent management, alternative forms of international assignments and non-employees into the discussion. *The International Journal of Human Resource Management*, 29(1), 165–187. doi.org/10.1080/09585192.2017.1380064

Cutcher-Gershenfeld, J., & Ford, K. (2005). *Valuable disconnects in organizational learning systems: Integrating bold visions and harsh realities.* New York: Oxford University Press.

D'Abate, C. P., Eddy, E. R., & Tannenbaum, S. I. (2003). What's in a name? A literature-based approach to understanding mentoring, coaching, and other constructs that describe developmental interactions. *Human Resource Development Review*, 2(4), 360–384. doi.org/10.1177/1534484303255033

Dahlsrud, A. (2008). How corporate social responsibility is defined: An analysis of 37 definitions. *Corporate Social Responsibility and Environmental Management*, 15(1), 1–13. doi.org/10.1002/csr.132

Dai, G., De Meuse, K. P., & Peterson, C. (2010). Impact of multi-source feedback on leadership competency development: A longitudinal field study. *Journal of Managerial Issues*, 22, 197–219. www.jstor.org/stable/20798905

Davis, S. (2015, July/August). The state of global leadership development. *Training Magazine*, pp. 30–33.

Deloitte Consulting. (2013). Predictions for 2013: Corporate talent, leadership and HR – Nexus of global forces drives new models for talent. Retrieved from www.deloitte.com/view/en_US/us/Services/consulting/human-capital/index.htm

De Meuse, K. P., Dai, G., & Lee, R. J. (2009). Evaluating the effectiveness of executive coaching: Beyond ROI?. *Coaching: An International Journal of Theory, Research and Practice*, 2(2), 117–134. doi.org/10.1080/17521880902882413

De Pater, I. E., Van Vianen, A. E., Bechtoldt, M. N., & Klehte, U. C. (2009). Employee's challenging job experiences and supervisors' evaluations of promotability. *Personnel Psychology*, 62(2), 297–325. doi.org/10.1111/j.1744-6570.2009.01139.x

DeRue, D. S., & Wellman, N. (2009). Developing leaders via experience: The role of developmental challenge, learning orientation, and feedback availability. *Journal of Applied Psychology*, 94, 859–875. doi.org/10.1037/a0015317

Doherty, N. T., & Dickmann, M. (2012). Measuring the return on investment in international assignments: An action research approach. *The International Journal of Human Resource Management*, 23(16), 3434–3454. doi.org/10.1080/09585192.2011.637062

Dorfman, P., Javidan, M., Hanges, P., Dastmalchian, A., & House, R. (2012). GLOBE: A twenty year journey into the intriguing world of culture and leadership. *Journal of World Business*, 47(4), 504–518. doi.org/10.1016/j.jwb.2012.01.004

Dragoni, L., Oh, I. S., Tesluk, P. E., Moore, O. A., VanKatwyk, P., & Hazucha, J. (2014). Developing leaders' strategic thinking through global work experience: The moderating role of cultural distance. *Journal of Applied Psychology*, 99(5), 867. doi.org/10.1037/a0036628

Dragoni, L., Oh, I. S., Vankatwyk, P., & Tesluk, P. E. (2011). Developing executive leaders: The relative contribution of cognitive ability, personality, and the accumulation of work experience in predicting strategic thinking competency. *Personnel Psychology*, 64(4), 829–864. doi.org/10.1111/j.1744-6570.2011.01229.x

Dragoni, L., Tesluk, P. E., Russell, J. E. A., & Oh, I. S. (2009). Understanding managerial development: Integrating developmental assignments, learning orientation, and access to developmental opportunities in predicting managerial competencies. *Academy of Management Journal*, 52, 731–743. doi.org/10.5465/amj.2009.43669936

Gentry, W. A., Manning, L., Wolf, A. K., Hernez-Broome, G., & Allen, L. W. (2013). What coaches believe are best practices for coaching: A qualitative study of interviews from coaches residing in Asia and Europe. *Journal of Leadership Studies*, 7(2), 18–31. doi.org/10.1002/jls.21285

Goldstein, A. P., & Sorcher, M. A. (1974). *Changing supervisory behavior*. New York: Pergoman Press.

Georgakakis, D., Dauth, T., & Ruigrok, W. (2016). Too much of a good thing: Does international experience variety accelerate or delay executives' career advancement? *Journal of World Business*, 51(3), 425–437. doi.org/10.1016/j.jwb.2015.11.008

Halman, F., & Fletcher, C. (2000). The impact of development centre participation and the role of individual differences in changing self-assessments. *Journal of Occupational and Organizational Psychology*, 73(4), 423–442. doi.org/10.1348/096317900167146

Herd, A. M., Alagaraja, M., & Cumberland, D. M. (2016). Assessing global leadership competencies: The critical role of assessment centre methodology. *Human Resource Development International*, 19(1), 27–43. doi.org/10.1080/13678868.2015.1072125

Javidan, M., Dorfman, P. W., De Luque, M. S., & House, R. J. (2006). In the eye of the beholder: Cross cultural lessons in leadership from project GLOBE. *Academy of Management Perspectives*, 20(1), 67–90. doi.org/10.5465/amp.2006.19873410

Jones, R. G., & Whitmore, M. D. (1995). Evaluating developmental assessment centers as interventions. *Personnel Psychology*, 48, 377–388. doi.org/10.1111/j.1744-6570.1995.tb01762.x

King, S. N., & Santana, L. C. (2010). Feedback-intensive programs. In Van Velsor, E., McCauley, C. D., & Ruderman, M. N. (Eds.), *The center for creative leadership handbook of leadership development* (Vol. 122, p. 97). New York: John Wiley & Sons.

Kleinmann, M., & Ingold, P. V. (2019). Toward a better understanding of assessment centers: A conceptual review. *Annual Review of Organizational Psychology and Organizational Behavior*, 6, 349–372. doi.org/10.1146/annurev-orgpsych-012218-014955

Latham, G. P., & Saari, L. M. (1979). Application of social-learning theory to training supervisors through behavioral modeling. *Journal of Applied Psychology*, 64(3), 239. doi.org/10.1037/0021-9010.64.3.239

Lopes, M. C., Fialho, F. A., Cunha, C. J., & Niveiros, S. I. (2013). Business games for leadership development: A systematic review. *Simulation & Gaming*, 44(4), 523–543. doi.org/10.1177/1046878112471509

Lord, R. G., & Hall, R. J. (2005). Identity, deep structure and the development of leadership skill. *The Leadership Quarterly*, 16(4), 591–615. doi.org/10.1016/j.leaqua.2005.06.003

McCall, M. W., & Lombardo, M. M. (1982). Using simulation for leadership and management research: Through the looking glass. *Management Science*, 28, 533–549. doi.org/10.1287/mnsc.28.5.533

McCauley, C. D. (2006). *Developmental assignments: Creating learning experiences without changing jobs*. Greensboro, NC: CCL Press.

McCauley, C. D., Ruderman, M. N., Ohlott, P. J., & Morrow, J. E. (1994). Assessing the developmental components of managerial jobs. *Journal of Applied Psychology*, 79(4), 544. doi.org/10.1037/0021-9010.79.4.544

Mendenhall, M. E., Stahl, G. K., Ehnert, I., Oddou, G., Osland, J. S., & Kuhlmann, T. M. (2004). Evaluation studies of cross-cultural training programs. In D. Landis, J. M. Bennett, & M. J. Bennett (Eds.), *Handbook of intercultural training* (pp. 129–143). Thousand Oaks, CA: Sage.

Mitchell, C., Ray, R. L., & van Ark, B. (2017, January), *The Conference Board CEO Challenge® 2017: Leading through risk, disruption and transformation.* New York: The Conference Board. www.conference-board.org

Nelson, J. K., Zaccaro, S. J., and Herman, J. L. (2010). Strategic information provision and experiential variety as tools for developing adaptive leadership skills. *Consulting Psychology Journal: Practice and Research* 62: 131–142. doi.org/10.1037/a0019989

Oddou, G. R., & Mendenhall, M. E. (2013). Global leadership development. In M. E. Mendenhall & Associates (Eds.), *Global leadership: Research, practice, and development* (pp. 215–239). New York: Routledge.

Ott, D. L., & Michailova, S. (2018). Cultural intelligence: A review and new research avenues. *International Journal of Management Reviews*, 20(1), 99–119. doi.org/10.1111/ijmr.12118

Pless, N. M., & Borecká, M. (2014). Comparative analysis of international service learning programs. *Journal of Management Development*, 33(6), 526–550. doi: 10.1108/JMD-04-2014-0034

Pless, N. M., Maak, T., & Stahl, G. K. (2011). Developing responsible global leaders through international service-learning programs: The Ulysses experience. *Academy of Management Learning & Education*, 10(2), 237–260. doi.org/10.5465/amle.10.2.zqr237

Pless, N. M., Maak, T., & Stahl, G. K. (2012). Promoting corporate social responsibility and sustainable development through management development: What can be learned from international service-learning programs? *Human Resource Management*, 51(6), 873–903. doi.org/10.1002/hrm.21506

Puck, J. F., M. G. Kittler, & Wright, C. (2008). Does it really work? Re-assessing the impact of pre-departure cross-cultural training on expatriate adjustment. *The International Journal of Human Resource Management*, 19(12), 2182–2197. doi.org/10.1080/09585190802479413

Raser, J. R. (1969). *Simulation and society: An exploration of scientific gaming.* Boston, MA: Allyn & Bacon.

Raver, J. L., & Van Dyne, L. (2017). Developing cultural intelligence. In K. G. Brown (Ed.), *The Cambridge handbook of workplace training and employee development* (p. 407). New York: Cambridge University Press.

Reiche, B. S., Bird, A., Mendenhall, M. E., & Osland, J. S. (2017). Contextualizing leadership: A typology of global leadership roles. *Journal of International Business Studies*, 48, 552–572. doi.org/10.1057/s41267-016-0030-3

Schwartz, M. S., & Carroll, A. B. (2003). Corporate social responsibility: A three-domain approach. Business ethics quarterly, 503–530.

Seibert, S. E., Sargent, L. D., Kraimer, M. L., & Kiazad, K. (2017). Linking developmental experiences to leader effectiveness and promotability: The mediating role of leadership self-efficacy and mentor network. *Personnel Psychology*, 70(2), 357–397. doi.org/10.1111/peps.12145

Sessa, V. I., & London, M. (2015). *Continuous learning in organizations: Individual, group, and organizational perspectives.* New York: Psychology Press.

Shadrick, S. B., & Lussier, I. W. (2009). Training complex cognitive skills: A theme-based approach to the development of battlefield skills. In E. A. Ericsson (Ed.), *Development of professional expertise: Toward measurement of expert performance and design of optimal learning environments* (p. 286). Cambridge, UK: Cambridge University Press.

Shadrick, S. B., Lussier, J. W., & Fultz, C. (2007). *Accelerating the development of adaptive performance: Validating the think like a commander training* (No.

ARI-RR-1868). Alexandria, VA: Army Research Institute for the Behavioral and Social Sciences.

Smither, J. W., London, M., & Reilly, R. R. (2005). Does performance improve following multisource feedback? A theoretical model, meta-analysis, and review of empirical findings. *Personnel Psychology*, 58(1), 33–66. doi.org/10.1111/j.1744-6570.2005.514_1.x

Smither, J. W., London, M., Vasilopoulos, N. L., Reilly, R. R., Millsap, R. E., & Salvemini, N. (1995). An examination of the effects of an upward feedback program over time. *Personnel Psychology*, 48(1), 1–34. doi.org/10.1111/j.1744-6570.1995.tb01744.x

Sonesh, S. C., Coultas, C. W., Lacerenza, C. N., Marlow, S. L., Benishek, L. E., & Salas, E. (2015). The power of coaching: A meta-analytic investigation. *Coaching: An International Journal of Theory, Research and Practice*, 8(2), 73–95. doi.org/10.1080/17521882.2015.1071418

Stewart, L. (1962). Management games today. In J. M. Kibbee, C. J. Kraft, & B. Nanus (Eds.), *Management games*. New York: Reinhold.

Taylor, P. J., Russ-Eft, D. F., & Chan, D. W. (2005). A meta-analytic review of behavior modeling training. *Journal of Applied Psychology*, 90(4), 692. doi.org/10.1037/0021-9010.90.4.692

Theeboom, T., Beersma, B., & van Vianen, A. E. (2014). Does coaching work? A meta-analysis on the effects of coaching on individual level outcomes in an organizational context. *The Journal of Positive Psychology*, 9(1), 1–18. doi.org/10.1080/17439760.2013.837499

Thornton III, G. C., & Krause, D. E. (2009). Selection versus development assessment centers: An international survey of design, execution, and evaluation. *The International Journal of Human Resource Management*, 20(2), 478–498. doi.org/10.1080/09585190802673536

Thornton III, G. C., & Rupp, D. E. (2006). *Assessment centers in human resource management: Strategies for prediction, diagnosis, and development*. New York: Psychology Press.

Triandis, H. C. (2006). Cultural intelligence in organizations. *Group & Organization Management*, 31(1), 20–26.

Volini, E., Schwartz, J., Indranil, R., Hauptmann, M., Durme, Y. V., Denny, B., & Bersin, J. (2019). Leadership for the 21st century: The intersection of the traditional and the new. *2019 global human capital trends*. New York: Deloitte.

Walker, A. G., & Smither, J. W. (1999). A five-year study of upward feedback: What managers do with their results matters. *Personnel Psychology*, 52(2), 393–423. doi.org/10.1111/j.1744-6570.1999.tb00166.x

Zenger, J. H., & Stinnett, K. (2006). Leadership coaching: Developing effective executives. *Chief Learning Officer*, 5(7), 44–47.

Yukl, G. (2012). Effective leadership behavior: What we know and what questions need more attention. *Academy of Management Perspectives*, 26(4), 66–85. doi.org/10.5465/amp.2012.0088

CHAPTER **11**

Organizational and Societal Issues

Questions

✓ What are the characteristics of a learning organization?
✓ What models can be adopted to facilitate the move to a learning organization?
✓ How are societies across the globe attempting to address issues of youth employment, worker skill obsolescence, and reemployment?

Some argue that the only sustainable advantage an organization will have in the future is its ability to learn faster than its competitors. This means that surviving and thriving requires learning at an increasingly rapid rate across all levels and functions. The building of "intellectual capital" and the institutionalization of learning within the organization is a key strategic weapon for improving competitiveness and for delivering effective services (Stewart, 2007). The increasing complexity of the changes occurring in the workplace such as the infusion of new technology require a highly developed workforce that is prepared to deal with those changing realities.

Government agencies are also increasing the amount of money and attention paid to learning and development such as preparing youths for jobs and helping displaced workers to more fully utilize their talents in the workforce. Facilitating learning within industries, within societies, and across global domains requires taking an integrated approach to developing human resources.

The first section of this chapter describes what it means to be a learning organization whereby learning is viewed as a core organizational value. The characteristics of a learning organization are identified. The second section presents organizational models and strategic approaches to building a learning organization. The third section examines the learning implications for meeting dual societal goals of developing and maintaining a competitive workforce in our global economy and enhancing the quality of life for individuals within one's country.

THE LEARNING ORGANIZATION

The concept of a learning organization has captured much attention. It has been described in different ways but has some core propositions. This section defines the concept of a learning organization and describes strategic leadership efforts to create an organizational learning culture.

Definition and Indicators

A learning organization refers to a systematic approach to change an organization's capacity for doing something new. This definition involves both learning and change. For example, one can examine the extent to which an organization has the motivation and capability to: (1) analyze the gap between the organization's evolving vision/values/purpose and current organizational practice; (2) determine what changes are necessary to reduce this gap; (3) build shared knowledge and skills of individuals, groups, and other organizations to approach the organization's evolving vision/values; and (4) monitor and revise action to continuously improve (Cutcher-Gershenfeld & Ford, 2005). Key attributes or components of becoming a learning organization include:

- Employees continually create, acquire, and transfer knowledge to help their company adapt (Garvin, Edmondson, & Gino, 2008).
- Individuals are working together across traditional organizational boundaries to solve problems and to create innovative solutions (Senge, 2006).
- The capacity to integrate people and structures in an organization to move towards continuous learning and change (Yang, Watkins, & Marsick, 2004).
- There is an emphasis on training, problem solving, and innovation for all organizational members (Goldstein & Ford, 2002).

A learning organization is intentional about helping the individual, team, and organization to improve and develop. The goal of a learning organization is to encourage everyone in the organization – employees, line managers, supervisors, and technical personnel – to become actively engaged in expanding their skills and improving organizational effectiveness. Learning becomes an everyday part of the job rather than being confined to formal training sessions in classrooms. Employees learn skills of others in their work unit, teach other employees in areas of expertise, and learn from one another on a day-to-day basis.

Clearly, creating a learning organization requires a heavy investment in training and a variety of other developmental activities as discussed in the previous chapters. This investment must be closely tied to the strategic goals of the organization. A driving force is the ability of employees to find or make opportunities to learn from whatever situation is presented to problem solve and innovate. Problem-solving and innovation skills require root cause analysis and the identification of improvement options. A learning organization has members who make choices about which improvement option has the greatest potential to add value to the organization and evaluate the effectiveness of the improvement effort.

An underlying dilemma for organizations is how to maintain efficient daily operations that satisfy a variety of organizational and external stakeholders while at the same time allocating time, resources, and energy towards addressing continual progress towards learning and development. It can take years for a transformation to a learning organization to unfold into a top management-supported, long-range effort to improve an organization's problem-solving and renewal process (French & Bell, 1999). The move to a learning organization therefore presents challenges as it often requires a major change in organizational values and norms. The move to a learning organization can expose the underlying clash in subcultures that exist within an organization as they do not understand each other very well and often work against one another (Schein, 2010). For example, shop floor operations work on quite a tight time frame while research and development groups work from a long-time frame such as creating a new innovative product. Therefore, time focused on creating collaborative learning structures might be easier to implement in the research and development groups and be more contested in the manufacturing operations. In support of this notion, Kislov, Walshe, and Harvey (2012) showed that knowledge sharing and diffusion is affected by existing functional and level boundaries in a health care system. Other barriers beyond divergent perspectives across teams, functions, and levels include issues such as lack of time and resources, high turnover, lack of clear responsibility concerning planning and implementation of learning goals, limits to evaluation and feedback for improvement, and overconfidence in the value of the existing practices and processes (Schilling & Kluge, 2009). Hogan and Coote (2014) find support for the premise that when values and norms are aligned across levels and functions in an organization around innovation, there is more innovative behaviors observed and those behaviors are linked to firm market and financial performance.

Despite harsh realities around the difficulties of becoming a learning organization, there is evidence from case studies that provides evidence that organizations can build their learning capabilities with intentional strategies and strong leadership support (Goh, 2003). These intentional strategies often revolve around open communication and information sharing, support for new idea generation, and resource availability (Kontoghiorghes et al., 2005). Building a learning organization has been linked to improvements in organizational innovation, performance, and effectiveness. There is evidence that organizations having higher levels on learning organization components are also more likely to show higher levels of financial performance assessed by return on investment, average productivity per employee, time to market for products and services, market share, and cost per business transaction (Bhaskar & Mishra, 2017; Davis & Daley, 2008; Ellinger, Ellinger, Yang, & Howton, 2002).

Leading a Learning Culture

Leadership's role in making the vision and plan for becoming a learning organization a reality is clearly critical for success. Leaders support the gathering of data, the sharing of knowledge, and the taking of collective action to improve system functioning. A positive learning environment occurs when individuals and teams know how their job/projects fits into the larger system, are assigned tasks that stretch and challenge them, and are provided the resources needed for success. In addition, there is an important leadership role relative to the recognition of learning, encouragement for risk taking and idea generation, tolerance for mistakes during learning, and minimizing constraints to learning.

Building a learning culture requires a commitment from leadership to seeing learning as a key strategic direction for the organization. One structural indicator of this commitment is elevating learning to the executive or "C" suite level through the creation of a formal learning and development role. The CEO Jack Welsh at General Electric is often cited as creating this new role at the executive level in 1989 – since that time a wide range of industries have created similar types of positions at the executive level (Oesch, 2018).

This position at the executive level can have different labels such as Chief Learning Officer (CLO) or Chief Talent Development Officer. Many organizations such as Caterpillar, IBM, and Ingersoll-Rand have elevated the role to one of being a business leader of corporate learning (Bersin, 2007). By appointing the CLO, the chief executive officer communicates to both internal employees and external stakeholder partnerships that the organization is making a long-term investment in learning and development. The CLO is responsible for driving value and aligning learning with business goals and strategies (Phillips, Phillips, & Elkeles, 2016). This can include building a vision for learning in the organization that builds capabilities to meet current needs as well as monitoring and developing approaches to meet future learning needs. This vision and alignment is necessary to create a positive learning culture.

A survey of CLOs finds that the top three tasks where they devote the greatest amount of time are strategy development and planning, communication with corporate executives, and management of the learning staff. They also report wanting to spend more time on performance improvement and knowledge management. One of their greatest challenges is measuring and communicating the value of learning to the organization as well as measuring and interpreting the level of performance improvement from learning initiatives (Sugrue & Lynch, 2006). The measurement needs of the job include tracking learning needs, understanding the efficiency of the learning function, and the level of improvement in the alignment of learning with business goals. The role can also include performance management and succession planning as well as the more traditional training and development domains (Bonner & Wagner, 2002). The evolving role of the CLO includes planning for and implementing mobile learning strategies as well as introducing cutting-edge learning technologies such as virtual reality training and artificial intelligence to better meet learning needs in the organization (BasuMallick, 2019). There is also greater pressure for the CLO to be a strategic change and innovation leader (Todd, Buckley, & Herring, 2014).

MODELS FOR BUILDING A LEARNING ORGANIZATION

There are numerous models of learning organizations to benchmark and there are now professional societies that focus exclusively on understanding and facilitating the move towards becoming a learning organization. One example of a center for organizational learning is the Society of Organizational Learning (www.solonline.org/).

Characteristics of a learning organization include the need to create continuous learning opportunities, promote inquiry and dialogue, establish systems to capture and share learning, empower people toward a collective vision, connect the organization to its environment, and promote/ advance a learning culture through strategic leadership around learning and

TABLE 11.1	Characteristics of a Learning Organization	
Characteristics of a Learning Organization	**Definition**	**Example**
Creating a learning culture through strategic leadership	Leaders model, champion, and support learning; leadership uses learning strategically for business results	Chief Learning Officer
Advance continuous learning	Learning designed into work so that people can learn on the job; opportunities are provided for ongoing education and growth	Corporate universities/ academies
Promote inquiry and dialogue	People gain productive reasoning skills to express their views and capacity to listen and inquire into views of others; the culture is changed to support questioning, feedback, and experimentation	Communities of practice
Establish systems to capture and share learning	Technology systems are created to aid sharing of learning and integrated with work; access is provided; systems are maintained	Knowledge management
Empower people towards a collective vision	Responsibility is distributed close to decision-making so that people are motivated to learn what they are held accountable for	Case study
Connect the organization to its environment	People are helped to see the effect of their work on the entire enterprise; people scan the environment and use information to adjust work practices; the organization Is linked to its communities	Organizational development
Encourage collaboration and team learning	Work is designed to use groups to access different modes of thinking; groups are expected to learn together and work together; collaboration is valued by the culture and rewarded	Team learning chapter (debriefs, team training, etc.)

Source: Adapted from Marsick, V. J., & Watkins, K. E. (2003). Demonstrating the value of an organization's learning culture: The dimensions of the learning organization questionnaire. *Advances in Developing Human Resources*, 5(2), 132–151. Copyright 2003 by Sage Publications. Reprinted by permission.

collaboration (Marsick & Watkins, 2003). Table 11.1 presents these characteristics, provides definitions and indicates an exemplar of each characteristic. Teams are expected to learn together and work together and collaboration is valued by the culture and rewarded. Chapter 9 highlighted ways to facilitate the development of this type of collaboration and team learning. Strategies to enhance the development of other characteristics of learning organization are discussed below and include creating corporate universities, encouraging communities of practice, developing knowledge management systems, and adapting to changing needs.

Creating Continuous Learning Opportunities

Many leading-edge organizations have made heavy investments in developing their work forces. One strategy in making this investment is promoting continuous learning through corporate universities. A corporate university approach "is an educational entity that is a strategic tool designed to assist its parent organization in achieving its mission by conducting activities that cultivate both individual and organizational learning, knowledge and wisdom" (Allen, 2007; p. 9). The idea behind a corporate university is to go beyond training and better link learning to organizational goals and objectives through (1) building a competency-based learning curriculum for all jobs, (2) providing employees with a common shared vision of the company, its values, and business context, (3) extending learning goals and activities to stakeholder groups such as customers and suppliers, and (4) experimenting with new and innovative approaches to learning and effective action planning (Rademakers, 2014). The goal of corporate universities is not just knowledge production but also knowledge application and transfer.

Corporate universities have grown globally over the last 20 years with over 4,000 in the United States alone (Lui Abel & Li, 2012). One indicator of this growth is that there is a Global Council of Corporate Universities (www.globalccu.com) whose goals include connecting Directors of Corporate Universities through a global network to learn from one another, contributing knowledge on how to create and improve corporate universities, and sharing innovative practices.

Motorola University is one company often cited as a benchmark for the concept of a corporate university. Motorola has a campus setting at each major company site worldwide and is heavily engaged in learning technologies to provide immediate access to new knowledge and information. The idea of Motorola University started in 1980 as a program developed outside the traditional human resources department. While traditional approaches to training continued, the vision of Motorola University is geared toward addressing special business needs such as retraining or updating workers and redefining jobs roles and responsibilities. The focus is on the necessity for organizational change, participation in solution generation, and developing new and more effective systems to push the standards of manufacturing. An initial success was the development of a two-week course that brought together manufacturing, product development, and marketing managers to discuss and improve the product development cycle. Based on the coordinated efforts of these teams, the production development cycle was reduced from a three- to seven-year cycle to an 18-month cycle. This success illustrates the direction of the University to not just focus on training but rather put the emphasis on what organizational excellence means in a changing business environment (Baldwin, Danielson, & Wiggenhorn, 1997). Motorola has partnered with a local community college to develop a two-year associate degree in applied science in areas such as electromechanical process technology. The curriculum includes up to 256 hours for developing process skills such as interpersonal, mentoring, and communication skills as well as up to 256 hours of job specific competencies that covered the more basic technical skills of the job.

Corporate academies vary in terms of broadness of scope, centralization of structure, type of governance system, types of learning services offered, and the role of information technology and learning (Baporikar, 2014). The roles of corporate academies continue to evolve given changes in technology, learner needs, and changing corporate strategies. Apple University targets leveraging learning as a cultural mechanism to accelerate knowledge creation and dissemination. Northwell Health's approach to leader development concentrates on executives as teachers so as to help high potentials to gain a better understanding of where the business is going and what skills are needed for the future. AT&T University, created in 2008, aligns learning systems given mergers and acquisitions. The emphasis now is on minimizing skill obsolescence and adding flexibility through reskilling in order to better prepare the organization for the future. More generally, there is also an expanding orientation from learning and business strategy and alignment to also enhancing employee engagement (Rio, 2018).

Corporate universities are embracing the digitization of business and its implications for blended instruction, gamification and skill development via virtual reality programs. Danone has a cloud-based "Danone Campus 2.0," which provides digital access for employees to share best practices, to enhance understanding of changing external demands, and to foster collaborative learning (Benson-Armer, Gast, & van Dam, 2016). There are also efforts to link business academies with four-year and graduate education institutions. The Australian company Coles Myer has formed a partnership between its academy institute with Deakin University in order to provide opportunities for Coles Myer's 55,000 staff to access undergraduate, postgraduate, and non-award qualifications, tailored to the needs of Cole (Riddiford, 2010).

Clearly, given the variety of types of corporate universities and academies, it is difficult to conduct research on the effectiveness of this learning organization movement. What criteria to use to determine effectiveness is certainly challenging. In addition, how to collect such information across enough entities to be able to analyze factors linked to effectiveness is daunting. The growth in the movement is due to the general feeling that leading companies have established corporate universities thus resulting in more companies following the trend. It will be interesting to see the future evolution of corporate universities.

Promoting Inquiry and Dialogue

Learning requires iterative cycles of knowledge and skill creation, knowledge sharing, and collective action (Ford & Foster-Fishman, 2012). Knowledge creation through the generation of data is the first step in creating a learning organization. For data to be turned into shared knowledge, organizational members need to interpret and then agree on the meaning of the data collected. Data such as tacit individual information is more likely to be transformed into shared organizational knowledge when organizational members engage in discovery processes where they, together, challenge existing assumptions, explore patterns, and inconsistencies within the data, and co-generate new meaning.

One strategy for creating opportunities for discovery and innovation is through the encouragement of communities of practice. Communities of practice (CoP) are differentiated from work and project teams as the goal of communities of practice is on knowledge sharing and collaborative learning that is outside the formal structure and tasks of the organization (Cordery & Wenzel, 2017). Learning communities are typically created by individuals who self-select into a highly autonomous group formed around an issue or domain that the individuals are passionate about exploring. The members spend time together examining their current realities and collect relevant data to discuss work practices and systems and innovations occurring outside organizational boundaries that could have implications for improving the organization's effectiveness (Wenger, McDermott, & Snyder, 2002b). Therefore, a learning community is where there is a desire by a group of people to examine a common work domain together and exchange data, information, and knowledge in an informal, nonhierarchical setting to develop an innovative approach in that domain of interest.

Table 11.2 describes a case of hospital staff creating a CoP to address the serious issue of sepsis in these settings. As can be seen in the case, the outcomes

TABLE 11.2   Community of Practice: Educating a Hospital about Sepsis
At the foundation of the Outreach Team there was a need for improving the diagnosis and treatment of sepsis. It had been believed by its leader, a clinical nurse specialist, that it was necessary to spread the active responsibility for diagnosing sepsis beyond intensive care (where very sick patients are treated). The reason for that need was that sepsis could occur anywhere in the hospital and therefore it was very important that as many practitioners as possible were confident about recognizing the symptoms early.
The Outreach Team comprises five senior nurses who specialize in sepsis and who all have experience in intensive care. Not only is the team responsible for quickly responding to cases of sepsis in the hospital, but they also educate the staff in the wards about diagnosis and first response, provide them with supporting tools and systems, and help to improve their communication about sepsis. An analysis highlighted the facilitation of education about sepsis "on the job" as the most significant (central) theme that enabled the whole hospital to develop its organizational ability to perform well in this area of strategic importance.
The range of regular actions of the team included: demonstrating to practitioners how to deal with sepsis "in practice"; mentoring junior doctors and junior nurses who are allowed to spend time with the team; organizing training courses about sepsis in the hospital, which are delivered by an interdisciplinary teaching team; designing objects that support interdisciplinary communication about sepsis such as small cards with key definitions, descriptions of symptoms and required actions, which are distributed among practitioners; and, convening interdisciplinary sepsis-related meetings where patient cases are discussed. As the leader of the Outreach Team commented:
We are a bridge between the intensive care and the ward areas. Historically, the intensive care was quite a secretive place. It was an inner sanctum that patients came to and then the nurses didn't see them again until they come back out again. And there wasn't any sort of joint working. And back where we started there was a nice term came out that "we should change and it should be critical care without walls." Not physical walls, but metaphorical walls. And that was our starting point. There was lots and lots of different things. We got nurses who were in intensive care to go out and spend time in the wards to see what it looks like. And we got nurses from the wards to come spend time in intensive care. And that served a lot of useful things. People get to know each other. And then we saw an opportunity for another sort of learning: that if student doctors, student nurses, staff nurses came and spent time with us and see what we do, that would increase their learning. And to this day that's growing and growing. So several student nurses as part of their training now they're asked to come and spend their time with us. And the student doctors as well. (The Outreach Team's leader)
Source: Adapted from Pyrko, I., Dörfler, V., & Eden, C. (2017). Thinking together: What makes communities of practice work? *Human Relations*, 70(4), 389–409. Copyright 2017 by Sage Publishing. Reprinted by permission.

of this effort include enhanced problem-solving and the creation of innovative solutions to enduring organizational problems. In other cases, CoPs can determine which best practices in other organizations are relevant and provide persuasive arguments to leaders as to the benefits of pursuing new strategies and approaches. Once new approaches are considered for implementation, community of practice members are often called on to help facilitate the change process.

Evidence points to a strong sense of a common vision as one key to the success of a CoP (Kimble, Hildreth, & Wright, 2001). High-level leadership support for and empowerment of members of communities of practice such as helping members manage the operational demands of the job and their role in the CoP is a critical best practice (Retna & Tee Ng, 2011). The team members' level of commitment and mastery goal orientation to address the issues underlying why the CoP was originally formed are also critical success factors (Hirst et al., 2011). A study of 30 CoP teams with globally dispersed members virtually connected in mining and mineral firms found that a factor for success was feelings of psychological safety and the richness of the communication systems in use (Kirkman et al., 2011). High levels of nationality diversity led to better community of practice experiences and performance outcomes than those that have moderate levels of diversity (Kirkman et al., 2013). Finally, an interesting study investigated the impact of ten communities of practice teams on organizational change over a five-year period in three refineries operated by a multinational company. The findings showed that CoP teams benefited the organizations by accelerating the adoption of best practices leading to enhanced organizational routines and operational procedures (Cordery et al., 2015).

As a cautionary tale, research has also found that attempts by high level leaders to intentionally form communities of practice in a top-down rather than emergent manner can fail. Harvey et al. (2013) studied an organization that was high on dimensions of bureaucratic structure and functions within a labor union. Over the course of 16 months, they found that initial enthusiasm for a CoP around sustainable development waned as the freedom to explore topics led to participants and leaders feeling that progress was not being made. This lack of progress led to decreased participation and difficulty in regaining traction. The structure that people were used to on a day-to-day basis was inconsistent with the lack of structure and high levels of autonomy that were part of the CoP.

Establishing Systems to Capture and Share Knowledge

In order for knowledge to be a key strategic asset, organizations need to be intentional about setting up effective knowledge management systems to acquire, share, and apply information regarding issues such as evidence-based best practices. Knowledge management involves this intentional strategy and approach to formalize and enhance access to the experience and expertise within the organization to drive the diffusion of new capabilities that enable superior performance (Beckman, 1999). Building this capability requires having the appropriate technology, structure, and culture in place. Figure 11.1 provides a framework that identifies three types of knowledge infrastructure needed and the four knowledge processes

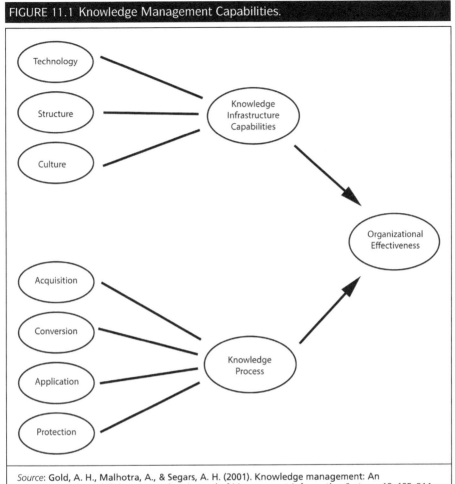

FIGURE 11.1 Knowledge Management Capabilities.

Source: Gold, A. H., Malhotra, A., & Segars, A. H. (2001). Knowledge management: An organizational capabilities perspective. *Journal of Management Information Systems*, 18, 185–214. Copyright 2001 Taylor & Francis. Reprinted by permission.

required to drive improved organizational effectiveness around knowledge management (Gold, Malhotra, & Segars, 2001).

In terms of enhancing capabilities, the model highlights the importance of incorporating the appropriate technology needed to store organizational relevant knowledge and then to build in capacities to allow for easy access to that knowledge as well as simple ways to update the knowledge. The organizational structure needs to be designed for flexible rather than rigid boundaries across functions and departments. In addition, structurally, organizations need to have individuals who span multiple teams and departments so as to help integrate the differentiated functions within the organization. In essence, the organizational structure needs to be more organic than bureaucratic so that the structure encourages collaboration and sharing rather than inhibiting cooperation across units. This points to the need to have some level of decentralization and empowerment with a cultural focus on continuous improvement that allows for experimentation and decisions at the source of an issue or problem. There also needs to be a strong incentive system that rewards knowledge acquisition, sharing, and application. This requires intentional efforts to identify what type of knowledge is valued and to develop norms that are supportive of knowledge sharing and diffusion across the organization.

In terms of knowledge process issues, acquiring data and information is the way in which organizational members can identify new knowledge. This new knowledge is generated from a range of ideas that point to new direction or the identification of activity that uncovers a best practice that might be useful to diffuse throughout the organization. Before the new knowledge can be adopted, it needs to be integrated into the existing knowledge base of the organization and shared, and then converted into a proposition so that decisions can be made as to the possible value of this new knowledge for the organization. Once a decision is made that the new knowledge is valuable the knowledge can be exploited for the benefit of the organization by being transformed into a new approach or product that is applied to the organization. This new approach or perspective then needs to be protected to make sure the approach or product is appropriately integrated into new procedures and processes in the organization. If the new approach or product provides a competitive advantage, there also needs to be strategies to preserve that advantage. This is an ongoing process to "continuously transform knowledge and ideas into new products, processes and systems for the benefit of the firm and its stakeholders" (Lawson & Samson, 2001; p. 384). Table 11.3 summarizes the key problems faced and some solutions organizations can implement to further their knowledge management system.

The knowledge management system can focus on the accumulation and diffusion of explicit knowledge that has already been codified and is accessible (e.g., evidence-based best practice write-ups, procedural manuals) as well as what has been called tacit knowledge. Tacit knowledge is personal based on individual and team learnings from experiences on the job. It is the linkage of personal and context specific experiences that has developed over time in an individual or team that goes beyond simple factual and procedural knowledge to include insights and wisdom that comes with valuable experiences. Capturing and disseminating expert tacit knowledge can lead to a tangible learning path for others to follow. Tacit knowledge includes the technical know-how of completing job tasks as well as the mental models and schemata that has developed within a person that has led the person to be considered an expert (Seideler-de Alwis & Hartmann, 2008). One way to capture both the technical and cognitive aspects was described in Chapter 3 as part of a cognitive task analysis. In this way an individual's or team's knowledge base that has accumulated can become organizational knowledge. This organizational knowledge can be part of an effective succession planning process so when experts retire, their accumulated wisdom can be imparted to and speed up the acquisition of expertise for the next generation of employees. It can also be a key strategy for risk analysis and management for systems such as healthcare by codifying the experiential knowledge of clinicians (Waring & Currie, 2009).

There is evidence that the development of knowledge management systems is related to valued organizational outcomes. Survey-based evidence from executives finds that both the level of knowledge infrastructure capability and degree of knowledge process capability are important factors affecting organizational effectiveness (Gold et al., 2001). Mishra and Bhaskar (2011) studied an IT company in India that was considered high and one that was low

TABLE 11.3   Knowledge Management Framework

Knowledge Capabilities	Components	Problem	Solution
Build Infrastructure Capabilities	Technology	Fragmented information flows	Integrate information and communication systems
	Structure	Individualistic behavior and hording of information by units	Design for flexibility and self-organization
	Culture	Status quo orientation	Communicate vision and values around collaboration and knowledge sharing
Enhance Knowledge Process Capabilities	Acquisition	Limited efforts and experience in recognizing and capturing new knowledge	Benchmarking and identifying knowledge gaps
	Conversion	Lack of consistency of standards across units on what knowledge is valued and lack of a common language around the sharing knowledge	Eliminate excess volume and target key information need
	Application	Limited attention to and evaluation of outcomes from application of knowledge	Develop effective storage and retrieval mechanisms to allow quick access when needed
	Protection	Limited security measures to protect organization from illegal or inappropriate use of new knowledge or innovations	Go beyond trademark and other property laws to enact employee conduct rules and develop technology that restricts and tracks access to new knowledge

Source: Adapted from Gold, A. H., Malhotra, A., & Segars, A. H. (2001). Knowledge management: An organizational capabilities perspective. *Journal of Management Information Systems*, 18, 185–214.

on the characteristics of a learning organization. They conducted interviews in both companies around their knowledge management systems. They found striking differences in the approaches to knowledge creation, knowledge sharing and refinement, and knowledge retention. For example, those with a high number of characteristics of a learning organization had more formal processes for rewarding idea generation and had greater decentralized and multi-channel interaction structure built into the organization. Another study of over 400 New Zealand firms discovered that knowledge management practices particularly around knowledge acquisition and being adaptable to changing situations were the same firms that were more likely to show a pattern of innovative practices (Darroch & McNaughton, 2002). A survey of CEOs from a diverse set of industries found that strategies for capturing both tangible/explicit and tacit knowledge into the day-to-day organizational routines led to more innovative practices and enhanced financial performance (Darroch, 2005). Finally, Harlow (2008) developed a measure of an organization's tacit knowledge in terms of approaches used to identify expertise, lessons learned, and capturing content and linked the level of tacit knowledge to innovative practices. This firm level study showed that the extent to which there were intentional approaches to capturing and disseminating tacit knowledge the greater the amount of innovative practices.

Empowering People towards a Collective Vision

A learning organization recognizes the need to delegate and decentralize responsibility to those closest to the issues and problems that arise. A learning organization also recognizes that learning must be pointed in the direction of a vision for the company moving forward. An example of this notion of empowering people is provided by a small manufacturing company that I have worked with over a long period of time. The company totally re-invented itself from a traditional manufacturing structure to a team-based learning organization. The team-based system transformed front-line employees into owners of a manufacturing process leading to a finished product.

This change effort began with the creation of an overall vision and underlying values that the organization wanted to pursue and create. The vision and values were generated by a team of employees and management. The vision included the following components: (1) to remain competitive, we must continually improve quality, productivity, and profitability; (2) everyone in the company will have access to business knowledge and understand the company's financial performance and share in the long-term success; and (3) the focus must be on meeting and exceeding customer needs and maintaining long-term relationships with valued customers. The underlying values by which the vision would be accomplished were identified as: (1) the operative principle is one of teamwork, involvement, empowerment, and responsibility among its members; (2) interactions among members will embody a climate of trust, mutual respect, and open communication; and (3) we will be characterized by continuous learning that integrates problem-solving, technical updating, and people skills.

Interventions to move the organization towards its vision and values included grouping like problems to exploit similarities in product and processes in efforts to simply and control the quality of work. The manufacturing process was reorganized around manufacturing cells that operate as discrete, "focused" factories within the company. All aspects of operation, production, and quality are controlled by the teams of people who operate and set them up. A production focus is on building and designing quality at the source with the primary responsibility for quality belonging to the team members. To make it right the first time, the operator was given the resources, responsibilities, and the tools to do the job.

These interventions were implemented through the shared efforts of management and line workers. Company-wide teams were created to operationalize the vision by developing a prototype for the plant, evaluating its success, and developing procedures for generalizing from the pilot program to diffusion throughout the shop floor. Ad hoc teams were formed to develop guidelines for safety procedures, quality, machine maintenance, and tooling. Other teams were formed to develop a standardized set of procedures on how to operate the various machines (hobs, lathes, drills, broaching) in the factory. Within each team, weekly meetings were held to review quality and safety concerns and to consider ways to continuously improve cell processes.

An emphasis was placed on providing workers with extensive information on the company's financial situation so that employees could see the bigger picture around the change effort. Much effort and resources were also devoted to employee training. External consultants provided training in areas such as teamwork, running effective team meetings, improving internal and external customer relations, as well as enhancing problem-solving and seeking root causes to problems so that continuous improvements could be made. Consultants also developed train-the-trainer systems in which technical experts within the company were provided with skills on how to teach others within the organization to work effectively in team. In addition, internal technical training and cooperative educational programs have been utilized to improve skills in areas such as statistical process control, quality monitoring at the source, print reading, gauge usage, and geometric tolerance.

The change effort rested on the pillars of systems thinking, worker participation, and creating a learning culture. Rather than being solely the "transformation" part of the manufacturing process (e.g., drilling a hole into a piece of steel all day), each employee and team has become a mini system within the larger system. Each team is in charge of its inputs (e.g., determining what jobs to run), transformation (taking raw material and transforming it into a product), outputs (preparing output for shipping directly to the customer), and feedback (checking quality). Team members are empowered to set up the machines in whatever way makes sense and to calculate their own cycle times for getting the work done. Teams are able to review customer orders, schedule their own work to meet customer needs, do their own maintenance, make purchases to improve cell operations, and to improve daily operations.

One component for enhancing effectiveness is the standardization of work procedures. Another key component is extensive training and education of members in areas such as statistical process control, blueprint reading, advanced machine processes, machine set-up, basic maintenance issues, problem-solving skills, teambuilding, how to run effective team meetings, and internal and external customer relations. The change initiative to becoming a learning organization has been quite successful. The company made dramatic improvements in quality and on-time delivery. Profits went up and employee bonuses grew as they are learning and continuously improving.

Connecting the Organization to Its Environment

The environment surrounding an organization can be in flux affecting organizational stability. For example, the case example above is also a story of the organization losing much of its business to competitors and having to create a new vision of the company around precision manufacturing. Thus, the organization has now reinvented itself again after it had become wildly successful with the move to empowering people and encouraging collaboration and teamwork. This required scanning the environment for new opportunities and an intentional decision-making process to determine its future.

Zollo and Winter (2002) describe the modification of existing routines as an organization's dynamic capability to integrate, build, and reconfigure internal competencies and operations to address changing environments. This cyclical view of organizational knowledge includes scanning for new information, evaluating the legitimacy of the information, sharing the information across the organization, and enacting and routinizing a new set of policies, procedures, and actions.

Scanning is the formal term given to the process of acquiring information outside the boundaries of the organization to better understand the realities facing the organization. Information can be acquired about trends, events, or conditions occurring external to the organization so the organization can target a future course of action. Oftentimes, organizations are more reactive to changing demands that develop into an organizational crisis. A proactive approach occurs when scanning is of broad scope, intentional, and future oriented around what competitors are doing, the changing market conditions and advances in technology. Research has shown that what aspects in the environment are perceived as having strategic uncertainty get targeted for more intensive scanning. For example, it was found that Nigerian companies saw greater uncertainty that could impact their organization from political, legal, and economic sectors while Hong Kong and U.S. executives described greater levels of uncertainty that needed to be scanned in the technology sector. U.S. executives also pointed to socio-cultural factors like diversity and inclusion as an area of strategic uncertainty (Ebrahimi & Sawyerr, 2016).

Issues of scanning and acquiring information does not mean that the organization has the capacity to effectively interpret the information scanned and turn it into knowledge to gain insight. This calls for the organizations to have processes in place to link the acquisition of information into a well-developed data analytic system to gain those valuable insights from new knowledge from scanning (Jiang & Gallupe, 2015). A key factor relevant to this is building the internal capabilities to access and interpret the wealth of information available to an organization. This capability to value, assimilate, and use new knowledge has been called the absorptive capacity of an organization (Lane, Koka, & Pathak, 2006). High levels of absorptive capacity facilitate the exploration and application of new knowledge. Deciding to use new knowledge is necessarily a highly social endeavor, often involving numerous meetings and informal conversations. In fact, when organizational settings create participatory processes where members can openly explore and assess external best practice evidence, members are more likely to develop shared understandings about the evidence that can promote broader support for the new knowledge and implementation decisions (Honig, 2003).

The creation of internal information and decision-making routines that guide how information should be discussed and decisions made must be established (Winder, 2000). Many organizations make substantial investments in knowledge and learning functions only to not realize an optimal level of return due to poor governance structures around learning and knowledge creation and dissemination. Several studies have found that one of the most reported barriers to implementing best practice evidence is the lack of enough time to reflect and discuss ideas (e.g., Retsas, 2000). Effective internal knowledge management routines include having formalized processes and procedures in place that allocate agenda time for the consideration of trends, new ideas, and research findings (Foster-Fishman et al., 2001). In addition, reporting guidelines should be established for determining the value of new approaches for getting to the desired outcomes. Overall, the extent to which organizations create opportunities for and routines around the assessment of trends as well as best practices significantly influence the level of absorptive capacity. The strength of absorptive capacity has been found to affect an organization's ability to adopt and implement new ideas and practices (Zahra & George, 2002). For example, school districts were found to be more likely to use best practice evidence from external sources to guide their decisions when they had the capacity to acquire and make sense of this evidence (e.g., Honig & Coburn, 2008).

SOCIETAL CONCERNS

The increasing scope and complexity of changes occurring in the workplace require a well prepared and highly developed and sustainable workforce. These organizational realities have implications for the societies within which the organizations are embedded. There is a need for a robust education and training system across the globe so that individual members can function successfully and be gainfully employed. In the U.S. alone, estimates are that the federal government spends up to $19 billion on a variety of job training programs. Other countries commit to spending more per person. The broader issues of meeting societal needs with implications for learning are: (1) increasing the readiness of individuals to enter the workforce, (2) addressing skill obsolescence and helping individuals who have lost employment, and (3) ensuring fairness and opportunities within the workplace.

Increasing Workforce Readiness

There is a widening monetary gap between the highly educated and highly skilled and those less educated and lower skilled workers. These gaps have led to efforts to identify and enhance basic competencies so as to increase the readiness of individuals to join the workforce. Individuals who have limited basic skills needed for the job market or have other constraints make landing and retaining a job difficult.

A survey of adults in 24 countries (samples from age 16 to 65) showed a high percentage of low levels in basic literacy, numeracy, and digital problem solving skills. In the U.S., 14% of the employed population were found to have low literacy skills while 23% had low numeracy skills. A majority (62%) had low problem-solving skills (Rampey et al., 2016). A low level on problem-solving was defined as adults who can complete tasks in which the goal is explicitly stated and can solve problems that have only a small number of steps and a small number of operations to consider (OECD, 2013). There are many programs and approaches around the world to address literacy and basic competency issues. For example, in the Philippines college-aged students can be attend a Literacy Training Service, which provides approaches for teaching literacy and numeracy skills to schoolchildren, at risk youths, and prison inmates (Lopez, 2019).

A United Nations report on the future of work noted that there are 1.2 billion young people aged 15–24 (16% of world population). The report on youth development noted that the primary issues of concern for this group is around education and employment. In terms of employment, the report estimates that 71 million young people are unemployed with 156 million youth living in poverty even though they are employed. Many others are in low quality and poorly paid jobs that lead to insecurities as to future prospects. Youth are also at a greater risk of being on temporary employment. The global action agenda from the United Nations includes a number of target goals (see Table 11.4) including countries helping support the development of small- to medium-sized enterprises to promote job creation while at the same time providing support for increasing workplace readiness (United Nations World Youth Report, 2018).

One area of emphasis is the transition from school to work and the development of strategies to build skills that allow youth to be better positioned to enter the job market. Strategies include apprenticeships (Chapter 8) and cooperative education agreements that allow students to gain work experience while continuing to attend school. The Australian Government's Department of Education is working to bring schools and businesses together so young

TABLE 11.4 Example Youth and Employment Targets for Sustainable Development Goals for 2030
Ensure equal access to affordable and quality technical, vocational and tertiary education, including university.
Increase the number of youth and adults who have relevant skills, including technical and vocational skills, for employment, decent jobs and entrepreneurship.
Recognize and value unpaid care and domestic work through the provision of public services, infrastructure and social protection policies.
Ensure women's full and effective participation and equal opportunities for leadership at all levels of decision-making.
Achieve higher levels of economic productivity through diversification, technological upgrading and innovation in high-value added and labor-intensive sectors.
Promote development-oriented policies that support the growth of micro small- and medium-sized organizations including access to financial services to enhance job creation and entrepreneurship.
Achieve full and productive employment and decent work for all and equal pay for work of equal value.
Substantially reduce the proportion of youth not in employment, education, or training.
Protect labor rights and promote safe and secure working environments for all workers including those in precarious employment.
Promote inclusive and sustainable industrialization while increasing industry's share of employment and gross domestic product.
Source: United Nations Department of Economic and Social Affairs (2018). *Work youth report: Youth and the 2030 agenda for sustainable development*. New York: United Nations.

people can gain the types of skills to be a productive member of the work-force. One program called the Pathways in Technology offers high school-aged students an industry supported pathway to science and technology fields in which they are provide with hands-on project-based learning in schools and in the workplace (www.ptech.org.au/).

A major issue of concern within the European Union is youth unemployment and underemployment. To help meet this school to work need, the European Commission founded the Youth Employment Initiative (and Youth Guarantee) for those up to 25 years old to provide financial support for apprenticeships, traineeships (internships), job placement help, and additional educational opportunities to meet job qualifications within four months of leaving school or becoming unemployed (https://ec.europa.eu/social/main.jsp?catId=950&langId=en). Traineeships are limited time period positions in organizations to help young people gain practical and professional experience to improve employability or to help transition to full-time employment. Twenty million young people have taken up this offer of a Youth Guarantee. Within three years of its launch, the EU has seen a drop of 2.4 million fewer youths unemployed from 2013 to 2018. Nevertheless, concerns have been raised about the quality of the traineeships as many jobs are menial and have little to no learning component. Consequently, the Commission developed a list of recommended quality elements for traineeships. These recommendations include the following: (1) require that traineeship agreements include learning objectives; (2) promote best practices to meet the learning objectives; (3) encourage organizations to have a mentor to guide the trainee through the assigned tasks; (4) ensure a reasonable length of time in the traineeship to allow the individual to gain skills; and (5) create certifications that validate the knowledge, skills, and competencies gained during the experience (Council of the European Union, 2014).

Another strategy to aid school to work transition is identifying and building up the workplace readiness factors. Competences identified by the American Council of Testing (ACT) include areas such as:

- Problem-solving
- Critical thinking
- Reading and using work-related text
- Applying information from workplace documents to solve problems
- Applying mathematical reasoning to work-related problems
- Setting up and performing work-related mathematical calculations
- Locating, synthesizing, and applying information that is presented graphically
- Comparing, summarizing, and analyzing information presented in multiple related graphics.

With competencies identified ACT created the WorkKeys system that includes assessment and development leading to a National Career Readiness Certificate. This certification asserts that the person is workforce ready for particular jobs given their scores on the key competencies for each job.

The WorkKeys curriculum is delivered through a mobile-based learning management system. Table 11.5 presents two examples of curriculum topics for graphics literacy and for applied technology for mechanics. The curriculum has a set of course topics divided into levels (from 3 to 7) that signify a

Level	Graphic Literacy	Applied Technology/Mechanics
TABLE 11.5 WorkKeys Curriculum and Levels Example		
3	Finding Information in Tables Reading Simple Charts & Graphs Reading and Using Forms Simple Gauges Reading Simple Flowcharts	Force & Pressure Friction & Inertia Planes & Levers Torque & Gears Wheels & Pulleys Springs & Stored Energy
4	Understanding Tables Interpreting Charts & Graphs Understanding Dashboards Identifying Trends	Screws Acceleration Rotation Center of Gravity Troubleshooting Exercises
5	Scatter Plots Combination Charts & Graphs with a Secondary Y-Axis Complex Diagrams Choosing Effective and Accurate Graphics Real-World Decisions with Graphics	Bearings Lubrication Conveyers Sound & Vibration Troubleshooting Exercises
6	Interpreting Graphics with a Secondary Y-Axis Uncommon Charts & Graphs Real-World Decisions with Graphics Interpreting & Comparing Trends	Gas Engines Alternative Power Hybrid Engines Troubleshooting Exercises
7	Making Decisions with Complex Maps & Diagrams Analyzing Financial Data in Graphs Interpreting Trends & Making Predictions	
Source: ACT WorkKeys (2019). ACT WorkKeys curriculum administration guide. Iowa City, IA.		

progressively more advanced set of knowledge and skills. For the mechanics course, a lower level includes a basic course on torque and gears (level 3) while the more advanced courses include a section on how to work with hybrid engines (level 6). There are assessments that lead to each participant getting a level score in their dashboard for each set of curricula. WorkKeys also creates a skill profile for a variety of jobs linked to the WorkKeys curricula. For a mobile heavy equipment mechanic, the necessary level of skill for graphic literacy is 3 while for applied technology it is level 4 with an applied math level of 3. Research indicates that individuals with the same education level but with higher proficiency levels on WorkKeys curricula competencies have higher incomes (Steedle & LeFebvre, 2018). In 2016, nonqualifiers on WorkKeys curricula were earning about $20,000 while those who obtained levels on the WorkKeys beyond what was needed for the job were averaging close to $35,000. Case studies such as Boeing hiring assembly workers point to success gained from hiring those with the certification in required areas in terms of lower formal training time, a reduction in on-the-job training costs, and improved retention (Street, 2017).

Other school-to-work programs that prepare students for work have been found to be effective. In one study, graduates of vocational schools (18–19-year-olds) were randomly assigned to a "school-to-work" career management training program or to a control condition. The program consists of 20 hours over 5 days of a highly structured group counseling program to enhance employment preparedness. Preparedness is defined as readiness to take advantage of employment opportunities and the capacity to deal with setbacks. Participants were given counseling around effective job searching strategies as well as active practice on key skills based on the social learning theory and the behavioral modeling approached discussed in Chapter 10. Participants were given strategies on how to behave successfully in a job interview and watched a demonstration of a person modeling the wrong way to approach a job interview. Participants then discussed problems with the modeled approach and generated ways to improve the job interview. Based on this input, trainers modeled the improved way and then the participants role-played the correct approach and were given targeted feedback for improvement. Participants were also able to interview employers to gain knowledge of recruitment and organizational socialization expectations for new hires. Participants in the control condition were given content on job search strategies and prepared a job application to an advertisement found on the internet. Analysis ten months after the intervention showed benefits for the trained group in terms of higher levels of employment preparedness, which in turn was related to higher employment rates. The higher employment rates also reduced the individual's perceptions of financial strain and depression symptoms (Koivisto, Vuori, & Vinokur, 2010).

Upgrading Skills for Reemployment

According to the McKinsey Global Institute (2018), by 2030 as many as 375 million workers – or roughly 14% of the global workforce – may need to switch occupational categories as the move to digitization, automation, robotics, artificial intelligence, and machine learning affect the future world of work in terms of what jobs will be lost and which types of jobs will be opened. Higher cognitive skills such as quantitative and statistical skills, project management, and complex information processing and interpretation will become more important leading to the displacement of jobs that now require only basic cognitive skills. More specifically, in the banking and insurance industries it is projected that the top growing jobs will be around financial analysis, information systems managers, software developers, and computer systems analysis while the declining jobs will be bill and account collectors, data entry clerks, tellers, computer user support specialists, and insurance sales agents. And as noted about the future of work "today's skills will not match the jobs of tomorrow and newly acquired skills may quickly become obsolete" (Global Commission on the Future of Work, 2019; p. 10). The critical issues for organizations and governments are how to reduce the potential for talent shortages while at the same time minimize impact on unemployment or income disparity.

Upskilling includes learning activities that are designed to enhance or transform existing skills with significantly improved knowledge and skills so that the job incumbent can successfully continue in the same field of work for the organization. Reskilling also includes learning activities designed to help the incumbent gain new knowledge and skills to enable them to perform new jobs. A survey of talent development leaders across a variety of types of organizations worldwide revealed that over half the companies provide upskilling, reskilling or both. The respondents also recognize the need to accelerate these efforts as they cite skill gaps, pipeline concerns and an aging workforce in addition to automation and artificial intelligence as key drivers of this need. Unfortunately, the respondents also noted the limited support and inadequate resource allocations leading to rating the usefulness of the skills training they currently provide as low with only 25% saying that they upskilled people effectively. Another set of respondents who provide upskilling and reskilling stated that the usefulness of the programs was unclear as evaluation data was not being systematically collected (Ketter et al., 2018).

There are a number of efforts underway that show promise. Major approaches to upskilling or reskilling are in-house efforts, tuition reimbursement programs, and external partnerships. These approaches begin with a thorough needs assessment to identify skill gaps and future skill needs as we talked about in Chapter 3. Efforts include special programs developed in local colleges to help incumbents learn new skills identified by the company as critical. For example, AK Steel partners with a local technical school to provide certification to employees in structural welding and electrical maintenance. SAP, a software company, has created programs in house and mapped out learning journeys for thousands of employees to transition them into new roles and responsibilities (see Business Roundtable, 2017 for a description of over 60 reskilling and upskilling initiatives). AT&T has spent one billion dollars on retraining (Chapter 1) its workforce through partnerships with a variety of educational platforms (Donovan & Benko, 2016). Some evidence is now emerging in Europe regarding the positive return on investment for retraining efforts especially around advanced technology skills and working with artificial intelligence (McKinsey & Company, 2017).

Displaced workers are defined as persons aged 20 years or older who have lost or left jobs because their organization closed or moved, there was insufficient work for them to do, or their position or shift was abolished. Reentering the job market is clearly even more difficult for what has been termed the hard core unemployed – people who have been out of the job market for an extended time. Individuals and their families can pay a heavy price when a job loss occurs. Affective consequences include depression and other mental health issues while behavioral consequences can include antisocial behaviors, substance abuse, and increased violent actions (Price & Burgard, 2008). Many organizations attempt to ameliorate the problems associated with downsizing by providing outplacement services for their employees. The outplacement services can range from simply providing a place for employees to seek out employment opportunities (long-distance phone calling to employers, copying résumés, etc.) to more full-blown services that impart job search skills, provide outplacement counseling, and identify retraining opportunities to aid in the reemployment effort.

Governmental agencies have taken a proactive stance regarding addressing issues surrounding displaced workers such as enacting policies around unemployment benefits. European countries tend to provide higher levels of benefits for a longer time than the U.S. There are a variety of job search and job training programs for the unemployed that have been implemented. In Australia, there is a government campaign to promote the benefits of employing and retaining workers as part of a productive workforce. Payroll tax

FIGURE 11.2 Factors Affecting Reemployment Success.

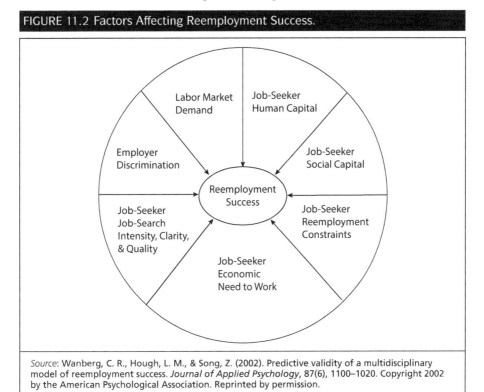

Source: Wanberg, C. R., Hough, L. M., & Song, Z. (2002). Predictive validity of a multidisciplinary model of reemployment success. *Journal of Applied Psychology*, 87(6), 1100–1020. Copyright 2002 by the American Psychological Association. Reprinted by permission.

incentives are available to employers who take on long-term unemployed people (Suleyman, 2016).

Figure 11.2 displays a conceptual model of seven factors that are related to success in gaining reemployment. These factors include (1) labor market demand for the particular skills of the job seeker; (2) the ability and skill level (human capital) of the job seeker; (3) the social network or social capital that the job seeker can find support; (4) constraints that limit potential job options (e.g., not being able to move due to family responsibilities); (5) the level of economic need to find work to support oneself or others; (6) job commitment to and clarity regarding effective job-seeking behaviors; and (7) employer preferences and/or discrimination. These factors impact reemployment success that is defined in terms of the speed of obtaining reemployment, quality (and person/organizational fit) of the job obtained, and the pay level of the new job. One study found that skill level (human capital) predicted the quality of the job obtained as well as pay level. Job search intensity predicted the number of job offers obtained and the quality of the job obtained. The job searcher level of confidence related to the pay level of the job that was obtained (Wanberg, Zhang, & Diehn, 2010).

There are benefits of programs that have been carefully created to provide the knowledge, skills and attitudes that help job seekers who have been displaced to find work. A long-term research effort called the JOBS program addresses the problem facing the unemployed and their families by promoting reemployment and enhancing coping skills. The JOBS program consists of five half-day sessions held over a one- to two-week period. The sessions target "effective job search strategies, improving participant job search skills and increasing the self-esteem, confidence, and motivation of participants to engage in and persist in job search activities until they become reemployed" (Price, Friedland, Choi, & Caplan, 1998; p. 202). The positive impact of the JOBS program has been documented in randomized experimental trials that show the program returns the unemployed to new jobs quickly and at a high rate of pay while at the same time reducing stress and mental health problems. The researchers attribute much of the success of the program to the fact that individuals gain an enhanced sense of control or mastery over the job search process rather than feeling they have no control (Vinokur, Schul, Vuori, & Price, 2000).

The success of the JOBS program has led to collaborative efforts in countries as diverse as Finland, Ireland, and China to help participants become more active job seekers and provide guidance on labor market issues. A randomized field study of 1,261 unemployed Finnish job seekers found that six months after the job intervention program the trained group benefited in terms of quality of reemployment and decreased stress (Vuori et al., 2002). A key factor in the success of the Finnish program was its impact on the individual's job search preparedness and job search self-efficacy as well as strategies for coping effectively with job search setbacks (Vuori & Vinokur, 2005).

A recent meta-analysis of 47 studies on job search interventions (including the JOBS intervention) found evidence that the odds of obtaining reemployment were 2.6 times higher for participants in such interventions than individuals in a control condition (Liu, Huang, & Wang, 2014). The components of successful interventions included the teaching of job search and self-presentation skills, boosting job search proactivity, setting of job search goals, and building social support networks. These findings support the need to focus not only on skill development but also on enhancing job seeker motivation. The meta-analytic findings also showed that interventions were more effective for those who had been unemployed for a shorter period of time, for younger and older participants (rather than middle age) and for those with special needs in comparison to the job seekers in general.

Enhancing Fairness and Creating Opportunities

The issues of employment practices, fairness, and equality have become major areas of interests at both societal and organizational levels. Two areas of particular concern are gender equality and workforce diversity and inclusion. Women's rights and gender equality is a goal that is leading to newly enacted international policies and expanded national laws across a number of counties (Nishii & Özbilgin, 2007). The goals include equal access to jobs, development, and promotions. While the share of women in organizations (in the U.S.) has risen to 53% at entry level positions, the pipeline becomes more constrained as there is movement up the hierarchy. One study found that the percentage of women in manager level jobs is 40%, 35% at the director level, 27% at the vice president level, and 19% in the C-suite (Barsh & Yee, 2012).

Equal employment laws have traditionally focused attention on the selection of people into the workplace. In areas where a more diverse workforce has successfully entered the job market, issues are shifting from employment opportunity (which are still important but beyond the scope of this book) to career opportunities. For example, concerns over glass ceiling and artificial barrier effects on women and minorities advancing in organizations have led to increased efforts at growing the pipeline of talent. From a learning perspective, there is more attention given to the identification of high-potential employees and the need for equal access and selection into such programs. The goal is to increase opportunities for training, mentoring, and other leader development activities.

Global companies face interesting tensions around taking a universalistic approach towards gender equality consistent with their home country and the need for local adaptation – especially in highly patriarchal societies. The attempt to transfer gender equality approaches from Western to non-Western cultures, for example, are challenging given that equal employment laws on equality are often more rudimentary with few court cases to provide a legal foundation around equality issues. It has been noted that in many countries there are policies on the books for gender equality but concerns are raised about the implementation of policies and the lack of monitoring and penalizing of discriminatory practices in order to make meaningful changes happen (Özbilgin, Syed, Ali, & Torunogulu, 2012).

A survey of global Fortune 500 companies shows that respondents acknowledge global diversity as an important issue to address (Dunavant & Heiss, 2005). Workforce diversity is defined as the composition of work units across levels and functions in the organizations in terms of salient cultural and demographic characteristics. The desire to enhance diversity has led to efforts at diversity management, which involves strategic managerial plans and actions aimed at increasing diversity and promoting positive and productive working relationships at work. The planning can also include a focus on inclusion and how to actively value differences and using them constructively to build a climate of support and wellbeing in the organization (Jonsen, Maznevski, & Schneider, 2011). Similar to issues around gender equality, significant cultural, religious and socioeconomic differences across a variety of countries pose challenges to meeting diversity goals. There is divergence in what forms of discrimination are seen as unlawful across countries and variation in how equal opportunity issues are interpreted and implemented. Sippola and Smale (2007) report on a study of a European company that attempted to integrate diversity management globally through its worldwide operations. While this intensive effort over two years was able to move to consistency across its worldwide operations at the level of a diversity philosophy, it was forced to have a multi-local approach to what diversity policies and practices to implement. A review of diversity management practices in India shows a wide range of approaches from simple legal compliance to viewing diversity management as a strategic initiative. From a strategic perspective, the goals involves encouraging diverse thinking to foster innovation, providing work-life balance and pushing for integration through cultural awareness training (Cooke & Saini, 2010). Managing global diversity, then, requires understanding cross-national differences in how diversity is defined and understood. This makes global diversity management a complex and evolving concept for organizations.

The major learning intervention in organizations consists of diversity and inclusion training. The diversity instructional programs developed often attempt to broaden participant's perspectives towards others so as to facilitate positive interactions, reduce stereotyping and discrimination as well as enhancing skills and motivation to interact positively with all people. The training can target the understanding of specific employee groups (e.g., race, gender, age) or emphasize the concept of inclusiveness and the need for working in a way that enhances the contribution of all employees. The training programs differ in terms of the emphasis on raising awareness about assumptions and biases to being more behavioral based and attempting to build skills around communication skills and responding to actions in a more inclusive way. Therefore, possible outcomes of diversity training include attitude or affective changes as well as knowledge and skill changes. These changes could include things such as being more tolerant towards others different from oneself, a better understanding of the legal landscape to be in compliance, and how to respond in a more positive way to individual and team situations at work.

The findings from reviews of diversity training are clearly mixed in terms of the extent to which expected learning outcomes are achieved. Concerns have been raised that poorly designed or implemented programs can even reinforce stereotypes and lead to a more hostile work environment. A recent meta-analytic study of 40 years of research of 260 studies on diversity training provides some window into understanding the complex effects of diversity training. The studies included in the meta-analysis made use of a pre-test–post-test design with a control or comparison group. The vast majority of studies were conducted in the United States and therefore cannot address the global tension points discussed above. The overall findings are that diversity training (across all types) has its largest effect on immediate positive reactions to the training by participants and on enhancing participant knowledge of diversity relevant issues. There were smaller effects of the training on attitudinal and behavioral changes. The meta-analytic study also found that the strength of the impact of the training diminished over time for attitudes and behaviors while remaining strong for the knowledge outcomes – people continued to remember the key knowledge being conveyed in the training but initial changes in attitude and behaviors tended to decay or revert back to levels closer to the pre-training level. Longer training programs were found to have more impact on learning outcomes than shorter programs. Probably the most important finding in terms of practical recommendations is that the effects of diversity training on attitude and behavioral change are enhanced when complemented by sustained strategic efforts relevant to other diversity initiatives conducted within the organization prior to and after the training (Bezrukova et al., 2016). While certainly common sense, it bears stating that standalone diversity and inclusion training programs tend not to have long-term effects – it must be part of an overall and larger strategic or diversity management plan that is rolled out over time.

CONCLUSION

This chapter has concentrated on learning from a broader systems perspective. From this perspective, learning and developmental activities are nested within a larger organizational learning system. The larger system conveys information regarding the importance of learning and continuous development through strategic decisions about resource allocation, the reward and promotion system within the organization, and through enacted policies and prcodures. The increasing scope and complexity of changes occurring in the workplace places a premium on a highly skilled workforce. Progressive organizations have devoted considerable resources to developing employees to be better prepared to deal with the changing realities of the workplace.

This chapter has also focused on the problems of the knowledge and skill gaps that are global in scope. The "supply" of highly skilled and talented individuals is not keeping up with the "demands" of the expanding and globally competitive job market. There is clearly an important role for innovative learning approaches for enhancing the likelihood that youths can be gainfully employed, that employees are treated fairly, and that displaced workers find new employment. The government, educational systems, and private sector have all been involved in this effort.

For people in learning and development research and practice, there is a growing knowledge base to derive best practices. While many issues remain unresolved, the demands of society, and work organizations seeking ways to enhance learning and development makes for exciting possibilities. The hope is that this book stimulates ideas and efforts for improving our understanding of learning and the factors that impact both individual, team, leadership, and organizational effectiveness as well as employee well-being.

References

ACT WorkKeys (2019). *ACT WorkKeys curriculum administration guide*. Iowa City, IA: ACT.

Allen, M. (2007). *The next generation of corporate universities: Innovative approaches for developing people and expanding organizational capabilities*. New York: Pfeiffer & Co.

Baldwin, T. T., Danielson, C., & Wiggenhorn, W. (1997). The evolution of learning strategies in organizations: From employee development to business redefinition. *Academy of Management Perspectives*, 11(4), 47–58. doi.org/10.5465/ame.1997.9712024838

Baporikar, N. (2014). Corporate university edification in knowledge society. *Journal of Strategic Change Management*, 5, 125–139.

Barsh, J. & Yee, L. (2012). Unlocking the full potential of women at work. Report for Wall Street Journal Executive Task Force for Women in the Economy, McKinsey & Co. New York, New York. www.mckinsey.com/client_service/organization/latest_thinking/women_at_work

BasuMallick, C. (2019, February 15). The role of the chief learning officer in the age of AI. *HR Technologist*. www.hrtechnologist.com/articles/learning-development/the-role-of-the-chief-learning-officer-in-the-age-of-ai/

Beckman, T. (1999). The current state of knowledge management. In J. Liebowitz (Ed.), *Knowledge management handbook*. Boca Raton, FL: CRC Press.

Benson-Armer, R., Gast, A., & van Dam, N. (2016). Learning at the speed of business. *McKinsey Quarterly*, (2), 115–121.

Bersin, J. (2007). The new chief learning officer: 2008 and beyond. *Bersin Newletter*. https://joshbersin.com/2007/07/the-new-chief-learning-officer-2008-and-beyond, accessed August 12, 2019.

Bezrukova, K., Spell, C. S., Perry, J. L., & Jehn, K. A. (2016). A meta-analytical integration of over 40 years of research on diversity training evaluation. *Psychological Bulletin*, 142(11), 1227–1274. doi.org/10.1037/bul0000067

Bhaskar, A. U., & Mishra, B. (2017). Exploring relationship between learning organizations dimensions and organizational performance. *International Journal of Emerging Markets*, 12(3), 593–609. doi.org/10.1108/IJoEM-01-2016-0026

Business Roundtable. (2017). *Work in progress: How CEOs are helping close America's skill gap*. Washington, DC: Business Round Table.

Bonner, D., & Wagner, S. (2002). Meeting the new chief learning officers. *Training and Development*, 56 (5), 80–89.

Cooke, F. L., & Saini, D. S. (2010). Diversity management in India: A study of organizations in different ownership forms and industrial sectors. *Human Resource Management*, 49, 477–500. doi. org/10.1002/hrm.20360

Cordery, J., & Wenzel, R. (2017). Organizational communities of practice and autonomous learning. In *Autonomous learning in the workplace* (pp. 78–94). New York: Routledge.

Cordery, J. L., Cripps, E., Gibson, C. B., Soo, C., Kirkman, B. L., & Mathieu, J. E. (2015). The operational impact of organizational communities of practice: A Bayesian approach to analyzing organizational change. *Journal of Management*, 41(2), 644–664. doi.org/10.1177/0149206314545087

Council of the European Union. (2014). Council recommendation of 10 March 2014 on a Quality Framework for Traineeships. *Official Journal of the European Union*, 88, 88/1–88/4.

Cutcher-Gershenfeld, J., & Ford, K. (2005). *Valuable disconnects in organizational learning systems: Integrating bold visions and harsh realities*. New York: Oxford University Press.

Davis, D., & Daley, B. J. (2008). The learning organization and its dimensions as key factors in firms' performance. *Human Resource Development International*, 11(1), 51–66. doi. org/10.1080/13678860701782352

Darroch, J. (2005). Knowledge management, innovation and firm performance. *Journal of Knowledge Management*, 9(3), 101–115. doi. org/10.1108/13673270510602809

Darroch, J., & McNaughton, R. (2002). Examining the link between knowledge management practices and types of innovation. *Journal of Intellectual Capital*, 3(3), 210–222. doi. org/10.1108/14691930210435570

Donovan, J., & Benko, C. (2016). Inside AT&Ts talent overhaul. *Harvard Business Review*, 94(10): 68–73.

Dunavant, B.M., & Heiss, B. (2005). *Global diversity 2005*. Washington, DC: Diversity Best Practices.

Ebrahimi, B. & Sawyerr, O. (2016). *Executive environmental scanning and strategic uncertainty: The impact of institutional context*. Academy of management proceedings. Briarcliff Manor, NY: Academy of Management. doi. org/10.5465/ambpp.2016.16981

Ellinger, A. D., Ellinger, A. E., Yang, B., & Howton, S. W. (2002). The relationship between the learning organization concept and firms' financial performance: An empirical assessment. *Human Resource Development Quarterly*, 13(1), 5–22. doi.org/10.1002/hrdq.1010

Ford, J. K., & Foster-Fishman, P. (2012). Organizational development and change: Linking research from the profit, nonprofit, and public sectors. In *The Oxford handbook of organizational psychology* (Vol. 2, pp. 956–992). Oxford: Oxford University of Press.

Foster-Fishman, P. G., Berkowitz, S. L., Lounsbury, D. W., Jacobson, S., & Allen, N. A. (2001). Building collaborative capacity in community coalitions: A review and integrative framework. *American Journal of Community Psychology*, 29, 241–261. doi. org/10.1023/A:1010378613583

French, W. L., & Bell, C. H. (1999). *Organization development* (6th ed.). Upper Saddle River, NJ: Prentice-Hall.

Garvin, D. A., Edmondson, A. C., & Gino, F. (2008). Is yours a learning organization? *Harvard Business Review*, 86(3), 109.

Global Commission on the Future of Work. (2019). *Work for a brighter future*. Geneva: International Labor Organization

Goh, S. C. (2003). Improving organizational learning capability: Lessons from two case studies. *The Learning Organization*, 10(4), 216–227. doi. org/10.1108/09696470310476981

Gold, A. H., Malhotra, A., & Segars, A. H. (2001). Knowledge management: An organizational capabilities perspective, *Journal of Management Information Systems*, 18(1), 185–214, doi: 10.1080/07421222.2001.11045669

Goldstein, I. L., & Ford, J. K. (2002). *Training in organizations: Needs assessment, development, and evaluation* (4th ed.). Belmont, CA: Wadsworth.

Harlow, H. (2008). The effect of tacit knowledge on firm performance. *Journal of Knowledge Management*, 12(1), 148–163. doi.org/10.1108/13673270810852458

Harvey, J. F., Cohendet, P., Simon, L., & Dubois, L. E. (2013). Another cog in the machine: Designing communities of practice in professional bureaucracies. *European Management Journal*, 31(1), 27–40. doi.org/10.1016/j.emj.2012.07.008

Hirst, G., Van Knippenberg, D., Chen, C. H., & Sacramento, C. A. (2011). How does bureaucracy impact individual creativity? A cross-level investigation of team contextual influences on goal orientation–creativity relationships. *Academy of Management Journal*, 54(3), 624–641. doi.org/10.5465/amj.2011.61968124

Hogan, S. J., & Coote, L. V. (2014). Organizational culture, innovation, and performance: A test of Schein's model. *Journal of Business Research*, 67(8), 1609–1621. doi.org/10.1016/j.jbusres.2013.09.007

Honig, M. I. (2003). Building policy from the practice: District central office administrators' roles and capacity for implementing collaborative education policy. *Education Administration Quarterly*, 39, 292–338. doi.org/10.1177/0013161X03253414

Honig, M. I., & Coburn, C. (2008). Evidence-based decision making in school district central offices: Toward a policy and research agenda. *Educational Policy*, 22(4), 578–608. doi.org/10.1177/0895904807307067

Jiang, J., & Gallupe, R. B. (2015, August). Environmental scanning and business insight capability: the role of business analytics and knowledge integration. In *Proceedings of the twenty-first Americas conference on information systems*, Puerto Rico (pp. 13–15).

Jonsen, K., Maznevski, M. L., & Schneider, S. C. (2011). Special Review Article: Diversity and its not so diverse literature: An international perspective. *International Journal of Cross Cultural Management*, 11(1), 35–62. https://doi.org/10.1177/1470595811398798

Ketter, P., Jones, M., Cole, M., Coppel, C., Sanchez, I., & Robinson, S. (2018). *Upskilling and reskilling: Turning disruption and change into new capabilities*. ATD research. Alexandria, VA: Association for Talent Development.

Kimble, C., Hildreth, P. & Wright, P. (2001). Communities of practice: Going virtual. In Y. Malhotra (Ed.), *Knowledge management and business model innovation* (pp. 220–234). Hershey, PA: IGI Publishing.

Kirkman, B. L., Cordery, J. L., Mathieu, J., Rosen, B., & Kukenberger, M. (2013). Global organizational communities of practice: The effects of nationality diversity, psychological safety, and media richness on community performance. *Human Relations*, 66(3), 333–362.

Kirkman, B. L., Mathieu, J. E., Cordery, J. L., Rosen, B., & Kukenberger, M. (2011). Managing a new collaborative entity in business organizations: Understanding organizational communities of practice effectiveness. *Journal of Applied Psychology*, 96(6), 1234. doi.org/10.1037/a0024198

Kislov, R., Walshe, K., & Harvey, G. (2012). Managing boundaries in primary care service improvement: A developmental approach to communities of practice. *Implementation Science*, 7(1), 97. doi.org/10.1186/1748-5908-7-97

Koivisto, P., Vuori, J., & Vinokur, A. D. (2010). Transition to work: Effects of preparedness and goal construction on employment and depressive symptoms. *Journal of Research on Adolescence*, 20(4), 869–892. doi.org/10.1111/j.1532-7795.2010.00667.x

Kontoghiorghes, C., Awbre, S. M., & Feurig, P. L. (2005). Examining the relationship between learning organization characteristics and change adaptation, innovation, and organizational performance. *Human Resource Development Quarterly*, 16(2), 185–212. doi.org/10.1002/hrdq.1133

Lane, P. J., Koka, B. R., & Pathak, S. (2006). The reification of absorptive capacity: A critical review and rejuvenation of the construct. *Academy of Management Review*, 80, 833–863. doi.org/10.5465/amr.2006.22527456

Lawson, B., & Samson, D. (2001). Developing innovation capability in organisations: A dynamic capabilities approach. *International Journal of Innovation Management*, 5(03), 377–400. doi.org/10.1142/S1363919601000427

Lui Abel, A., & Li, J. (2012). Exploring the corporate university phenomenon: Development and implementation of a comprehensive survey. *Human Resource Development Quarterly*, 23(1), 103–128. doi.org/10.1002/hrdq.21122

Liu, S., Huang, J. L., & Wang, M. (2014). Effectiveness of job search interventions: A meta-analytic review. *Psychological Bulletin*, 140(4), 1–33. doi.org/10.1037/a0035923

Lopez, E. L. F. (2019). Application of the literacy training service component of the National Service Training Program in New Bilibid Prison (Philippines). *International Review of Education*, 65, 755–784. https://doi.org/10.1007/s11159-019-09799-w

Marsick, V. J., & Watkins, K. E. (2003). Demonstrating the value of an organization's learning culture: The dimensions of the learning organization questionnaire. *Advances in Developing Human Resources*, 5(2), 132–151. doi.org/10.1177/1523422303005002002

McKinsey & Company. (2017). Shaping the future of work in Europe's digital front-runners. www.mckinsey.com/featured-insights/europe/shaping-the-future-of-work-in-europes-nine-digital-front-runner-countries

McKinsey Global Institute. (2018). *Skill shift: Automation and the future of the workforce*. San Francisco, CA: McKinsey & Company. www.mckinsey.com/mgi

Mishra, B., & Uday Bhaskar, U. A. (2011). Knowledge management process in two learning organisations. *Journal of Knowledge Management*, 15(2), 344–359. doi.org/10.1108/13673271111119736

Nishii, L. H., & Özbilgin, M. F. (2007). Global diversity management: Towards a conceptual framework. *International Journal of Human Resource Management*, 18(11), 1883–1894. doi:10.1080/09585190701638077

OECD. (2013), *Time for the U.S. to reskill?: What the survey of adult skills says, OECD skills studies*. Paris: OECD Publishing. doi.org/10.1787/9789264204904-en

Oesch, T. (2018). The role of the chief learning officer in the digital era. *Training industry*, www.traininindustry.com/articles/stratgy-alginment-and-planning, accessed August 7, 2019.

Özbilgin, M. F., Syed, J., Ali, F., & Torunoglu, D. (2012). International transfer of policies and practices of gender equality in employment to and among Muslim majority countries. *Gender, Work & Organization*, 19, 345–369.

Phillips, J., Phillips, P., & Elkeles, T. (2016). *Chief talent officer: The evolving role of the chief learning officer*. London: Routledge.

Price, R. H., & Burgard, S. A. (2008). The new employment contract and worker health in the United States. In R. F. Schoeni, J. S. House, G. A. Kaplan, & H. Pollack (Eds.), *Social and economic policy as health policy: Rethinking America's approach to improving health* (pp. 201–227). New York: Russell Sage.

Price, R. H., Friedland, D. S., Choi, J. N., & Caplan, R. D. (1998). Job-loss and work transitions in a time of global economic change. In X. B. Arriaga & S. Oskamp (Eds.), *The Claremont symposium on applied social psychology. Addressing community problems: Psychological research and interventions* (pp. 195–222). Thousand Oaks, CA: Sage Publications, Inc.

Pyrko, I., Dörfler, V., & Eden, C. (2017). Thinking together: What makes communities of practice work? *Human Relations*, 70(4), 389–409. doi.org/10.1177/0018726716661040

Rademakers, M. F. (2014). *Corporate universities: Drivers of the learning organization*. New York: Routledge.

Rampey, B. D., Finnegan, R., Goodman, M., Mohadjer, L., Krenzke, T., Hogan, J., & Provasnik, S. (2016). *Skills of U.S. unemployed, young, and older adults in sharper focus: Results from the program for the international assessment of adult competencies (PIAAC) 2012/2014: First look* (NCES 2016-039). Washington, DC: U.S. Department of Education, National Center for Education Statistics. http://nces.ed.gov/pubs2016/2016039.pdf

Retsas, A. (2000). Barriers to using research evidence in nursing practice. *Journal of*

Advanced Nursing, 31(3), 599–606. doi. org/10.1046/j.1365-2648.2000.01315.x

Retna, K. S., & Tee Ng, P. (2011). Communities of practice: Dynamics and success factors. *Leadership & Organization Development Journal*, 32(1), 41–59. doi. org/10.1108/01437731111099274

Riddiford, M. (2010). Corporate learning a growth industry. *The Australian*. www.theaustralian.com.au/higher-education/corporate-learning-a-growth-industry/news-story/cb624ad92822a6ebe0b867779273c41c

Rio, A. (2018). The future of the corporate university. *Chief Learning Officer*, 17(4), 36–56.

Schein, E. H. (2010). *Organizational culture and leadership* (Vol. 2). Hoboken, NJ: John Wiley & Sons.

Schilling, J., & Kluge, A. (2009). Barriers to organizational learning: An integration of theory and research. *International Journal of Management Reviews*, 11(3), 337–360. https://doi.org/10.1111/j.1468-2370.2008.00242.x

Seidler-de Alwis, R. & Hartmann, E. (2008). The use of tacit knowledge within innovative companies: Knowledge management in innovative enterprises. *Journal of Knowledge Management*, 12, 133–147. doi.org/10.1108/13673270810852449

Senge, P. M. (2006). *The fifth discipline: The art and practice of the learning organization*. New York: Broadway Business.

Sippola, A. & Smale, A. (2007). The global integration of diversity management: A longitudinal case study. *The International Journal of Human Resource Management*, 18, 1895–1916. doi.org/10.1080/09585190701638101

Steedle, J. T., & LeFebvre, M. (2018). *Income trends for ACT NCRC earners. ACT research & policy technical brief.* Iowa City, IA: ACT.

Street, D. G. (2017). Boeing improves retention while reduction training time. www.act.org/content/dam/act/unsecured/documents/pdfs/CS-Workforce-Boeing.pdf

Stewart, T. A. (2007). *The wealth of knowledge: Intellectual capital and the twenty-first century organization.* New York: Crown Business.

Strong, B., Davenport, T., & Prusak, L. (2008). Organizational governance of knowledge and learning. *Knowledge and Process Management*, 15, 150–157.

Sugrue, B., & Lynch, D. (2006, February). Profiling a new breed of learning executive. *Training and Development*, 60, 51–56.

Suleyman, A. (2016, November). Generous South Australian payroll tax incentives. www.pitcher.com.au/news/generous-south-australian-payroll-tax-incentives

Todd, R., Buckley, L., & Herring, S. (2014, November). The innovator chief learning officer. *Talent Development*, 68, 35–41.

United Nations Department of Economic and Social Affairs. (2018). *World youth report: Youth and the 2030 agenda for sustainable development.* New York: United Nations.

Vinokur, A. D., Schul, Y., Vuori, J., & Price, R. H. (2000). Two years after a job loss: Long-term impact of the JOBS program on reemployment and mental health. *Journal of Occupational Health Psychology*, 5(1), 32. doi.org/10.1037/1076-8998.5.1.32

Vuori, J., Silvonen, J., Vinokur, A. D., & Price, R. H. (2002). The Työhön Job Search Program in Finland: Benefits for the unemployed with risk of depression or discouragement. *Journal of Occupational Health Psychology*, 7(1), 5. doi.org/10.1037/1076-8998.7.1.5

Vuori, J., & Vinokur, A. D. (2005). Job-search preparedness as a mediator of the effects of the Työhön Job Search Intervention on re-employment and mental health. *Journal of Organizational Behavior*, 26(3), 275–291. doi.org/10.1037/1076-8998.7.1.5

Wanberg, C. R., Hough, L. M., & Song, Z. (2002). Predictive validity of a multidisciplinary model of reemployment success. *Journal of Applied Psychology*, 87(6), 1100–1120. doi.org/10.1037/0021-9010.87.6.1100

Wanberg, C. R., Zhang, Z., & Diehn, E. W. (2010). Development of the "Getting Ready for Your Next Job" inventory for unemployed individuals. *Personnel Psychology*, 63(2), 439–478. doi.org/10.1111/j.1744-6570.2010.01177.x

Waring, J., & Currie, G. (2009). Managing expert knowledge: Organizational challenges and managerial futures for the UK medical profession. *Organization Studies*, 30(7), 755–778. doi.org/10.1177/0170840609104819

Wenger, E., McDermott, R. A., & Snyder, W. (2002b). *Cultivating communities of practice: A guide to managing knowledge.* Boston, MA: Harvard Business Press.

Winder, C. (2000). Integrating OHS, environmental, and quality management standards. *Quality Assurance*, 8, 105–135. doi.org/10.1080/105294100317173880

Yang, B., Watkins, K. E., & Marsick, V. J. (2004). The construct of the learning organization: Dimensions, measurement, and validation. *Human Resource Development Quarterly*, 15(1), 31–55. doi.org/10.1002/hrdq.1086

Zahra, S. A., & George, G. (2002). Absorptive capacity: A review, reconceptualization, and extension. *Academy of Management Review*, 27, 185–203. doi.org/10.5465/amr.2002.6587995

Zollo, M., & Winter, S. G. (2002). Deliberate learning and the evolution of dynamic capabilities. *Organization Science*, 13, 339–351. doi.org/10.1287/orsc.13.3.339.2780

Appendix

LEARNING BY DOING!

We can learn much from hands-on projects that allow the learner to experience what it is like to make decisions about training and learning opportunities. This project focuses on the development of a training program for a new hire to a job and then a discussion of strategies for accelerating the development of the newcomer over the first 6 to 12 months on the job after the initial training.

The project requires picking a job and interviewing at least the job incumbent (and hopefully others who know the job). The job should be one that includes a number of observable tasks that a newcomer would need to learn quickly to start a job. The project can be done individually but if it makes sense to do so, a two-person team can be formed. A final report of the project(s) addresses the project steps below. If instructors would like to modify the project steps to better meet their course needs, an electronic version can be sent by contacting me at fordjk@msu.edu.

Step 1: Identify the Job and Job Context

1. Provide a short description of the job selected and why this job is appropriate for this project.
2. Describe who will be interviewed in terms of tenure in the job in question. If interviewing other individuals describe how knowledgeable the person(s) is about the job).
3. Provide an overview of the company including how many people are employed (if the company is large and in multiple locations, describe the local facility where the job is located), and what the organizational structure looks like (organizational hierarchy, type of

functions in the company). Where does the job fit within the organizational structure and how many people are in the job you have selected?

Step 2: Conduct a Needs Assessment

1. Conduct a simplified organizational analysis by describing the overall strategic goals of the organization including the vision and values that the organization has communicated to their employees. Describe the interviewee's perspective about the climate for learning in the organization and what constraints there are for development and growth (see Chapter 3 for examples of issues to discuss). What type of training is mandated by external agencies or by the organization for this job?
2. Interview the job incumbent to develop a list of tasks that are typically performed as part of this job. Start by asking what a typical day is like for the incumbent. From the responses you have collected, write task statements consistent with the material in Chapter 3 in the form of "adjusts work schedules to meet emergency conditions" and "inspects police vehicles to determine that they are properly serviced and maintained." Make sure to also ask about less frequently performed or non-routine tasks that are performed. A list of 30 to 50 tasks can easily be generated from such an interview.
3. Use the task statements to ask the interviewee what knowledge and skills are required to perform the

various job tasks. For example, ask "for the administrative tasks you mentioned, what are the knowledge and skills one needs to have to successfully perform those tasks?" After the interview, place the responses into statements in the form of "knowledge of standard accounting principles and procedures" and "skill in adjusting cutting blades on labeling machine."

4. Examine the task statements and develop task clusters that capture the similarity of tasks (see Chapter 3 for examples). Place the individual tasks under the appropriate task cluster. Then list the knowledge and skills required to complete the various tasks under that task clusters. At this point there is likely between four and seven task clusters with a list of tasks under each cluster as well as a list of the knowledge and skills required to perform the tasks identified (the knowledge and skills can be placed within each task cluster or be provided as a separate list). An example for one task cluster for the job of mortgage banker is provided.

Task Cluster 2: Administration

1. Pull customers' credit reports to determine eligibility for a mortgage loan using company software on a company computer.
2. Write mortgage loans in order to make a sale by telephone.
3. Enter customer information into mortgage loan paperwork using organization's software program on company computers.
4. Enter payment information into point of sale system.
5. Upload important documentation (including W-2, pay stubs, S documentation) to computer software program.
6. Send important documentation to underwriters in order to close the loan.
7. Shred notes or identifying paperwork related to customer loans promptly once the information has

been inputted in the software program and the loan has been closed.

Knowledge Required	Skills Required
1. Knowledge of residency requirements for loans 2. Knowledge of items that can be found on a credit report 3. Knowledge of types of debts 4. Knowledge of types of property 5. Knowledge of different loans: conventional loan, FHA loan, veteran's loan 6. Knowledge of eligibility requirements/ organizational thresholds for each loan 7. Knowledge to pass the Secure and Fair Enforcement for Mortgage Licensing Act of 2008 (SAFE) exam 8. Knowledge of differences in regulations between states	1. Skill in operating computer and access internet 2. Skill in performing database searches for mortgage guidelines in different states 3. Skill in operating mortgage loan software program 4. Skill in operating computer software program (mortgage writing program) 5. Skill in using email and telephone 6. Skill in building rapport with many different types of customers 7. Skill in analyzing credit reports 8. Skill in inputting information into the computer software program

5. Collect information such as ratings of importance of tasks and knowledge and skills for job performance and especially important for newcomers to be able to do. This information will be used in the next step to prioritize which tasks and knowledge and skills to train a new hire.
6. Identify one task that requires problem-solving and decision-making. Make sure the task has some degree of complexity. Conduct a cognitive task analysis with the job

incumbent to understand how the person approaches the problem-solving task and comes up with a solution. An example from the mortgage loan banker:

I'll start with the profile call where I'm assessing the client…kind of figure out what they want to do. Starting from the beginning, I get their information, exchange my contact information, and then start talking about their goals. Figure out what they want to do with their refinance. Generally, there's three directions: you're looking to lower your payment, cut years off your loan, or take cash out. From there, I look at four main areas – I have this exact same spiel I tell them when on the call: I look at their income property, assets, and credits. So I'll ask them about their job, what they do for a living, how they're paid, how often they get paid, if they get bonuses, if they write anything off on their taxes, what their property is worth, any repairs they did, anything that will get in the way of us appraising their home. I then pull their credit report, to make sure they make their payments, have good credit, no delinquencies, and, finally, I ask about their assets: what they have in reserves, money in the bank, 401k, anything they could use to substantiate the loan documents. So, that's the profile call.

Note: The training need assessment provides the framework for the content of the training program. Thus, devote time and energy now so as not to have to revisit assessment issues later.

Step 3: Create Training Objectives

1. Based on information collected, determine the most important tasks and knowledge and skills to include in training of a new hire. One cannot just train a newcomer on every aspect of the job. Justify why a newcomer needs to be able to perform these tasks and have a reasonable amount of knowledge and skills in order to perform these

tasks soon on the job. In particular, select between five and ten knowledge and skills to be trained in on your program. Include some knowledge and skills in the list to be trained. In addition, discuss why some tasks and knowledge and skills will not be part of the initial training but will be gained over time on the job.

2. Provide one example of effective behavior and one example of an ineffective behavior that people have exhibited relevant to each of the tasks to be trained. These critical incidents should be written to include the performance (this nurse observed changes in a chronic nephritis patient's ability to read a newspaper), the conditions surrounding the performance (the nurse had just gotten on the shift and was checking on the patients), and the outcome of the actions taken (e.g., the identification of the problem led to treatment that was effective and the patient recovered more quickly than would have occurred if the nurse had not discovered the problem). This provides information about what to do on the job and what to avoid doing, which can be helpful in developing a training plan.

3. Write a training objective for *each* of the knowledge and skill statements that have been retained for inclusion in the initial training program. Each statement must include a condition, behavior, and criterion as noted in Chapter 4. Remember that objectives focus on what the learner will be able to do now at the end of training (not on the job yet!) that they could not do before the training. Two examples are below:

Without using reference materials, describe three types of debts that can be seen on a credit report within 10 minutes.

With an example credit report and personal information at hand, determine the example customer's eligibility for an FHA loan within 15 minutes.

4. Justify the conditions of performance and the criterion standards set for each objective in the training program.

Step 4: Develop Plans of Instruction

1. Place training objectives into sequenced order (i.e., which objective would you train first, second, third etc.) and describe why this would be the best way to sequence learning in your training program to maximize learning and retention. The sequencing of training content is often done on the basis of (1) logical order – present the least difficult material first and build to the most difficult; (2) problem-centered order – focus on a general problem and develop various ways to solve the problem prior to moving to another problem area; (3) job performance order – order based on the sequence in which a job or task is actually performed; or (4) psychological order – moving from abstract concepts to more concrete examples and hands-on experience.

2. Each objective is now to be turned into a training module. Therefore, if there are five objectives, five training modules are to be created. For each module, develop an overall plan of instruction by describing (1) how the objective for the module is to be introduced, (2) what the core part of the training for this module would look like, and (3) what will happen at the end of each module. Provide an outlined list of what is to be covered rather than actually producing the training material. For example, if there is a lecture and discussion for a module, outline what would be in the lecture and what questions would be part of the discussion. If the instructor

would demonstrate a skill, state how the demonstration would be conducted. If the trainee is to do a role-play, describe what scenario(s) would be part of the role-play and how the role-play would be conducted.

3. For each module, identify one or two learning principles to incorporate into the design of the training and how they would be incorporated. Justify the choices relevant to how incorporating the learning principle will aid in encoding, retention, and/or transfer of training.

4. Provide a time estimate for each training module (e.g., how much time for lecture and discussion, and demonstration and role play). Include time for testing/evaluation of whether the trainee has meet the objective for each module.

Step 5: Facilitate Transfer

1. Describe pre-training strategies to incorporate to facilitate readiness and motivation to learn from the upcoming training you have created.

2. At the end of training, discuss what would be done to help trainees retain the knowledge and skills gained in the training and what the trainee would be asked to do at the end of the training (and before going on the job) to enhance learning transfer (remember discussion of post-training interventions in Chapter 5).

3. Describe what the supervisor of the newcomer should do on the job after training to facilitate training transfer (be specific)?

Step 6: Develop a Training Evaluation Plan

1. Describe a plan for formative evaluation around the key issues to observe to help determine how to improve the course.

2. Describe what information to obtain from the trainees after training is completed about their reactions to the training and how that information would be helpful in determining how to improve the training for the next group of trainees?
3. For each training module, discuss how learning validity would be evaluated (i.e., what would be the strategy for measuring the level of knowledge or skill obtained by the trainee) and whether it meets the criterion set in each training objective.
4. For each module, identify the behaviors that the trainee should demonstrate on the job after the training to show that learning transfer occurred.
5. Detail how to measure the behaviors identified above in a way that leads to high reliability and high levels of criterion relevancy while minimizing criterion deficiency and criterion contamination.

Step 7: Facilitate Onboarding

1. Ask the job incumbent (interviewee) to describe the onboarding process (first day, orientation sessions) that this person experienced with this company the first week on the job.
2. Detail the strengths and weaknesses of this onboarding process from the job incumbent's perspective.
3. Based on material in Chapter 8, identify three ways the onboarding process could be improved (including how to make the first day more special) to better acclimate a newcomer into the job and the organization.

Step 8: Accelerate Development

1. Have the interviewee describe the socialization process or what occurred during the period of learning and adjustment over the first three to six months on the job so that person gained a greater and perhaps more realistic understanding of the values, norms, and expected behaviors to participate effectively as a member of the organization.
2. Detail the strengths and weaknesses of this socialization process from the job incumbent's perspective.
3. Based on the material on socialization in Chapter 8, identify three ways the process could be improved to help speed up learning and adjustment.
4. What additional training, guided instruction, on-the-job experiences, or self-directed learning would have been helpful in accelerating the growth and development of the job incumbent during the first year on the job?

Step 9: Lessons Learned

1. Discuss how an evidence-based approach to deriving best practices helped when completing this project as well as aspects of the project where the evidence-based approach was not helpful in your decision making process.
2. Describe three to five lessons learned regarding the process of developing a training program for new hires and the development of effective onboarding and socialization processes. This discussion should include why the lessons are personally important ones to take away from doing this project.

INDEX

Page numbers in *italic* indicate figures.
Page numbers in **bold** indicate tables.